NATIVE CANADIAN
ANTHROPOLOGY
AND HISTORY

NATIVE CANADIAN ANTHROPOLOGY AND HISTORY

A Selected Bibliography

Revised Edition

By SHEPARD KRECH III

Foreword by Jennifer S. H. Brown

University of Oklahoma Press : Norman and London

By Shepard Krech III

Praise the Bridge that Carries You Over: The Life of Joseph Sutton (Cambridge, Mass., 1981)

Native Canadian Anthropology and History: A Selected Bibliography (Winnipeg, Man., 1986; Norman, 1994)

(ed.) *Indians, Animals, and the Fur Trade* (Athens, Ga., 1981)

(ed.) *The Subarctic Fur Trade: Native Social and Economic Adaptations* (Vancouver, 1984)

A Victorian Earl in the Arctic: The Travels and Collections of the Fifth Earl of Lonsdale, 1888–9 (Seattle, 1989)

Library of Congress Cataloging-in-Publication Data

Krech, Shepard, 1944-
    Native Canadian anthropology and history : a selected bibliography / by Shepard Krech III ; foreword by Jennifer S.H. Brown. —Rev. ed.
        p. cm.
    Includes index.
    ISBN 0-8061-2617-5 (alk. paper)
    1. Indians of North America—Canada—Bibliography. 2. Inuit—Canada—Bibliography. I. Title.
Z1209.2.C2K74 1994
[E78.C2]
016.971'00497—dc20   93-37591
                                             CIP

Text design by Cathy Carney Imboden.

    1   2   3   4   5   6   7   8   9   10

To my students

CONTENTS

FOREWORD

In the 1990s, Canada's Aboriginal history and peoples are drawing unprecendented interest and attention. Native issues and concerns have been in the foreground across Canada in recent years, particularly since the events at Oka in the summer of 1990 when the Mohawks and their supporters confronted the Quebec police and Canadian military forces in a land dispute with deep historical roots. Authors and publishers have responded to the growing public interest in Native people with an outpouring of new works, and it is a continuing challenge to keep up with all the printed materials that are appearing.

The first edition of Shepard Krech III's *Native Canadian Anthropology and History: A Selected Bibliography* appeared in 1986 as one of the first publications of the Rupert's Land Research Centre at the University of Winnipeg. The print run was small and the format simple, but the book sold out rather quickly, and requests for it have been arriving ever since. The events of 1990 intensified interest in a new edition, and it gives me great pleasure to introduce the present volume, updated and much enlarged. The publication process itself has consumed many months, so naturally it has not been possible to add items which have appeared while the book was in production. Nonetheless, the new edition should prove highly useful to students, scholars, and general readers in a wide variety of fields for several years to come.

The entries are conveniently organized alphabetically by author under major regional and subject headings, and the index helps to trace authors' works that may appear under various headings. I would strongly encourage readers to begin, however, with a close look at Shepard Krech's carefully crafted Introduction, which offers basic guidelines for the most effective use of this bibliography.

As editor of the Rupert's Land Research Centre publications series, I would like to offer particular thanks to Shepard Krech for his dedication and patience in the preparing of this new edition, and to all those who have assisted him in gathering and entering bibliographic data since the last edition appeared. My thanks also to John Drayton, Editor-in-Chief of the University of Oklahoma Press, whose interest in the history of Rupert's Land and in the Aboriginal history of North America made him an encouraging and warm supporter of the idea of co-publishing the second edition of the bibliography with our Centre.

JENNIFER S. H. BROWN

University of Winnipeg

ACKNOWLEDGMENTS

In compiling both editions of this bibliography I have indebted myself to many people who responded generously to requests for citations or for organizational advice, and I wish to acknowledge with gratitude their aid: Michael Asch, Donald W. Clark, Thomas Abler, Charles Bishop, Margaret Blackman, Philip Bock, Hartwell Bowsfield, Jennifer Brown, Sarah Carter, Norman Chance, Bruce Cox, David Damas, Olive Dickason, Kate Duncan, William Eccles, Harvey Feit, Robin Fisher, A. D. Fisher, Thomas Flanagan, John Foster, Milton Freeman, Barry Gough, Gary Granzberg, Robert Grumet, Cornelius Jaenen, Alice Kehoe, Carmen Lambert, Douglas Leighton, Tony Lussier, Harold McGee, David McNab, Charles Martijn, Donald Mitchell, Virginia Miller, Toby Morantz, George Parsons, Trudy Nicks, Graeme Patterson, Palmer Patterson, Richard Preston, John Price, Arthur J. Ray, Robin Ridington, Edward S. Rogers, Margaret Seguin, Donald Smith, Shirlee Anne Smith, Irene Spry, Elisabeth Tooker, François Trudel, Ruth Whitehead, Robert Williamson, James Waldram, and Sally Weaver. Several either commented on the entire manuscript or on major portions of it; Jennifer Brown, Olive Dickason, and Toby Morantz especially deserve thanks.

Also participating in this project were Stella Bryans-Munson, Barbara Warner, and Paula Brizee, all of whom were enrolled in 1984 in Native Canadian Ethnology and History (Anthropology 399) at George Mason University and helped compile—and used—the initial version of this bibliography. Two people provided fundamental assistance with production: Marilyn Taylor-Berry, on the first edition, and Ann McMullen, a graduate student in anthropology at Brown University, whose labors on the second edition were indispensable; I am grateful to both.

The effort to compile and publish this bibliography would have come to naught had it not been for the timely support of the Canadian Embassy and the Rupert's Land Research Centre. The Canadian Embassy assisted through its Faculty Enrichment Grants Programme, administered by Norman London, Academic Relations Officer. And Rupert's Land Research Centre, through Tim Ball, Director, and Jennifer Brown, General Editor of the Rupert's Land Record Society, has assisted in every way the publication of both editions of this bibliography. Finally, I finished the copyediting on this revised edition while a fellow of the Woodrow Wilson International Center for Scholars and the National Humanities Center. Thanks to all.

—SHEPARD KRECH III

NATIVE CANADIAN
ANTHROPOLOGY
AND HISTORY

INTRODUCTION

In 1984, with the support of a Faculty Enrichment Grant from the Canadian Embassy, I developed and taught a seminar on Native Canadian anthropology and history. My students attended one of Virginia's newer state universities, whose library holdings were limited. The quality of their research was heavily dependent on their ability to supplement materials obtained on campus with interlibrary loans or by visiting one of the older, more-comprehensive libraries nearby. As a consequence, one of the first priorities was to compile a bibliography of then-current sources on Native Canadians as a resource for research projects. The result was the original version of *Native Canadian Anthropology and History: A Selected Bibliography,* whose revision and first publication was supported by the Rupert's Land Research Centre (Krech 1986).

The usefulness of the first edition has led the Rupert's Land Research Centre to copublish with the University of Oklahoma Press a revised, updated edition of *Native Canadian Anthropology and History.* The new edition pretends to broad coverage, especially of recently published materials, but because brevity has also been a goal, the sources listed have been rigorously selected. Before the first edition was published, I asked several scholars for their critique. Some spotted defects. Others thought the bibliography curiously nonanthropological. Many brought to attention sources that had been missed altogether. Many were encouraging. Above all, almost all responded generously, for which they have my gratitude; their names appear in the Acknowledgments. On the basis of their suggestions as well as broader searches through the literature, many new sources were added, several sections were rethought, and when the first edition appeared, it listed well over two thousand sources in nineteen sections.

For this revised edition, over one thousand new sources have been added, mainly publications between 1984 and 1991; all citations in the bibliography proper have been indexed by author; and this introduction has been rewritten. The first edition's nineteen sections, which were grouped in three parts, remain identical: Part One ("Reference, Comparative, and Basic Historical Sources"), as its name implies, lists reference materials, comparative analyses overlapping other sections, and historical sources; Part Two ("Regional and Ethnic Sources") contains eight sections on "nations," "tribes," or ethnic groups, which are grouped in culture areas mainly on the basis of such conventional criteria as cultural and linguistic affiliation and geographical area. Finally, the eight "Special Topics," in Part Three, remain as salient for research today as in 1984.

SEVERAL CAVEATS AND STRENGTHS

Several cautions voiced to users of the first edition still apply. First, the bibliography is of necessity selected, in particular for sources published before 1980, and more so the farther back in time one looks. Second, some chapters in the books listed as "General and Comparative," or in some of the more-comprehensive ethnographic studies listed in Part Two, may elude students interested in specific topics—in education or the impact of missionaries, for example—unless they become familiar with this Introduction. Third, despite their frequent appearance, no attempt has been made to list comprehensively the numerous papers and reports produced by various federal, provincial, and territorial offices, or unpublished theses and dissertations, or unpublished works that were produced on contract or through other means. The last—the so-called grey literature—are notoriously difficult to obtain. Fourth, works that are nonanthropological or nonhistorical, or that were greeted by strongly negative critiques when they appeared, have *not* been omitted as some thought they should be. Each person who wishes must investigate these sources critically. Fifth, with very few exceptions, sources have not been listed more than once. Sixth, in a very few cases, references are listed despite being incomplete, in the belief that even though the full citation of a particular work is not readily available, the source appears to be pertinent. Seventh and finally, even though works published after 1991 have not been listed in the bibliography, this Introduction mentions several important books that have appeared since 1991.

Given those caveats, one might well wonder wherein lie the strengths of this bibliography. Three particular ones come to mind. First, a singular emphasis has been placed on listing recent, post-1980 sources on Canadian Native people, especially in the topical sections of Part Three. By starting with these sources, and by using standard research techniques, one can readily identify pre-1980 works to consult.

Second, in Part Two an attempt has been made to identify and list basic ethnographic sources, regardless of date of publication, for each Native Canadian ethnic group. (The terms *tribe, band,* and increasingly, *nation* are used often, despite the well-publicized drawbacks, for the major meaningful sociopolitical units. Today, many Native people prefer "First Nations" to refer to themselves.) There is a tendency to privilege (and list) in Part Two scholars whose work continues to be of theoretical interest today to broad constituencies—such as A. Irving Hallowell—or to single out for mention a particular part of a scholar's work—for example, Frank Speck's work on family hunting territories—because of widespread continuing interest. Neither tendency, however, is to the detriment of a wide range of other ethnographic writings, although no attempt is made here to duplicate what can be found in such comprehensive sources as the *Ethnographic Bibliography of North America* (Murdock and O'Leary 1975).

The organization in Part Two is mainly by culture area, a concept, that despite well-deserved criticism, nevertheless continues to have considerable heuristic value. Consequently, sources are included on some Native people whose territories were or are mainly south or west of Canada's border with the United States. The territories of some groups who speak closely related languages or dialects and share many aspects of culture straddle the political borders; for example, the Gwich'in (Loucheux/Kutchin) and other Northern Athapaskans, or the Tlingit in northwestern Canada and Alaska. In other cases, there have been contacts and movements of people across the border during the historical period, for example, among various Iroquoian groups. In this Introduction, standard spellings and names of tribal groups are used most often (the standard I tend to follow is the *Handbook of North American Indians*), even though some attention has been given to current ethnonymic usages, which, however, are subject to fashion. The labels *Native Canadian* and *Canadian Native* are used interchangeably to refer to all who self-identify as such, as are *Native American* and *American Indian.* Many Native people tend to use them interchangeably, and also often refer to themselves as simply *Indian* or *Native,* although in the Columbus quincentenary year just past, some contested anew the appropriateness of *American* and *Indian* for the indigenous people of the New World.

While the division into nineteen sections is to some extent arbitrary, it does provide a useful way to order a sprawling and diverse literature. Some sources that deal comprehensively with particular issues concerning Native people seem to defy placement within a single section, but despite that obvious difficulty, each work is listed only once, with very few exceptions. Many comprehensive sources are listed as "General and Comparative" and identified in the following description of Section 2.

One hope is that this bibliography, used in conjunction with others listed in Section 1, "Bibliography and Reference," as well as with the references cited in the recently published materials listed throughout, will lay the groundwork for well-researched student projects. Other audiences, including scholars who already possess extensive knowledge of Canadian Native ethnology and history, will surely discover in this bibliography sources of which they were unaware. But they may also regard, with some justification, the lack of systematic coverage of more inaccessible governmental or research-center reports—the grey literature referred to above—as a drawback. In contrast, to judge by reception of the first edition, students in Native studies and in anthropology and history courses, for whom this bibliography is especially intended, should find this edition useful. It will understandably be most advantageous if they can supplement it with some of the more-comprehensive bibliographies listed under "Bibliography and Reference," and if their research can be guided by teachers who possess a broad knowledge of Canadian Native people.

SOME MAJOR JOURNALS AND SERIES

Before commenting on each section, mention should be made of some of the principal sources for information on Native Canada. For example, students using key words, or simply browsing tables of contents or entire runs of journals, may examine with profit the relevant volumes of the *Handbook of North American Indians,* the papers of each year's Algonquian Conference, the *Dictionary of Canadian Biography,* the series or occasional-paper publications of various departments and divisions in such national institutions as the Canadian Museum of Civilization, as well as such provincial series as the Archaeological Survey of Alberta, plus the following periodicals: *Acadiensis, Anthropologica, Arctic, Arctic Anthropology, The Beaver, BC Studies, Canadian Historical Review, Canadian Journal of Native Education, Canadian Journal of Native Studies, Canadian Review of Sociology and Anthropology, Culture, Études/Inuit/Studies, Muse, Native Studies Review, The Northern Review, Plains Anthropologist, Recherches amérindiennes au Québec,* and *Revue d'histoire de l'Amérique française.* Among the more useful indexes are the *Canadian Periodical Index, Index for the Social Sciences,* and *Index for the Humanities.* Finally, the citations of recent literature that appear in each number of the *Canadian Historical Review* frequently include articles, essays, and books on Native Canadians.

A GUIDE TO THIS BIBLIOGRAPHY

In the remainder of this Introduction, brief comments are made on the bibliography's nineteen sections, both as a guide to each section and as a way to identify sources on particular topics or people listed in other sections. Reading these comments first, or skimming them at the very least, is strongly advised, beginning with "Bibliography and Reference" (Section 1) and "General and Comparative" (Section 2), where many works that pertain to the remaining sections of the bibliography appear. My hope is that by becoming familiar with the organization of this bibliography, with its regularities as well as—one hopes—its few oddities, students at all levels will find it to be maximally "friendly" and useful.

Part One. Reference, Comparative, and Basic Historical Sources

1. Bibliographies and Reference

Among the bibliographies, bibliographical essays, and reference works are a traditional bibliography of anthropological sources on North American Indian and Inuit tribes, organized by culture area (Murdock and O'Leary 1975), and a comparative bibliography on the United States (Prucha 1977). The many other reference works cover Arctic (Burch 1979, Condon 1990, Dekin 1978, Millar and Ervin 1981), the Northwest Coast and Plateau British Columbia (Adams 1981, Duff 1973, Legros 1984, Scherer 1990), early sources on the Northeast (Quinn 1981), Métis (Brown 1987, Friesen and Lusty 1980, Madill 1983, Martin and Makahonuk 1985), language (Campbell and Mithun 1979, Parr 1974, Pentland and Wolfart 1982; see also the remarks on "Linguistics" at the end of this Introduction), health (McCardle 1981, Meiklejohn and Rokala 1986), missionaries (Ronda and Axtell 1978), demography, the fur trade, and other topics of historical interest (Calloway, ed. 1988, Hoxie, ed. 1988, Swagerty, ed. 1984), Canadian Indian sources published during the 1960s (Abler and Weaver 1974), Native studies in Canada (Allen 1984), and dissertations and theses on Canadian Natives (Gadacz and Asch 1984). Not all of the sources listed in Section 1 are specifically mentioned here, but those that are should give a good appreciation of the range.

Among the most helpful general reference works and bibliographical aids to appear in recent years is the *Handbook of North American Indians,* which is under the general editorship of William C. Sturtevant and published periodically by the Smithsonian Institution. Volumes entitled *Northeast* (Trigger, ed. 1978), *Subarctic* (Helm, ed. 1981), *Arctic* (Damas, ed. 1984), *History of Indian-White Relations* (Washburn, ed. 1988), and *Northwest Coast* (Suttles, ed. 1990) have been published; *Plains* (Vol. 13) and other volumes that include essays on Canadian Na-

tive people will appear in due course. Specific *Handbook* chapters are of great aid, although data on the particular groups or culture areas that are the basis of *Handbook* organization should be supplemented by bibliographical information contained in other sources (e.g., for Northern Algonquians [Section 5], in addition to Trigger, ed. [1978], see Deer [1974a, 1974b], Dominique and Deschenes [1980], and Proulx [1984a, 1984b]; for Northern Athapaskans [Section 9], in addition to Helm, ed. [1981], see Burch [1979], Helm and Kurtz [1984], Krech [1980a, 1980b], and Slobodin [1975]). The *Handbook* volumes have been subject to some critical scrutiny and ought to be read as critically as any other source. When a volume appears, it is reviewed in a major review essay in *Ethnohistory,* and often in the *American Anthropologist,* which readers may wish to consult. For example, for critical reviews of *Subarctic,* see Krech (1984) and Ray and Roberts (1985), both listed in "General and Comparative"; several reviews of the *Arctic* volume of the *Handbook* have been reprinted in *Études/Inuit/Studies.*

Another useful bibliographical series is that published for the Newberry Library. Volumes of selected sources introduced by critical essays pertaining to Native Canadians have appeared on the Subarctic (Helm 1979), the Northwest Coast (Grumet 1979), the Ojibwas (Tanner 1976), the Northeast (Tooker 1978), missionaries (Ronda and Axtell 1978), and Canadian Indian policy (Surtees 1982). See also Swagerty's (1984) edited collection of essays.

Several essays listed in Section 1 discuss the development and current status of anthropological research in Anglophone and Francophone Canada and make for rewarding reading, especially for Francophone Canada, where an emphasis has been placed on community studies (including Native communities) and applied anthropology in Quebec. See in particular Gold and Tremblay (1982), Inglis (1982), and Tremblay (1982).

Finally, several essays listed in Section 12, "Writing the History of Native Canadians," contain useful bibliographical notes or listings. See especially Axtell (1978), Fisher (1982), Iverson (1984), McGee (1981), Trigger (1982a), and Walker (1971, 1983).

2. General and Comparative

Listed in this section are various monographs, reports, edited collections, and essays that are comparative in ethnographic scope or that provide detailed coverage on more than one of the special topics of Part Three, making placement in one particular section inadvisable. Some works contain useful bibliographies; this is particularly true of several introductory general books on Native North America—for example, Boxberger (1990), Driver (1969), Kehoe (1981), Newcomb (1974), Oswalt (1987), Owen, Deetz, and Fisher (1967), and Spencer and Jennings (1965). Driver's *Indians of North America* is organized by topics (such as subsistence patterns, art, property and inheritance), but the others are organized by culture area or by a group ("tribe") considered in some way representative of a culture area. One can find in these works sections—or collections of articles in the case of Owen, Deetz and Fisher—on the Northwest Coast (Tlingit for Oswalt), Iroquoia and Huronia (Iroquois for Oswalt), Northern Athapaskan and Northern Algonquian sections of the Subarctic (Chipewyan for Oswalt), and Arctic (Caribou Eskimos for Oswalt). Several works are exclusively on Native Canadian ethnology or history: Cox, ed. (1973, 1987), Fisher and Coates (1988), Jenness's (1977) classic *Indians of Canada,* McMillan (1989), Miller (1989), Miller, ed. (1991), and Price (1979). Not listed in the bibliography, because it bears a 1992 publication date, is an important new major work: Olive Dickason's *Canada's First Nations: A History of Founding Peoples* (Toronto and Norman, 1992).

The contents of several edited collections listed in Section 2 are diverse. Morrison and Wilson (1986) consists of essays on Native Canadians. Cox (1973) includes articles, some reprinted, others written for this collection, on cultural ecological approaches. In Getty and Lussier (1983), one can find essays on land cessions, treaties, Indian Affairs policy, Indian administration beginning in the eighteenth century, alcoholism, Métis, the Cypress Hills massacre, Inuit politics, and the justice system. In Getty and Smith (1978) are essays on fur-trade history, the history and contemporary situation of Indians in the Treaty 7 region, British Columbia Indian organizations in the nineteenth and early twentieth centuries, the Sioux, and Cree-Ojibwa art. The collection edited by Lotz and Lotz (1971) contains articles on missionization among the Tsimshian, Champlain's Indian policy, Beaver Indian religion, psychological research in the North, Arctic demography, and Mackenzie Delta frontier culture. In Wonders, ed. (1971), a general book on the North, appear several essays of historical interest and several specifically pertaining to Native settlements and economic resources.

An important group of essays and books listed in Section 2 is concerned with the "Heroic Age" and the interpretation of the historical record in New France, and should be looked at closely by those interested in Algonquians and Beothuks of the Eastern Maritimes (Section 4), Northern Algonquians of the Eastern Subarctic and of the Great Lakes Region (Section 5), and Iroquoia and Huronia (Section 6). Some of the more-important works to mention here, as starting points for this topic, are by Dickason (1977, 1979, 1984), Eccles (1969, 1972), Jacobs (1988), Jaenen (1969–86; especially *Friend and Foe* [1976]), Jones (1988), Slattery (1980), Surtees (1988a, 1988b), Wade (1988), and Trigger's (1985) *Natives and Newcomers,* in which there is an extended discussion of the historiography of Native Canada and of the Huron and Iroquois, as well as an extensive bibliography. See also Denys Delâge—an essay (1991) and *Bitter Feast: Amerindians and Europeans in the American Northeast, 1600–64* (Vancouver, 1993).

A work of seminal importance for the interpretation of the historical era in eastern Canada, among Algonquians of the Maritimes and of the Eastern Subarctic, is Bailey's (1969) *The Conflict of European and Eastern Algonkian Cultures, 1504–1700,* which has truly stood the test of time and remains a starting point for many whose interests lie in making sense of Native-white relations in the sixteenth and seventeenth centuries. Also listed in "Comparative and General" are publications that address interethnic relations (when the ethnic groups are in different culture areas and hence in separate sections of this bibliography) or whose concern is multiethnic communities. For example, for works on the North dealing with Inuit, on the one hand, and Northern Algonquians or Northern Athapaskans, or both, on the other, see Barger (1980), Beaudry (1988), Brody (1987), Clairmont (1963), Coates (1985), Coates and Morrison (1988), Coates and Morrison, eds. (1989), Crowe (1974), Graburn and Strong (1973), Helm and Damas (1963), Honigmann (1952, 1962, 1965, 1970, 1972, 1973), Honigmann and Honigmann (1970, 1975), Janes (1973), Kinietz (1986), Maclaren (1991), and Smith's (1979) edited collection. Some of these works, in particular those by the Honigmanns, also discuss the Métis. Placed in this category also are comparative works on Northern Algonquians and Northern Athapaskans: see Brumbach and Jarvenpa (1989), Helm and Leacock (1971), Helm, Rogers, and Smith (1981), Krech (1984), Krech, ed. (1980), Ray and Roberts (1985), Riches (1982), and Rogers and Smith (1981). At least two works (Burch 1972, Bergerud 1984) discuss a resource—caribou—harvested by various Inuit and Indian groups. A newly published work on entrepreneurship in the North is Wanda Wultenee's *In Business for Ourselves* (Montreal, 1992). An award-winning new work which has a bearing on Algonquians and Iroquoians in the Great Lakes region is Richard White's *The Middle Ground: Indians, Empires, and the Republics in the Great Lakes Region, 1650–1815* (Cambridge, 1991).

A large and significant group of authors have addressed the contemporary scene, sometimes with historical background: see, for example, Adams (1975 [1989]), Cardinal (1969, 1977), Coates (1985), Coates and Powell (1989), Comeau and Santin (1990), Dacks and Coates, eds. (1990), Dyck (1990), Frideres (1974, 1983), Hawthorn (1966–67), Hedican (1991), Krotz (1990), Manuel and Poslums (1974), Richardson, ed. (1989), Robertson (1970), Waubegeshig (1970), Wilson (1977), and Wuttunee (1971). These analyses take up to some degree issues covered comprehensively in Section 19, "Political, Legal, and Constitutional Issues."

Section 2 also lists many articles focused variously on mostly contemporary economic, social, or political patterns, on deviance, on the link between criminal justice and drinking, or a combination of those subjects. The precise subject matter can usually be discerned from the title. Consult Bernèche et al. (1980), Bienvenue and Latif (1974), Billson (1988), E. Boldt, ed., et al. (1983), M. Boldt (1980, 1981a–c), Bonta (1989), Dunning (1959), Durst (1991), Fisher (1976), Hagen (1974), Harding (1991), Hobart (1982), Inglis (1971), Kellough (1980), Lane et al. (1978), La Prairie (1988, 1990), Monture (1989), Morse (1976), Morse, ed. (1985), Parkinson (1988), Price (1982, 1983), Robinson and Ghostkeeper (1987), Ryan (1987), Schmeiser (1976), Scott (1989), Starr (1978), Weick (1988), York (1989), Young and McDermott (1988), Zentner (1963, 1970). Again, several of those address matters that are taken up systematically in Section 19, "Political, Legal, and Constitutional Issues," or Section 16, "Health and Disease."

Several works listed in Section 2 concern urban Natives: Dosman (1972), McCaskill (1981), Nagler (1973), Ryan (1978), Stanbury (1975).

Since the first edition of this bibliography, a strong interest in Native Canadian literature and writers has emerged. Through New (1990) and Petrone (1990) one can gain access to these works. See also Petrone (1983, 1985) and other works listed in Section 15, "Education," as well as the comments for that section.

3. Some Major Published Primary Historical Sources

This category ("Historical Sources," hereafter) is of utmost importance for any bibliography on Native anthropology and history. Approximately seventy-five basic historical sources, most of which are primary, have been selected and are listed. Many provide information on groups from more than one culture area. The student need not be daunted at the prospect of locating these sources, because many are available in reprint editions.

Section 3 especially presented a great challenge to the selection of sources: while few will dispute the importance of the sources that have been listed, some will argue cogently that many that should be included have not been. Indeed, if the intense interest shown in the Columbus quincentenary is any indication, the (re)translation, annotation, and analysis of primary historical documents containing observations of Native people, as well as accounts of European-Native relations, will be a sustained interest long into the future. The Columbus industry of 1992 may have held little immediate relevance to Native Canadians, but the "encounter" in general did, does, and will; and the recent concern for, say, contextualizing culturally and historically the texts of André Thevet and others may be seen in that light.

It is best for the student to be guided beyond the historical sources listed in this section by the specialist who has broad knowledge of a particular region, or to be pointed toward the specialty bibliographies in "Bibliography and Reference" that list a variety of documents and other historical sources. In addition, most essays in the *Handbook of North American Indians* contain sections on sources that list historical documents and a variety of unpublished, archival materials. Alternatively, one may wish to consult a major document series such as that of the Hudson's Bay Record Society or the publications of the Champlain Society; several volumes from both series are listed here.

Several works listed in Section 2 provide insight into the lives of Algonquians and Beothuks of the Eastern Maritimes (for the cultural and geographical boundaries of this and other regions, see Sections 4–10 in Part Two). For example, consult Cartier for information on the sixteenth-century Micmac; Nicolas Denys and Chrestien Le Clercq, a Recollect, on the seventeenth-century Micmac; and James Howley (a compilation of primary sources), on the Beothuk. Sieur de Dièreville, Lescarbot, Rand, and Thwaites also are basic for this region. A recent edition of *The Voyages of Jacques Cartier* is introduced by Ramsay Cook (Montreal, 1993).

The number of important sources increases greatly for the Northern Algonquians of the Eastern and Central Subarctic and of the Great Lakes Region. Thwaites again is basic for the region. See Sagard-Théodat on the seventeenth-century Montagnais and Samuel de Champlain on seventeenth-century Algonquians. The sources on eighteenth-century Cree include the elder Alexander Henry; Andrew Graham; Bacqueville de La Potherie (in Emma Blair's *The Indian Tribes of the Upper Mississippi Valley and the Region of the Great Lakes* [1911]); David Thompson (on the nineteenth century also); James Isham; Samuel Hearne; Chouart, Groseilliers, and Radisson (all in Grace Nute's *Caesars of the Wilderness* [1943], which includes information on the Ottawa as well); Alexander Mackenzie; and others in Davies and Johnson (1963). For the Ojibwa in the seventeenth and eighteenth centuries, see the observations of Nicolas Perrot and La Potherie (in Blair, ed. and trans. 1911), James Isham, John Long (Quaife, ed. 1922), and Baron de Lahontan, and the Jesuit Pierre de Charlevoix (for the eighteenth-century Ojibwa and the Great Lakes region). For the nineteenth-century Montagnais and Naskapi, consult Davies and Johnson, eds. (1963), Henry Hind, and John McLean.

The following provide information on Iroquoia and Huronia: Thwaites's *Jesuit Relations;* Cartier, on the sixteenth century; Champlain's *Works;* Joseph François Lafitau, Baron de Lahontan, and John Long (Quaife, ed.), on the eighteenth-century Iroquois and Huron; Sagard-Théodat, a Recollect, on the seventeenth-century Huron and Iroquois. For Indians of the Prairies and Plains, see the journals and writings of Anthony Henday (Hendry), Matthew Cocking, Henry Kelsey, François La Rocque, Duncan McGillivray, the younger Alexander Henry, and David Thompson.

Several sources pertain to the Indians of the Northwest Coast and Plateau British Columbia. For eighteenth-century comments on the Nootka, see Captain James Cook's records of his voyages (and the contributions by James King and David Samwell in Cook's *Journals*). Espinoza is also important for the Nootka, as are the turn-of-the-nineteenth-century journals of George Dixon (on Haida and Tlingit) and of Vancouver, La Pérouse, and Lisiansky (all on Tlingit). Erna Gunther has used many eighteenth-century documents in *Indian Life of the Northwest Coast of North America* (listed in Section 8, "Indians of the Northwest Coast and Plateau British Columbia"). For the nineteenth century, consult documents by Gabriel Franchère and John Jewitt (the latter for the early-nineteenth-century Nootka) and the letters of John McLoughlin (Rich, ed. 1941, 1943, 1944). Also important for this region, especially the land-based inland trade, are the journals of Alexander Mackenzie, Simon Fraser, David Thompson, and Peter Skene Ogden.

For eighteenth-century Northern Athapaskans of the Western Subarctic, see Samuel Hearne, Alexander Mackenzie, and Peter Fidler. For the nineteenth century, one can consult works by the following writers: George Back; Bishop Bompas (in Hiram Cody [1908]) on the Slavey; John Franklin (both narratives), on Mackenzie-drainage groups; Daniel Harmon, on the Carrier, Sekani, and Beaver; Wentzel and Keith (in Masson); A. H. Murray, on the Kutchin; Simon Fraser, on the Carrier and Sekani; Emile Petitot, the Oblate priest, on the Gwich'in, Hare, Slavey, and other Mackenzie-drainage groups; George Simpson, on Chipewyans and others; and Samuel Black on the early part of the century, John Richardson on the mid-1800s, and Frank Russell on the 1890s, all in the Mackenzie drainage.

For important ethnographic information on the Inuit of the Arctic, see especially John Franklin's two narratives, John Richardson, and some of the writings of Emile Petitot; and supplement those with the observations of the numerous explorers who searched for the Northwest Passage and then the remains of John Franklin, as well as other sources listed in the *Arctic* volume (Damas 1984) of the *Handbook of North American Indians.*

Finally, for some brief thoughts on historical research, see the comments below for Section 12, "Writing the History of Native Canadians."

Part Two: Regional and Ethnic Sources

As stated above, the intent in this part is to identify and list basic ethnographic sources on Native Canadian ethnic groups, or as they are more frequently termed, bands, tribes, and nations, or "First Nations," the term increasingly used in Canada. The organization by culture area corresponds to some degree to the major physiographic or biotic regions in Canada.

4. Algonquians and Beothuks of the Eastern Maritimes

Included here are the Beothuk, the Micmac, and the Maliseet-Passamaquoddy, whose traditional territories were in modern-day Newfoundland, Nova Scotia, New Brunswick, Prince Edward Island (and a small section of eastern Maine for some Passamaquoddy speakers), and on Quebec's Gaspé peninsula. The Western Abenaki are also included, even though their traditional territory in Canada was not in the Eastern Maritimes but in Quebec, directly north of the border with New Hampshire and Vermont, as well as in those two states.

For major ethnographic and historical sources, consult Bock (1966a), Day (1981), Howley (1915—in Section 3), Mechling (1958–59), K. M. Morrison (1984), Speck (1922, 1940), and Wallis and Wallis (1955, 1957); for a general edited collection, McGee (1974, 1983); for historical works, Bailey (1969—in Section 2), Sévigny (1976), Upton (1979), and Whitehead (1991); and in Trigger, ed. (1978), *Northeast* volume of the *Handbook of North American Indians,* the essays by Bock, Day, Erickson, Reynolds, and Snow.

As is the case with all sections of Part Two, some sources on the Native people of this region are listed in other sections of Parts One and Three. In all cases, in order to identify these sources, the best starting point is in Part One: in Section 1, "Bibliography and Reference"; Section 2, "General and Comparative" (be sure not to neglect Bailey's *The Conflict of European and Eastern Algonkian Cultures*); or Section 3, "Historical Sources." Of the sections of Part Three, note especially Section 17, "Art and Material Culture," which contains several important sources on Algonquians of the Eastern Maritimes; they are identified in the comments for that section.

5. Northern Algonquians of the Eastern and Central Subarctic and of the Great Lakes Region

Included in this section (hereafter referred to as "Northern Algonquians") are groups that range across an enormous expanse of territory: the Innu (or Montagnais as they are traditionally known in the literature), the Naskapi, the Attikamek (Tête de Boule), the Algonquin, the Ottawa, the Delaware, the Potawatomie, the Nipissing, many bands of Crees (the largest group in Canada, with over 90,000 in 1980), and the group variously known as the Ojibwe (Ojibwa), Chippewa, or Saulteaux (Canada's second largest, with over 60,000). The traditional territories exploited by those groups are located on the present-day Labrador peninsula and in Quebec, Ontario, Manitoba, northern Saskatchewan, and northeastern and north-central Alberta. The area is diverse ecologically, ranging from taiga in the north, to boreal forest in the vast central portions of the Canadian Shield, to parkland on the edge, and a mixture of coniferous and deciduous forest in the southern portions. All of the Indians who inhabited the region spoke an Algonquian language.

Major anthropological and historical contributions on the Native peoples of this region include Brown and Brightman (1988), Driben (1986), Driben and Trudeau (1983), Dunning (1959), Hallowell (1955, 1976), Hedican (1986a), Hickerson (1970, 1988), Hodgins and Benidickson (1989), Honigmann (1961, and in Section 2, 1962), Jenness (1935, in Section 5), Kinietz (1947, 1965), Knight (1968), Landes (1937, 1968), Leacock (1954), Mason (1967), McGhee (1961), Rogers (1962, 1963b, 1973), Shkilnyk (1985), Skinner (1911), Speck (1977), Tanner (1979), and Turner (1890); see also Stymeist (1975) and Wills (1985). Many chapters in the *Northeast* and *Subarctic* volumes of the *Handbook of North American Indians* are listed here: Barger (1981), Bishop (1981), Callender (1978), Clifton (1978), Day (1978), Day and Trigger (1978), Feest and Feest (1978), Helm, Rogers, and Smith (1981, in Section 2), Henriksen (1981), Honigmann (1981), Leacock (1981), McNulty and Gilbert (1981), Preston (1981), Rogers and Leacock (1981), Rogers and Taylor (1981), J. G. E. Smith (1981), Steinbring (1981).

Because the Great Lakes Region has often been treated as a separate area, it may be helpful to draw together here the numerous sources on Northern Algonquians who live around and near them (for which generally, consult H. Tanner 1986): for the Chip-

pewa, see Densmore (1929), Hickerson (1960, 1967a, 1967b, 1970, 1971), Hilger (1951), Kinietz (1947, 1965), Ritzenthaler (1978), and Vizenor (1984); for the Ojibwa, see Holmer (1954), Jenness (1935), Johnston (1976), Landes (1937, 1968), and Rogers (1978); for the Potawatomie, consult Clifton (1975, 1978); for the Ottawa, see Feest and Feest (1978); and for the Delaware, see Goddard (1978b), Heckewelder (1876 [1818], in Section 3), Newcomb (1956), and Weslager (1972). See also Goddard (1978a), on language; Brose (1978), on prehistory; and Bleasdale (1975), Callender (1978), Day (1978), Day and Trigger (1978), Leighton (1977), Rhodes (1984a, 1984b), Rogers (1962, 1978), Sosin (1965), and Stanley (1950). See also Charles E. Cleland's *Rites of Conquest: The History and Culture of Michigan's Native Americans* (Ann Arbor, 1992), which pertains to Canada as well as Michigan; and Richard White's *The Middle Ground* in Section 2, "General and Comparative."

Two issues that have attracted almost perennial attention concern Northern Algonquian hunting territories and windigo, and accordingly sources are listed on each. For hunting territories, see Bishop (1970), Bishop and Morantz, eds. (1986), Cooper (1939), Hallowell (1949), Knight (1965), Leacock (1954), Morantz (1978b, 1986), Rogers (1963b), Snow (1968, in Section 4), Speck (1915, 1923), Speck and Eiseley (1939), and Tanner (1971, 1973). And for windigo, see Bishop (1975c), Brightman (1988), Brown (1971), Flannery, Chambers, and Jehle (1981), Fogelson (1965), Hay (1971), Marano (1982), Norman (1982), Parker (1960), Preston (1977, 1978b, 1980b), Rohrl (1970), J. G. E. Smith (1976a), Teicher (1960), Turner (1977), and Waisberg (1975). Scapulimancy has also attracted attention; see Moore (1957), Slaughter (1981), and Tanner (1978).

To locate sources on Northern Algonquians in other sections, begin again with the three sections in Part One, looking for pertinent reference, comparative, and historical materials. In Part Three, see especially Section 13, "The Fur Trade"; Section 14, "Missionaries," where there are several relevant essays and books; and Section 15, "Education," where some items on bilingual education and other issues pertain to Northern Algonquians. Most discussions of contemporary resource use and extraction are listed in Section 19, "Political, Legal, and Constitutional Issues," but there are such exceptions as Hodgins's and Benidickson's (1989) study of forestry, aboriginal rights, and tourism and Waldram's work on hydroelectric projects in Manitoba and farther west. But for major works on the James Bay hydroelectric project and land-claims settlement, see the comments below on Section 19 and the citations in that section.

6. Iroquoia and Huronia

Included in this section are the Huron, the Neutral, the Petun, the St. Lawrence Iroquoians, and the Northern Iroquoians who were members of the Five Nations (Mohawk, Oneida, Onondaga, Cayuga, and Seneca). Those groups lived in southeastern Ontario, along the St. Lawrence in Quebec, and in New York. Section 6, perhaps more than any other, includes Native peoples whose territories were located, and whose lives were led, primarily south of the border. In some cases, many people actually went to Canada, so that a complete understanding of the history or culture of Canadian Iroquoians is premised on understanding the history or culture of Iroquoians who lived across what became the border with the United States. For example, the Mohawk in the seventeenth and eighteenth centuries established communities in Canada, as did some Oneida who moved to Ontario in the nineteenth century (and today they number over 16,000 and 3,000, respectively). Moreover, Handsome Lake's Longhouse religion spread from New York Seneca to Canadian Iroquois communities.

Major traditional and contemporary ethnographic sources and historical works are included here: Chafe (1961), Delâge (1985), Desrosiers (1947), Fenton (1936, 1953), Goldstein (1969), Graymont (1972), Hauptman (1986), Heidenreich (1971, 1972), Hunt (1940), Jennings (1984, 1988), Jennings, ed. (1985), Kelsay (1984), Morgan (1851), Richter and Merrell, eds. (1987), Shimony (1961), Tooker (1964), Trigger (1969, 1976, 1990, and others), Wallace (1969), and Weaver (1972, 1975). The

edited collection by Foster, Campisi, and Mithun (1984) contains a variety of analyses as well as a bibliography of William Fenton's numerous contributions. Also listed in this section are essays in the *Northeast* volume of the *Handbook of North American Indians,* edited by Bruce Trigger (1978): Abler and Tooker; Blau, Campisi and Tooker; Campisi; Fenton; Fenton and Tooker; Frisch; Garrad and Heidenreich; Heidenreich; Lounsbury; Morissonneau; Tooker (several); Trigger and Pendergast; Tuck; Wallace; Weaver; White; and White, Engelbrecht, and Tooker. In 1992, Daniel K. Richter published his major study, *The Ordeal of the Longhouse: The Peoples of the Iroquois League in the Era of European Colonization* (Chapel Hill, 1992), which should be consulted in addition to his other works listed in this section.

For works on Iroquoia and Huronia in other sections, see especially Trigger (1985) and the analyses of Jaenen, Eccles, and others listed in "General and Comparative"; Sioui's *Pour une autohistoire amérindienne* (or *For an Amerindian Autohistory*), listed in and discussed below in the comments for Section 12; and isolated works in Part Three, identified in the comments below on each topical section.

7. Indians of the Prairies and Plains

Included here are the several Blackfoot groups (Blackfoot, Piegan, Blood), the Assiniboine, the Sarci, the Gros Ventre, the Sioux, the Plains Cree, and the Plains Ojibwe (Plains Ojibwa) or Plains Saulteaux, otherwise known as the Bungi. These Natives lived in prairie and plains ecosystems in south-central and southwestern Manitoba, in central and southern Saskatchewan, and in central and southern Alberta. The several basic ethnographic and historical works included in Section 7 are Carter (1990), Denig and Hewitt (1930), Barbeau's (1960) collection of reminiscences, several of Dempsey's works (e.g. 1968, 1976, 1978a, 1978b, 1980, 1984), Elias (1988), Ewers (1955, 1974, 1985), Friesen (1984), Goldfrank (1945), Hanks and Hanks (1950), Howard (1965, 1984), Hungry Wolf (1977), Jenness (1938), Kehoe (1989), Laviolette (1944), Lowie (1910), Mandelbaum (1940, 1979), Samek

(1987), Tarasoff (1980), Wissler (1912, 1913, 1918), Wissler and Duvall (1908), and Witmer (1982). Two contemporary monographs are by Lithman (1984) and Meyer (1985); the latter is also very useful for its historical perspective.

Among the edited collections to note are Ubelaker and Viola (1982), in which are essays on the Blood and the Blackfoot and on Plains clothing styles; and Wood and Liberty (1980), which includes a couple of essays on Canadian Natives, although most of the articles are on United States Plains Indian groups. Another edited work, not listed because it was published in 1992, is *Buffalo* (Edmonton, 1992), edited by John Foster, Dick Harrison, and I. S. MacLaren; it includes one dozen essays on the archaeology, history, ecology, and representations of that animal. See also Bryan (1991) for a recent archaeological view of Plains dwellers.

Several analyses of the conflict on the Plains from the 1870s through the late 1880s are listed: for the Cypress Hills massacre of 1873, see, for example, Goldring (1973) and Sharp (1954); and for the events of the late 1870s and mid-1880s, including the Frog Lake incident and the careers of Big Bear, Poundmaker, and other leaders, consult, among others, Ahenakew (1960), Allen (1972), Bingaman (1975), Dempsey (1984), Fraser (1966), Hughes (1976), Tobias (1983), and Wiebe (1973, 1975). For the analysis of policy, see Helen Buckley's *From Wooden Ploughs to Welfare* (Montreal, 1992).

For works on the Plains and Prairies in other sections, see in particular Albers and Medicine's (1983) edited collection mentioned in Section 18, "Gender," and several identified in Section 17, "Art and Material Culture."

8. Indians of the Northwest Coast and Plateau (British Columbia)

The following coastal groups, from north to south, are included in this section: Haida, Tsimshian, Kwakiutl, Haisla, Bella Coola, Nootka, and Coast Salish (for the various alternative names used for Northwest Coast groups, see Suttles, ed. 1990, in Section 1). Sources on the Tlingit are an important addition to this bibliography, especially in Section

17, "Art and Material Culture," because of what they represent in a full analysis of the Northwest Coast region and its major institutions, beginning with the potlatch, even though, except for the middle Stikine River, Tlingit territory is located in Alaska. Also listed in this section are references on various Indians living on the mountainous Plateau in interior southeastern British Columbia: the Kutenai, various Interior Salish groups (Lillooet, Thompson, Shuswap, Okanagan, Lake), and the Athapaskan-speaking Nicola. Other Athapaskan speakers who live farther north (Carrier and Chilcotin, for example) are included in Section 9, "Northern Athapaskans of the Western Subarctic."

Several general works and edited collections should draw one's attention first: Drucker (1955, 1965) and Woodcock (1977) have authored general works on the region; important edited collections by McFeat (1966) and Abbott (1981), which contain several essays listed here and many mentioned in "Art and Material Culture"; Miller and Eastman (1984), which is mainly on the Tsimshian; Seguin, ed. (1984), on the Tsimshian; and of course, Suttles's (1990) edited *Northwest Coast* volume of the *Handbook of North American Indians*. Listed from the *Handbook* are essays, all bearing a 1990 date, by Amoss, Arima and Dewhirst, Blackman, Boyd, Carlson (two), Codere, Cole and Darling, Cybulski (two), De Laguna, Dunn and Booth, Fladmark et al., Halpin and Seguin, Hamori-Torok, Hilton, Hobler, Holm, Kennedy and Bouchard (two), Kew (two), Kinkade, Lohse and Sundt, Mitchell, Nelson, Renker and Gunther, Stearns, Suttles (four), Suttles and Jonaitis, and Webster.

Many substantial ethnographic or historical contributions are listed in Section 8: Amoss (1978a), Arima (1983), Assu and Inglis (1989), Barnett (1955), Barbeau (1973), all of Franz Boas's, Boelscher (1988), Carstens (1991), Collins (1974) on Coast Salish of Washington, De Laguna (1960, 1972), Drucker (1951), Ford (1941), Goldman (1975), Krause (1956), McIlwraith (1948), Oberg (1973), Rohner and Rohner (1970), Stearns (1981), Swanton (1909), Teit (1898, 1900, 1906, 1909), and Walens (1981). Works that are largely historical in focus are by Fisher (1977) and Duff (1964)—both of which are fundamental—and by Gough (1980, 1984), Gunther (1972; an important discussion of sources), and La Violette (1973). Contemporary analyses to note are by Hawthorn, Belshaw, and Jamieson (1958), Knight (1978), Lewis (1970), and Stanbury and Siegel (1975).

The most famous Northwest Coast institution, and one that has attracted a great deal of attention over the decades, is the potlatch. Discussions of the potlatch are sprinkled throughout many of the works cited in the preceding paragraph; in addition, see the following, which are devoted specifically to understanding the nature of this noted Northwest Coast institution: Adams (1973), Barnett (1938), Clutesi (1969), Codere (1950), Cole and Chaikin (1990), Drucker and Heizer (1967), Dundes (1979), all of Kan's work on the Tlingit, Murdock (1936), Orans (1975), Piddocke (1965), Riches (1984), Ringel (1979), Rosman and Rubel (1971, 1972), Spradley (1969), and Suttles (1960).

Additional information on Northwest Coast and Plateau Indians can be found in other sections, in particular in Section 17, "Art and Material Culture," where many sources are listed on all of the Northwest Coast groups, especially the Tlingit; and in Section 13, "The Fur Trade." See also the reference works by Adams, Duff, and Grumet listed in "Bibliography and Reference." Noteworthy also is Blackman's (1982) *During My Time,* the life history of Florence Davidson Edenshaw (in "Gender"), and works identified below in the comments for Section 14, "Missionaries." Three recently published works are Brian Hayden's *A Complex Culture of the British Columbia Plateau* (Vancouver, 1992); *To the Charlottes: George Dawson's 1878 Survey of the Queen Charlotte Islands,* edited by Douglas Cole and Bradley Lockner (Vancouver, 1993); and Barry Gough's *The Northwest Coast British Navigation, Trade, and Discoveries to 1812* (Vancouver, 1992).

9. Northern Athapaskans of the Western Subarctic
This section lists works on Northern Athapaskans who live in the Arctic drainage and in Canadian sections of the Cordillera: from south to north (roughly),

the Chilcotin, the Carrier, the Tsetsaut, the Tahltan, the Sekani, the Beaver, the Chipewyan, the Yellowknife, the Slavey, the Dogrib, the Hare, the Mountain Indians, the Kaska, the Inland Tlingit, the Tagish, the Tutchone, the Han, and the Gwich'in (Loucheux, Kutchin). A very small section of the homeland of the Tanana was also within Canadian territory. This vast region encompasses parts of four Canadian provinces and both territories: northern Manitoba and Saskatchewan, northern and northwestern Alberta, the central and northern interior of British Columbia, the forested and taiga portions of the Northwest Territories west of Hudson Bay, and most of the Yukon Territory.

As with all sections in this bibliography, consult Section 1, "Bibliography and Reference," for pertinent reference material; and Section 2, "General and Comparative," for analyses of the relations between Northern Athapaskans and other ethnic groups such as the Northern Algonquians and the Inuit, and for accounts of the multiethnic settings shared by Northern Athapaskans and members of other ethnic groups.

A good starting point for the ethnography of this region is Van Stone's (1974) general work, *Athapaskan Adaptations*. Other major ethnographic contributions are Balikci (1963), Christian and Gardner (1977), Cruikshank (1991), Emmons (1911), Goddard (1916), Guédon (1974), Hara (1980), Helm (1961), Helm and Lurie (1961), Honigmann (1946, 1949, 1954), Jarvenpa (1980), Jenness (1937, 1943), McClellan (1975b), McKennan (1959, 1965), Nelson (1973), Osgood (1931, 1936a, 1971), Ridington (1978b, 1989, 1990b), Rushforth (1984), Rushforth and Chisholm (1991), Savishinsky (1974), Sharp (1979, 1988), Slobodin (1962), David Smith (1982), and Van Stone (1965). See also Guy Lanoue's *Brothers: The Politics of Violence among the Sekani of Northern British Columbia* (New York/Oxford, 1992). When it appeared, Clark (1975) was a crucial set of essays on Northern Athapaskans, two of them are separately listed here (De Laguna 1975, McClellan 1975). Other important edited collections are J. G. E. Smith (1976), on Chipewyan adaptations, and Lantis (1970). Listed also are analyses from the

Subarctic volume of the Handbook of North American Indians, edited by June Helm (1981)—but see the remarks above in "Bibliography and Reference" on the Handbook, as well as on bibliographical materials for this region.

In other sections, see especially additional works by Julie Cruikshank listed in Section 18, "Gender"; the essays and books by Asch (1976), Coates (1982, 1984), Krech (1976, 1981, 1982, 1983, 1984), McCormack (1984), Sloan (1979), Yerbury (1976, 1981, 1985), and others in Section 13, "The Fur Trade"; and Section 19, "Political, Legal, and Constitutional Issues," where works pertaining to Dene land claims and the exploitation and transportation of hydrocarbon resources are listed and identified. The North has been extraordinarily active politically in recent years, with both Inuit and Northern Athapaskan claims (the Inuit claim for Nunavut, and the Fort McPherson Gwich'in claim for land in the northwest corner of the Northwest Territories), and many works are devoted to describing the changing political scene.

10. Inuit of the Arctic

Canadian Inuit lived in bands distributed from the Mackenzie Delta and Yukon coast in the west to the Labrador coast in the East, and today they inhabit towns throughout that area. The tribal or tribelike groupings (as identified in Damas's [1984] Arctic volume of the Handbook), west to east, are the Inuvialuit, or Mackenzie Delta Eskimo, the Copper Eskimo, the Netsilik, the Caribou Eskimo, the Iglulik, the Sallirmiut, the Baffinland Eskimo, the Inuit of Quebec, and the Labrador Coast Eskimo. Native political associations, many Natives, and the Canadian government prefer the name Inuit to Eskimo, but the Mackenzie Delta Eskimo prefer Inuvialuit to Inuit as a self-designation.

General works that serve as introductions to the Inuit are by Birket-Smith (1959), Dumond (1977), M. A. Freeman (1975), Jenness (1959), Mary-Rousselière (1980), Metayer (1971), Pitseolak and Eber (1975), and Stefánsson (1913, 1921). For historical periods when commercial whaling was important, see Ross (1975) and Francis (1984).

Included in Section 10 are major monographs on traditional and contemporary ethnography. The more traditional ethnographic works, including analyses of kinship, adoption, alliance, and the like, are by Balikci (1970), Birket-Smith (1929, 1945), Boas (1901–1907, 1964), Damas (1963), Graburn (1964), Guemple (1972a), Guemple, ed. (1979), Jenness (1922), Rasmussen (1929, 1930a, 1930b, 1931, 1932), Saladin d'Anglure (1967), Smith (1991), Steenhoven (1959), and Turner (1894). Not as comprehensive as the above, but also noteworthy, are several analyses of female infanticide (Balikci 1967, Riches 1974, Schrire and Steiger 1974, 1981), literature (McGrath 1984), suicide (Balikci 1960b), the patterning of emotions (Briggs 1970), and music (Cavanaugh 1982, Lutz 1982, Eckert and Newmark 1980, Nattiez 1980).

Other works are focused more on contemporary settings (Condon 1983, 1987, Graburn 1969, Honigmann and Honigmann 1965, Usher 1970, Vallee 1967b, Wenzel 1981, Williamson 1974), and some are concerned with Inuit-white relations (Balikci 1961, Ben-Dor 1966, Brody 1975, Jenness 1964, 1965, 1968, Paine 1977b, Paine, ed. 1971, Vallee 1967a). A recent work discussing both traditional and contemporary life is John Matthiasson's Living on the Land: Change among the Inuit of Baffin Island (Peterborough, Ont., 1992).

For essays on various Inuit groups, on language, on contemporary Inuit, and on other issues in Damas's (1984) Arctic volume of the Handbook of North American Indians, see essays by the following, all bearing the 1984 date: Arima, Balikci, Brantenberg and Brantenberg, Damas (two), Freeman (two), Kemp, McGhee, Mary-Rousselière, Maxwell, Neatby, Saladin d'Anglure (two), D. G. Smith, Taylor, Woodbury, and Vallee, Smith and Cooper.

Arctic archaeology has been especially active in recent years, including some work in the Northern Athapaskan region (e.g., see Gordon's work in Section 5 for the Inuit also). Accordingly, a substantial number of archaeological analyses are listed in this section; see comments under "Archaeology" below for this literature.

For information on the Inuit in other sections, see

Section 2, "General and Comparative," where sources pertaining to the historical and contemporary relationship between Inuit and Indians are listed. Consult especially Section 17, "Art and Material Culture," for sources on traditional and contemporary art, and Section 19, "Political, Legal, and Constitutional Issues," for sources on land claims including the Nunavut. In other sections of Part Three additional works pertaining to the Inuit can almost always be identified from their titles or by comments (e.g., see remarks on Section 16, "Health and Disease" below).

11. Métis

The literature on the Métis and their most visible representative, Louis Riel, underwent a virtual explosion in the 1980s. Some works on Riel and the 1885 rebellion are readily identified by their title. Of the several major biographies listed in Section 11, the student can begin with Bowsfield (1969, 1971), Flanagan (1983a), Stanley (1963, 1970), or the bibliographical essay by Lafontaine (1979); see also Brown (1987), in "Bibliographies and Reference." Additional insights into Riel's thoughts are contained in Flanagan's (1976a) *The Diaries of Louis Riel,* but for a comprehensive examination of Riel's writings, see the five-volume collection by G. F. G. Stanley and his associates (1986).

There is also a rapidly expanding literature on Métis history, identity, and ethnicity, as well as on Métis rights and claims. Many of the issues are addressed in works listed in Section 11. The best introduction is provided by two fairly recently published collections: *The New Peoples,* edited by Jacqueline Peterson and Jennifer S. H. Brown (1985), which contains articles on the origins of the Métis and on Métis ethnicity, including revised versions of Peterson (1982) and Dickason (1982), and other topics; and Waldram and Barron's (1985) edited collection, *1885 and After,* which contains eighteen essays on Riel, the Métis rebellion, and the aftermath. See also a special issue of *Canadian Ethnic Studies,* guest edited by Thomas Flanagan and John Foster (1985), in which essays on federal policy making for Métis, on Métis identity, and on other issues appear. Other

essays on federal policy and Native rights are by Flanagan (1983a), Pelletier (1974), Sealey (1975), Sprague (1980a, 1980b, 1988), and Taylor (1983); see also Frideres (1983) in "General and Comparative." For information on the Métis in other sections see comments above in "General and Comparative" as well as Adams's (1975) *Prison of Grass* listed there; the works of Jennifer Brown (in particular, her *Strangers in Blood* [1980]), Carol Judd, and Sylvia Van Kirk, listed in Section 13, "The Fur Trade"; and the analyses of Brown and Van Kirk (especially the latter's *Many Tender Ties* [1980]) and Campbell's *Halfbreed,* in Section 18, "Gender."

Part Three: Special Topics

As stated earlier, the original intent in Part Three was to bring together references on eight topics that were topical in the mid-1980s. They are as relevant today. Indeed, the vast expansion of interest in areas such as art and material culture (and museums) and political and constitutional issues, and the perennial interest in others such as the fur trade, seem to confirm the continued usefulness of the initial selection.

12. Writing the History of Native Canadians

In recent years the historiography of Native Canada and the United States has been a sustained interest. In one sense this reflects much wider concerns: the historiography of indigenous peoples in general; historicizing anthropology, as well as anthropologizing history; and multiculturalism. For Canadian Native people, perhaps the most critical question is, What constitutes an adequate history of a Canadian Native group, of Canadian Native-white relations, or of a particular issue or problem involving Canadian Native people? Historiography involves minimally the interpretation of primary historical materials (for example, the "Historical Sources" of Section 3), as well as a wide range of archival materials found in repositories like the Hudson's Bay Company Archives, the National Archives of Canada, and provincial and ecclesiastical archives. Thus, in order to write the history of any group, both published and unpublished documentary materials must be analyzed. Yet to deal with certain types of historical problems (perhaps all) and certain eras (perhaps all), one might argue that a history that is also an ethnohistory should combine the analysis of documentary and archival materials with oral history and other information obtained, as it were, in the ethnographic field or in ethnographic archives.

Then, of course, there is the matter of interpretation, of theory. Ethnohistory, or anthropological history, draws on a greater range of sources than more traditional forms of history. In the past, it was used most often by anthropologists and historians interested primarily in the past of a people among whom anthropologists conducted ethnographic work (such as Canadian Native people). In contrast to history or anthropology, ethnohistory is not a discipline with its own theory. It lacks theory separate from theory in history or anthropology—although the very label "ethnohistory" contains assumptions about what is an appropriate ethnos for an ethnohistory, assumptions with which a reflexive historiography might be in conflict, preferring instead a label like anthropological history or historical anthropology. That matter aside, the play between anthropology and history has been extraordinarily active in recent years, and accordingly the selection of essays and books for Section 12 was difficult. For extended discussion of all the issues, see Krech (1991).

A great range of viewpoints is included in this section. Some argue that a history of a Native Canadian group must be ethnohistorical in the sense that the term is cognate with others in which ethno- is a prefix; others assert that the Native group, wherever it happens to be located, must be placed in the broader context of global processes and the wider world, which should be considered in any "history" of a particular group. For examples of the first perspective, see Raymond Fogelson's (1985) "Night Thoughts," in which he talks about the great importance of Native ideas of time, duration, event, and person for writing Native history; Bruner's (1986) important essay on narratives that, through time, have structured American Indian historiography; and Clifton's (1979) critique of several works in the

"tribal history" genre. For examples of the second, global perspective, see White (1983) or Eric Wolf's *Europe and the People Without History,* which contains a chapter on the fur trade in Canada and elsewhere. Wolf argues, in the general style of F. Braudel, I. Wallerstein and others, that understanding the exchange for furs requires that it be put in the context of global processes and expanding European economic systems.

There is much between those two poles, some of which is revealed in critical essays on particular bodies of literature (Axtell 1978, Fisher 1982, Iverson 1984, McGee 1981, Trigger 1982a, Walker 1971, 1983)—all recommended as good introductions to many issues.

Another set of essays focuses on understanding the Native-white relations, cultural encounters, and the worlds of both Indians and Europeans. James Axtell (1981 and elsewhere) has been particularly active in this regard, publishing several collections of essays; his most recent collection, *Beyond 1492* (New York, 1992), was published in the Columbus quincentenary year. Trigger (1971, 1981, 1982b, 1984, 1991) has also actively presented revisionist views of Indian-white relations in New France; his (1985) *Natives and Newcomers: Canada's "Heroic Age" Reconsidered* (see "General and Comparative") is one of the more significant of his many historiographical analyses of the relations between Champlain and other Europeans and the Huron and other Natives of New France. The evaluation of European writings and attitudes is as important as plumbing Native perspectives for a proper understanding of Native history, as Trigger, Cornelius Jaenen (1978, 1983, 1984; see also "General and Comparative"), Olive Dickason, and others have emphasized. So also is an understanding of invented traditions (Clifton, ed. 1990; see Bruner 1986, Hobsbawm and Ranger, eds. 1983).

As Native people increasingly write their own history, their historical methods and assumptions occasionally stand in sharp contrast to mainstream history—which makes Native historiography challenging and lively. One acerbic dispute in the United States is over how to weigh the contribution, if any, of Iroquois political thought to the U.S. Constitution. The extent of the polemic can be seen in reactions to James Clifton's edited collection, *The Invented Indian* (1990), and in several books that appeared in 1992: Ward Churchill's *Fantasies of the Master Race,* edited by M. Annette Jaimes (Monroe, Me., 1992); *Struggle for the Land: Indigenous Resistance to Genocide, Ecocide, and Expropriation in Contemporary North America* (Monroe, Me., 1992) and *The State of Native America: Genocide, Colonization, and Resistance,* both edited by M. Annette Jaimes (Boston, 1992). For a new departure for Native Canada that reflects writings in other parts of the world, see Sioui's *Pour un autohistoire amérindienne* (the English edition, *For an Amerindian Autohistory* [Montreal, 1992] appeared recently), a polemic on history from a Native point of view, by a Native historian, for Native purposes.

Because so many works throughout this bibliography pertain to the writing of Native history, issues that are historiographical in nature are implied throughout, whether or not they are explicitly acknowledged. In "Writing the History of Native Canadians," as in no other section, publications are included that have nothing directly to do with Native Canada but are fundamental for writing history; See Cohn (1987), Hobsbawm and Ranger, eds. (1983), Keesing (1990), and White (1983). Again, and finally, for a recent discussion of many of the issues raised in this literature, as well as of theoretical agendas that underlie ethnohistories, see "The State of Ethnohistory" (Krech 1991).

13. The Fur Trade
For the best recent introduction to pre-1984 literature on the fur trade, see Peterson and Anfinson's (1984) comprehensive critical review. Consult also the remarks in the introduction of *The Subarctic Fur Trade* (Krech, ed. 1984). The comments that follow here provide a guide to sources that pertain to the fur trade included in this section and found elsewhere.

A number of monographs and edited collections, plus several general works, are listed in Section 13. Many of them provide immediate access to literature as well as insights into the issues discussed by fur-

trade scholars; see especially Bishop (1974), Brown (1980), Francis and Morantz (1983), Heidenreich and Ray (1976), Innis (1970), Krech (1988), Krech, ed. (1981, 1984), Martin (1978), Miller and Hamell (1986), Ray (1974), Ray and Freeman (1978), Thistle (1986), Tough (1988), and Yerbury (1985). Fur Trade Conference selected proceedings (Bolus 1972, Buckley 1984, Judd and Ray 1980, Trigger et al. 1986) are also useful collections. A recent multi-part narrative of the trade, written expressly for a popular audience (for the first two parts, see Newman 1985, 1987), has attracted both attention and substantial critique (e.g., Brown 1986, Fisher 1988).

Virtually all of Canada's ethnographic regions are represented by at least several analyses of the fur trade in Section 13. To those should be added works that pertain in part to the fur trade but are listed in the ethnographic sections. For example, for Northern Algonquians of the Eastern Maritimes, Subarctic, or Great Lakes (Sections 4 and 5), see, in Section 13, Arthur (1985), Bishop (1972, 1974, 1981), Burley (1981), Francis and Morantz (1983), Hickerson (1956), Krech (1988), Lytwyn (1986), Martin (1975), Morantz (1980, 1982, 1983, 1984), Preston (1975), Rogers (1983), and Tanner (1978). To those add from Section 4 ("Algonquians and Beothuks"), Brasser (1978), Martin (1974), Seeber (1984), and especially Upton's (1979) *Micmacs and Colonists;* and from Section 5 ("Northern Algonquians"), the essays on hunting territories (see the comments for that Section above), Hickerson's *Chippewa and Their Neighbors* (1970—in Section 5) and his other essays, Grant (1983), Greenberg and Morrison (1982), Hanks (1982), Murphy and Steward (1957), Taylor (1972), and many of the works of Charles Bishop, Eleanor Leacock, Toby Morantz, and Edward Rogers and Mary Black-Rogers.

For Iroquoia and Huronia, see in Section 13, Calloway (1987), Dickinson (1987), Eccles (1988), Miller and Hamell (1986), and Norton (1974). For the role of the Iroquois in the West, see Karamanski (1982), Nicks (1980), and Trelease (1962). Add from Section 6 the works of Conrad Heidenreich and Bruce Trigger (especially the latter's *The Children of Aataentsic),* Abler (1975), and a few others.

For the Indians of the Plains and Prairies, consult in Section 13, Ewers (1972), Schilz (1984), and Wood and Thiessen (1984), and add from Section 7 the rest of Ewers's works and Goldfrank's. For the Northwest Coast, see in Section 13, Fisher (1977), Grumet (1984), and Harris and Ingram (1972), to which add from Section 8, de Laguna (1972), Codere (1950), Duff (1964), and particularly Fisher's (1977) *Contact and Conflict.* Also relevant, but not listed in any section, is James R. Gibson's *Otter Skins, Boston Ships, and China Goods: The Maritime Fur Trade of the Northwest Coast, 1785–1841* (Seattle, 1992). For the Northern Athapaskan region, examine in Section 13, Asch (1976), Coates (1982, 1984), Holmgren (1984), Janes (1975), Janes and Losey (1974), Jarvenpa and Brumbach (1984), Jarvenpa and Zenner (1979), Karamanski (1983), Krech (1976, 1981, 1982, 1983, 1984, 1987), McCormack (1984), Parker (1976), Sloan (1979), and Yerbury (1976, 1981, 1985); and from Section 9, Bishop (1980, 1983), Gillespie (1970, 1975a, 1975b, 1976), Helm (1978, 1980), Janes (1976), Krech (1978a, 1978b, 1980, 1982, 1983, 1984), Sharp (1977a), D. M. Smith (1982), J. G. E. Smith (1976b), Yerbury (1977, 1978), plus several studies of contemporary trapping, Savishinsky (1978), Sharp (1975b), Slobodin (1969b), Tetso (1970), and Van Stone (1963a).

Other important works in "General and Comparative" should be mentioned here: Bailey's *Conflict of European and Eastern Algonkian Cultures* is of utmost importance, as is Trigger's *Natives and Newcomers,* mentioned in other contexts above; see also Jaenen (1984), Krech, ed. (1980), Krech (1984), Martin (1980), Ray and Roberts (1985), and the essay by Ray in Getty and Smith, ed. (1978). Numerous fur traders' journals and narratives and even more of their comments on the trade are to be found in Section 3, "Historical Sources." In Section 12, "Writing the History of Native Canadians," see the chapter on the fur trade in Wolf's *Europe and the People Without History.* And consult the work of Jennifer Brown and Sylvia Van Kirk in the sections "Métis" and "Gender."

It is difficult to summarize succinctly this vast literature. Fundamental issues are the nature of the trade; whether or not it produced dependence; whether economic or political dimensions were more important; whether or not it promoted fundamental social, economic and cultural changes; and the reasons for Native participation in the trade. These questions were raised years ago by Innis, Bailey, and Rich, and have been debated ever since; there are ongoing debates on all of the points. Innis's work has undergone revisionist critique (Eccles 1972, 1981; Grant 1981); the creative roles played by Indians in the trade have been stressed (Ray 1974, Ray and Freeman 1978, Fisher 1977 [in Section 8]); economic and ideological dimensions of participation in the trade are debated (Martin 1978, Krech, ed. 1981); alternative chronological frameworks, with implicit assumptions of stability and change embedded in each framework, are proposed for the historical period (Bishop and Ray 1976; the essays of Helm and her colleagues and Rogers and Smith 1981 [in "General and Comparative"], Krech 1984, Ray and Roberts 1985 [in General and Comparative], Krech, ed. 1984); the political and economic dimensions of the trade are discussed (e.g., Eccles 1979, 1983; Rotstein 1972, Ray 1985); it is actively debated whether the fur trade produced a common experience (e.g., Hickerson 1973, Wolf's 1982 essay in Section 12), or a range of responses; and the growth of settlement populations and the nature of fur-trade families are analyzed (Brown 1976, 1977, 1980, 1982; Judd 1980a, 1980b, 1986; Van Kirk 1980).

Those are issues that have been raised during the last few years. The Fur Trade Conference proceedings give some indication of interests at the time that each conference was held (see Bolus, ed. 1972; Judd and Ray, eds. 1980, Buckley, ed. 1984). The essays published following the 1985 conference were selected primarily because they addressed the nature of the early fur trade in North America (Trigger et al., eds. 1986).

14. Missionaries

For decades there has been strong interest in the impact of Christianity on Native religions and lives; in recent years, this has included the analysis of the accommodation, or indigenization, of Christianity to persistent Native systems of symbol and thought. One impact of missionization, of course, has been on the formal education of Native people, which in the early years government left in the hands of missionaries (see Section 15, "Education"). For evidence that the relationship of Christian and Native thought can occasion great debate, see reaction to Sam Gill's (1987) *Mother Earth.*

Inasmuch as Native religions are a principal focus of this section, it may help to list several sources from which one can gain familiarity with the continental breadth of religions and religious traditions: Dooling and Jordan-Smith, eds. (1989), Gill (1982, 1983), Hultkrantz (1979, 1987), Sullivan, ed. (1989), Tedlock and Tedlock, eds. (1975), and Vecsey, ed. (1990) are good places to begin; collectively the essays in the edited volumes are broad ranging, both topically and areally, and some are directly concerned with such Canadian Native peoples as the Inuit, the Ojibwa, and the Dunne-za. Although his works are not listed here, Mircea Eliade, through *The Sacred and the Profane: The Nature of Religion* (New York, 1959) and many other books, has had a lasting influence on many scholars of religion.

The best starting points with issues that arise from Native Canadian experiences with missionaries may be in three book-length studies published during the 1980s and in a critical bibliography: *The Invasion Within: The Contest of Cultures in Colonial North America,* by James Axtell (1985); *American Indians and Christian Missions: Studies in Cultural Conflict,* by Henry Bowden (1981); *Moon of Wintertime: Missionaries and the Indians of Canada in Encounter Since 1534,* by John W. Grant (1984); and *Indian Missions: A Critical Bibliography,* by James Ronda and James Axtell (1978), listed in "Bibliography and Reference." Three of those four discuss the mission experience on the American side of the border as well as in Canada, a comparative dimension which is not a drawback in analysis of the Canadian Native encounter with missionaries. Berkhofer's (1965) *Salvation and the Savage* remains fundamental on many issues. Various topics may be pursued, including the nature of conversion, the degree to which aboriginal religious systems changed

or persisted, the establishment of ideal religious communities, the attitudes of missionaries towards Indians (and of Native Canadians toward missionaries), the roles of Indian catechists, missionary strategies and tactics, and the relation between missionaries and the fur trade (and fur traders) or between missionaries and the potlatch. That list is by no means exhaustive, but merely representative of the sources in Section 14.

The sources in "Missionaries" are weighted heavily, not by design, toward certain selected regions of Native Canada. Much has been written on the Northwest Coast, for example, but comparatively less on the mission experience for Natives living in the Arctic, the Athapaskan and Algonquian sections of the Subarctic, or the Plains. For the Northwest Coast and Plateau, see Bolt (1983), Fisher (1977), Gough (1982, 1983), Gresko (1982), Henderson (1974), Kan (1985), La Violette (1951), Lemert (1954), Mulhall (1986), Murray (1988), Patterson (1981, 1982a, 1982b), Rettig (1980), Stevenson (1986, 1990), Usher (1968, 1971b, 1974), Whitehead (1981a, 1981b), Whitehead, ed. (1988), and Zaslow (1966). A recent analysis of Native-missionary relations is Clarence Bolt's *Thomas Crosby and the Tsimshian* (Vancouver, 1992). These studies cover a wide range of topics, including the nature of conversion, missionaries and the potlatch, reactive and nativistic movements, missionary theory, history, tactics and strategies, the role of Indian catechists, and the development of model communities. Several monographs listed in "Indians of the Northwest Coast and Plateau British Columbia" contain significant data on religion and the mission experience: Duff's *The Indian History of British Columbia,* Fisher's *Contact and Conflict,* Gough's *Gunboat Frontier,* La Violette's *The Struggle for Survival,* and Spradley's *Guests Never Leave Hungry* (which chronicles the life of James Sewid, a Kwakiutl Indian) are most important here.

Books in other ethnographic sections also contain significant information on the impact of missionary ideas and policies on Native religion and ideology. Bruce Trigger's *The Children of Aataentsic* and A. F. C. Wallace's *Death and Rebirth of the Seneca* are of the greatest significance for "Iroquoia and Huronia," where they are found, as well as for analyses in other regions. See also in Section 6, Blanchard (1982), Burns (1966), Delâge (1982), Harrod (1984), Moore (1982), and other works by Trigger and Axtell. Trigger's *Natives and Newcomers* and Cornelius Jaenen's (1984) *The French Relationship with the Native Peoples,* both listed in "General and Comparative," should also be consulted. Several major works discuss missionary impact and religious change (or persistence) in the Algonquian-speaking regions of eastern and central Canada: Morrison, *The Embattled Northeast*; Upton, *Micmacs and Colonists*; Vecsey, *Traditional Ojibwa Religion and Its Historical Changes*; Gray (1956), on the Moravian presence among the Delaware; and to a lesser extent, Bailey, *Conflict of European and Eastern Algonkian Cultures.* Adrian Tanner's *Bringing Home Animals* should be read in conjunction with those, as should some of Richard Preston's works (listed in "Northern Algonquians"), in order to discern the degree of religious persistence or change. C. L. Miller's *Prophetic Worlds,* (1985), an analysis of nineteenth-century events on the Columbia Plateau, just south of the border, pertains to Plateau Natives in Canada as well; however, this work has been forcefully critiqued.

Several works in "Historical Sources" contain valuable historical information on missionary-Native relations, beginning with the 73-volume *Jesuit Relations,* edited by Thwaites, and the journals and observations of others who are identified there as Oblates, Recollects, and so forth. The role of Christianity in Louis Riel's thought, covered in publications in Section 11, "Métis," also should not be overlooked.

Finally, the mission experience has been the focus of many twentieth-century comments: see, for example, Cardinal's *Unjust Society* ("General and Comparative") or Fumoleau's *As Long as This Land Shall Last* ("Legal, Political, and Constitutional Issues") for insights into the role of missionaries in the treaty-making process.

15. Education

With respect to education—which here means formal education—the two issues most dealt with are the widespread perception that formal education has often been and still is a source of cultural conflict for many Native Canadians, and Native people's growing involvement in the education of their children by incorporating culturally sensitive materials and Native languages into the curriculum. The beginning point is with Hawthorn's *A Survey of the Contemporary Indians of Canada,* the so-called Hawthorn Report, on education; and with several reactions published after the Hawthorn Report, notably Harold Cardinal's *The Rebirth of Canada's Indians* and *The Unjust Society* (all of these are listed in "General and Comparative"). See also the recently published *Indian Education in Canada,* volume 1, *The Legacy,* and volume 2, *The Challenge,* both edited by Barman, Hébert, and McCaskill, which are collections of essays on the history of Native education in both mission and federal residential schools and on contemporary attempts by Natives to control the education in their communities. The history of Native education in Canada is tied to mission-run schools, and several works investigate the mission-school experience (see Chalmers 1976, Fisher 1981, Gladstone 1967, Gresko 1975, Krech 1978, and Wilson 1974; see also C. S. Ford's (1941) *Smoke from Their Fires,* Spradley's (1969) *Guests Never Leave Hungry,* and Fisher's (1977) *Contact and Conflict,* all listed in Section 8, "Indians of the Northwest Coast and Plateau British Columbia"; and Grant's (1984) *Moon of Wintertime,* in "Missionaries"). An important ethnographic report on education is King's (1967) *School at Mopass.*

Analyses of bilingualism, literacy, the development of Native-language orthographies, the involvement of Native teachers, and the assumption by Natives of control over their education are listed in Section 15; see especially Allison (1983), Beaudoin (1977b), special issue on education in *Canadian Association in Support of Native Peoples Bulletin,* Burnaby (1980, 1982, 1983, 1984, 1985, 1987), Burnaby, ed. (1985), Clarke and Mackenzie (1980), Leavitt (1987, 1989), McGrath (1991–92), Murdoch (1982), Preston (1979), Toohey (1983, 1985), Tschanz (1980), and Wyatt (1978). Burnaby (1985) contains an important set of twenty articles on implementing Native orthographies in Micmac, Montagnais, Cree, Dene, and Inuktitut, among other languages.

Another set of analyses explores adult education and vocational education; see Carney (1982, 1983) and Dieleman (1983) in particular. Other works are concerned with the roles evaluated highly by students: see McElroy (1979), Matthiasson (1979), and Smith (1974).

Several essays explore the impact of television in Native Canadian communities; for example, Coldevin and Wilson (1982), Graburn (1982), Hanks (1981), Hanks et al. (1983), Molohon (1984), and Watson (1980).

In other sections, consult especially Honigmann and Honigmann's (1970) *Arctic Townsmen,* Robertson's (1970) *Reservations Are for Indians,* and Nagler's (1973) *Indians in the City* (in "General and Comparative"); Driben and Trudeau's (1983) *When Freedom Is Lost* and Lithman's (1984a) *The Community Apart* (in "Northern Algonquians"); Berger's (1977) *Northern Frontier, Northern Homeland* and Watkins, ed. (1977), *Dene Nation* (in "Political, Legal, and Constitutional Issues"); and Brody's (1975) *People's Land* (in "Inuit of the Arctic").

16. Health and Disease

This section of the bibliography can be understood as the result of long-standing and continuing interests, first, in Native theories of disease and death (which change as Western theories supplement and supplant traditional theories), and second, in mortality both from the epidemics introduced by Europeans and on contemporary reserves. Among the articles discussing in general terms either historical or contemporary health, disease, and demographic patterns for Native Canada, Brady (1983), Graham-Cumming (1967), Hurlich (1983), Jarvis and Boldt (1982), Piche (1973), Stymeist (1976), Trovato (1987), and Young (1979, 1983, 1984) are good starting points. The literature on health and disease in the Arctic, reported in *Proceedings of the Circumpolar Health Conferences* and elsewhere, is especially strong; see, for example, Christie and Halpern (1990), Fortuine, ed. (1985), Grondin

(1989), Harvald and Hansen, eds. (1982), Shepherd and Itoh, eds. (1976), Milan, ed. (1980), Duval and Thérien (1982), J.-P. Thouez et al. (1989, 1990), and Tremblay (1981).

The use of alcohol by Native people and the link between alcohol abuse and mortality patterns, including suicide, has attracted much attention in Canada, as it has in the United States. This interest is reflected in numerous sources listed in Section 16: Bagley (1991), Balikci (1968), Brody (1971, 1977), Clairmont (1962), Dailey (1968), a collection edited by Hamer and Steinbring (1980), Hobart (1978), Honigmann (1945), Lemert (1954), Lithman (1979), Lurie (1969), MacAndrew and Edgerton (1969), McLeod (1963), Minorr (1991), Robbins (1973), Savishinsky (1977), Schumann (1982), Steinbring (1980), Vachon (1960), and Waddell (1985); see also Shkilnyk (1985) in "Northern Algonquians." For the link between alcohol use and the criminal justice system, see the comments above on Section 2, "General and Comparative."

Other specific topics addressed in articles listed here are cancer (Hodgson 1983), diabetes (Hagey 1984), tuberculosis (Hodgson 1982, T. K. Young et al. 1990), mental and psychological issues (Carey 1988; Christie and Halpern 1990; Fritz and D'Arcy 1983; Jilek 1974, 1980; Vallee 1966, 1968), and the role of Native healers and intermediaries (Jilek 1982, Kennedy 1984, Kaufert and Koolage 1984).

Numerous analyses of the impact of diseases during various historical periods (see Decker 1991, Zubrow 1991) are in Section 16, where they can easily be identified by title, and elsewhere: for example, Miller (1982), for Algonquians and Beothuks of the Eastern Maritimes; La Rocque (1980), Schlesier (1976), and Trigger (1976, 1981), for Iroquoia and Huronia; Krech (1978, 1983), for Northern Athapaskans; and Yarmie (1968), for Indians of the Northwest Coast. For a major study of the impact of mercury pollution on a Native community, see also Shkilnyk (1985), in "Northern Algonquians"; and for the link between seasonality and health among the Inuit, consult Condon's (1983) *Inuit Behavior and Seasonal Change in the Canadian Arctic.*

17. Art and Material Culture

The increase in interest in material culture and art during the 1980s was remarkable and, if one includes the analysis of museums and exhibitions in which Native Canadian art and artifacts are shown, shows no signs of abating. The size of Section 17 reflects both that recent trend and the constant, long-term interest in the traditional and market art of Northwest Coast Indians and Inuit. Although the following list does not exhaust the large number of titles listed in this section, it should give some indication of the great diversity.

For general discussions of traditional and historical patterns in Inuit art, see Carpenter (1973) and Martijn (1964); for archaeological studies, Harp (1969/70), Jordan (1979/80), McGhee (1981), and Maxwell (1983); for material culture studies, Arima (1963, 1964, 1967, 1975), Arima, ed. (1991), Jenness (1946), Krech (1989b), Oakes (1991), Pearce (1987), Shackleton and Roberts (1983), Sherman (1972), and Taylor (1974); for catalogues of art objects, Blodgett (1979a, 1983), Collins et al. (1973), Smith (1980), and Swinton (1972); for contemporary drawings and prints, Berlo (1990), Blodgett (1985), Canada (1977), Eber (1971), and Houston (1955); for sculpture, Brundege and Fisher (1990), Graburn (1986), and Hessel (1990); and for tourist or market art, Graburn (1967, 1976, 1978a, 1978b), Houston (1952, 1980), Ipellie (1980), Simard (1982), Stuart (1972), and Vastokas (1971), among others.

Studies of Northwest Coast art and material culture are as numerous as are those for the Inuit, and range widely in subject matter: for collecting, see Ames (1981), Cole (1982, 1985), and Jonaitis (1988); for architecture and totem poles, Barbeau (1951), Halpin (1981), and MacDonald (1983a, 1983b, 1984); for masks, Halpin (1983), Holm (1972), King (1979), Lévi-Strauss (1979), Waite (1966), and Walens in Crumrine and Halpin (1983); for basketry, Laforet (1984); for graphics, Hall, Blackman, and Richard (1981); for weaving, Jensen and Sargent (1987), MacDonald (1981b), Gustafson (1982), and Samuel (1987). Numerous studies exist of market or tourist art (including Haida argillite carving); among them are Jonaitis (1976), Sheehan (1981), Wyatt (1984), Duffek (1983), and Halpin (1978); see also Vaughn and Holm (1982). In some works more than others, iconographical issues are discussed, although this is very difficult to separate out; see especially Boas (1927), Duff (1967, 1975), Holm (1970), Inverarity (1950), Jonaitis (1981a, 1981b, 1983), McLaren (1978), and Duff, Hoover, Holm, Halpin, and MacDonald in Abbott, ed. (1981). These various interests show no sign of abating—for example, Black (1989), Bringhurst (1991), Jonaitis (1989), and Rosman and Rubel (1990). It should be emphasized that the possibilities are not exhausted here, and interested students should look carefully through the titles of articles, catalogues, and books for relevant materials.

Compared with the two regions just discussed, materials on art and material culture are less extensive for other areas of Native Canada: for Algonquians and Beothuks of the Eastern Maritimes, see Marshall (1985), Pelletier (1979, 1982), Speck (1914), Walker (1984), and Whitehead (1978, 1980, 1982); for Northern Algonquians, see Anderson and Hussy-Arntson (1986), Dewdney (1975, 1978), Fieber (1978), Fulford (1989), Garte (1985), Gidmark (1985, 1988a, 1988b), King (1982), Levesque (1976), Luegar (1981), McLuhan and Hill (1984), Nelson (1983, 1984), Oberholtzer (1990, 1991), Phillips (1984a, 1984b), Rogers (1967), Sinclair and Pollock (1979), Speck (1937), Speck and Heye (1921), Tanner (1984), Van Stone (1982b, 1985, 1988), and Whiteford (1986); for Iroquoia and Huronia, see Ceci (1982), Fenton (1971, 1987, 1989), Hamell (1983), Kenyon and Kenyon (1983), Mathews (1980, 1981a, 1981b), and Sturtevant in Crumrine and Halpin (1983); for Indians of the Prairie and Plains, see Bebbington (1982), Ewers (1986), Gilman and Schneider (1987), Pohrt (1989), Van Stone (1983), Walton et al. (1985), and Wissler (1910, 1912); for Northern Athapaskans, see Brandson (1981), Duncan (1984, 1989), Duncan and Carney (1988), Hail and Duncan (1989), Krech and Hail, eds. (1991), Siebert (1980), Simeone and Van Stone (1986), Van Stone (1981, 1982a), and Thompson (1972); and for

Métis, see Duncan (1981), Morier (1979), and Thompson (1983).

Also listed are some general books on Canadian Native art, among them Brasser (1976), Burnham (1981), Dickason (1972), Hallett (1981), Nicks (1982), Patterson (1973), and Turner (1976); and one on architecture (Nabokov and Easton 1989).

Exhibitions and museums themselves have come under scrutiny in recent years. In Canada sharp debate has accompanied major exhibitions like "The Spirit Sings" (Ames 1988c, Feest 1989, Graburn and Lee 1988, Harrison 1988a–c, Livingstone 1988). For discussions of other topics in museology, including repatriation, see Ames (1985a, 1985b, 1987, inter alia), Ames et al. (1988), Clark (1982, 1986), Duffek (1988), Fenton (1989), Hill (1989), Krech (1989a), Lee and Graburn (1988), MacDonald (1987, 1988), and Webster (1988). As with other topics in this section, discussions of the various issues continue apace: Atleo (1991), Houle (1991), Isseenman (1991), McMaster (1990), Podedworny (1991), and Townsend-Gault (1991). Discussions of many museum- and exhibition-related topics can be found in each issue of *Muse*. Michael Ames's *Cannibal Tours and Glass Boxes: The Anthropology of Museums* (Vancouver, 1992) brings many issues up to date.

18. Gender

The surge in women's studies and feminist scholarship may be a relatively recent phenomenon, but for Native Canada it builds on a long-standing interest in women's roles and status among the Iroquois and other Native people. Nevertheless, the traditional ethnography of Canadian Native peoples suffers, as did ethnographic work elsewhere, from the often-exclusionary focus of men on men, and not until recent times have scholars, and Native people themselves, started to correct this gender asymmetry. Labeled Gender, this section concerns women and lists sources that shed light on and analyze women's lives, roles, and status, contemporary and past. But in researching these interests, one should not neglect, despite the drawbacks just mentioned, the basic ethnographic materials listed in the ethnographic sections of Part Two and contained in many

of Part One's "Major Published Primary Historical Sources." Several texts on Native North Americans in general deserve attention in "General and Comparative," e.g., Axtell's (1981) excerpts from primary sources, which contains sections on birth, coming of age, and love and marriage.

Listed in this section on Gender are works on Iroquoian women (Anderson 1988, Brown 1970, 1975; Castellano 1989, Clermont 1983; Tooker 1984); on Micmac (Gonzales 1981, 1982); on Montagnais (Anderson 1988, Beaudet 1984, Drapeau 1984, Kapesh 1976, Leacock 1981, Vincent 1983); on Attikamèque (Labrecque 1984a, 1984b; Routhier 1984); on Cree (Preston 1980, 1982); on Ojibwa (Castellano 1989, Landes 1938); on the Plains (Albers and Medicine 1983, Swampy 1982); on the Northwest Coast (Blackman 1981, 1982); on Athapaskans (Cruikshank 1975, 1976, 1979, 1983; Perry 1979; Ridington 1983); on Inuit (Guemple 1986, McElroy 1975, 1989); and on Métis and fur-trade families (Brown 1983 as well as other sources by Brown listed in Section 13, "The Fur Trade," Campbell 1973, Willis 1972, Van Kirk 1972, 1976, 1977, 1980, 1983). Several comparative pieces are mentioned, e.g., Brizinski (1981), Brodniff (1984), Jamieson (1984), Leacock (1978), and Séguin (1981). For an emergent Native women's literature, see Godard (1990) in Section 15, "Education."

For introductions to issues on Native women's rights, see Canada (1982), Corrigan (1974), Sanders (1975), and Weaver (1983).

19. Political, Legal, and Constitutional Issues

The struggle of the Lubicon Lake Cree, the confrontation at Oka, the land-claims settlements of the Gwich'in and Inuit in northern Canada, the negotiation between the Native people of British Columbia and the province for compensation in exchange for aboriginal title, the Native desire that empowerment or self-government be written into Canada's constitution—those are just five areas in which there has been significant play with respect to the numerous political, policy, status, constitutional, legal, and other issues grouped in this section. To initiate an inquiry into these issues, consult six recently published works: Surtees's (1982) bibliography, *Canadian Indian Policy* (in "Bibliography and Reference"); *Pathways to Self-Determination,* edited by Little Bear, Boldt, and Long (1984); *The Quest for Justice,* edited by Boldt and Long (1985b); Asch's (1984) *Home and Native Land; Aboriginal Peoples and the Law,* edited by Morse (1985); and Ponting and Gibbens's (1980) *Out of Irrelevance.* Each is important. Surtees's work is a critical review of almost 300 sources on the policies of French, British, and Canadians toward Natives in Canada. *Pathways to Self-Determination* contains essays by Native Canadians and others on governmental policies, sovereignty, self-government, self-determination, and Indian perspectives on aboriginal and treaty rights and other matters. *The Quest for Justice* develops some of the themes in *Pathways* in twenty-three essays on constitutional questions, aboriginal rights, and the concerns of some Métis, Inuit, and status and non-status Indians. Asch's *Home and Native Land* is on the Canadian constitution and Native and aboriginal rights. Comprehensive collections continue to appear; Menno Boldt's *Surviving As Indians* (Montreal, 1993) and *People's Canada,* edited by Noel Dyck and James B. Waldram (Montreal, 1993) are recent examples.

For background discussions of treaties and aboriginal rights, see Badcock (1976), Barber (1976), Clark (1987, 1990), Green (1970, 1972), Green and Dickason (1989), Harper (1947), Hawkes (1989), McCardle (1982), Purich (1986), Sanders (1973a), and Berger (1983). For essays on status, see especially Dyck (1980), Imai and Laird (1982) and Sanders (1972).

The complex relationship of Native Canadians with the Canadian constitution, and the implications of that relationship, are discussed in such publications as Anderson (1982), Barsh and Henderson (1982), Moss (1980–81), Opekoken (1980), Sanders (1983a), Schwartz (1986). For self-government, see Long, Little Bear, and Boldt (1982); for sovereignty, see Eccles (1984), Boldt and Long (1984), and Flanagan (1985); and for trusteeship and matters concerning international law, see Green (1983).

Other articles in Section 19 explore different is-

sues concerning Native rights. For historical perspectives, see Dickason (1977), Donohue (1991), Eccles (1984), Fisher (1971–72), Grant (1984), Hall (1977), Montgomery (1963), Morrison (1979–80), McInnis (1969), Patterson (1983), Raby (1972, 1973), Sprague (1980), Stanley (1973), Surtees (1968), Titley (1983), Tobias (1976), and Upton (1973). For the Indian Act, see Bartlett (1978) and Harper (1945, 1946), among others. For discussions of the relationship between Indians and the federal Department of Indian Affairs and Northern Development, and for discussions of Indian politics and lobbying, see, among others, Dunning (1976), Dyck (1981, 1983a), Elias (1976), Tanner (1980), Tennant (1983), Weaver (1981, 1982), and Woodward and George (1984).

For territorial claims and political changes in the North in general, consult Abeele (1987), Canadian Arctic Resources Committee (1984, 1988a, 1988b), Coates and Powell (1989), Crowe (1979), Cumming (1977), Ervin (1983), Frideres (1981), Frideres and Reeves (1987), Fumoleau (1988), Jull (1981), Morisset (1979), Puddicombe (1991), Sanders (1973b), Usher (1982b), and Wonders (1987, 1988). The northern claims that have attracted the most attention have been in the James Bay region of northern Quebec and in the Northwest Territories, although several recent publications focus on British Columbia. In-depth studies of development and claims in the North continue to appear; Mark Dickerson's *Whose North?: Political Change, Political Development, and Self-Government in the Northwest Territories* (Vancouver, 1992) and Roger Hutchinson's *Prophets, Pastors, and Public Choices: Canada's Churches and the Mackenzie Valley Pipeline Debate* (Waterloo, 1992) are recent examples.

The James Bay settlement has been discussed in journals. See especially Bariteau (1991), Chance (1974), Chance and Pothier (1967), Charest (1980, 1981, 1982a, 1982b), Coon-Come (1991), Diamond (1991), Feit (1979, 1980, 1982), McDonnell (1991), Preston (1983), Richardson (1975), Rouland (1978), Salisbury (1979, 1986), and Trudel (1977). The settlement was above all about hydroelectric power and the desire of government and industry to extract energy, a desire that often, in Native America, is in conflict with many native people. In this regard, it may be valuable to consult, in "Northern Algonquians," Waldram's work on hydroelectric development.

An important group explores the issues stemming from early 1970s hearings on pipeline construction and on Native claims and the rights of the Dene in the Northwest Territories. The literature is vast. Included here are Asch (1979, 1982a, 1982b, 1983, 1984, 1985), Berger (1977, 1981), Bissett (1973, 1974), Bissonnette (1981), Bliss (1978), Cox (1971), Dacks (1977, 1979, 1981), Davis (1977), Fumoleau (1975), Hamelin (1976), Helm (1980), Krech (1984), McConnell (1978), McCullum and McCullum (1975), Morisset (1979, 1981), O'Malley (1976), Stabler (1977), Watkins (1977), and Watkins, ed. (1977).

A second highly visible claim in the Northwest Territories in recent years has been that of the Inuit for the territory they call Nunavut; see Bickenback (1980), Cumming and Aalton (1973–74), Jull (1986, 1988, 1989, 1991), McInnis (1981), Merritt et al. (1989), Morrison (1986), *Musk Ox* (1976), Weller (1988), and the essays listed above on northern claims. See also Keeping (1989) for the Inuvialuit agreement, which affected people and land adjacent to Nunavut.

Another group of writers have explored fishing, hunting, and wildlife rights: Alison (1977), Brown (1981), Gottesman (1983), Knoll (1979), Lysyk (1966), Pibus (1983), Sanders (1973–74). For a recent cultural analysis of Inuit technology, hunting, and subsistence, framed by animal-rights advocacy, see Wenzel's (1991) *Animal Rights, Human Rights* and the recent *Arctic Wars, Animal Rights, Endangered Peoples,* by Finn Lynge (Hanover, 1992).

For the conflicts at Oka in the summer of 1990, consult "Bibliographic Guide to Oka," by Olive Dickason, a listing of over eighty sources in Rupert's Land Research Centre *Newsletter* 8, nos. 1–2 (1992).

In other sections, see in particular, in Section 11, "Métis" the analyses of Flanagan that pertain to Métis rights (Flanagan 1983b, 1985b, 1987); and the essays specifically identified above in Section 2,

"General and Comparative," as dealing with political, legal, and constitutional issues.

Archaeology and Linguistics: A Guide
The absence of sections on linguistics and archaeology in this bibliography does not mean that either is unimportant for analyses of Native Canada—whether one is concerned with traditional society and culture, ethnohistory, contemporary educational reforms, museums and repatriation, land claims, and so on. And, in fact, neither linguistics nor archaeology has been neglected, as a quick perusal of the description above of the ethnographic sections in Part Two will show. In those sections, considerable effort has been devoted to listing representative examples of recent publications, particularly in archaeology, despite the difficulty of obtaining the so-called grey literature spoken of earlier. To aid the interested user, these sources are discussed here briefly so that archaeology and linguistics can be more systematically investigated.

Archaeology. In addition to the specific works listed below, readers should examine, in "Bibliography and Reference," various chapters in the culture-area volumes of the *Handbook of North American Indians* for their archaeological contributions: *Northeast* (Trigger ed., 1978), *Subarctic* (Helm, ed., 1981), *Arctic* (Damas, ed., 1985), and *Northwest Coast* (Suttles, ed., 1990). See also, in "Bibliography and Reference," Abler and Weaver (1974), Burch (1979), Dekin (1978), Gadacz and Asch (1984), Helm and Kurtz (1984), and other bibliographies for their listings; and in "General and Comparative," consult Boxberger (1990), Jennings (1978), Kehoe (1981), McGhee, Archambeault, and Foster (1989), Nash, ed. (1983), Snow (1980), Snow, ed. (1981), and Wright (1985), among others.

The following are works in archaeology in the ethnographic sections in Part Two of this bibliography: in "Algonquians and Beothuk of the Eastern Maritimes," Bragdon (1990), Penney and Nicol (1984), Snow (1978b), Such (1978), and Tuck (1976, 1984); in "Northern Algonquians," Brose (1978), Hanna and Kooyman, eds. (1982), Meyer (1987), Meyer and Russell (1987), Tisdale (1987), and

Wright (1979, 1981); in "Iroquoia and Huronia," Abler (1970), Bibeau (1978), Chapdelaine (1982, 1984), Clermont (1978, 1980a and b, and others), Clermont and Chapdelaine (1980), Fitzgerald (1982), J. Jamieson (1983), S. Jamieson (1981), La Rocque (1980), Noble (1982, 1984), Tooker, ed. (1967), Trigger (1970, 1976, 1978b, 1979, 1981, and others), Tuck (1978), and Wright (1966, 1970, 1982); in "Indians of the Prairies and Plains," Bryan, ed. (1991), Burley, ed. (1985), Davis (1983), Moore, ed. (1981), Quigg (1984), Reeves (1983), Verbicky-Todd (1984), and Walker (1983); in "Indians of the Northwest Coast and Plateau British Columbia," Abbott, ed. (1981 passim), Borden (1979), Croes (1976), Drucker (1955, 1965), Fladmark (1975, 1980–81a, 1980–81b, 1982), Fladmark, Ames and Sutherland (1990), Hester and Nelson (1978), Inglis and MacDonald, eds. (1979), Mitchell (1990), Murray (1982), Nelson (1990), and Pokotylo and Froese (1983); in "Northern Athapaskans of the Western Subarctic," Cinq-Mars (1979), Clark (1982, 1983a, 1983b), Clark and Clark (1983), Clark and Morlan (1982), Derry and Hudson (1975), Gordon (1975, 1976, 1981), Gordon and Savage (1974), Greer and Leblanc (1983), Gruhn (1981), Hanks and Winter (1983), Helmer, Van Dyke, and Kense (1977), Janes (1983a, 1983b), Jopling, Irving, and Beebe (1981), Morlan (1970, 1972a, 1972b, 1973), and Morrison (1984); in "Inuit of the Arctic," Arnold (1983, 1988), Arnold and Stimmel (1983), Bielawski (1988), Dumond (1987), Fitzhugh (1980, 1985), Fitzhugh, ed. (1975), Jacobs and Stenton (1985), Jordan and Kaplan (1980), Kaplan (1980, 1985a, 1985b), McCartney and Savelle (1985), McGhee (1974–88), Maxwell (1980a, 1984, 1985), Morrison (1987, 1989, 1990a, 1990b), Schindler (1985), and Tuck (1976).

Articles of an archaeological nature appear in many different journals, including *The Canadian Journal of Archaeology, Arctic, Arctic Anthropology, Études/Inuit/Studies, American Antiquity* (where annual reports on field season activity also appear), *Plains Anthropologist, Man in the Northeast, Recherches Amérindiennes au Québec,* and *BC Studies,* among others. The Canadian Museum of Civilization has an active publications agenda of books

for the general public as well as reports for the specialist. A vast amount of archaeological work appears in reports, occasional papers, and so on, from various agencies of the federal, provincial, and territorial governments or from various consulting companies. Some are listed in this bibliography, but others have not been, and so it may be useful to mention here some of the major governmental and educational series in which archaeological work appears: National Museum of Man, Mercury Series, Archaeological Survey of Canada; History and Archaeology Series, National Historic Parks and Sites Branch, Parks Canada; Historic Resources Division, Department of Culture, Recreation, and Youth, Government of Newfoundland and Labrador; Culture and Historical Resources, Fredericton, New Brunswick; Conservation Archaeology Report, Ontario Ministry of Citizenship and Culture, Heritage Branch; Royal Ontario Museum Publications in Archaeology; Papers in Manitoba Archaeology, Manitoba Department of Cultural Affairs and Historical Resources; Occasional Papers of the Archaeological Survey of Alberta; Human History Occasional Papers, Provincial Museum of Alberta; Anthropological Series, Saskatchewan Museum of Natural History; and Publications of the Department of Archaeology, Simon Fraser University.

Linguistics. In addition to the specific essays listed below, a vast amount of linguistic data is scattered throughout chapters in the volumes of the *Handbook of North American Indians.* See also Abler and Weaver (1974), Campbell and Mithun, eds. (1979), Helm and Kurtz (1984), Parr (1974), and Pentland (1982), all listed in "Bibliography and Reference." One steady source for essays on language are the *Papers of the Algonquian Conferences,* edited by William Cowan and published annually. Special issues devoted to language appear from time to time in a range of journals including *Études/Inuit/Studies* and *Recherches Amérindiennes au Québec.* Substantial material on language, not necessarily comprehensive and difficult to summarize here, is in both traditional and contemporary ethnographic reports; and a literature is emerging on orthography and the use of Native languages in schools (see Section 15, "Education").

In addition to the sources mentioned above, see the following essays and monographs on language and linguistics: for Algonquians and Beothuks of the Eastern Maritimes, Goddard (1978); for Northern Algonquians, Goddard (1978), Nichols (1988), Rhodes (1982), and Rhodes and Todd (1981); for Iroquoia and Huronia, Foster, ed. (1974), Lounsbury (1978), and Mithun (1979); for Indians of the Northwest Coast and Plateau British Columbia, Haig-Brown (1983); for Northern Athapaskans, Krauss (1973), Krauss and Golla (1981), and Scollon and Scollon (1979); for Inuit of the Arctic, Woodbury (1984); and for the Métis, Crawford (1983) and Douaud (1980, 1985).

Part One

Reference, Comparative, and Basic Historical Sources

Section One

🍁

BIBLIOGRAPHIES AND REFERENCE

Abler, Thomas S., Sally M. Weaver, et al.
1974   *A Canadian Indian Bibliography, 1960–1970.* Toronto: University of Toronto Press.

Adams, John W.
1981   Recent Ethnology of the Northwest Coast. *Annual Review of Anthropology* 10:361–92.

Allen, Robert S.
1984   *Native Studies in Canada: A Research Guide.* 2d ed. Ottawa: Research Branch, Department of Indian and Northern Affairs.

Annis, R. C., ed.
1984   *Abstracts of Native Studies.* Brandon, Man.: Abstracts of Native Studies Press.

Artibise, Alan F. J., ed.
1990   *Interdisciplinary Approaches to Canadian Literature.* Kingston and Montreal: McGill-Queen's University Press.

Brown, Jennifer S. H.
1987   People of Myth, People of History: A Look at Recent Writings on the Metis. *Acadiensis* 17(1): 150–62.

Burch, Ernest S., Jr.
1979   The Ethnography of Northern North America: A Guide to Recent Research. *Arctic Anthropology* 16(1):62–146.

Calloway, Colin G.
1988   *New Directions in American Indian History.* Norman: University of Oklahoma Press.

Campbell, Lyle, and Marianne Mithun, eds.
1979   *The Languages of Native America: Historical and Comparative Assessment.* Austin: University of Texas Press.

Condon, Richard, G.
1990   Arctic Bibliography: A Guide to Current Arctic and Subarctic Periodicals. *Arctic Anthropology* 27(2):113–22.

Cooke, Alan, and Clive Holland
1978   *The Exploration of Northern Canada, 500 to 1920: A Chronology.* Toronto: Arctic History Press.

Damas, David, ed.
1985   *Handbook of North American Indians,* vol. 5, *Arctic.* Washington: Smithsonian Institution Press.

Deer, A. Brian
1974a   *Bibliography of the Cree, Montagnais, and Nas-*

kapi Indians. Quebec: Rupert House Band Council/Cree Way Project.

1974b   *Bibliography on the History of the James Bay People Relating to the Cree People.* Quebec: Rupert House Band Council/Cree Way Project.

Dekin, A. A.
1978   *Arctic Archaeology: A Bibliography and History.* New York: Garland.

Dictionary of Canadian Biography. Vols. 1–12 (A.D. 1000–1900). Toronto: University of Toronto Press.

Dominique, Richard
1976   *Bibliographie thématique sur les montagnais-naskapi.* Service d'Archéologie et d'Ethnologie Dossier 21. Montreal: Ministère des Affaires Culturelles.

Dominique, Richard, and Jean-Guy Deschenes, eds.
1980   *Bibliographie thématique sur les montagnais-naskapi.* Montreal: Ministère des Affaires Culturelles.

Duff, Wilson, et al.
1973   A Select Bibliography of Anthropology of British Columbia. *BC Studies* 19:73–121.

Feit, Harvey A., M. E. Mackenzie, José Mailhot, and Charles A. Martijn
1972   Bibliography: Native Peoples, James Bay Region. *Recherches amérindiennnes au Québec,* Bulletin d'Information 2 (1 spécial). Montreal.

Friesen, John W., and Terry Lusty
1980   *The Metis of Canada: An Annotated Bibliography.* Toronto: Ontario Institute for Studies in Education.

Gadacz, René R., and Michael I. Asch
1984   *Thesis and Dissertation Titles and Abstracts on the Anthropology of Canadian Indians, Inuit, and Metis, from Canadian Universities. Report 1, 1970–1982.* Mercury Series, Canadian Ethnology Service Paper 95. Ottawa: National Museum of Man.

Gold, Gerald L., and Marc-Adélard Tremblay
1982   After the Quiet Revolution: Quebec Anthropology and the Study of Quebec. *Ethnos* 47:103–32.

Green, H., and D. Sawyer
1983   *The NESA Bibliography Annotated for Native Studies.* Vancouver: Tillacum Library.

Griffiths, Curt Taylor, and Linda F. Weafer
1984   *Native North Americans: Crime, Conflict, and Criminal Justice.* Vancouver: Criminology Research Centre, Simon Fraser University and the Northern Conference.

Grumet, Robert Stephen
1979   *Native Americans of the Northwest Coast: A Critical Bibliography.* Bloomington: Indiana University Press.

Harris, R. Cole, and Geoffrey J. Matthews
1987   *Historical Atlas of Canada.* Vol. 1, *From the Beginning to 1800.* Toronto: University of Toronto Press.

Helm, June
1979   *The Indians of the Subarctic: A Critical Bibliography.* Bloomington: Indiana University Press.

Helm, June, ed.
1981   *Handbook of North American Indians.* Vol. 6, *Subarctic.* Washington: Smithsonian Institution Press.

Helm, June, and Royce Kurtz
1984   *Subarctic Athapaskan Bibliography—1984.* Iowa City: Department of Anthropology, University of Iowa.

Hoxie, Frederick E., ed.
1988   *Indians in American History.* Chicago and Arlington Heights: Newberry Library and Harlan Davidson.

Inglis, Gordon B.
1982   In Bed with the Elephant: Anthropology in Anglophone Canada. *Ethnos* 47:82–102.

Jamieson, Kathleen
1983   *Native Women in Canada, A Selected Bibliography.* Ottawa: Social Sciences and Humanities Research Council.

Krech, Shepard III
1980a   Northern Athapaskan Ethnology: An Annotated Bibliography of Published Materials, 1970–79. *Arctic Anthropology* 17(2):68–105.
1980b   Northern Athapaskan Ethnology in the 1970s. *Annual Review of Anthropology* 9:83–100.
1984   *Native Canadian Anthropology and History: A Selected Bibliography.* Winnipeg: Rupert's Land Research Centre.

Legros, Dominique
1984   Bibliographie des amérindiens de la côte nord-ouest (1973–1982). *Recherches amérindiennnes au Québec* 14(2):57–70.

Lerner, Loren R., and Mary F. Williamson
1991   *Art and Architecture in Canada: A Bibliography and Guide to the Literature.* Toronto: University of Toronto Press.

Leslie, John, and R. Maguire, eds.
1979   *Selected Bibliography of Canadian Indian Treaties and Related Subjects.* Ottawa: Department of Indian Affairs and Northern Development.

McCardle, Bennett Ellen
1981   *Bibliography of the History of Canadian Indian and Inuit Health.* Edmonton: Indian Association of Alberta, Treaty and Aboriginal Rights Research Unit.

Madill, D.
1983   *Select Annotated Bibliography on Metis History and Claims.* Ottawa: Research Branch, Department of Indian Affairs and Northern Development.

Martijn, Charles A., ed.
1988   *Bibliographie préliminaire—la présence autochtone dans le détroit de Belle-Isle, Est du Canada.* Quebec: Ministère des Affaires Culturelles.

Martin, Shirley, and Glen Makahonuk, eds.
1985   *Louis Riel and the Rebellions in the Northwest: An Annotated Bibliography of Material in Special Collections, University of Saskatchewan Library.* Saskatoon.
1982   *Indian History and Claims: A Research Handbook.* Vol. 1, *Research Projects.* Ottawa: Treaties and Historical Research Centre, Department of Indian Affairs and Northern Development.

Meiklejohn, Christopher, and D. A. Rokala
1986   *The Native Peoples of Canada: An Annotated Bibliography of Population Biology, Health, and Illness.* Mercury Series, Archaeological Survey of Canada Paper 134. Ottawa: Canadian Museum of Civilization.

Millar, James F. V., and Alexander M. Ervin
1981   A Status Report and Bibliography of Cultural Studies in the Canadian Arctic to 1976. *Musk-Ox,* Special Publication.

Miska, John
1990   *Ethnic and Native Canadian Literature: A Bibliography.* Toronto: University of Toronto Press.

Murdock, George Peter, and Timothy J. O'Leary
1975   *Ethnographic Bibliography of North America.* 5 vols. 4th ed. New Haven: Human Relations Area Files.

Parr, Richard T.
1974   *A Bibliography of the Athapaskan Languages.* Mercury Series, Canadian Ethnology Service Paper 14. Ottawa: National Museum of Man.

Pentland, David H., and H. Christoph Wolfart
1982   *Bibliography of Algonquian Linguistics.* 2d ed. Winnipeg: University of Manitoba Press.

Proulx, Jean-René
1984a   *Bilan des recherches ethnohistoriques concernant les groupes autochtones du Québec.* Vol. 2, *Bibliographie des ouvrages ethnohistoriques, 1960–1983.* Montreal: Ministère des Affaires Culturelles du Québec.
1984b   *Bilan des recherches ethnohistoriques concernant les groupes autochtones du Québec.* Vol. 3, *Bibliographie des sources publiés.* Montreal: Ministère des Affaires Culturelles du Québec.

Prucha, F. Paul
1977   *A Bibliographical Guide to the History of Indian-White Relations in the United States.* Chicago: University of Chicago Press.

Quinn, David B.
1977   *North America from Earliest Discovery to First Settlement: The Norse Voyages to 1612.* New York: Harper and Row.
1979   *New American World: A Documentary History of North America to 1612.* 5 vols. New York: Arno Press and Hector Bye.
1981   *Sources for the Ethnography of Northeastern North America to 1611.* Mercury Series, Canadian Ethnology Service Paper 76. Ottawa: National Museum of Man.

Ronda, James P., and James Axtell
1978   *Indian Missions: A Critical Bibliography.* Bloomington: Indiana University Press.

Scherer, Joanna C.
1990   Repository Sources of Northwest Coast Indian Photographs. *Arctic Anthropology* 27(2):40–50.

Senkpiel, Aron, and N. Alexander Easton
1988   New Bearings on Northern Scholarship. *Northern Review* 1:9–26.

Slobodin, Richard
1975   Canadian Subarctic Athapaskans in the Literature to 1965. *Canadian Review of Sociology and Anthropology* 12:278–89.

Surtees, Robert J.
1982   *Canadian Indian Policy: A Critical Bibliography.* Bloomington: Indiana University Press.

Suttles, Wayne, ed.
1990   *Handbook of North American Indians.* Vol. 7, *Northwest Coast.* Washington: Smithsonian Institution Press.

Swagerty, William R., ed.
1984   *Scholars and the Indian Experience: Critical Reviews of Recent Writing in the Social Sciences.* Bloomington: Indiana University Press.

Tanner, Helen Hornbeck
1976   *The Ojibwas: A Critical Bibliography.* Bloomington: Indiana University Press.

Tooker, Elisabeth
1978   *The Indians of the Northeast: A Critical Bibliography.* Bloomington: Indiana University Press.

Tremblay, Marc-Adélard
1982   Les études amérindiennes au Quebec, 1960–1981: Etat des travaux et principales tendances. *Culture* 2(1):83–106.

Trigger, Bruce G., ed.
1978   *Handbook of North American Indians.* Vol. 15, *Northeast.* Washington: Smithsonian Institution Press.

Venne, Sharon, ed.
1981   *Indian Acts and Amendments, 1868–1975: An Indexed Collection.* Saskatoon: University of Saskatchewan Native Law Centre.

Washburn, Wilcomb, ed.
1988   *Handbook of North American Indians.* Vol. 4, *History of Indian-White Relations.* Washington: Smithsonian Institution Press.

Section Two

♦

GENERAL AND COMPARATIVE

Adams, Howard
1975   *Prison of Grass: Canada from the Native Point of View.* Toronto: New Press. Rev. ed. Saskatoon: Fifth House, 1989.

Axtell, James, ed.
1981   *The Indian Peoples of Eastern America: A Documentary History of the Sexes.* New York: Oxford University Press.

Bailey, Alfred G.
1969   *The Conflict of European and Eastern Algonkian Cultures, 1504–1700.* 1937. 2d ed. Toronto: University of Toronto Press.

Barger, W. K.
1980   Inuit and Cree Adaptation to Northern Colonialism. In *Political Organization of Native North Americans,* edited by E. L. Schusky, pp. 189–214. Washington: University Press of America.

Barron, F. Laurie
1988   The Indian Pass System in the Canadian West, 1882–1935. *Prairie Forum* 21(1):25–42.

Barsh, Russel L.
1987   Europe's Role in Displacing Native Canadians. In *Indians and Europe: An Interdisciplinary Collection of Essays,* edited by Christian Feest, pp. 563–84. Aachen: Rader Verlag.

Beaudry, Nicole
1988   Singing, Laughing, and Playing: Three Examples from the Inuit, Dene, and Yupik Traditions. *Canadian Journal of Native Studies* 8(2):275–90.

Bergerud, A. T., et al.
1984   The Buffalo of the North: Caribou (Rangifer tarandus) and Human Developments. *Arctic* 37:7–22.

Berkes, Fikret
1990   Native Subsistence Fisheries: A Synthesis of Harvest Studies in Canada. *Arctic* 43(1):35–42.

Bernèche, F., J. A. Fernandez, and D. Gauvreau
1980   Les mariages d'indiennes et de non-indiens au Québec: caractéristiques et conséquences démographiques. *Recherches amérindiennnes au Québec* 9(4):313–22.

Berry, John W.
1981   Native Peoples and the Larger Society. In *A*

Canadian Social Psychology of Ethnic Relations, edited by R. C. Gardner and R. Kalin, pp. 214–30. Toronto: Methuen.

Bienvenue, Rita M., and A. H. Latif
1974   Arrests, Dispositions, and Recidivism: A Comparison of Indians and Whites. *Canadian Journal of Criminology and Corrections* 16(2): 1–12.

Billson, Janet M.
1988   Social Change, Social Problems, and the Search for Identity: Canada's Northern Native Peoples in Transition. *American Review of Canadian Studies* 18:295–316.

Boldt, Edward D., et al.
1983   Presentence Reports and the Incarceration of Natives. *Canadian Journal of Criminology* 25:269–76.

Boldt, Menno
1980   Canadian Native Indian Leadership: Context and Composition. *Canadian Ethnic Studies* 12(1):15–33.
1981a   Social Correlates of Nationalism: A Study of Leadership in an Internal Colony. *Ethnic Groups* 3:307–32.
1981b   Enlightenment Values, Romanticism, and Attitudes Toward Political Status: A Study of Native Leaders in Canada. *Canadian Review of Sociology and Anthropology* 18:545–65.
1981c   Social Correlates of Nationalism: A Study of Native Indian Leaders in a Canadian Internal Colony. *Comparative Political Studies* 14:205–32.

Bone, Robert M., and Milford B. Green
1984   Jobs and Access—A Northern Dilemma. *Journal of Canadian Studies* 18(3):90–101.

Bonta, James
1989   Native inmates: Institutional response, risk, and needs. *Canadian Journal of Criminology* 31:49–62

Boxberger, Daniel L., ed.
1990   *Native North Americans: An Ethnohistorical Approach.* Dubuque, Iowa: Kendall/Hunt Publishing Company.

Brody, Hugh
1987   *The Living Arctic: Hunters and Trappers of the Canadian North.* Vancouver: Douglas and Mc-

Intyre. Rev. ed. Seattle: University of Washington Press, 1990.

Brumbach, Hetty Jo, and Robert Jarvenpa
1989   *Ethnoarchaeological and Cultural Frontiers: Athapaskan, Algonquian, and European Adaptations in the Central Subarctic.* New York: Peter Lang.

Burch, Ernest S., Jr.
1972   The Caribou/Wild Reindeer as a Human Resource. *American Antiquity* 37:339–68.
1991   Herd following reconsidered. *Current Anthropology* 32:439–45.

Burnaby, Barbara
1986   Speakers of Canadian Aboriginal Languages: Perspectives from the 1981 Census. In *Actes du dix-septième congrès des algonquinistes,* edited by William Cowan, pp. 47–64. Ottawa: Carleton University.

Cardinal, Harold
1969   *The Unjust Society: The Tragedy of Canada's Indians.* Edmonton: Hurtig.
1977   *The Rebirth of Canada's Indians.* Edmonton: Hurtig.

Cassidy, Frank
1990   Aboriginal Governments in Canada: An Emerging Field of Study. *Canadian Journal of Political Science* 23:73–99.

Chartrand, Paul
1991   "Terms of division": Problems of "outside naming" for aboriginal peoples in Canada. *Journal of Indigenous Studies* 2(2):1–22.

Christopher, Robert
1988   Narrators of the Arctic: Images and Movements in Northland Narratives. *American Review of Canadian Studies* 18:259–70.

Clairmont, D. H.
1963   Deviance Among Indians and Eskimos in Aklavik, N.W.T. NCR 63–9. Ottawa: Northern Coordination and Research Centre, Department of Northern Affairs and National Resources.

Clifton, James A., ed.
1989   *Being and Becoming Indian: Biographical Studies of North American Frontiers.* Chicago: Dorsey Press.

Coates, Kenneth S.
1985   *Canada's Colonies: A History of the Yukon and*

Northwest Territories. Toronto: James Lorimer and Company.

1988 On the Outside in Their Homeland: Native People and the Evolution of the Yukon Economy. *Northern Review* 1:73–89.

Coates, Kenneth S., and William R. Morrison
1988 *Land of the Midnight Sun: A History of the Yukon.* Edmonton: Hurtig.

Coates, Kenneth S., and William R. Morrison, eds.
1989 *Interpreting Canada's North: Selected Readings.* Toronto: Copp Clark Pitman.

Coates, Kenneth S., and Judith Powell
1989 *The Modern North: People, Politics, and the Rejection of Colonialism.* Toronto: James Lorimer and Company.

Comeau, Pauline, and Aldo Santin
1990 *The First Canadians: A Profile of Canada's Native People Today.* Toronto: James Lorimer and Company.

Cooke, G. A.
1981 The Boreal Institute for Northern Studies—Resources on Native Education. *Canadian Journal of Native Education* 8(4):19–21.

Cornell, Stephen
1988 The Transformation of the Tribe: Organization and Self-Concept in Native American Ethnicities. *Ethnic and Racial Studies* 11(1):27–47.

Cox, Bruce A.
1985 Prospects for the North Canadian Native Economy. *Polar Record* 22.

Cox, Bruce A., ed.
1973 *Cultural Ecology: Readings on the Canadian Indians and Eskimos.* Toronto: McClelland and Stewart.
1987 *Native Peoples, Native Lands: Canadian Indians, Inuit, and Metis.* Ottawa: Carleton University.

Cronk, Sam, Beverly Cavanagh, and Franziske von Rosen
1987 Celebration: Native Events in Eastern Canada. *Folklife Annual* 1987.

Crowe, Keith J.
1974 *A History of the Original Peoples of Northern Canada.* Montreal: McGill-Queens University Press and Arctic Institute of North America.

Dacks, Gurston, and Kenneth Coates, eds.
1990 *Northern Communities: Prospects for Empower-*

ment. Edmonton: Boreal Institute for Northern Studies, University of Alberta.

Davis, Richard C., ed.
1988 *Rupert's Land: A Cultural Tapestry.* Waterloo: Wilfred Laurier University Press.

Delâge, Denys
1991 Amérindiens dans l'imaginaire des Québécois. *Liberté* 33(4–5):15–28.

Demay, Jöel
1991 Clarifying ambiguities: The rapidly changing life of the Canadian aboriginal print media. *Canadian Journal of Native Studies* 11(1):95–112.

Dempsey, James
1983 The Indians and World War I. *Alberta History,* September, 1–8.

Dewdney, Selwyn
1975 *They Shared to Survive: The Native Peoples of Canada.* Toronto: Macmillan.

Dickason, Olive Patricia
1977 The Concept of l'homme sauvage and Early French Colonialism in the Americas. *Revue française d'histoire d'outre-mer* 64:5–32.
1979 Europeans and Amerindians: Some Comparative Aspects of Early Contact. *Historical Papers/Communications historiques* 1979:182–202.
1984 *The Myth of the Savage and the Beginnings of French Colonialism in the Americas.* Edmonton: University of Alberta Press.

Dickinson, John A.
1985 L'image de l'autre: Européens et Amérindiens. *Revue d'histoire de l'Amérique français* 39(2):263–70.

Dominique, Richard
1984 Les etudes sur la récolte autochtone au Canada. *Recherches amérindiennnes au Québec* 14(1):60–66.

Donald, Leland
1985 Captives or Slaves? A Comparison of Northeastern and Northwestern North America by Means of Captivity Narratives. *Culture* 5(2):17–23.

Dosman, Edgar J.
1972 *Indians: The Urban Dilemma.* Toronto: McClelland and Stewart.

Driver, Harold E.
1969   *Indians of North America.* 2d ed. rev. Chicago: University of Chicago Press.

Dunning, R. W.
1959   Ethnic Relations and the Marginal Man in Canada. *Human Organization* 18(3):117–22.

Dunston, William
1963   Canadian Indians Today. *Canadian Geographic Journal,* pp. 182–93.

Durst, D.
1991   Conjugal violence: Changing attitudes in two northern native communities. *Community Mental Health Journal,* 27:359–73.

Dyck, Noel
1990   Cultures, communities, and claims: Anthropology and native studies in Canada. *Canadian Ethnic Studies* 22(3):40–55.

Eccles, William J.
1969   *The Canadian Frontier, 1534–1760.* Albuquerque: University of New Mexico Press.
1972   *France in America.* New York: Harper and Row.

Eisen, George
1977   Voyageurs, Black-Robes, Saints, and Indians. *Ethnohistory* 24:191–205.

Embree, J.
1977   *Let Us Live: The Native People of Canada.* Don Mills, Ont.: J. M. Dent and Sons.

Fisher, Anthony D.
1976   The Dialectic of Indian Life in Canada. *Canadian Review of Sociology and Anthropology* 13:458–64.

Fisher, Robin, and Kenneth Coates, eds.
1988   *Out of the Background: Readings on Canadian Native History.* Mississauga, Ont.: Copp Clark Pitman.

Francis, Daniel
1986   *Discovery of the North: The Exploration of Canada's Arctic.* Edmonton: Hurtig.

Frideres, James S.
1974   *Canada's Indians: Contemporary Conflicts.* Scarborough: Prentice-Hall of Canada.
1983   *Native People in Canada: Contemporary Conflicts.* Scarborough: Prentice-Hall.

Gaffen, Fred
1985   *Canada's Forgotten Soldiers.* Penticton: Theytus Books.

Getty, Ian A. L., and Antoine S. Lussier, eds.
1983   *As Long as the Sun Shines and Water Flows.* Vancouver: University of British Columbia Press.

Getty, Ian A. L., and Donald B. Smith, eds.
1978   *One Century Later: Western Canadian Reserve Indians Since Treaty 7.* Vancouver: University of British Columbia Press.

Goldie, Terry
1989   *Fear and Temptation: The Image of the Indigene in Canadian, Australian, and New Zealand Literatures.* Kingston and Montreal: McGill-Queen's University Press.

Gooderman, Kent, ed.
1969   *I Am an Indian.* Don Mills, Ont.: J. M. Dent.

Gough, Barry M.
1991   The return of the Canadian native. *Contemporary Review* 258:176–83.

Graburn, Nelson H. H., and B. Stephen Strong
1973   *Circumpolar Peoples: An Anthropological Perspective.* Pacific Palisades, Calif.: Goodyear Publishing Company.

Griffiths, Curt Taylor, J. Colin Yerbury, and Linda F. Weafer
1987   Canadian Natives: Victims of Socio-Structural Deprivation? *Human Organization* 46:277–82.

Hagen, J.
1974   Criminal Justice and Native People: A Study of Incarceration in a Canadian Province. *Canadian Review of Sociology and Anthropology,* special issue, 220–36.

Hamell, George R.
1986–87 Strawberries, Floating Fields, and Rabbit Captains: Mythical Realities and European Contact in the Northeast During the Sixteenth and Seventeenth Centuries. *Journal of Canadian Studies* 21:72–94.

Harding, Jim
1991   Policing and Aboriginal Justice. *Canadian Journal of Criminology* 33:363–83.

Harris, R. Cole, ed., and G. J. Matthews, cartographer
1987   *Historical Atlas of Canada.* Vol. 1, *From the Beginning to 1800.* Toronto: University of Toronto Press.

Hauch, Christopher
1985   *Coping Strategies and Street Life: The Ethnog-*

raphy of Winnipeg's Skid Row. Institute of Urban Studies Report 11. University of Winnipeg.

Hawthorn, Harry B., ed.
1966–67 *A Survey of the Contemporary Indians of Canada.* 2 vols. Ottawa: Queen's Printer.

Hedican, Edward J.
1991 On the ethnopolitics of Canadian native leadership and identity. *Ethnic Groups* 9(1):1–15.

Helm, June, and David Damas
1963 The Contact-traditional All-Native Community of the Canadian North: The Upper Mackenzie "Bush" Athapaskans and the Igluligmiut. *Anthropologica* 5(1):9–21.

Helm, June, and Eleanor B. Leacock
1971 The Hunting Tribes of Subarctic Canada. In *North American Indians in Historical Perspective,* edited by E. B. Leacock and N. O. Lurie, pp. 343–74. New York: Random House.

Helm, June, Edward S. Rogers, and James G. E. Smith
1981 Intracultural Relations and Cultural Change in the Shield and Mackenzie Borderlands. In *Handbook of North American Indians,* vol. 6, *Subarctic,* edited by June Helm, pp. 146–57. Washington: Smithsonian Institution Press.

Hill, Frederick I.
1986 Commentary on "Prospects for the North Canadian Native Economy." *Polar Record* 23(142):91–96.

Hobart, Charles W.
1982 Industrial Employment of Rural Indigenes: The Case of Canada. *Human Organization* 41:54–63.

Honigmann, John J.
1952 Intercultural Relations at Great Whale River. *American Anthropologist* 54:510–22.
1962 *Social Networks in Great Whale River: Notes on an Eskimo, Montagnais-Naskapi, and Euro-Canadian Community.* Bulletin 178. Anthropological Series 54. Ottawa: National Museum of Canada.
1965 Social Disintegration in Five Northern Canadian Communities. *Canadian Review of Sociology and Anthropology* 2(4):199–214.
1970 Field Work in Two Northern Canadian Communities. In *Marginal Natives: Anthropologists at Work,* edited by Morris Freilich, pp. 39–72. New York: Harper and Row.

1971 Northern Townsmen. *Northwest Anthropological Research Notes* 5(1):97–122.
1972 Housing for New Arctic Towns. In *Technology and Social Change,* edited by H. Russell Bernard and Pertti J. Pelto, pp. 228–44. New York: Macmillan.
1973 Integration of Canadian Eskimo, Indians, and Other Persons of Native Ancestry in Modern Economic and Public Life: Evidence from Inuvik. In *Circumpolar Problems: Habitat, Economy, and Social Relations in the Arctic,* edited by G. Berg, pp. 61–72. Oxford: Pergamon Press.

Honigmann, John J., and Irma Honigmann
1970 *Arctic Townsmen: Ethnic Backgrounds and Modernization.* Ottawa: Canadian Research Centre for Anthropology.
1975 Five Northern Towns. *Anthropological Papers of the University of Alaska* 17(1):1–68.

Howard, James H.
1983 Pan-Indianism in Native American Music and Dance. *Ethnomusicology* 27(1):71–82.

Inglis, Gordon B.
1971 Canadian Indian Reserve Populations: Some Problems of Conceptualization. *Northwest Anthropological Research Notes* 5(1):23–36.

Jacobs, Wilbur R.
1988 British Indian Policies to 1783. In *Handbook of North American Indians,* vol. 4, *History of Indian-White Relations,* edited by Wilcomb E. Washburn, pp. 5–12. Washington: Smithsonian Institution Press.

Jaenen, Cornelius J.
1969 The Indian Problem in the 17th Century. In *Documentary Problems in Canadian History,* edited by J. M. Bumsted, pp. 1–24. Georgetown, Ont.: Irwin-Dorsey.
1972 Problems of Assimilation in New France, 1603–1645. In *Documentary Problems in Canadian History: Pre-Confederation,* edited by J. M. Bumsted, pp. 40–58. Georgetown, Ont.: Irwin-Dorsey.
1973 The Meeting of French and Amerindians: A Reinterpretation of Cultural Clash in the Seventeenth Century. *Revue de l'Université d'Ottawa* 43(1):128–44.
1974 Amerindian Views of French Culture in the

Seventeenth Century. *Canadian Historical Review* 55:261–91.

1976 *Friend and Foe: Aspects of French-Amerindian Cultural Contact in the Sixteenth and Seventeenth Century.* Toronto: McClelland and Stewart.

1978 Conceptual Framework for French Views of America and Amerindians. *French Colonial Studies* 2:1–22.

1980 French Attitudes Towards Native Society. In *Old Trails and New Directions,* edited by C. M. Judd and A. J. Ray, pp. 59–72. Toronto: University of Toronto Press.

1982 "Les sauvages amériquains": Persistence into the 18th Century of Traditional French Concepts and Constructs for Comprehending Amerindians. *Ethnohistory* 29:43–56.

1983 L'esperienza del contatto tra i Francesi e le culture amerindie del Nord America. In *Canadiana problemi de storia canadese,* edited by Luca Codignola, pp. 65–90. Venice: Marsilic Editori.

1984 *The French Relationship with the Native Peoples of New France and Acadia.* Ottawa: Department of Indian Affairs and Northern Development, Research Branch.

1986 French Sovereignty and Native Nationhood During the French Regime. *Native Studies Review* 2(1).

Janes, Robert R.
1973 Indian and Eskimo Contact in Southern Keewatin: An Ethnohistorical Approach. *Ethnohistory* 29:39–54.

Jenness, Diamond
1977 *Indians of Canada.* 1932. 7th ed. Toronto: University of Toronto Press.

Jennings, Jesse D., ed.
1978 *Ancient Native Americans.* San Francisco: Freeman.

Jones, Dorothy V.
1988 British Colonial Indian Treaties. In *Handbook of North American Indians,* vol. 4, *History of Indian-White Relations,* edited by Wilcomb E. Washburn, pp. 185–94. Washington: Smithsonian Institution Press.

Joseph, Shirley
1991 Assimilation tools: Then and now. *BC Studies* 89:65–79.

Kawashima, Yasuhide
1989 Forest Diplomats: The Role of Interpreters in Indian-White Relations on the Early American Frontiers. *American Indian Quarterly* 13(1):1–14.

Kehoe, Alice B.
1981 *North American Indians: A Comprehensive Account.* Englewood Cliffs, N.J.: Prentice-Hall.

Kellough, Gail
1980 From Colonialism to Economic Imperialism: The Experience of the Canadian Indian. In *Structured Inequality in Canada,* edited by John Harp and J. R. Hofley, pp. 343–77. Scarborough: Prentice-Hall of Canada,

Kerr, Donald, and Deryck W. Holdsworth, eds.
1987 *Historical Atlas of Canada.* Vol. 3. *Addressing the Twentieth Century, 1891–1961.* Toronto: University of Toronto Press.

Kinietz, A.
1986 Ethnic Identity in Northern Canada. *Journal of Ethnic Studies* 14(1):129–34.

Krech, Shepard III
1984 Ethnohistory and Ethnography in the Subarctic. *American Anthropologist* 86:80–86.

Krech, Shepard III, ed.
1980 Reconsiderations of Aboriginal Social Organization in the North American Subarctic. *Arctic Anthropology* 17(2):1–67.

Krotz, Larry
1980 *Urban Indians: The Strangers in Canada's Cities.* Edmonton: Hurtig.

1990 *Indian Country: Inside Another Canada.* Toronto: McClelland and Stewart.

Lane, E. B., et al.
1978 The Incarcerated Native. *Canadian Journal of Criminology* 20(3):308–16.

Lane, Theodore
1987 *Developing America's Northern Frontier.* Lanham, Md.: University Press of America.

La Prairie, Carol P.
1988 Community Types, Crime, and Police Services on Canadian Indian Reserves. *Journal of Research in Crime and Delinquency* 25:375–91.

1990 The Role of Sentencing in the Over-representation of Aboriginal People in Correctional

Institutions. *Canadian Journal of Criminology* 32(3):429–40.

LaRocque, Emma
1975   *Defeathering the Indian.* Agincourt, Ont.: Book Society of Canada.

Leach, Douglas E.
1988   Colonial Indian Wars. In *Handbook of North American Indians,* vol. 4, *History of Indian-White Relations,* edited by Wilcomb E. Washburn, pp. 128–43. Washington: Smithsonian Institution Press.

Lederman, Anne
1988   Old Indian and Métis Fiddling in Manitoba: Origins, Structure, and Questions of Syncretism. *Canadian Journal of Native Studies* 8(2):205–30.

Lewis, Henry T., and T. A. Ferguson
1988   Yards, Corridors, and Mosaics: How to Burn a Boreal Forest. *Human Ecology* 16:57–77.

Lewis, Malcolm
1980   Indian Maps. In *Old Trails and New Directions,* edited by Carol M. Judd and Arthur J. Ray, pp. 9–23. Toronto: University of Toronto Press.

Long, J. Anthony, and Menno Boldt
1983   Political Attitudes of Members of an Internal Colony: A Study of Native Indian University Students in Canada. *Foundation for the Study of Plural Societies* 14(¾):85–98.

Lotz, Pat, and Jim Lotz, eds.
1971   *Pilot Not Commander: Essays in Memory of Diamond Jenness.* Ottawa: Canadian Research Centre for Anthropology.

McCaskill, Don
1981   The Urbanization of Indians in Winnipeg, Toronto, Edmonton, and Vancouver: A Comparative Analysis. *Culture* 1(1):82–89.

McCormack, Patricia A., and R. Geoffrey Ironside, eds.
1990   *Proceedings of the Fort Chipewyan and Fort Vermilion Bicentennial Conference.* Edmonton: Boreal Institute for Northern Studies, University of Alberta.

McGhee, Robert, G. Archambeault, and H. Foster
1989   *Ancient Canada.* Ottawa: Canadian Museum of Civilization/Libre Expression.

MacLaren, I. S.
1991   Samuel Hearne's Accounts of the Massacre at

Bloody Fall, 17 July 1771. *Ariel* 22 (January):25–51.

McMahon, Kevin
1988   *Arctic Twilight: Reflections on the Destiny of Canada's Native Land and People.* Toronto: James Lorimer.

McMillan, Alan D.
1989   *Native Peoples and Cultures of Canada: An Anthropological Overview.* Vancouver: Douglas and McIntyre.

Manuel, George, and Michael Poslums
1974   *The Fourth World: An Indian Reality.* Toronto: Collier-Macmillan.

Martin, Calvin
1980   Subarctic Indians and Wildlife. In *Old Trails and New Directions,* edited by Carol M. Judd and Arthur J. Ray, pp. 73–84. Toronto: University of Toronto Press.

Matijasic, Thomas D.
1987   Reflected Values: Sixteenth-century Europeans View the Indians of North America. *American Indian Culture and Research Journal* 11(2):31–50.

Miller, J. R.
1989   *Skyscrapers Hide the Heavens: A History of Indian-White Relations in Canada.* Toronto: University of Toronto Press.

Miller, J. R., ed.
1991   *Sweet Promises: A Reader in Indian-White Relations in Canada.* Toronto: University of Toronto Press.

Monture, Patricia A.
1989   Vicious Circle: Child Welfare and the First Nations. *Canadian Journal of Women and the Law* 3(1):1–17.

Moreau, Jean-François
1984   Les sociétés de pêcheurs-collectrices. *Recherches amérindiennnes au Québec* 14(1):3–16.

Morisset, Jean
1980   Miroir indigène/reflet eurogène. Essai sur l'américanité et la fabrication de l'identité canadienne. *Recherches amérindiennnes au Québec* 9(4):285–312.

Morrison, Bruce, and Roderick C. Wilson, eds.
1986   *Native Peoples: The Canadian Experience.* Toronto: McClelland and Stewart.

Morse, Bradford N.
1976   Native People and Legal Services in Canada. *McGill Law Journal* 22:504–40.

Morse, Bradford N., ed.
1985   *Aboriginal People and the Law: Indians, Metis, and Inuit Rights in Canada.* Ottawa: Carleton University.

Moses, L. G.
1984   Wild West Shows, Performers, and the Image of the American Indian, 1887–1914. *South Dakota History* 14:193–221.

Muise, D. A., ed.
1977   *Approaches to Native History in Canada: Papers of a Conference Held at the National Museum of Man, October, 1975.* Ottawa: National Museum of Man.

Nagler, Mark
1973   *Indians in the City.* Ottawa: Canadian Research Centre for Anthropology, St. Paul University.

Nash, Ronald J., ed.
1983   *The Evolution of Maritime Cultures on the Northeast and the Northwest Coasts of America.* Publication 11. Burnaby, B.C.: Simon Fraser University, Department of Archaeology.

New, W. H.
1990   *Native Writers and Canadian Writing.* Vancouver: University of British Columbia Press.

Newcomb, William W., Jr.
1974   *North American Indians: An Anthropological Perspective.* Pacific Palisades, Calif.: Goodyear Publishing.

Nichols, Roger L.
1989   The United States, Canada, and the Indians: 1865–1876. *Social Science Journal* 26:249–63.

Normandeau, Louise, et Victor Piche, eds.
1984   *Les populations amérindiennes et inuit du Canada. Aperçu démographique.* Montreal: Presses de l'Université de Montréal.

Oswalt, Wendell H.
1987   *This Land Was Theirs: A Study of North American Indians.* 4th ed. Mountain View, Calif.: Mayfield.

Owen, Roger C., James J. F. Deetz, and Anthony D. Fisher, eds.
1967   *The North American Indians: A Sourcebook.* Boston: Little, Brown.

Paper, Jordan
1989   *Offering Smoke: The Sacred Pipe and Native American Religion.* Edmonton: University of Alberta Press.

Parent, Raynald
1978   Inventaire des nations amérindiens au début du XVIIe siècle. *Recherches amérindiennnes au Québec* 7(3–4):5–19.

Parkinson, John M.
1988   Sources of Capital for Native Businesses: Problems and Prospects. *Canadian Journal of Native Studies* 8(1):27–58.

Patterson, E. Palmer II
1972   *The Canadian Indian: A History Since 1500.* Don Mills, Ontario.: Collier-Macmillan Canada.

Petrone, Penny
1990   *Native Literature in Canada: From the Oral Tradition to the Present.* Toronto: University of Toronto Press.

Price, A. Grenfell
1972   *White Settlers and Native Peoples.* Westport, Conn.: Greenwood Press.

Price, John A.
1978   *Native Studies: American and Canadian Indians.* Toronto: McGraw-Hill Ryerson
1979   *Indians of Canada: Cultural Dynamics.* Scarborough: Prentice-Hall of Canada.
1982   Historical Theory and the Applied Anthropology of U.S. and Canadian Indians. *Human Organization* 41:43–53.
1983   Canadian Indian Families. In *The Canadian Family,* edited by K. Ishwaran, pp. 72–83. Toronto: Gage.

Purdy, Barbara
1988   American Indians After A.D. 1492: A Case of Forced Cultural Change. *American Anthropologist* 90:640–54.

Ray, Arthur J., and Arthur Roberts
1985   Approaches to the Ethnohistory of the Subarctic. *Ethnohistory* 32:270–80.

Reeves, W., and J. Frideres
1981   Government Policy and Indian Urbanization: The Alberta Case. *Canadian Public Policy* 7:584–95.

Richardson, Boyce
1987   Kind Hearts or Forked Tongues? The Indian

Ordeal: A Century of Decline. *Beaver* 67(1):16–41.

Richardson, Boyce, ed.
1989   *Drumbeat: Anger and Renewal in Indian Country.* Toronto: Summerhill Press.

Riches, David
1982   *Northern Nomadic Hunter-Gatherers: A Humanistic Approach.* London: Academic Press.

Robinson, Michael, and Elma Ghostkeeper
1987   Native and Local Economies: A Consideration of Economic Evolution and the Next Economy. *Arctic* 40:138–44.

Robertson, Heather
1970   *Reservations Are for Indians.* Toronto: Lewis and Samuel.

Robinson, Patricia
1985   Language retention among Canadian Indians: A simultaneous equations model with dichotomous endogenous variables. *American Sociological Review* 50:515–29.

Rogers, Edward S., and James G. E. Smith
1981   Environment and Culture in the Shield and Mackenzie Borderlands. In *Handbook of North American Indians,* vol. 6, *Subarctic,* edited by June Helm, pp. 130–45. Washington: Smithsonian Institution Press.

Ruggles, Richard I.
1990   *A Country So Interesting: The Hudson's Bay Company and Two Centuries of Mapping, 1670–1870.* Kingston and Montreal: McGill-Queen's University Press.

Ryan, Joan
1978   *Wall of Words: Betrayal of Urban Indians.* Toronto: Peter Martin Associates.
1987   Aboriginal Peoples in Canada: Contemporary Dimensions of Political Dominance. *American Indian Quarterly* 11:315–24.

Sanders, Douglas E.
1988   Government Indian Agencies in Canada. In *Handbook of North American Indians,* vol. 4, *History of Indian-White Relations,* edited by Wilcomb E. Washburn, pp. 276–83. Washington: Smithsonian Institution Press.

Schmeiser, Douglas A.
1976   The Native Offender in Canada. In *Les facettes de l'identité amérindiennne,* edited by Marc-Adélard Tremblay, pp. 133–51. Quebec: Presses de l'Université Laval.

Scott, Colin
1989   Custom, Tradition, and Aboriginal Self-Government in Canada. In *Social Change and Space: Indigenous Nations and Ethnic Communities in Canada and Finland,* edited by Ludger Müller-Wille, pp. 81–108. Montreal: McGill Minor in Northern Studies Program.

Simard, Jean-Jacques
1980   Les aumoniers du régiment et le Québec amérindien. *Recherches amérindiennnes au Québec* 9(4):269–84.

Slattery, Brian
1980   Official French Attitudes Toward American Indian Territories, 1500–1599. *Canadian Historical Review* 61(4).

Smith, Donald B.
1974a   *Le "sauvage": The Native People in Quebec. Historical Writing on the Heroic Period (1534–1663) of New France.* Mercury Series, History Division Paper 6. Ottawa: National Museum of Man.
1974b   *Le "sauvage" pendant la période héroique de la Nouvelle-France (1534–1663) d'après les historiens canadiens-français de XIXe et XXe siècles.* Montreal: Hurtubise HMH.

Smith, James G. E., ed.
1979   Indian-Eskimo Relations: Studies in the Interethnic Relations of Small Societies. *Arctic Anthropology* 16(2):1–195.

Snow, Dean R.
1980   *The Archaeology of New England.* New York: Academic Press.

Snow, Dean R., ed.
1981   *Foundations of Northeast Archaeology.* New York: Academic Press.

Spencer, Robert F., Jesse D. Jennings, et al.
1965   *The Native Americans.* New York: Harper and Row.

Stabler, Jack C.
1989   Dualism and Development in the Northwest Territories. *Economic Development and Cultural Change* 37:805–39.
1990   A utility analysis of activity patterns of native

males in the Northwest Territories. *Economic Development and Cultural Change* 39:47–60.

Stanbury, William T.
1975   *Success and Failure: Indians in Urban Society.* Vancouver: University of British Columbia Press.

Starr, Fred M.
1978   Indians and the Criminal Justice System. *Canadian Journal of Criminology* 20:317–23.

Surtees, Robert J.
1971   *The Original People.* Toronto: Holt, Rinehart and Winston of Canada.
1988a   Canadian Indian Policies. In *Handbook of North American Indians,* vol. 4, *History of Indian-White Relations,* edited by Wilcomb E. Washburn, pp. 81–95. Washington: Smithsonian Institution Press.
1988b   Canadian Indian Treaties. In *Handbook of North American Indians,* vol. 4, *History of Indian-White Relations,* edited by Wilcomb E. Washburn, pp. 202–10. Washington: Smithsonian Institution Press.

Trigger, Bruce G.
1985   *Natives and Newcomers: Canada's "Heroic Age" Reconsidered.* Kingston and Montreal: McGill-Queen's University Press.

Trudel, François
1990   Les relations entre indiens et inuit dans l'est de la baie d'Hudson (1800–1840). In *Papers of the Twenty-First Algonquian Conference,* edited by William Cowan, pp. 356–69. Ottawa: Carleton University.

Upton, L. F. S.
1980   Contact and Conflict on the Atlantic and Pacific Coasts of Canada. *BC Studies* 45:103–15.

Usher, Peter J.
1982   Les autochtones et les chasseurs sportifs peuvent-ils coexister? *Recherches amérindiennes au Québec* 12(4):263–68.

Vanderburgh, Rosamond M.
1988   The Impact of Government Support for Indian Culture on Canada's Aged Indians. In *North American Elders: United States and Canadian Perspectives,* edited by E. Rathbone-McCuan and B. Havens. New York: Greenwood Press.

Vincent, Sylvie, et Bernard Arcand
1979   *L'image de l'amérindien dans les manuels scolaires du Québec ou comment les québécois ne sont pas des sauvages.* Montreal: Hurtubise HMH.

Wade, Mason
1988   French Indian Policies. In *Handbook of North American Indians,* vol. 4, *History of Indian-White Relations,* edited by Wilcomb E. Washburn, pp. 20–28. Washington: Smithsonian Institution Press.

Waubageshig
1970   *The Only Good Indian.* Toronto: New Press.

Weeks, Philip, ed.
1988   *The American Indian Experience: A Profile: 1524 to the Present.* Arlington Heights, Ill.: Forum Press.

Weick, Edward R.
1988   Northern Native People and the Larger Canadian Society: Emerging Economic Relations. *American Review of Canadian Studies* 18:317–30.

White, Richard
1991   *The Middle Ground: Indians, Empires, and Republics in the Great Lakes Region, 1650–1815.* Cambridge: Cambridge University Press.

Wilson, James
1977   *Canada's Indians.* Report 21. London: Minority Rights Group.

Wiseman, N.
1991   The native issue in Canada. *Capital and Class* 44:15–22.

Wonders, William C., ed.
1971   *Canada's Changing North.* Toronto: McClelland and Stewart.

Wright, James V.
1985   The Development of Prehistory in Canada, 1935–1985. *American Antiquity* 50:421–33.

Wuttunee, William I. C.
1971   *Ruffled Feathers: Indians in Canadian Society.* Alberta: Bell Books.

York, Geoffrey
1989   *The Dispossessed: Life and Death in Native Canada.* Toronto: Lester and Orpen Dennys.

Young, R. A., and Peter McDermott
1988   Employment Training Programs and Accul-

turation of Native Peoples in Canada's Northwest Territories. *Arctic* 41:195–202.

Zeman, Brenda
1988　*To Run with the Longboat: Twelve Stories of Indian Athletes in Canada.* Edmonton: GMS2 Ventures Inc.

Zentner, Henry
1963　Factors in the Social Pathology of a North American Indian Society. *Anthropologica* 5:119–30.

1970　The Impending Identity Crisis Among Native Peoples. In *Prairie Perspectives,* edited by D. P. Gagan, pp. 78–89. Toronto: Holt, Rinehart and Winston of Canada.

Zimmerly, D. W.
1975　*Cain's Land Revisited: Culture Change in Central Labrador, 1775–1972.* Institute of Social and Economic Research Studies 16. St. John's: Memorial University of Newfoundland.

Section Three

🍁

SOME MAJOR PUBLISHED PRIMARY HISTORICAL SOURCES

Back, Sir George
1836   *Narrative of the Arctic Land Expedition to the Mouth of the Great Fish River, and Along the Shores of the Arctic Ocean, in the Years 1833, 1834, and 1835.* London.

Black, Samuel
1955   A Journal of a Voyage from Rocky Mountain Portage in Peace River to the Sources of Finlay's Branch and North West Ward in Summer 1824. Edited by E. E. Rich. London: Hudson's Bay Record Society.

Blair, Emma Helen, ed. and trans.
1911   *The Indian Tribes of the Upper Mississippi Valley and the Region of the Great Lakes as Described by Nicolas Perrot, . . . Bacqueville de la Potherie, . . . Morrell Marston, . . . and Thomas Forsyth.* 2 vols. Cleveland: Arthur H. Clark.

Cartier, Jacques
1924   *The Voyages of Jacques Cartier.* Edited and translated by H. P. Biggar. Publications of the Public Archives of Canada 11. Ottawa.

Champlain, Samuel de
1922–36 *The Works of Samuel de Champlain.* 6 vols. Edited by H. P. Biggar. Toronto: Champlain Society.

Charlevoix, Pierre de
1761   *Journal of a Voyage to North-America.* 2 vols. London.

Cocking, Matthew
1908   *An Adventurer from Hudson Bay. Journal of Matthew Cocking from York Factory to the Blackfeet Country, 1772–1773.* Edited by L. J. Burpee. Transactions of the Royal Society of Canada, series 3, vol. 2.

Cody, Hiram A.
1908   *An Apostle of the North: Memoirs of the Right Reverend William Carpenter Bompas, D. D.* London: Seeley.

Cook, James
1955   *The Journals of Captain James Cook on His Voyages of Discovery.* Vol. 3, parts 1 and 2, *The Voyage of the "Resolution" and "Discovery," 1776–1780,* edited by J. C. Beaglehole. Cambridge: Hakluyt Society.

Coues, Elliott, ed.
1965   *New Light on the Early History of the Greater*

Northwest: The Manuscript Journals of Alexander Henry [the Younger] . . . and of David Thompson. 1897. Minneapolis: Ross and Haines.

Davies, Kenneth G., and A. M. Johnson, eds.
1963   *Northern Quebec and Labrador Journals and Correspondence, 1819–35.* London: Hudson's Bay Record Society.
1965   *Letters from Hudson Bay, 1703–40.* London: Hudson's Bay Record Society.

Denys, Nicolas
1980   *The Description and Natural History of the Coasts of North America (Acadia).* Edited by William F. Ganong. Toronto: Champlain Society.

Désy, Pierrette
1983   *Trente ans de captivité chez les Indiens Ojiwa. Récit de John Tanner.* Paris: Payot.

Dièreville, Sieur de
1933   *Relation of the Voyage to Port Royal in Acadia or New France.* Edited by J. C. Webster. Toronto: Champlain Society.

Dixon, George
1789   *A Voyage Round the World; but more Particularly to the North-West Coast of America: Performed in 1785, 1786, 1787 and 1788 in the "King George" and "Queen Charlotte," Captains Portlock and Dixon.* London.

Dobbs, Arthur
1744   *An Account of the Countries Adjoining to Hudson's Bay in the North-west Part of America.* London.

Espinoza y Tello, José
1930   *A Spanish voyage to Vancouver Island and the northwest coast of America, being the Narrative of the voyage made in the year 1792 by the schooners Sutil and Mexicana to explore the Strait of Fuca.* Translated by Cecil Jane. London.

Fidler, Peter
1934   Journal of a Journey with the Chipewyans or Northern Indians to the Slave Lake and to the East and West of the Slave River, in 1791 and 1792. In *Journals of Samuel Hearne and Phillip Turnor Between the Years 1774 and 1792,* edited by J. B. Tyrrell, pp. 493–556. Toronto: Champlain Society.

Franchère, Gabriel
1969   *Journal of a Voyage to the Northwest Coast of North America During the Years 1811, 1812, 1813, and 1814, by Gabriel Franchère.* Edited by W. Kaye Lamb. Toronto: Champlain Society.

Franklin, Sir John
1823   *Narrative of a Journey to the Shores of the Polar Sea in the Years 1819, 20, 21 and 22.* London.
1828   *Narrative of a Second Expedition to the Shores of the Polar Sea in the Years 1825, 1826 and 1827 Including an Account of the Progress of a Detachment to the Eastward.* London.

Fraser, Simon
1960   *The Letters and Journals of Simon Fraser, 1806–1808.* Edited by W. Kaye Lamb. Toronto: Macmillan.

Graham, Andrew
1969   *Andrew Graham's Observations on Hudson's Bay, 1767–1791.* Edited by Glyndwr Williams. London: Hudson's Bay Record Society.

Harmon, Daniel W.
1957   *Sixteen Years in Indian Country: The Journal of Daniel Williams Harmon, 1800–1816.* Edited by W. Kaye Lamb. Toronto: Macmillan.

Hearne, Samuel
1958   *A Journey from Prince of Wales's Fort in Hudson's Bay to the Northern Ocean in the Years 1769, 1770, 1771, 1772.* 1795. Edited by Richard Glover. Toronto: Macmillan.

Heckewelder, John G. E.
1876   *History, Manners and Customs of the Indian Natives Who Once Inhabited Pennsylvania and the Neighboring States.* 1818. Rev. ed. Memoirs of the Pennsylvania Historical Society 12. Philadelphia.

Hendry [Henday], Anthony
1907   *York Factory to the Blackfoot Country, the Journal of Anthony Hendry, 1754–55.* Edited by L. J. Burpee. Proceedings and Transactions of the Royal Society of Canada, 3d. ser., vol. 1.

Henry, Alexander [the Elder]
1901   *Travels and Adventures in Canada and the Indian Territories Between the Years 1760 and 1776.* Edited by James Bain. Boston: Little, Brown.

Henry, Alexander [the Younger]
1988   *The Journal of Alexander Henry the Younger 1799–1814*, vol. 1. Edited by Barry M. Gough. Toronto: Champlain Society.

Hind, Henry Y.
1863   *Explorations in the Interior of the Labrador Peninsula, the Country of the Montagnais and Nasquapee Indians.* 2 vols. London.
1969   *Narrative of the Canadian Red River Exploring Expedition of 1857 and of the Assiniboine and Saskatchewan Exploring Expedition of 1858.* 1860. New York: Greenwood Press.

Hoffman, Bernard G.
1961   *Cabot to Cartier: Sources for a Historical Ethnography of Northeastern North America, 1497–1550.* Toronto: University of Toronto Press.

Howley, James P.
1915   *The Beothuks, or Red Indians: The Aboriginal Inhabitants of Newfoundland.* Cambridge: Cambridge University Press.

Isham, James
1949   *Observations on Hudson's Bay, 1743, and Notes and Observations on a Book Entitled a Voyage to Hudsons Bay in the Dobbs Galley, 1749.* Edited by E. E. Rich. Toronto: Champlain Society for Hudson's Bay Record Society.

Jewitt, John R.
1974   *The Adventures and Sufferings of John R. Jewitt, Captive Among the Nootka, 1803–05.* Toronto: McClelland and Stewart.

Kelsey, Henry
1929   *The Kelsey Papers.* Edited by A. G. Doughty and Chester N. Martin. Ottawa: Public Archives of Canada.

Lafitau, Joseph François
1974–77 *Customs of the American Indians Compared with the Customs of Primitive Times.* 2 vols. Edited and translated by William N. Fenton and Elizabeth L. Moore. Toronto: Champlain Society.

Lahontan, Louis Armand de Lom d'Arce, baron de
1905   *New Voyages to North America by the Baron de Lahontan.* 1703. Edited by Reuben G. Thwaites. 2 vols. Chicago: A. C. McClurg.

La Pérouse, Jean François Galoup de
1798   *La Pérouse Voyage Round the World Per-formed in the Years 1785–1788.* 2 vols. Translated from the French. London.

LaRocque, François
1910   *Journal of Larouque from the Assiniboine to the Yellowstone.* 1805. Publications of the Public Archives of Canada 5. Ottawa.

La Vérendrye, Pierre Gaultier de Varennes de
1927   *Journals and Letters of Pierre Gaultier de Varennes de la Vérendrye and His Sons. . . .* Edited by L. J. Burpee. Toronto: Champlain Society.

Le Clercq, Chrestien
1910   *New Relation of Gaspesia with the Customs and Religion of the Gaspesian Indians.* Edited and translated by William F. Ganong. Toronto: Champlain Society.

Lescarbot, Marc
1907–14 *The History of New France.* 1618. Translated by W. L. Grant. 3 vols. Toronto: Champlain Society.
1928   *Nova Francia: A Description of Acadia.* Edited by H. P. Biggar. London: Routledge.

Lisiansky, Urey
1814   *Voyage Round the World in 1803, 4, 5, 6.* London.

McGillivray, Duncan
1929   *The Journal of Duncan McGillivray of the Northwest Company at Fort George on the Saskatchewan, 1794–1795.* Edited by A. S. Morton. Toronto.

Mackenzie, Sir Alexander
1970   *The Journals and Letters of Sir Alexander Mackenzie* [1789–1819]. Edited by W. Kaye Lamb. Cambridge: Hakluyt Society.

McLean, John
1932   *John McLean's Notes of a Twenty-five Years' Service in the Hudson's Bay Territory.* 1849. Edited by W. S. Wallace. Toronto: Champlain Society.

Masson, Louis F. R., ed.
1960   *Les bourgeois de la Compagnie du Nord-ouest: récits de voyages, lettres, et rapports inédits relatifs au Nord-ouest canadien.* 1889–90. 2 vols. New York: Antiquarian Press.

Murray, Alexander H.
1910   *Journal of the Yukon, 1847–48.* Edited by L. J.

Burpee. Publications of the Public Archives of Canada, no. 4. Ottawa.

Nute, Grace Lee
1943   *Caesars of the Wilderness: Médard Chouart, Sieur des Groseilliers, and Pierre Esprit Radisson, 1618–1710.* New York: D. Appleton-Century. Reprint. St. Paul: Minnesota Historical Society Press, 1978.

Ogden, Peter Skene
1950   *Peter Skene Ogden's Snake Country Journals, 1824–25 and 1825–26.* Edited by E. E. Rich. London: Hudson's Bay Record Society.

Oldmixon, John
1741   *The British Empire in America, Containing the History of the Discovery, Settlement, Progress, and State of the British Colonies on the Continent and Islands of America. . . . 2d ed. 2 vols.* London.

Petitot, Emile
1876   *Monographie des Dènè-Dindjié.* Paris.
1888   *En route pour la mer glaciale.* 2d ed. Paris.
1889   *Quinze ans sous le cercle polaire: Mackenzie.* Paris.
1891   *Autour du Grand Lac des Esclaves.* Paris.
1893   *Exploration de la région du Grand Lac des Ours (fin de quinze ans sous le cercle polaire).* Paris.

Quaife, Milo M., ed.
1922   *John Long's Voyages and Travels in the Years 1768–1788.* Chicago: R. R. Donnelley and Sons.

Radisson, Pierre E.
1885   *Voyages of Peter Esprit Radisson, Being an Account of His Travels and Experiences Among the North American Indians, from 1652–1684.* Boston.

Rand, Silas T.
1850   *A Short Statement of Facts Relating to the History, Manners, Customs, Language, and Literature of the Micmac Tribe of Indians in Nova-Scotia and P. E. Island.* Halifax.

Rich, E. E., ed.
1941   *The Letters of John McLoughlin from Fort Vancouver to the Governor and Committee, First Series, 1825–1838.* London: Hudson's Bay Record Society.
1943   *The Letters of John McLoughlin from Fort Vancouver to the Governor and Committee, Second Series, 1839–1844.* London: Hudson's Bay Record Society.
1944   *The Letters of John McLoughlin from Fort Vancouver to the Governor and Committee, Third Series, 1844–1846.* London: Hudson's Bay Record Society.

Richardson, Sir John
1851   *Arctic Searching Expedition: A Journal of a Boat Voyage Through Rupert's Land and the Arctic Sea, in Search of the Discovery of Ships Under Command of Sir John Franklin with an Appendix on the Physical Geography of North America.* 2 vols. London.

Russell, Frank
1898   *Explorations in the Far North: Being the Report of an Expedition Under the Auspices of the University of Iowa During the Years 1892, '93, and '94.* Iowa City.

Sagard-Théodat, Gabriel
1939   *Father Gabriel Sagard: The Long Journey to the Country of the Hurons.* 1632. Edited by George M. Wrong. Toronto: Champlain Society.

Simpson, Sir George
1938   *Journal of Occurrences in the Athabasca Department by George Simpson, 1820 and 1821, and Report.* Edited by E. E. Rich. Toronto: Champlain Society.
1947   *Part of a Despatch from George Simpson Esqr. Governor of Ruperts Land to the Governor and Committee of the Hudson's Bay Company London, March 1, 1829. Continued and completed March 24 and June 5, 1829.* London: Hudson's Bay Record Society.

Tanner, John
1956   *A Narrative of the Captivity and Adventures of John Tanner During Thirty Years' Residence Among the Indians in the Interior of North America.* Edited by Edwin James. Minneapolis: Ross and Haines.

Thevet, André
1986   *André Thevet's North America.* Edited by Roger Schlesinger and Arthur P. Stabler. Kingston: McGill-Queen's University Press.

Thompson, David
1962   *David Thompson's Narrative, 1784–1812.* Edited by Richard Glover. 2d ed. Toronto: Champlain Society.

Thwaites, Reuben Gold
1896–1901 *The Jesuit Relations and Allied Documents.* 73 vols. Cleveland.

Tyrrell, J. B., ed.
1934 *Journals of Samuel Hearne and Philip Turnor Between the Years 1774 and 1792.* Toronto: Champlain Society.

Vancouver, George
1798 *A voyage of discovery to the North Pacific Ocean, and Round the World . . . Performed in the Years 1790, 1791, 1792, 1793, 1794 and 1795, in the "Discovery" Sloop of War and Armed Tender "Chatham," under the Com-* mand of Captain George Vancouver. 3 vols. London.

Walker, Alexander
1982 *An Account of a Voyage to the North West Coast of America in 1785–1786 by Alexander Walker.* Edited by Robin Fisher and J. M. Bumsted. Vancouver and Toronto: Douglas and McIntyre.

Wood, W. Raymond, and Thomas D. Thiessen, eds.
1984 *Early Fur Trade on the Northern Plains: Canadian Traders Among the Mandan and Hidatsa Indians, 1738–1818.* Norman: University of Oklahoma Press.

Part Two

Regional and Ethnic Sources

Section Four

♣

ALGONQUIANS AND BEOTHUKS OF THE EASTERN MARITIMES

Anger, Dorothy C.
1981   The Micmacs of Newfoundland: A Resurgent Culture. *Culture* 1:78–81.

Bakker, Peter
1988   Basque Pidgin Vocabulary in European-Algonquian Trade Contacts. In *Papers of the Nineteenth Algonquian Conference,* edited by William Cowan, pp. 7–15. Ottawa: Carleton University.
1989   A Basque-Amerindian Pidgin in use between Europeans and Native Americans in North America, ca. 1540–ca. 1640. *Anthropological Linguistics.*

Bartels, Dennis, and Olaf Ume Janzen
1990   Micmac migration to western Newfoundland. *Canadian Journal of Native Studies* 10(1):71–96.

Black, David, and Ruth Holmes Whitehead
1988   Prehistoric Shellfish Preservation and Storage on the Northeast Coast. *North American Archaeologist* 9(1):17–30.

Bock, Philip K.
1964   Patterns of Illegitimacy on a Canadian Indian Reserve: 1860–1960. *Journal of Marriage and the Family* 26:142–48.
1966a   *The Micmac Indians of Restigouche: History and Contemporary Description.* Anthropological Series, no. 77. Bulletin 213. Ottawa: National Museum of Canada.
1966b   Social Time and Institutional Conflict. *Human Organization* 25:96–102.
1978   Micmac. In *Handbook of North American Indians,* vol. 15, *Northeast,* edited Bruce G. Trigger, pp. 109–22. Washington: Smithsonian Institution Press.

Bourque, Bruce J.
1989   Ethnicity on the Maritime Peninsula, 1600–1789. *Ethnohistory* 36:257–84.

Bragdon, Kathleen J.
1990   The Northeast. In *Native North Americans: An Ethnohistorical Approach,* edited by Daniel L. Boxberger, pp. 91–133. Dubuque Iowa: Kendall/Hunt Publishing Company.

Brasser, Ted J. C.
1971   The Coastal Algonkians: People of the First Frontiers. In *North American Indians in Historical Perspective,* edited by E. B. Leacock

and N. O. Lurie, pp. 64–91. New York: Random House.

1978   Early Indian-European Contacts. In *Handbook of North American Indians,* vol. 15, *Northeast,* edited by Bruce G. Trigger, pp. 78–88. Washington: Smithsonian Institution Press.

Clark, Andrew Hill
1968   *Acadia: The Geography of Early Nova Scotia to 1760.* Madison: University of Wisconsin Press.

Day, Gordon M.
1978   Western Abenaki. In *Handbook of North American Indians,* vol. 15, *Northeast,* edited by Bruce G. Trigger, pp. 148–59. Washington: Smithsonian Institution Press.
1981   *The Identity of the St. Francis Indians.* Mercury Series, Canadian Ethnology Service Paper 71. Ottawa: National Museum of Man.

Deblois, Albert D.
1991   *Micmac Texts.* Mercury Series, Canadian Ethnology Service Paper 117. Ottawa: Canadian Museum of Civilization.

Dickason, Olive Patricia
1976   Louisbourg and the Indians: A Study in Imperial Race Relations, 1713–1760. *History and Archaeology* (Ottawa), vol. 6.

Erickson, Vincent
1978   Maliseet-Passamaquoddy. In *Handbook of North American Indians,* vol. 15, *Northeast,* edited by Bruce G. Trigger, pp. 123–36. Washington: Smithsonian Institution Press.

Goddard, Ives
1978   Eastern Algonquian Languages. In *Handbook of North American Indians,* vol. 15, *Northeast,* edited by Bruce G. Trigger, pp. 70–77. Washington: Smithsonian Institution Press.

Gould, G. P., and A. J. Semple, eds.
1980   *Our Land: The Maritimes.* Fredericton: Saint Anne's Point Press.

Guillemin, Jeanne
1975   *Urban Renegades.* New York: Columbia University Press.

Hamilton, W. D., and S. A. Spray, eds.
1977   *Source Materials Relating to the New Brunswick Indians.* Fredericton.

Hutton, Elizabeth A.
1963   Indian Affairs in Nova Scotia, 1760–1834.

Collections of the Nova Scotia Historical Society 34:33–54.

Larsen, Tord
1977   *Negotiating Identity: Ethnic Incorporation Among the Nova Scotia Micmacs.* Oslo: Institute for Social Anthropology.
1983   Negotiating Identity: The Micmac of Nova Scotia. In *The Politics of Indianness,* edited by Adrian Tanner, pp. 37–136. St. John's: Memorial University of Newfoundland, Institute of Social and Economic Research.

McFeat, Tom
1983   An Affair to Remember: Winoque, 1965. *Culture* 3(1):79–90.
1989   Rise and Fall of the Big Men of the Northeast: Maliseet Transformations. In *Actes du vingtième congrès des algonquinistes,* edited by William Cowan, pp. 232–49. Ottawa: Carleton University.

McGee, Harold F., Jr.
1983   No Longer Neglected: A Decade of Writing Concerning the Native Peoples of the Maritimes. In *The Native Peoples of Atlantic Canada: A History of Indian-European Relations,* edited by H. F. McGee, Jr., pp. 209–18. Ottawa: Carleton University.

McGee, Harold F., Jr., ed.
1974   *The Native Peoples of Atlantic Canada: A Reader in Regional Ethnic Relations.* Toronto: McClelland and Stewart.
1983   *The Native Peoples of Atlantic Canada: A History of Indian-European Relations.* Ottawa: Carleton University.

Marshall, Ingeborg C. L.
1977   An Unpublished Map Made by John Cartwright Between 1768 and 1773 Showing Beothuck Indian Settlements and Artifacts and Allowing a New Population Estimate. *Ethnohistory* 24:223–50.
1988a   Beothuk and Micmac: Re-examining Relationships. *Acadiensis* 17(2):52–82.
1988b   *Beothuks of Newfoundland: A Vanished People.* St. John's, Nfld.: Breakwater Books.
1988c   Newfoundland Beothuk Illustrated. *Man in the Northeast* 35:47–70.
1989   *Reports and Letters by George Christopher Pulling Relative to the Beothuk of Newfoundland.* St John's: Breakwater Books.

1990   Evidence for Two Beothuk Subsistence Economies. In *Papers of the Twenty-First Algonquian Conference,* edited by William Cowan, pp. 216–26. Ottawa: Carleton University.

Martijn, Charles A.
1989   An Eastern Micmac Domain of Islands. In *Actes du vingtième congrès des algonquinistes,* edited by William Cowan, pp. 208–31. Ottawa: Carleton University.

Martijn, Charles A., ed.
1986   *Les Micmacs et la mer.* Montreal: Recherches amérindiennnes au Québec.

Martin, Calvin
1974   The European Impact on the Culture of a Northeastern Algonquian Tribe: An Ecological Interpretation. *William and Mary Quarterly* 31:3–26.

Martin, Peggy
1979   Micmac Indians as Witches in the Newfoundland Tradition. In *Papers of the Tenth Algonquian Conference,* edited by W. Cowan, pp. 173–80. Ottawa: Carleton University.

Mechling, W. H.
1958–59 The Malecite Indians, with Notes on the Micmacs. *Anthropologica* 7–8:1–274.

Miller, Virginia P.
1976   Aboriginal Micmac Population: A Review of the Evidence. *Ethnohistory* 23:117–28.
1982   The Decline of Nova Scotia Micmac Population. *Culture* 2(3):107–20.
1983   Social and Political Complexity on the East Coast: The Micmac Case. In *The Evolution of Maritime Cultures on the Northeast and Northwest Coasts of America,* edited by Ronald J. Nash, pp. 41–55. Department of Archaeology Publication 11. Burnaby, B.C.: Simon Fraser University.

Morrison, Alvin H.
1990   Dawnland Dog-Feast: Wabanaki Warfare, c. 1600–1760. In *Papers of the Twenty-First Algonquian Conference,* edited by William Cowan, pp. 258–78. Ottawa: Carleton University.
1991   Dawnland Directors' Decisions: 17th-Century Encounter Dynamics on the Wabanaki Frontier. In *Papers of the Twenty-Second Algonquian Conference,* edited by William Cowan, pp. 225–45. Ottawa: Carleton University.

Morrison, Ann
1991   Voces Cantantes in Vestro: History of Research on Music Among the Wabanaki. In *Papers of the Twenty-Second Algonquian Conference,* edited by William Cowan, pp. 246–63. Ottawa: Carleton University.

Morrison, Kenneth M.
1984   *The Embattled Northeast: The Elusive Ideal of Abenaki-Euramerican Relations.* Berkeley: University of California Press.

Nash, Ronald J., and Virginia P. Miller
1987   Model Building and the Case of the Micmac Economy. *Man in the Northeast* 34:41–56.

Nicholas, Andrea Bear
1986   Maliseet Aboriginal Rights and Mascarene's Treaty, Not Dummer's Treaty. In *Actes du dix-septième congrès des algonquinistes,* edited by William Cowan, pp. 215-30. Ottawa: Carleton University.
1991   Wabanaki and French relations: Myth and reality. *Interculture* 24:12–34.

Passchier, Françoise
1985   Le système économique micmac—perspective ethnohistorique au XVIIe siècle. *Paléo-Québec* 17. Montreal.

Pastore, Ralph
1990   Native history in the Atlantic region during the colonial period. *Acadiensis* 20(1):200–25.

Pelletier, Gaby
1980   The Micmac Dilemma at the End of the Seventeenth Century. *Journal of the New Brunswick Museum,* pp. 103–11.

Penney, Gerald
1990   Frank Speck and the Newfoundland Micmac. In *Papers of the Twenty-First Algonquian Conference,* edited by William Cowan, pp. 295–302. Ottawa: Carleton University.

Penney, Gerald, and H. Nicol
1984   Burnt Knaps: A Micmac Site in Newfoundland. *Canadian Journal of Archaeology* 8:57–69.

Prins, Harald E. L.
1986   Micmacs and Maliseets in the St. Lawrence River Valley. In *Actes du dix-septième congrès des algonquinistes,* edited by William Cowan, pp. 263–78. Ottawa: Carleton University.

Quinn, David B.
1982   Newfoundland in the Consciousness of Europe in the Sixteenth and Early Seventeenth Centuries. In *Early European Settlement and Exploitation in Atlantic Canada,* edited by G. M. Storey, pp. 9–30. St. John's: Memorial University of Newfoundland.

Raynauld, Francoy
1984   Les pêcheurs et les colons anglais n'ont pas exterminé les Béothuks de Terre-Neuve. *Recherches amérindiennnes au Québec* 14(1):45–59.

Reid, John G.
1990   Mission to the Micmac. *Beaver* 70(5):15–22.

Reynolds, Barrie
1978   Beothuk. In *Handbook of North American Indians,* vol. 15, *Northeast,* edited by Bruce G. Trigger, pp. 101–8. Washington: Smithsonian Institution Press.

Rothschild, Nan A.
1983   The Recognition of Leadership in Egalitarian Societies of the Northeast. In *The Development of Political Organization in Native North America,* edited by E. Tooker, pp. 165–82. Washington: American Ethnological Society.

Rowe, Frederick W.
1977   *Extinction: The Beothuks of Newfoundland.* Toronto: McGraw Hill-Ryerson.

Seeber, Pauleena MacDougall
1984   The European Influence on Abenaki Economics Before 1615. In *Papers of the Fifteenth Algonquian Conference,* edited by William Cowan, pp. 201–16. Ottawa: Carleton University.

Sévigny, P.-André
1976   *Les Abenaquis: habitat et migrations (17e et 18e siècles).* Montreal: Bellarmin.

Smith, Nicholas N.
1957   Notes on the Malecite of Woodstock, New Brunswick. *Anthropologica* 5:1–40.
1983   The Wabenaki-Mohawk Conflict: A Folkhistory Tradition. In *Actes du quatorzième congrès des algonquinistes,* edited by William Cowan, pp. 49–56. Ottawa: Carleton University.

Snow, Dean R.
1968   Wabanaki "Family Hunting Territories." *American Anthropologist* 70:1143–51.
1978a   Eastern Abenaki. In *Handbook of North American Indians,* vol. 15, *Northeast,* edited by Bruce G. Trigger, pp. 137–47. Washington: Smithsonian Institution Press.
1978b   Late Prehistory of the East Coast. In *Handbook of North American Indians,* vol. 15, *Northeast,* edited by Bruce G. Trigger, pp. 58–69. Washington: Smithsonian Institution Press.

Speck, Frank G.
1922   *Beothuk and Micmac.* Indian Notes and Monographs, misc. ser., 22. New York: Museum of the American Indian, Heye Foundation.
1940   *Penobscot Man.* Philadelphia: University of Pennsylvania Press.

Such, Peter
1973   *Riverrun.* Toronto: Clarke.
1978   *Vanished Peoples: The Archaic, Dorset, and Beothuk People of Newfoundland.* Toronto: NC Press.

Tuck, James A.
1976   *Newfoundland and Labrador Prehistory.* Ottawa: National Museum of Man.
1984   *Maritimes Provinces Prehistory.* Chicago: University of Chicago Press.

Upton, L. F. S.
1974   Indian Affairs in Colonial New Brunswick. *Acadiensis* 4:6–26.
1975a   Colonists and Micmacs. *Journal of Canadian Studies* 10:44–56.
1975b   Indian Policy in Colonial Nova Scotia, 1783–1871. *Acadiensis* 5:3–31.
1976   Indians and Islanders: The Micmacs in Colonial Prince Edward Island. *Acadiensis* 6:21–42.
1977   The Extermination of the Beothucks of Newfoundland. *Canadian Historical Review* 58:133–53.
1979   *Micmacs and Colonists: Indian-White Relations in the Maritimes, 1713–1867.* Vancouver: University of British Columbia Press.
1980   Contact and Conflict on the Atlantic and Pacific Coasts of Canada. *BC Studies* 45:103–15.

Wallis, Wilson D., and Ruth S. Wallis
1955   *The Micmac Indians of Eastern Canada.* Minneapolis: University of Minnesota Press.
1957   *The Malecite Indians of New Brunswick.* National Museum of Canada Bulletin 148.

Whitehead, Ruth Holmes
1991   *The Old Man Told Us: Excerpts from Micmac History 1500–1950.* Halifax: Nimbus Publishing.

Whitehead, Ruth Holmes, and H. F. McGee, Jr.
1983   *The Micmac: How They Lived Five Hundred Years Ago.* Halifax: Nimbus Publishing.

Whitley, Barbara
1966   *The Beothuks and Other Primitive Peoples.* St. John's: Centre for Newfoundland Studies.

Wien, Fred
1986   *Rebuilding the Economic Base of Indian Communities: The Micmac in Nova Scotia.* Montreal: Institute for Research on Public Policy.

Winter, Keith
1975   *Shananditte.* North Vancouver: J. J. Douglas.

Section Five

✤

NORTHERN ALGONQUIANS
OF THE EASTERN AND
CENTRAL SUBARCTIC AND
THE GREAT LAKES REGION

Adams, Gary
1983   Tipi Rings at York Factory: An Archaeological-Ethnographic Interface. *Plains Anthropologist* 28 (no. 102, pt. 2):7–15.

Angus, James T.
1989   How the Dokis Indians Protected Their Timber. *Ontario History* 81:181–99.

Armitage, Peter, and John C. Kennedy
1989   Redbaiting and Racism on Our Frontier: Military Expansion in Labrador and Quebec. *Canadian Review of Sociology and Anthropology* 26:798–817.

Arnason, T., R. Hebda, and T. Johns
1981   Use of Plants for Food and Medicine by Native Peoples of Eastern Canada. *Canadian Journal of Botany* 59:2189–325.

Barger, W. K.
1981   Great Whale River, Quebec. In *Handbook of North American Indians,* vol. 6, *Subarctic,* edited by June Helm, pp. 673–82. Washington: Smithsonian Institution Press.
1982   Cultural Adaptation: A Model from the Canadian North. *Anthropology and Humanism Quarterly* 7(2–3):17–21.

Beck, Jane C.
1972   The Giant Beaver: A Prehistoric Memory? *Ethnohistory* 19:109–22.

Berkes, Fikret
1979   An Investigation of Cree Indian Domestic Fisheries in Northern Quebec. *Arctic* 32:46–70.
1982   Waterfowl Management and Northern Native Peoples with Reference to Cree Hunters of James Bay. *Musk-Ox* 30:23–35.
1986   Chisasibi Cree Hunters and Missionaries: Humour as Evidence of Tension. In *Actes du dix-septième congrès des algonquinistes,* edited by William Cowan, pp. 15–26. Ottawa: Carleton University.

Berkes, Fikret, and Carole Farkas
1978   Eastern James Bay Cree Indians: Changing Patterns of Wild Food Use and Nutrition. *Ecology of Food and Nutrition* 7:155–72.

Bernier, Pierre
1981   Pêche côtière, intervention de l'état et développement des forces productives à rivière St. Paul. *Anthropologie et sociétés* 5:97–115.

Bishop, Charles A.
1970   The Emergence of Hunting Territories Among the Northern Ojibwa. *Ethnology* 9:1–15.
1975a   Ojibwa, Cree, and the Hudson's Bay Company in Northern Ontario: Culture and Conflict in the Eighteenth Century. In *Western Canada Past and Present,* edited by A. W. Rasporich, pp. 150–62. Calgary: McClelland-Stewart West.
1975b   The Origin of the Speakers of the Severn Dialect. In *Papers of the Sixth Algonquian Conference,* edited by William Cowan. Ottawa: Carleton University.
1975c   Northern Algonkian Cannibalism and Windigo Psychosis. In *Psychological Anthropology,* edited T. R. Williams, pp. 237–48. The Hague: Mouton.
1976   The Emergence of the Northern Ojibwa: Social and Economic Consequences. *American Ethnologist* 3:39–54.
1978   Cultural and Biological Adaptations to Deprivation: The Northern Ojibwa Case. In *Extinction and Survival in Human Populations,* edited by Charles Laughlin, Jr., and Ivan Brady, pp. 208–30. New York: Columbia University Press.
1981   Territorial Groups Before 1821: Cree and Ojibwa. In *Handbook of North American Indians,* vol. 6, *Subarctic,* edited by June Helm, pp. 158–60. Washington: Smithsonian Institution Press.
1982   The Indian Inhabitants of Northern Ontario at the Time of Contact: Socio-Territorial Considerations. In *Approaches to Algonquian Archaeology,* edited by M. G. Hanna and B. Kooyman, pp. 253–73. Calgary: University of Calgary.
1983   The Western James Bay Cree: Aboriginal and Early Historic Adaptations. *Prairie Forum* 8:147–55.
1986   Territoriality Among Northeastern Algonquians. *Anthropologica* 28(1–2):37–63.
1989   The Question of Ojibwa Clans. In *Actes du vingtième congrès des algonquinistes,* edited by William Cowan, pp. 43–61. Ottawa: Carleton University.

Bishop, Charles A., and Toby Morantz, eds.
1986   À qui appartient le castor? Les régimes fonciers algonquins du nord remis en cause/Who Owns the Beaver? Northern Algonquian Land Tenure Reconsidered. *Anthropologica* 28(1–2):1–216.

Black, M. Jean
1989   Nineteenth-century Algonquin Culture Change. In *Actes du vingtième congrès des algonquinistes,* edited by William Cowan, pp. 62–69. Ottawa: Carleton University.

Black, Mary B.
1969   Eliciting Folk Taxonomy in Ojibwa. In *Cognitive Anthropology,* edited by S. A. Tyler, pp. 165–89. New York: Holt, Rinehart and Winston.
1977a   Ojibwa Power Belief System. In *The Anthropology of Power,* edited by R. D. Fogelson and R. N. Adams, pp. 141–51. New York: Academic Press.
1977b   Ojibwa Taxonomy and Percept Ambiguity. *Ethos* 5:90–118.

Black-Rogers, Mary
1987   L'application des principes de l'ethnoscience. *Recherches amérindiennnes au Québec* 17(4):5–16.
1990   Fosterage and Field Data: The Round Lake Study 1889. In *Papers of the Twenty-First Algonquian Conference,* edited by William Cowan, pp. 51–71. Ottawa: Carleton University.

Black-Rogers, Mary, and Edward S. Rogers
1983   The Cranes and Their Neighbors, 1770–1970. In *Actes du quatorzième congrès des algonquinistes,* edited by William Cowan, pp. 91–124. Ottawa: Carleton University.

Bleasdale, Ruth
1975   Manitowaning: An Experiment in Indian Settlement. *Ontario Historical Society* 66:147–57.

Brightman, Robert A.
1988   The Windigo in the Material World. *Ethnohistory* 35:337–79.
1990   Primitivism in Missinippi Cree Historical Consciousness. *Man* 25:108–28.

Brose, David S.
1978   Late Prehistory of the Upper Great Lakes Area. In *Handbook of North American Indians,* vol. 15, *Northeast,* edited by Bruce G. Trigger, pp. 569–82. Washington: Smithsonian Institution Press.

Brown, Jennifer S. H.
1971   The Cure and Feeding of Windigos: A Critique. *American Anthropologist* 73:20–22.

1985 Central Manitoba Saulteaux in the 19th Century. In *Papers of the Sixteenth Algonquian Conference,* edited by William Cowan, pp. 1–8. Ottawa: Carleton University.

1987 A. I. Hallowell and William Berens Revisited. In *Papers of the Eighteenth Algonquian Conference,* edited by William Cowan, pp. 17–28. Ottawa: Carleton University.

1989 "A Place in Your Mind for Them All": Chief William Berens. In *Being and Becoming Indian: Biographical Studies of North American Frontiers,* edited by James Clifton, pp. 204–25. Chicago: Dorsey Press.

Brown, Jennifer S. H., and Robert Brightman, eds.
1988 *The Orders of the Dreamed: George Nelson on Cree and Northern Ojibwa Religion and Myth, 1823.* Winnipeg: University of Manitoba Press; St. Paul: Minnesota Historical Society Press.

Burleson, Richard
1987 Opposition of Musical Order in a Cree Round-Song Dance. In *Papers of the Eighteenth Algonquian Conference,* edited by William Cowan, pp. 29–38. Ottawa: Carleton University.

Callender, Charles
1978 Great Lakes-Riverine Sociopolitical Organization. In *Handbook of North American Indians,* vol. 15, *Northeast,* edited by Bruce G. Trigger, pp. 610–12. Washington: Smithsonian Institution Press.

Chance, Norman A.
1966 The Changing World of the Cree. *Natural History* 76:16–23.

1968 Implications of Environmental Stress for Strategies of Developmental Change in the North. *Archives of Environmental Health* 17:571–77.

1972 Economic Opportunity and Cultural Viability Among the Canadian Cree. In *Circumpolar Problems,* edited by C. Berg, pp. 45–51. Oxford: Pergamon Press.

Chance, Norman A., ed.
1968 *Conflict in Culture: Problems of Developmental Change Among the Cree.* Ottawa: St. Paul University.

1969 *Les cris du Québec.* Ottawa: ARDA.

Chance, Norman A., and J. Trudeau
1963 Social Organization, Acculturation, and Integration Among the Eskimo and Cree: A Comparative Study. *Anthropologica* 5(1):47–56.

Charest, Paul
1975 Les ressources naturelles de la Côte Nord. *Recherches amérindiennnes au Québec* 5(2): 32–52.

Charron, C. Y., and C. Lévesque
1979 Le mouvement coopératif au Nouveau-Québec. *Recherches amérindiennnes au Québec* 8:307–10.

Clément, Daniel
1991 Homme-caribou: L'analyse ethnoscientifique du mythe. *Canadian Journal of Native Studies* 11(1):49–93.

Clermont, Norman
1977 La transformation historique des systèmes économiques algonquiens. In *Papers of the Eighth Algonquian Conference,* edited by William Cowan, pp. 182–87. Ottawa: Carleton University.

1978 Les kokotchés à Weymontachie. *Recherches amérindiennnes au Québec* 8(2):139–46.

1980 Le contrat avec les animaux. Bestiaire sélectif des indiens nomades du Québec au moment du contact. *Recherches amérindiennnes au Québec* 10(1–2):91–109.

Clifton, James A.
1975 *A Place of Refuge for All Time: Migration of the American Potawatomie into Upper Canada, 1830 to 1850.* Mercury Series, Canadian Ethnology Service Paper 26. Ottawa: National Museum of Man.

1978 Potawatomi. In *Handbook of North American Indians,* vol. 15, *Northeast,* edited by Bruce G. Trigger, pp. 725–42. Washington: Smithsonian Institution Press.

Collin, Dominique
1985 Du travail indien au travail pour les Indiens. *Culture* 5(1):17–34.

Cooke, Alan
1979 L'indépendance des Naskapis et le caribou. *Recherches amérindiennnes au Québec* 9(1–2):99–104.

1985 The Montagnais. *Beaver* 316(1):13–19.

Cooper, John M.
1939 Is the Algonquian Family Hunting Ground

System Pre-Columbian? *American Anthropologist* 41:66–90.

Cowan, William
1987   Ojibwa Vocabulary in Longfellow's Hiawatha. In *Papers of the Eighteenth Algonquian Conference,* edited by William Cowan, pp. 59–68. Ottawa: Carleton University.

Cox, Bruce A.
1971   Modernization Among the Mistassini-Waswanipi Cree: A Comment. *Canadian Review of Sociology and Anthropology* 7(3):212–15.

Craik, Brian
1975   The Formation of a Goose Hunting Strategy and the Politics of the Hunting Group. In *Proceedings of the Second Congress of the Canadian Ethnology Society,* edited by Jim Freedman and Jerome H. Barkow, 2:450-65. Mercury Series, Canadian Ethnology Service Paper 28. Ottawa: National Museum of Man.
1979   We Are Divided by the Light: Experience and Belief in a Cree Society. In *Papers of the Tenth Algonquian Conference,* edited by W. Cowan, pp. 66–78. Ottawa: Carleton University.

Cummins, Bryan
1990   Attawapiskat Cree Land Use and State Intervention. In *Papers of the Twenty-First Algonquian Conference,* edited by William Cowan, pp. 100–13. Ottawa: Carleton University.

Darnell, Regna
1984   Interaction et langage chez les cris. *Recherches amérindiennnes au Québec* 14(4):42–50.

Day, Gordon M.
1953   The Indian as an Ecological Factor in the Northeastern Forest. *Ecology* 34:329–46.
1978   Nipissing. In *Handbook of North American Indians,* vol. 15, *Northeast,* edited by Bruce G. Trigger, pp. 787–91. Washington: Smithsonian Institution Press.

Day, Gordon M., and Bruce G. Trigger
1978   Algonquin. In *Handbook of North American Indians,* vol. 15, *Northeast,* edited by Bruce G. Trigger, pp. 792–97. Washington: Smithsonian Institution Press.

Densmore, Frances
1929   *Chippewa Customs.* Bureau of American Ethnology Bulletin 86. Washington: Smithsonian Institution Press.

Denton, David
1979   L'exploitation historique récente du caribou et les schèmes d'établissement dans la région de Caniapiscau. *Recherches amérindiennnes au Québec* 9(1–2):105–16.

Désveaux, Emmanuel
1983   Mythologie et astronomie des indiens de Big Trout Lake. In *Actes du quatorzième congrès des algonquinistes,* edited by William Cowan, pp. 203–18. Ottawa: Carleton University.
1984   La fonction gélinotte. In *Papers of the Fifteenth Algonquian Conference,* edited by William Cowan, pp. 33–48. Ottawa: Carleton University.
1988   *Sous le signe de l'ours. Mythes et temporalité chez les ojibwa septentrionaux.* Paris: Éditions de la Maison des sciences de l'homme.

Dominique, Richard
1979   Le caribou est un animal indien. *Recherches amérindiennnes au Québec* 9(1–2):47–54.

Drage, T. F.
1982   An Ethnographic Account of the Northern Cree, 1748. *Manitoba Archaeological Quarterly* 6(1):1–40.

Drapeau, Lynn
1984   Le traitement de l'information chez les montagnais. *Recherches amérindiennnes au Québec* 14(4):24–35.

Driben, Paul
1986   *Aroland Is Our Home: An Incomplete Victory in Applied Anthropology.* New York: AMS Press.

Driben, Paul, and Robert S. Trudeau
1983   *When Freedom Is Lost: The Dark Side of the Relationship Between Government and the Fort Hope Band.* Toronto: University of Toronto Press.

Dunk, Thomas W.
1987   Indian Participation in the Industrial Economy on the North Shore of Lake Superior, 1869–1940. *Thunder Bay Historical Museum Society* 3–13.

Dunning, R. W.
1959   *Social and Economic Change Among the Northern Ojibwa.* Toronto: University of Toronto Press.

1964   Some Problems of Reserve Indian Communities: A Case Study. *Anthropologica* 6:3–38.

Dyke, A. P.
1970   Montagnais-Naskapi or Montagnais and Nascaupi? An Examination of Some Tribal Differences. *Ethnohistory* 17:43–48.

Feest, Johanna E., and Christian F. Feest
1978   Ottawa. In *Handbook of North American Indians,* vol. 15, *Northeast,* edited by Bruce G. Trigger, pp. 772–86. Washington: Smithsonian Institution Press.

Feit, Harvey A.
1971a   L'ethno-écologie des cris waswanipis, ou comment des chasseurs peuvent aménager leurs ressources. *Recherches amérindiennnes au Québec,* Bulletin d'Information 1(4–5):84–93.
1971b   Exploitation des ressources naturelles en expansion dans la région de la baie James. *Recherches amérindiennnes au Québec,* bulletin d'information 1(4–5):22–26.
1973   The Ethno-Ecology of the Waswanipi Cree, or How Hunters Can Manage Their Resources. In *Cultural Ecology: Readings on the Canadian Indians and Eskimos,* edited Bruce Cox, pp. 115–25. Toronto: McClelland and Stewart.
1982   The Income Security Program for Cree Hunters in Quebec: An Experiment in Increasing the Autonomy of Hunters in a Developed Nation State. *Canadian Journal of Anthropology/Revue canadienne d'anthropologie* 3(1):59–70.

Fisher, Anthony J.
1971   The Cree of Canada: Some Ecological and Evolutionary Considerations. *Western Canadian Journal of Anthropology* 1(1):7–19.

Flannery, Regina
1962   Infancy and Childhood Among the Indians of the East Coast of James Bay. *Anthropos* 57(3–6):475–82.
1971   Some Magico-religious Concepts of the Algonquians on the East Coast of James Bay, Canada. In *Themes in Culture: Essays in Honor of Morris Opler,* edited by Mario D. Zamora, J. Michael Mahar, and Henry Orenstein, pp. 31–39. Quezon City, Philippines: Kayumanggi Publishers.

Flannery, Regina, and Mary Elizabeth Chambers
1985   Each Man Has His Own Friends: The Role of

Dream Visitors in Traditional East Cree Belief and Practice. *Arctic Anthropology* 22(1):1–22.

Flannery, Regina, Mary Elizabeth Chambers, and Patricia A. Jehle
1981   Witiko Accounts from the James Bay Cree. *Arctic Anthropology* 18(1):57–77.

Fogelson, Raymond D.
1965   Psychological Theories of Windigo "Psychosis" and a Preliminary Application of a Models Approach. In *Context and Meaning in Cultural Anthropology,* edited by Melford E. Spiro, pp. 74–99. New York: Free Press; London: Collier-Macmillan.
1982   Person, Self, and Identity: Some Anthropological Retrospects, Circumspects, and Prospects. In *Psychosocial Theories of the Self,* edited by B. Lee, pp. 67–109. New York: Plenum Press.

Foster, John E.
1977   *The Home Guard Cree and the Hudson's Bay Company: The First Hundred Years; Approaches to Native History in Canada.* Mercury Series, Canadian History Division Paper 25. Ottawa: National Museum of Man.

Fulford, George
1990   A Structural Analysis of Mide Chants. In *Papers of the Twenty-First Algonquian Conference,* edited by William Cowan, pp. 126–58. Ottawa: Carleton University.

Gadacz, René R.
1979   Acculturation as Paradigm in Historical Ethnology: The Montagnais Example. *Ethnohistory* 26:265–76.

Gagnon, Jo Ann
1982   Le régime de chasse, de pêche et de trappage et les conventions du Quebec nordique. *Collection Nordicana* 45. Laval: Centre d'études nordiques.

Garrad, Charles
1987   Michabous and the White Beaver: An Indian came to Michilimackinac to kill the Commandant—Why did he hesitate? *Beaver* 67(1): 50–55.

George, Peter J.
1989   Native Peoples and Community Economic Development in Northern Ontario. *British Journal of Canadian Studies* 4(1):58–73.

George, Peter J., and Richard J. Preston III
1987   "Going In Between": The Impact of European Technology on the Work Patterns of the West Main Cree of Northern Ontario. *Journal of Economic History* 47:447–60.

Gibson, Kathleen R., Mary Ellen Thames, and Kathryn T. Molohon
1991   Mating Patterns and Genetic Structure of Two Native North American Communities in Northern Ontario. In *Papers of the Twenty-second Algonquian Conference,* edited by William Cowan, pp. 145–56. Ottawa: Carleton University.

Goddard, Ives
1978a   Central Algonquian Languages. In *Handbook of North American Indians,* vol. 15, *Northeast,* edited by Bruce G. Trigger, pp. 583–87. Washington: Smithsonian Institution Press.
1978b   Delaware. In *Handbook of North American Indians,* vol. 15, *Northeast,* edited by Bruce G. Trigger, pp. 213–39. Washington: Smithsonian Institution Press.

Graburn, Nelson H. H.
1975   Naskapi Family and Kinship. *Western Canadian Journal of Anthropology* 5(2):56–84.

Graham, Janice E.
1987   After the Flood: Relocation to the Promised Land. In *Papers of the Eighteenth Algonquian Conference,* edited by William Cowan, pp. 137–46. Ottawa: Carleton University.
1988   Knowing the Cycle: Cognitive Control and Cree Death. In *Papers of the Nineteenth Algonquian Conference,* edited by William Cowan, pp. 81–88. Ottawa: Carleton University.

Grant, Valerie
1983   The Crane and Sucker Indians of Sandy Lake, 1870–1970: A Research Report. In *Actes du quatorzième congrès des algonquinistes,* edited by William Cowan, pp. 75–90. Ottawa: Carleton University.
1991   Users' Guide to the Round Lake Study Database with Special Attention to Sandy Lake. In *Papers of the Twenty-second Algonquian Conference,* edited by William Cowan, pp. 182–92. Ottawa: Carleton University.

Granzberg, Gary
1989   From Ritual to Theater in a Northern Manitoba Cree Community. *Anthropologica* 31:103–19.

Greenberg, Adolph M., and James Morrison
1982   Group Identities in the Boreal Forest: The Origin of the Northern Ojibwa. *Ethnohistory* 29:75–102.

Hallowell, A. Irving
1926   Bear Ceremonialism in the Northern Hemisphere. *American Anthropologist* 28(1):1–175.
1928   Recent changes in the kinship terminology of the St. Francis Abenaki. In *Acti del XXII congresso internazionale degli americanisti,* 2:97–145. Rome: Riccardo Garroni.
1930   Was Cross-cousin Marriage Practiced by the North-central Algonkian? In *Proceedings of the 23d International Congress of Americanists, 1928,* pp. 519–44. New York.
1936   The Passing of the Midewiwin in the Lake Winnipeg Region. *American Anthropologist* 38(1):32–51.
1938   Fear and Anxiety as Cultural and Individual Variables in a Primitive Society. *Journal of Social Psychology* 9:25–47.
1942   The Role of Conjuring in Saulteaux Society. *Publications of the Anthropological Society* 2. Philadelphia.
1949   The Size of Algonkian Hunting Territories: A Function of Ecological Adjustment. *American Anthropologist* 51(1):35–45.
1955   *Culture and Experience.* Philadelphia: University of Pennsylvania Press.
1960   Ojibwa Ontology, Behavior, and World View. In *Culture in History: Essays in Honor of Paul Radin,* edited by Stanley Diamond, pp. 19–52. New York: Columbia University Press.
1976   *Contributions to Anthropology: Selected Papers of A. Irving Hallowell.* Chicago: University of Chicago Press.

Hanks, Christopher C.
1982   The Swampy Cree and the Hudson's Bay Company at Oxford House. *Ethnohistory* 29:103–15.

Hanks, Christopher C., Gary Granzberg, and Jack H. Steinbring
1983   Social Changes and the Mass Media: The Oxford House Cree, 1909–83. *Polar Record* 21(134):459–65.

Hanna, Margaret G., and Brian Kooyman, eds.
1982   *Approaches to Algonquian Archaeology.* Calgary: Archaeology Association of the University of Calgary.

Hansen, Lise C.
1981   Revocation of Surrender and Its Implications for a Canadian Indian Band's Development. *Anthropologica* 23:121–44.
1983   Thirty-five Dollars: The Politics of Economic Development on Nipissing Reserve. *Canadian Journal of Native Studies* 2:269–83.

Hay, Thomas H.
1971   The Windigo Psychosis: Psychodynamic, Cultural, and Social Factors in Aberrant Behavior. *American Anthropologist* 73(1):1–19.

Hedican, Edward J.
1982a   Governmental Indian Policy, Administration, and Economic Planning in the Eastern Subarctic. *Culture* 2(3):25–36.
1982b   Some Implications of Contemporary Economic Activity Among the Ojibwa of Northern Ontario. In *Papers of the Thirteenth Algonquian Conference,* edited by William Cowan, pp. 275–84. Ottawa: Carleton University.
1985   Modern Economic Trends Among the Northern Ojibwa. *Man in the Northeast* 30:1–25.
1986a   *The Ogoki River Guide: Emergent Leadership Among the Northern Ojibwa.* Waterloo: Wilfred Laurier University Press.
1986b   Sibling Terminology and Information Theory: An Hypothesis Concerning the Growth of Folk Taxonomy. *Ethnology* 25:229–39.
1990   On the rail-line in northwestern Ontario: Non-reserve housing and community change. *Canadian Journal of Native Studies* 10(1):15–32.

Henriksen, Georg
1971   The Transactional Basis of Influence: White Men Among Naskapi Indians. In *Patrons and Brokers in the East Arctic,* edited by Robert Paine, pp. 22–33. Newfoundland Social and Economic Papers 2. St. John's: Memorial University of Newfoundland, Institute of Social and Economic Research.
1981a   Davis Inlet, Labrador. In *Handbook of North American Indians,* vol. 6, *Subarctic,* edited by June Helm, pp. 666–72. Washington: Smithsonian Institution Press.
1981b   *Hunters in the Barrens: The Naskapi on the Edge of the White Man's World.* St. John's: Memorial University of Newfoundland, Institute for Social and Economic Research.

Herring, D. Ann, Paul Driben, and L. A. Sawchuk
1983   Historic Fertility Patterns in a Northern Ojibwa Community: The Fort Hope Band. *Anthropologica* 25:147–62.

Hickerson, Harold
1959   Journal of Charles Jean Baptiste Chaboillez, 1797–1798. *Ethnohistory* 6:265–316, 363-427.
1960   The Feast of the Dead Among the Seventeenth Century Algonkians of the Upper Great Lakes. *American Anthropologist* 62:81–107.
1963   The Sociohistorical Significance of Two Chippewa Ceremonials. *American Anthropologist* 65:67–85.
1966   The Genesis of Bilaterality Among Two Divisions of Chippewa. *American Anthropologist* 68:1–26.
1967a   Land Tenure of the Rainy Lake Chippewa at the Beginning of the 19th Century. *Smithsonian Contributions to Anthropology* 2(4):37–63.
1967b   Some Implications of the Theory of Particularity, or "Atomism," of Northern Algonkians. *Current Anthropology* 8:313–43.
1970   *The Chippewa and Their Neighbors: A Study in Ethnohistory.* Toronto: Holt, Rinehart and Winston.
1971   The Chippewa of the Upper Great Lakes: A Study in Sociopolitical Change. In *North American Indians in Historical Perspective,* edited by E. B. Leacock and N. O. Lurie, pp. 167–99. New York: Random House. Reprint. Prospect Heights, Ill.: Waveland Press, 1988.
1988   *The Chippewa and Their Neighbors.* Rev. ed. Prospect Heights, Ill.: Waveland Press.

Hilger, Inez
1951   *Chippewa Child Life and Its Cultural Background.* Bureau of American Ethnology Bulletin 146. Washington.

Hodgins, Bruce W., and Jamie Benidickson
1989   *The Temagami Experience: Recreation, Resources, and Aboriginal Rights in the Northern Ontario Wilderness.* Toronto: University of Toronto Press.

Holden, David E. W.
1969   Modernization Among Town and Bush Cree in Quebec. *Canadian Review of Sociology and Anthropology* 6(4):237–48.

Holmer, N. M.
1954   *The Ojibway on Walpole Island, Ontario (A Linguistic Study)*. Uppsala Canadian Studies, no. 4. Lund, Sweden.

Holzkamm, Tim E.
1986   Ojibwa Horticulture in the Upper Mississippi and Boundary Waters. In *Actes du dix-septième congrès des algonquinistes*, edited by William Cowan, pp. 143–54. Ottawa: Carleton University.
1987   Sturgeon Utilization by the Rainy River Ojibwa Bands. In *Papers of the Eighteenth Algonquian Conference*, edited by William Cowan, pp. 155–64. Ottawa: Carleton University.

Holzkamm, Tim E., Victor P. Lytwyn, and Leo G. Waisberg
1988   Rainy River Sturgeon: An Ojibway Resource in the Fur Trade Economy. *Canadian Geographic* 32:194–205.

Honigmann, John J.
1953   Social Organization of the Attawapiskat Cree Indians. *Anthropos* 48(5–6):809–16.
1956   The Attawapiskat Swampy Cree. *Anthropological Papers of the University of Alaska* 5:23–82.
1958   Attawapiskat—Blend of Tradition. *Anthropologica* 6:57–67.
1961   *Foodways in a Muskeg Community: An Anthropological Report on the Attawapiskat Indians*. NCRC 62–1. Ottawa: Department of Northern Affairs and National Resources, Northern Coordination and Research Centre, Ottawa.
1968   Interpersonal Relations in Atomistic Communities. *Human Organization* 27(3):220–29.
1981   West Main Cree. In *Handbook of North American Indians*, vol. 6, *Subarctic*, edited by June Helm, pp. 217–30. Washington: Smithsonian Institution Press.

Hopper, M., and G. Power
1991   Fisheries of an Ojibwa Community in northern Ontario. *Arctic* 44:267–74.

Houston, C. Stuart, and Robert H. Buhr
1988   Swaddling of Indian Infants in Northern Saskatchewan. *Musk-Ox* 36:5–14.

James, Deborah
1986   Foreground and Background in Moose Cree Narratives. In *Actes du dix-septième congrès des algonquinistes*, edited by William Cowan, pp. 155–74. Ottawa: Carleton University.

Jarvenpa, Robert, and Hetty Jo Brumbach
1985   Occupational States, Ethnicity, and Ecology: Metis Cree Adaptation on a Canadian Trading Frontier. *Human Ecology* 13:309–29.

Jenness, Diamond
1935   *The Ojibwa Indians of Parry Island*. Department of Mines Bulletin 78. Ottawa: National Museum of Canada.

Johnston, Basil
1976   *Ojibwa Heritage*. Toronto: McClelland and Stewart.
1988   *Ojibway Heritage: The Ceremonies, Rituals, Songs, Dances, Prayers, and Legends of the Ojibway*. Toronto: McClelland and Stewart.

Keller, Robert H.
1988   Lac la Croix: Rumour, Rhetoric, and Reality in Indian Affairs. *Canadian Journal of Native Studies* 8(1):59–72.

Kilroe, Patricia
1991   Spatial Marking Affixes and the Expression of Time in Ojibwa. In *Papers of the Twenty-second Algonquian Conference*, edited by William Cowan, pp. 193–202. Ottawa: Carleton University.

Kinietz, W. Vernon
1947   Chippewa Village: The Story of Katikitegon. *Cranbrook Institute of Science Bulletin* (Bloomfield Hills, Mich.), vol. 25.
1965   *The Indians of the Western Great Lakes, 1615–1760*. 1940. Ann Arbor: University of Michigan Press.

Knight, Rolf
1965   A Re-examination of Hunting, Trapping, and Territoriality Among the Northeastern Algonkian Indians. In *Man, Culture, and Animals: The Role of Animals in Human Ecological Adjustments*, edited by Anthony Leeds and Andrew P. Vayda, pp. 27–42. Publication 78. Washington: American Association for the Advancement of Science.
1968   *Ecological Factors in Changing Economy and Social Organization Among the Rupert House Cree*. Anthropology Paper 15. Ottawa: National Museum of Canada.

Landes, Ruth
1937   *Ojibwa Sociology*. Columbia University Contributions to Anthropology 29. New York.

1968   *Ojibwa Religion and the Midéwiwin.* Madison: University of Wisconsin Press.

Lane, K. S.
1952   The Montagnais Indians, 1600–1640. *Publications of the Kroeber Anthropological Society* 7:1–62.

Leacock, Eleanor B.
1954   *The Montagnais "Hunting Territory" and the Fur Trade.* American Anthropological Association Memoir 78. Washington.
1955   Matrilocality in a Simple Hunting Economy (Montagnais-Naskapi). *Southwestern Journal of Anthropology* 11:31–47.
1958   Status Among the Montagnais-Naskapi of Labrador. *Ethnohistory* 5:200–9.
1969   The Montagnais-Naskapi Band. In *Contributions to Anthropology: Band Societies,* edited by David Damas, pp. 1–17. Anthropological Series 84, Bulletin 228. Ottawa: National Museum of Canada.
1980   Les relations de production parmi les peuples chasseurs et trappeurs des régions subarctiques du Canada. *Recherches amérindiennnes au Québec* 10(1–2):79–90.
1981   Seventeenth-century Montagnais Social Relations and Values. In *Handbook of North American Indians,* vol. 6, *Subarctic,* edited by June Helm, pp. 190–95. Washington: Smithsonian Institution Press.

Leacock, Eleanor B., and Jacqueline Goodman
1976   Montagnais Marriage and the Jesuits in the Seventeenth Century: Incidents from the Relations of Paul Le Jeune. *Western Canadian Journal of Anthropology* 6(3):77–91.
1983   Ethnohistorical Investigation of Egalitarian Politics in Eastern North America. In *The Development of Political Organization in Native North America,* edited by E. Tooker, pp. 17–31. Washington: American Ethnological Society.

Leclaire, Jacques
1987   Une tradition ancienne: Les camps de chasse des montagnais dans les bois d'après le témoinage du Père Paul Le Jeune (SJ 1634). *Études canadiennes/Canadian Studies* 23:41–52.

Leighton, Anna L.
1985   *Wild Plant Use by the Woods Cree (Nihithawak) of East-Central Saskatchewan.* Mercury Series,

Canadian Ethnology Service Paper 101. Ottawa: National Museum of Man.

Leighton, Douglas
1977   The Manitoulin Incident of 1863: An Indian-White Confrontation in the Province of Canada. *Ontario Historical Society* 69:113–24.

Lips, Julius E.
1939   Naskapi Trade. *Journal de la Société des Américanistes* 31:129–95.
1947a   Naskapi Law. *Transactions of the American Philosophical Society* 37:379–492.
1947b   Notes on Montagnais-Naskapi Economy. *Ethnos* 12:1–78.

Lithman, Yngve Georg
1984a   *The Community Apart: A Case Study of a Canadian Indian Reserve Community.* Winnipeg: University of Manitoba Press.
1984b   When Tomorrow is Today: Development as the Idiom of Routine. *Ethnos* 49:250–65.

Long, John S.
1988   Narratives of Early Encounters Between Europeans and the Cree of Western Bay. *Ontario History* 80:227–46.
1989   The Cree Prophets: Oral and Documentary Accounts. *Journal of the Canadian Church Historical Society* 31(1):3–14.

MacDonald, J. M.
1991   Undefeated: 300 Years of Ojibwa History. *Beaver* 71(2):29–32.

McGhee, John T.
1961   *Cultural Stability and Change Among the Montagnais Indians of the Lake Melville Region of Labrador.* Catholic University of America Anthropological Series, no. 19. Washington.

McNulty, Gérard, and Louis Gilbert
1981   Attikamek (Tête de Boule). In *Handbook of North American Indians,* vol. 6, *Subarctic,* edited by June Helm, pp. 208–16. Washington: Smithsonian Institution Press.

Mailhot, José
1983a   A moins d'être son esquimau, on est toujours le naskapi de quelqu'un. *Recherches amérindiennnes au Québec* 13(2):85–100.
1983b   La glorification du mâle dans le vocabulaire cri et montagnais. *Recherches amérindiennnes au Québec* 13(4):291–97.

1986a Beyond Everyone's Horizon Stand the Naskapi. *Ethnohistory* 33:384–418.

1986b Territorial Mobility Among the Montagnais-Naskapi of Labrador. *Anthropologica* 28(1–2):92–107.

Mailhot, José, and Sylvie Vincent
1982 L'indien n'est pas un fou: quelques réflexions Montagnaises sur la gestion du territoire. *Recherches amérindiennnes au Québec* 12(4):245–50.

Marano, Louis
1982 Windigo Psychosis: The Anatomy of an Emic-Etic Confusion. *Current Anthropology* 23:385–412.

1983 Boreal Forest Hazards and Adaptations: The Present. In *Boreal Forest Adaptations,* edited by A. Theodore Steegmann, Jr., pp. 269–88. New York: Plenum Press.

Marshall, Susan
1982 L'allaitement maternel chez les cris de la baie de James: Crise dans les services de santé. *Recherches amérindiennnes au Québec* 12(1):33–40.

Martijn, Charles A.
1990 Innu (Montagnais) in Newfoundland. In *Papers of the Twenty-first Algonquian Conference,* edited by William Cowan, pp. 227–46. Ottawa: Carleton University.

Mason, Leonard
1967 *The Swampy Cree: A Study in Acculturation.* Anthropology Paper 13. Ottawa: National Museum of Canada.

Meyer, David
1975 Waterfowl in Cree Ritual—The Goose Dance. In *Proceedings of the Second Congress of the Canadian Ethnology Society,* edited by Jim Freedman and Jerome H. Barkow, 2:422–49. Mercury Series, Canadian Ethnology Service Paper 28. Ottawa: National Museum of Man.

1987 Time-Depth of the Western Woods Cree Occupation of Northern Ontario, Manitoba, and Saskatchewan. In *Papers of the Eighteenth Algonquian Conference,* edited by William Cowan, pp. 187–200. Ottawa: Carleton University.

Meyer, David, and Dale Russell
1987 The Selkirk Composite of Central Canada: A Reconsideration. *Arctic Anthropology* 24(2):1–31.

Moise, B.
1989 Temagami Wilderness Under Siege. *Canadian Geographic* 109:28–39.

Molohon, Kathryn T.
1983 Notes on a Contemporary Cree Community. In *Actes du quatorzième congrès des algonquinistes,* edited by William Cowan, pp. 189–202. Ottawa: Carleton University.

1985 Residence Patterns and Related Aspects of Kinship Organization in a Swampy Cree Community. In *Papers of the Sixteenth Algonquian Conference,* edited by William Cowan, pp. 119–30. Ottawa: Carleton University.

Moore, Omar Khayyam
1957 Divination: A New Perspective. *American Anthropologist* 59:68–74.

Morantz, Toby
1976 L'organisation sociale des cris de Rupert House, 1820–1840: quelques exemples de l'utilité des études ethnohistoriques. Translated by Daniel Chevrier and Claude Chapdelaine. *Recherches amérindiennnes au Québec* 6(2):56–64.

1977 James Bay Trading Captains of the Eighteenth Century: New Perspectives on Algonquian Social Organization. In *Papers of the Eighth Algonquian Conference,* edited by William Cowan, pp. 77–89. Ottawa: Carleton University.

1978a Practiques religieuses des cris de la baie de James aux XVIIIe et XIXe siècles (d'après les européens). *Recherches amérindiennnes au Québec* 8(2):113–22.

1978b The Probability of Family Hunting Territories in Eighteenth Century James Bay: Old Evidence Newly Presented. In *Papers of the Ninth Algonquian Conference,* edited by William Cowan, pp. 224–36. Ottawa: Carleton University.

1979 L'importance du caribou durant 200 ans d'histoire à la baie de James (1660–1870). *Recherches amérindiennnes au Québec* 9(1–2):117–28.

1982 A Reconstruction of Early Nineteenth Century Social Organization in Eastern James Bay. In *Papers of the Thirteenth Algonquian Conference,* edited by William Cowan, pp. 261–74. Ottawa: Carleton University.

1983 *An Ethnohistoric Study of Eastern James Bay*

Cree Social Organization, 1700–1850. Canadian Ethnology Service Paper 88. Ottawa: National Museum of Man.

1984 Oral and Recorded History in James Bay. In *Papers of the Fifteenth Algonquian Conference,* edited by William Cowan, pp. 171–92. Ottawa: Carleton University.

1986 Historical Perspectives on Family Hunting Territories in Eastern James Bay. *Anthropologica* 28(1–2):64–91.

1991 Colonial French Insights into Early 18th-century Algonquians of Central Quebec. In *Papers of the Twenty-second Algonquian Conference,* edited by William Cowan, pp. 213–24. Ottawa: Carleton University.

Moreau, Jean-François
1980 Réflexions sur les chasseurs-cueilleurs: les montagnais, décrits par Le Jeune en 1634. *Recherches amérindiennnes au Québec* 10(1–2):40–51.

Morrison, Alvin H., and David A. Ezzo
1985 Dawnland Dualism in Northeastern Regional Context. In *Papers of the Sixteenth Algonquian Conference,* edited by William Cowan, pp. 131–50. Ottawa: Carleton University.

Murphy, Robert F., and Julian H. Steward
1956 Tappers and Trappers: Parallel Process in Acculturation. *Economic Development and Cultural Change* 4(4):335–55.

Newcomb, William W., Jr.
1956 *The Culture and Acculturation of the Delaware Indians.* Anthropological Papers 10. Ann Arbor: University of Michigan Museum of Anthropology.

Nichols, John D., ed.
1988 *An Ojibwe Text Anthology.* Studies in the Interpretation of Canadian Native Languages and Cultures 2. London: Centre for Research and Teaching of Canadian Native Languages, University of Western Ontario.

Norman, Howard
1982 *Where the Chill Came From.* San Francisco: North Point Press.

Ogg, A. C.
1988 Four Cree Love Songs: The Intersection of Text and Music. *Canadian Journal of Native Studies* 8(2):231–50.

Ouellette, Françoise-Romaine
1977 Les cris du Québec, des sous-prolétaires. *Recherches amérindiennnes au Québec* 6(3–4):8–15.

Panasuk, Anne-Marie, and Jean-René Proulx
1979 Les rivières à saumon de la Côte-Nord ou "Défense de pêcher—Cette rivière est la propriété de. . . ." *Recherches amérindiennnes au Québec* 9(3):203–18.

Parker, Seymour
1960 The Wiitiko Psychosis in the Context of Ojibwa Personality and Culture. *American Anthropologist* 62(4):603–23.

Paul, Keltie Jean
1986 Community Reaction to Hunting Restrictions in Wood Buffalo National Park. In *Actes du dix-septième congrès des algonquinistes,* edited by William Cowan, pp. 231–38. Ottawa: Carleton University.

Peers, Laura L.
1987 Rich Man, Poor Man, Beggarman, Chief: Saulteaux in the Red River Settlement. In *Papers of the Eighteenth Algonquian Conference,* edited by William Cowan, pp. 261–70. Ottawa: Carleton University.

Pentland, David H.
1985 The Ashkee Indians. In *Papers of the Sixteenth Algonquian Conference,* edited by William Cowan, pp. 151–60. Ottawa: Carleton University.

Polson, Gordon, and Roger Spielmann
1990 "Once There Were Two Brothers . . .": Religious Tension in One Algonquian Community. In *Papers of the Twenty-first Algonquian Conference,* edited by William Cowan, pp. 303–12. Ottawa: Carleton University.

Preston, Richard J., III
1969–72 Functional Politics in a Northern Indian Community. In *Proceedings of the 38th International Congress of Americanists,* Stuttgart-Munich, 1968, 3:169–78. Munich: Klaus Renner.

1971 Problèmes humains reliés au développement de la baie James. *Recherches amérindiennnes au Québec* 1(4–5):58–68.

1975a Belief in the Context of Rapid Change: An Eastern Cree Example. In *Symbols and Society: Essays on Belief Systems in Action,* edited by Carole E. Hill, pp. 117–29. Athens: University of Georgia Press.

1975b   *Cree Narrative: Expressing the Personal Meaning of Events.* Mercury Series, Canadian Ethnology Service Paper 30. Ottawa: National Museum of Man.

1975c   A Survey of Ethnographic Approaches to the Eastern Cree-Montagnais-Naskapi. *Canadian Review of Sociology and Anthropology* 12(3):267–77.

1975d   Symbolic Aspects of Eastern Cree Goose Hunting. In *Proceedings of the 2d Congress of the Canadian Ethnology Society,* edited by J. Freedman and J. Barkow, pp. 479–89. Mercury Series, Canadian Ethnology Service Paper 28. Ottawa: National Museum of Man.

1976   Reticence and Self-expression: A Study of Style in Social Relationships. In *Papers of the Seventh Algonquian Conference,* edited by William Cowan, pp. 450–94. Ottawa: Carleton University.

1977   Wiitiko: Algonquian Knowledge and Whiteman Interest. In *Papers of the Eighth Algonquian Conference,* edited by William Cowan, pp. 101–6. Ottawa: Carleton University.

1978a   La relation sacrée entre les Cris et les oies. *Recherches amérindiennnes au Québec* 8(2): 147–52.

1978b   Ethnographic Reconstruction of Witigo. In *Papers of the Ninth Algonquian Conference,* edited by William Cowan, pp. 61–67. Ottawa: Carleton University.

1979   The Development of Self-control in the Eastern Cree Life Cycle. In *Childhood and Adolescence in Canada,* edited by K. Ishwaran, pp. 83–96. Toronto: McGraw-Hill Ryerson.

1980a   Eastern Cree Notions of Social Grouping. In *Papers of the Eleventh Algonquian Conference,* edited by William Cowan, pp. 40–48. Ottawa: Carleton University.

1980b   The Witiko: Algonkian Knowledge and Whiteman Knowledge. In *Manlike Monsters on Trial: Early Records and Modern Evidence,* edited by M. Halpin and M. Ames, pp. 111–31. Vancouver: University of British Columbia Press.

1981   East Main Cree. In *Handbook of North American Indians,* vol. 6, *Subarctic,* edited by June Helm, pp. 196–207. Washington: Smithsonian Institution Press.

1982a   The Politics of Community Relocation: An Eastern Cree Example. *Culture* 2(3):37–49.

1982b   Towards a General Statement on the Eastern Cree Structure of Knowledge. In *Papers of the Thirteenth Algonquian Conference,* edited by William Cowan, pp. 299–306. Ottawa: Carleton University.

1985   Transformations musicales et culturelles chez les cris de l'est. *Recherches amérindiennnes au Québec* 15(4):19–28.

1986   Twentieth-century Transformations of the West Coast Cree. In *Actes du dix-septième congrès des algonquinistes,* edited by William Cowan, pp. 239–54. Ottawa: Carleton University.

1988   James Bay Cree Syncretism: Persistence and Replacement. In *Papers of the Nineteenth Algonquian Conference,* edited by William Cowan, pp. 147–55. Ottawa: Carleton University.

1990   The View from the Other Side of the Frontier: East Cree Historical Notions. In *Papers of the Twenty-first Algonquian Conference,* edited by William Cowan, pp. 313–28. Ottawa: Carleton University.

Preston, Sarah C.

1986a   *Let the Past Go: A Life History Narrated by Alice Jacob.* Mercury Series, Canadian Ethnology Service Paper 104. Ottawa: Canadian Museum of Civilization.

1986b   The Old Man's Stories: Lies or Truths? In *Actes du dix-septième congrès des algonquinistes,* edited by William Cowan, pp. 253–62. Ottawa: Carleton University.

1987   Is Your Cree Uniform the Same as Mine? Cultural and Ethnographic Variations on a Theme. In *Papers of the Eighteenth Algonquian Conference,* edited by William Cowan, pp. 287–96. Ottawa: Carleton University.

1988   Variation in James Bay Cree Narrative Themes. In *Papers of the Nineteenth Algonquian Conference,* edited by William Cowan, pp. 157–64. Ottawa: Carleton University.

Redsky, James, and James R. Stevens

1972   *Great Leader of the Ojibway: Mis-quona-queb.* Toronto: McClelland and Stewart.

Rhodes, Richard A.

1982   Algonquian Trade Languages. In *Papers of the Thirteenth Algonquian Conference,* edited by William Cowan, pp. 1–10. Ottawa: Carleton University.

1984a   Le baseball et l'emprunt culturel chez les

Ojibwés. *Recherches amérindiennnes au Québec* 14(4):9–16.

1984b   Baseball, Hotdogs, Apple Pie, and Chevrolets. In *Papers of the Fifteenth Algonquian Conference,* edited by William Cowan, pp. 373–88. Ottawa: Carleton University.

Rhodes, Richard A., and Evelyn M. Todd
1981   Subarctic Algonquian Languages. In *Handbook of North American Indians,* vol. 6, *Subarctic,* edited by June Helm, pp. 52–66. Washington: Smithsonian Institution Press.

Ribordy, François-Xavier
1988   Histoire sociologique du droit de la chasse et de la pêche en Ontario. *Anthropologica* 30: 155–73.

Ritzenthaler, Robert E.
1978   Southwestern Chippewa. In *Handbook of North American Indians,* vol. 15, *Northeast,* edited by Bruce G. Trigger, pp. 743–59. Washington: Smithsonian Institution Press.

Rogers, Edward S.
1962   *The Round Lake Ojibwa.* Art and Archaeology Division Occasional Paper 5. Toronto: Royal Ontario Museum.
1963a   Changing Settlement Patterns of the Cree-Ojibwa of Northern Ontario. *Southwestern Journal of Anthropology* 19(1):64–88.
1963b   *The Hunting Group-Hunting Territory Complex Among the Mistassini Indians.* Anthropological Series 63, Bulletin 195. Ottawa: National Museum of Canada.
1965   Leadership Among the Indians of Eastern Subarctic Canada. *Anthropologica* 7(2):263–84.
1967   *Subsistence Areas of the Cree-Ojibwa of the Eastern Subarctic: A Preliminary Study.* Anthropological Series 70, *Bulletin* 204:59–99. Ottawa: National Museum of Canada.
1969a   Band Organization Among the Indians of Eastern Subarctic Canada. In *Contributions to Anthropology: Band Societies,* edited by David Damas, pp. 21–50. Anthropological Series 84, Bulletin 228. Ottawa: National Museum of Canada.
1969b   Natural Environment—Social Organization—Witchcraft: Cree Versus Ojibwa—a Test Case. In *Contributions to Anthropology: Ecological Essays,* edited by David Damas, pp. 24–39.

Anthropological Series 86, Bulletin 230. Ottawa: National Museum of Canada.
1972   The Mistassini Cree. In *Hunters and Gatherers Today,* edited by M. G. Bicchieri, pp. 90–137. New York: Holt Rinehart and Winston.
1973   *The Quest for Food and Furs: The Mistassini Cree, 1953–1954.* Publications in Ethnology 5. Ottawa: National Museum of Man.
1978   Southeastern Ojibwa. In *Handbook of North American Indians,* vol. 15, *Northeast,* edited by Bruce G. Trigger, pp. 760–71. Washington: Smithsonian Institution Press.
1987   The Queen: A Cree Burial at Moose Factory, May 27, 1747. *Arctic Anthropology* 24(2):32–39.

Rogers, Edward S., and Mary B. Black
1976   Subsistence Strategy in the Fish and Hare Period, Northern Ontario: The Weagamow Ojibwa, 1880–1920. *Journal of Anthropological Research* 32:1–43.

Rogers, Edward S., and Eleanor B. Leacock
1981   Montagnais-Naskapi. In *Handbook of North American Indians,* vol. 6, *Subarctic,* edited by June Helm, pp. 168–89. Washington: Smithsonian Institution Press.

Rogers, Edward S., and Mary Black-Rogers
1978   Method for Reconstructing Patterns of Change: Surname Adoption by the Weagamow Ojibwa, 1870–1950. *Ethnohistory* 25:319–46.

Rogers, Edward S., and Jean H. Rogers
1959   The Yearly Cycle of the Mistassini Indians. *Arctic* 12(3):131–38.

Rogers, Edward S., and J. Garth Taylor
1981   Northern Ojibwa. In *Handbook of North American Indians,* vol. 6, *Subarctic,* edited by June Helm, pp. 231–43. Washington: Smithsonian Institution Press.

Rogers, Mary Black, and Edward S. Rogers
1980   Adoption of Patrilineal Surname System by Bilateral Northern Ojibwa: Mapping the Learning of an Alien System. In *Papers of the Eleventh Algonquian Conference,* edited by W. Cowan, pp. 198–230. Ottawa: Carleton University.
1982   Who Were the Cranes? Groups and Group Identity Names in Northern Ontario. In *Approaches to Algonquian Archaeology,* edited

by M. Hanna and B. Kooyman, pp. 147–88. Calgary: University of Calgary.

Rohrl, Vivian J.
1970   A Nutritional Factor in Windigo Psychosis. *American Anthropologist* 72(1):97–101.

Russell, Dale R.
1991   *Eighteenth-century Western Cree and Their Neighbors.* Mercury Series, Canadian Ethnology Service Paper 143. Ottawa: Canadian Museum of Civilization.

Ryan, James J.
1988   Economic Development and Innu Settlement: The Establishment of Sheshatshit. *Canadian Journal of Native Studies* 8(1):1–25.
1991–92 Eroding Innu cultural tradition: Individualization and communality. *Journal of Canadian Studies* 26(4):94–111.

Sangwine, Jean
1987   The Voice of Missahba: Self-help at Serpent River. *Beaver* 67(1).

Savard, Rémi
1969   L'hôte maladroit, essai d'analyse d'un conte montagnais. *Interprétation* 3(4):5–52.
1972   Note sur le mythe indien de ayasew à partir d'une version montagnaise. *Recherches amérindiennnes au Québec,* Bulletin d'Information 2(1):3–16.
1973   Structure du récit: l'enfant couvert de peaux. *Recherches amérindiennnes au Québec* 3(1–2):13–37.

Schmalz, P. S.
1984   The Role of the Ojibwa in the Conquest of Southern Ontario, 1650–1701. *Ontario History* 76:326–52.
1991   *The Ojibwa of Southern Ontario.* Toronto: University of Toronto Press.

Scott, Colin
1982   Production and Exchange Among Wemindji Cree: Egalitarian Ideology and Economic Base. *Culture* 2(3): 51–64.
1984   Between "Original Affluence" and Consumer Affluence: Domestic Production and Guaranteed Income for James Bay Cree Hunters. In *Affluence and Cultural Survival: Proceedings of the Spring Meeting of the American Ethnological Society,* edited by Richard Salisbury, pp. 74–86. Washington.

1988a   The Socio-economic Significance of Waterfowl Among Canada's Aboriginal Cree: Native Use and Local Management. In *The Value of Birds (Based on Proceedings at the XIX World Conference of the International Council for Bird Preservation),* pp. 49–62. ICBP Technical Publication 6. Cambridge.
1988b   Property, Practice, and Aboriginal Rights Among Quebec Cree Hunters. In *Hunters and Gatherers—Property, Power, and Ideology,* edited by James Woodburn, Tim Ingold, and David Riches, 2:35–51. London: Berg Publishers.
1989a   Ideology of Reciprocity Between the James Bay Cree and the Whiteman State. In *Outwitting the State,* edited by Peter Skalnik, pp. 81–108. New Brunswick, N.J.: Transaction Publishers.
1989b   Knowledge Construction Among Cree Hunters: Metaphors and Literal Understanding. *Journal de la Société des Américanistes* 75:193–208.
1991   Property, Practice, and Aboriginal Rights Among Quebec Cree Hunters. In *Hunters and Gatherers,* vol. 2, *Property, Power and Ideology,* edited by Tim Ingold, David Riches, and James Woodburn, pp. 35–51. Oxford: Berg.

Shkilnyk, Anastasia M.
1985   *A Poison Stronger than Love: The Destruction of an Ojibwa Community.* New Haven: Yale University Press.

Sioui, Anne-Marie
1979   Les amérindiens et les musées du Québec. *Recherches amérindiennnes au Québec* 8:249–65.

Skinner, Alanson
1911   Notes on the Eastern Cree and Northern Saulteaux. *Anthropological Papers of the American Museum of Natural History* 9:1–177.

Slaughter, Dale C.
1981   The Shoulder-blade Path Revisited: A Belated Response to Omar Khayyam Moore. *Arctic Anthropology* 18(2):95–103.

Smith, Donald B.
1975a   The Mississauga and David Ramsay. *Beaver* 305:4–8.
1975b   Who are the Mississauga? *Ontario History* 67(4):211–22.

1981   The Dispossession of the Mississauga Indians: A Missing Chapter in the Early History of Upper Canada. *Ontario History* 73(2):67–87.

1988   The Life of George Copway, or Kah-ge-ga-gah-bowh (1818–1869)—and a review of his writings. *Journal of Canadian Studies/Révue d'études canadiennes* 23(3):5–38.

Smith, James G. E.

1976a   Notes on the Wittiko. In *Papers of the Seventh Algonquian Conference,* edited by William Cowan, pp. 18–38. Ottawa: Carleton University.

1976b   On the Territorial Distribution of the Western Woods Cree. In *Papers of the Seventh Algonquian Conference,* edited by William Cowan, pp. 414–35. Ottawa: Carleton University.

1981   Western Woods Cree. In *Handbook of North American Indians,* vol. 6, *Subarctic,* edited by June Helm, pp. 256–70. Washington: Smithsonian Institution Press.

1987   The Western Woods Cree: Anthropological Myth and Historical Reality. *American Ethnologist* 14:434–48.

Smith, Nicholas N.

1980   Food Versus Nutrition: The Changing Diet of the Mistassini Cree. In *Papers of the Eleventh Algonquian Conference,* edited by William Cowan, pp. 128–34. Ottawa: Carleton University.

1984   The Cree Spring Goose Hunt. In *Papers of the Fifteenth Algonquian Conference,* edited by William Cowan, pp. 81–90. Ottawa: Carleton University.

Sosin, Jack

1965   The Use of Indians in the War of the American Revolution: A Reassessment of Responsibility. *Canadian Historical Review* 46:101–21.

Spaulding, J. M.

1985–86 Recent Suicide Rates Among Ten Ojibwa Indian Bands in Northeastern Ontario. *Omega* 16:347–54.

Speck, Frank G.

1915   The Family Hunting Band as the Basis of Algonkian Social Organization. *American Anthropologist* 17:289–305.

1923   Mistassini Hunting Territories in the Labrador Peninsula. *American Anthropologist* 25:452–71.

1926   Culture Problems in Northeastern North America. *Proceedings of the American Philosophical Society* 65(4):272–311.

1977   *Naskapi: The Savage Hunters of the Labrador Peninsula.* Norman: University of Oklahoma Press.

Speck, Frank G., and Loren C. Eiseley

1939   Significance of Hunting Territory Systems of the Algonkian in Social Theory. *American Anthropologist* 41:269–80.

Steegmann, A. Theodore, Jr., ed.

1983   *Boreal Forest Adaptations: The Northern Algonkians.* New York: Plenum Press.

Steinbring, Jack H.

1969–72 Acculturational Phenomena Among the Lake Winnipeg Ojibwa of Canada. In *Proceedings of the 38th International Congress of Americanists,* Stuttgart-Munich, 1968, 3:179–88. Munich: Klaus Renner.

1981   Saulteaux of Lake Winnipeg. In *Handbook of North American Indians,* vol. 6, *Subarctic,* edited by June Helm, pp. 244–55. Washington: Smithsonian Institution Press.

Stevens, James R., ed.

1971   *Sacred Legends of the Sandy Lake Cree.* Toronto: McClelland and Stewart.

1985   *Legends from the Forest.* Told by Chief Thomas Fiddler. Moonbeam, Ont.: Penumbra Press.

Stevens, James R., and Chief Thomas Fiddler

1985   *Killing the Shamen.* Moonbeam, Ont.: Penumbra Press.

Stone, Lyle M., and Donald Chaput

1978   History of the Upper Great Lakes Area. In *Handbook of North American Indians,* vol. 15, *Northeast,* edited by Bruce G. Trigger, pp. 602–9. Washington: Smithsonian Institution Press.

Strong, W. Duncan

1929   Cross-cousin Marriage and the Culture of the Northeastern Algonkian. *American Anthropologist* 31(2):277–88.

Stymeist, David H.

1975   *Ethnics and Indians: Social Relations in a Northwestern Ontario Town.* Toronto: Peter Martin.

Swan, Ruth
1987   Visual Images in Native History: Island Lake Manitoba. In *Papers of the Eighteenth Algonquian Conference,* edited by William Cowan, pp. 345–54. Ottawa: Carleton University.

Tanner, Adrian
1968   Occupation and Life Style in Two Minority Communities. In *Conflict in Culture: Problems of Developmental Change Among the Cree,* edited by Norman A. Chance, pp. 47–67. Ottawa: Saint Paul University, Canadian Research Centre for Anthropology.
1971   Existe-t-il des territoires de chasse? *Recherches amérindiennes au Québec,* Bulletin d'Information 1(4–5):69–83.
1973   The Significance of Hunting Territories Today. In *Cultural Ecology: Readings on the Canadian Indians and Eskimos,* edited by Bruce Cox, pp. 101–14. Toronto: McClelland and Stewart.
1975   The Hidden Feast: Eating and Ideology Among the Mistassini Cree. In *Papers of the Sixth Algonquian Conference,* edited by W. Cowan, pp. 291–313. Mercury Series, Canadian Ethnology Service Paper 23. Ottawa: National Museum of Man.
1978   Divination and Decisions: Multiple Explanations for Algonkian Scapulimancy. In *Yearbook of Symbolic Anthropology,* edited by E. Schwimmer, pp. 59–101. London: C. Hurst.
1979   *Bringing Home Animals: Religious Ideology and Mode of Production of the Mistassini Cree Hunters.* New York: St. Martin's Press.

Tanner, Helen Hornbeck
1986   *Atlas of Great Lakes Indian History.* Norman: University of Oklahoma Press.

Taylor, J. Garth
1972   Northern Ojibwa Communities of the Contact-traditional Period. *Anthropologica* 14(1):19–30.

Teicher, Morton I.
1960   Windigo Psychosis: A Study of a Relationship Between Belief and Behavior Among the Indians of Northeastern Canada. In *Proceedings of the 1960 Annual Spring Meeting of the American Ethnological Society.* Seattle: University of Washington Press.

Tisdale, M. A.
1987   Late Woodland Settlement Dynamics in the Central Boreal Forest: Clues from Pottery Technology. In *Papers of the Eighteenth Algonquian Conference,* edited by William Cowan, pp. 363–75. Ottawa: Carleton University.

Trudel, François
1991   Les relations entre les français et les indiens au Québec-Labrador méridional. In *Papers of the Twenty-second Algonquian Conference,* edited by William Cowan, pp. 359–73. Ottawa: Carleton University.

Turner, David H.
1977   Windigo Mythology and the Analysis of Cree Social Structure. *Anthropologica* 19(1):63–73.

Turner, Lucien M.
1890   Ethnology of the Ungava District. In *Eleventh Annual Report of the Bureau of American Ethnology* for the year 1889–90, pp. 159–84, 267–350. Washington.

Turner, Lucy W.
1983   Naskapi Trance: Counterbalance to the Mask. In *The Power of Symbols: Masks and Masquerade in the Americas,* edited by N. Ross Crumrine and Marjorie Halpin, pp. 30–38. Vancouver: University of British Columbia Press.

Vanderburgh, Rosamond M.
1982   When Legends Fall Silent Our Ways Are Lost: Some Dimensions of the Study of Aging Among Native Canadians. *Culture* 2(1):21–28.
1986   Modernization and Aging in the Anicinabe Context. In *Aging in Canada: Social Perspectives,* edited by V. W. Marshall. Markham, Ont.: Fitzhenry and Whiteside.

Vecsey, Christopher
1983   *Traditional Ojibwa Religion and Its Historical Changes.* Philadelphia: American Philosophical Society.
1984   Midewiwin Myths of Origin. In *Papers of the Fifteenth Algonquian Conference,* edited by William Cowan, pp. 445–67. Ottawa: Carleton University.
1987   Grassy Narrows Reserve: Mercury Pollution, Social Disruption, and National Resources: A Question of Autonomy. *American Indian Quarterly* 11:287–314.

Vennum, Thomas, Jr.
1988   *Wild Rice and the Ojibwa People.* St. Paul: Minnesota Historical Society Press.

Vincent, Sylvie
1973   Structure du rituel: la tente tremblante et le concept de mista-pe-w. *Recherches amérindiennnes au Québec* 3(1–2):69–83.
1978   Tradition orale et action politique montagnaises: Le case de la riviére Natashquan. In *Papers of the Ninth Algonquian Conference,* edited by William Cowan, pp. 138–45. Ottawa: Carleton University.
1982   La tradition orale montagnaise: comment l'interroger? *Cahiers de Clio* 70:5–26.

Vizenor, Gerald
1984   *The People Named the Chippewa.* Minneapolis: University of Minnesota Press.

Vollweiler, Lothar George, and Alison B. Sanchez
1983   Divination—"adaptive" from whose perspective? *Ethnology* 22:193–209.

Waisberg, Leo G.
1975   Boreal Forest Subsistence and the Windigo: Fluctuation of Animal Populations. *Anthropologica* 17(2):169–85.

Waldram, James B.
1980   Relocation and Political Change in the Manitoba Native Community. *Canadian Journal of Anthropology* 1:173–78.
1985   Hydroelectric Development and Dietary Delocalization in Northern Manitoba, Canada. *Human Organization* 44:41–49.
1987a   Native Employment and Hydroelectric Development in Northern Manitoba. *Journal of Canadian Studies/Révue d'études canadiennes* 22(3):62–76.
1987b   Relocation, Consolidation, and Settlement Pattern in the Canadian Subarctic. *Human Ecology* 15:117–31.
1988a   *"As Long as the Rivers Run": Hydroelectric Development and Native Communities in Western Canada.* Winnipeg: University of Manitoba Press.
1988b   Native People and Hydroelectric Development in Northern Manitoba, 1957–1987: The Promise and the Reality. *Manitoba History* 15:39–44.

Warren, William W.
1984   *History of the Ojibway People.* 1885. St. Paul: Minnesota Historical Society Press.

Weinstein, Martin S.
1977   Hares, Lynx, and Trappers. *American Naturalist* 111(980):806–8.

Weslager, C. A.
1972   *The Delaware Indians: A History.* New Brunswick, N.J.: Rutgers University Press.

Wills, Richard H.
1985   *Conflicting Perceptions: Western Economics and the Great Whale River Cree.* Chicago: Tutorial Press.

Winterhalder, Bruce
1980   Foraging Strategies in the Boreal Forest: An Analysis of Cree Hunting and Gathering. In *Hunter-Gatherer Foraging Strategies,* edited by Bruce Winterhalder and Eric Alden Smith, pp. 66–98. Chicago: University of Chicago Press.
1983   Boreal Foraging Strategies. In *Boreal Forest Adaptations,* edited by A. Theodore Steegmann, Jr., pp. 201–42. New York: Plenum Press.

Wolfart, H. Christoph
1989   Cree Midwifery: Linguistic and Literary Observations. In *Actes du vingtième congrès des algonquinistes,* edited by William Cowan, pp. 326–42. Ottawa: Carleton University.
1991   The scope of paternity tests in Cree myths. *Man* 26:737–40.

Wright, James V.
1979   *Quebec Prehistory.* Ottawa: National Museum of Man.
1981   Prehistory of the Canadian Shield. In *Handbook of North American Indians,* vol. 6, *Subarctic,* edited by June Helm, pp. 86–96. Washington: Smithsonian Institution Press.

Young, David E., Grant C. Ingram, and Lise Swartz
1989   *Cry of the Eagle: Encounters with a Cree Healer.* Toronto: University of Toronto Press.

Section Six

🍁

IROQUOIA AND HURONIA

Abler, Thomas S.

1970   Longhouse and Palisade: Northeastern Iroquois Villages of the Seventeenth Century. *Ontario History* 62:17–40.

1975   Presents, Merchants, and the Indian Department: Economic Aspects of the American Revolutionary Frontier. In *Proceedings of the Second Congress, Canadian Ethnological Society,* edited by Jim Freedman and Jerome H. Barkow, 1:603–21. Mercury Series, Canadian Ethnology Service Paper 28, Ottawa: National Museum of Man.

1980   Iroquois Cannibalism: Fact Not Fiction. *Ethnohistory* 27:309–16.

1987   Dendrogram and Celestial Tree: Numerical Taxonomy and Variants of the Iroquoian Creation Myth. *Canadian Journal of Native Studies* 7:195–221.

Abler, Thomas S., and Michael H. Logan

1988   The Florescence and Demise of Iroquoian Cannibalism: Human Sacrifice and Malinowski's Hypothesis. *Man in the Northeast* 35:1–26.

Abler, Thomas S., and Elisabeth Tooker

1978   Seneca. In *Handbook of North American Indians,* vol. 15, *Northeast,* edited by Bruce G. Trigger, pp. 505–17. Washington: Smithsonian Institution Press.

Allen, Robert S.

1988   His Majesty's Indian Allies: Native Peoples, the British Crown, and the War of 1812. *Michigan Historical Review* 14(2):1–24.

Aquila, Richard

1983   *The Iroquois Restoration: Iroquois Diplomacy on the Colonial Frontier, 1701–1754.* Detroit: Wayne State University Press.

Bibeau, Pierre

1978   Les palissades des sites iroquoiens. *Recherches amérindiennnes au Québec* 10(3):189–98.

Blanchard, David

1980   *Kahnawake: A Historical Sketch.* Caughnawaga, Que.

1983   High Steel. *Journal of Ethnic Studies* 11:41–60.

Blau, Harold, Jack Campisi, and Elisabeth Tooker

1978   Onondaga. In *Handbook of North American Indians,* vol. 15, *Northeast,* edited by Bruce G.

Trigger, pp. 491–99. Washington: Smithsonian Institution Press.

Bonvillain, Nancy, ed.
1980   *Studies on Iroquoian Culture.* Occasional Publications in Northeastern Anthropology, no. 6. Rindge, N.H.: Franklin Pierce College.

Bourgeois, Donald J.
1986   The Six Nations: A Neglected Aspect of Canadian Legal History. *Canadian Journal of Native Studies/Révue canadienne des études autochtones* 6(2):253–70.

Bradley, James W.
1989   *Evolution of the Onondaga Iroquois: Accommodating Change, 1500–1655.* Syracuse, N.Y.: Syracuse University Press.

Bruchac, Joseph
1991   Otstungo: A Mohawk village in 1491. *National Geographic* 180(4):68–83.

Buerger, Geoffrey E.
1989   Eleazar Williams: Elitism and Multiple Identity on Two Frontiers. In *Being and Becoming Indian: Biographical Studies of North American Frontiers,* edited by James Clifton, pp. 112–36. Chicago: Dorsey Press.

Campisi, Jack
1974   Consequences of the Kansas Claim to Oneida Tribal Identity. In *Proceedings of the First Congress, Canadian Ethnology Society,* edited by Jerome Barkow, pp. 35–47. Mercury Series, Canadian Ethnology Service Paper 17. Ottawa: National Museum of Man.
1978   Oneida. In *Handbook of North American Indians,* vol. 15, *Northeast,* edited by Bruce G. Trigger, pp. 481–90. Washington: Smithsonian Institution Press.
1982   The Iroquois and the Euro-American Concept of Tribe. *New York History,* April, 165–82.

Cardy, Michael
1989   The Iroquois in the Eighteenth Century: A Neglected Century. *Man in the Northeast* 38:1–20.

Chadoweic, Urzula
1972   La hantise et la practique: Le cannibalisme iroquois. *Nouvelle revue de psychanalyse* 6:55–69.

Chafe, Wallace L.
1961   *Seneca Thanksgiving Rituals.* Bureau of American Ethnology Bulletin 185. Washington.

Chapdelaine, Claude
1980   L'ascendence culturelle des Iroquoiens du Saint-Laurent. *Recherches amérindiennes au Québec* 10:145–52.
1982   Les pipes à plate-forme de la Pointe-du-Buisson: Un système d'échanges à définir. *Recherches amérindiennes au Québec* 12(3):207–16.
1984   Un campement de pêche iroquoien au royaume du Saguenay. *Recherches amérindiennes au Québec* 14(1):25–33.

Clermont, Norman
1978   Une figure iroquoise, Garakontie. *Recherches amérindiennes au Québec* 7(3–4):101–7.
1980a   L'augmentation de la population chez les iroquoiens préhistoriques. *Recherches amérindiennes au Québec* 10:159–64.
1980b   L'identité culturelle iroquoienne. *Recherches amérindiennes au Québec* 10:139–44.
1984   L'importance de la pêche en Iroquoisie. *Recherches amérindiennes au Québec* 14(1):17–24.

Clermont, Norman, et Claude Chapdelaine
1980   Le sédentarisation des groupes non agriculteurs dans la Plaine de Montréal. *Recherches amérindiennes au Québec* 10(3):153–58.

Dannin, Robert
1982   Forms of Huron Kinship and Marriage. *Ethnology* 21:101–10.

Dassonville, Dominique
1973   Problème d'ethnoconscience seneca: Manger de l'homme ou epouser des bêtes. *Recherches amérindiennes au Québec* 3(1–2):97–113.

Delâge, Denys
1985   *Le pays renversé: Amérindiens et européens en Amérique du nord-est, 1600–1664.* Montreal: Éditions du Boréal Express.

Desrosiers, Leo Paul
1947   *Iroquoisie: 1534–1646.* Montreal: Études de l'Institute d'histoire de l'Amérique française.

Dickinson, John A.
1980   The Pre-contact Huron Population: A Reappraisal. *Ontario History* 72:173–79.
1982   La guerre iroquoise et la mortalité en Nouvelle France, 1608–1666. *Revue d'histoire de l'Amerique française* 36(1):31–54.

Eccles, William J.
1955   Frontenac and the Iroquois, 1672–1682. *Canadian Historical Review* 36:1–16.

Eid, Leroy V.

1979   The Ojibwa-Iroquois War: The War the Five Nations Did Not Win. *Ethnohistory* 26:297–324.

Faux, David

1987   Iroquoian Occupation of the Mohawk Valley During and After the Revolution. *Man in the Northeast* 34:27–39.

Fenton, William N.

1936   *An Outline of Seneca Ceremonies at Coldspring Longhouse.* Yale University Publications in Anthropology, no. 9.

1940   Problems Arising from the Historic Northeastern Position of the Iroquois. In *Essays in Historical Anthropology of North America,* pp. 159–211. Smithsonian Miscellaneous Collections, no. 100. Washington.

1941a   Masked Medicine Ceremonies of the Iroquois. In *Annual Report of the Smithsonian Institution for 1940,* pp. 397–429. Washington.

1941b   Tonawande Longhouse Ceremonies: Ninety Years After Lewis Henry Morgan. In *Bureau of American Ethnology Bulletin 128,* pp. 140–65 (Anthropological Papers, no. 15). Washington.

1950   *The Roll Call of the Iroquois Chiefs: A Study of a Mnemonic Cane from the Six Nations Reserve.* Smithsonian Miscellaneous Collections 111(15).

1953   *The Iroquois Eagle Dance.* Bureau of American Ethnology Bulletin 156. Washington.

1962   "This Island, the World on the Turtle's Back." *Journal of American Folklore* 75(298):283–300.

1971   The Iroquois in History. In *North American Indians in Historical Perspective,* edited by Eleanor Burke Leacock and Nancy O. Lurie, pp. 129–68. New York: Random House. Reprint. Waveland Press.

1972   Return to the Longhouse. In *Crossing Cultural Boundaries: The Anthropological Experience,* edited by Solon T. Kimball and James B. Watson, pp. 102–18. San Francisco: Chandler.

1978a   Northern Iroquoian Culture Patterns. In *Handbook of North American Indians,* vol. 15, *Northeast,* edited by Bruce G. Trigger, pp. 296–321. Washington: Smithsonian Institution Press.

1978b   Problems in the Authentication of the League of the Iroquois. In *Neighbors and Intruders:*

An Ethnohistorical Exploration of the Indians of Hudson's River, edited by L. M. Hauptman and J. Campisi, no. 39, pp. 261–68.

Fenton, William N., recorder and ed.

1942   *Songs from the Iroquois Longhouse.* Folk Music of the United States, Archive of Folksong, album 6. Washington: Library of Congress.

Fenton, William N., ed.

1951   *Symposium on Local Diversity in Iroquois Culture.* Bureau of American Ethnology Bulletin 149. Washington.

Fenton, William N., and John Gulick, eds.

1961   *Symposium on Cherokee and Iroquois Culture.* Bureau of American Ethnology Bulletin 180. Washington.

Fenton, William N., and Elisabeth Tooker

1978   Mohawk. In *Handbook of North American Indians,* vol. 15, *Northeast,* edited by Bruce G. Trigger, pp. 466–80. Washington: Smithsonian Institution Press.

Ferdais, Marie

1980   Matrilinéarité et/ou matrilocalité chez les iroquoiens: remarques critiques et méthodologiques à l'usage des archéologues. *Recherches amérindiennes au Québec* 10:181–88.

Fitzgerald, William R.

1982   *Lest the Beaver Run Loose: The Early 17th Century Christianson Site and Trends in Historic Neutral Archaeology.* Archaeological Survey of Canada Paper, no. 111. Ottawa: National Museum of Man.

Foley, Denis P.

1977a   Six Nations Traditionalist Social Structure. *Man in the Northeast* 13:107–12.

1977b   The Rural Six Nations Traditionalist Belief System: 1870–1914. *Man in the Northeast* 14:19–33.

Foster, Michael K.

1974   *From the Earth to Beyond the Sky: An Ethnographic Approach to Four Longhouse Iroquois Speech Events.* Mercury Series, Canadian Ethnology Service Paper 20. Ottawa: National Museum of Man.

Foster, Michael K., ed.

1974   *Papers in Linguistics from the 1972 Conference on Iroquoian Research.* Mercury Series,

Canadian Ethnology Service Paper 10. Ottawa: National Museum of Man.

Foster, Michael K., Jack Campisi, and Marianne Mithun, eds.
1984   *Extending the Rafters: Interdisciplinary Approaches to Iroquoian Studies.* Albany: State University of New York Press.

Freilich, Morris
1958   Cultural Persistence Among the Modern Iroquois. *Anthropos* 53:473–83.

Frisch, Jack A.
1970   Tribalism Among the St. Regis Mohawks: A Search for Self-Identity. *Anthropologica* 12: 207–19.
1976   Some Ethnological and Ethnohistoric Notes on the Iroquois in Alberta. *Man in the Northeast* 12:51–64.
1978   Iroquois in the West. In *Handbook of North American Indians,* vol. 15, *Northeast,* edited by Bruce G. Trigger, pp. 544–46. Washington: Smithsonian Institution Press.

Garrad, Charles, and Conrad E. Heidenreich
1978   Khionontateronon (Petun). In *Handbook of North American Indians,* vol. 15, *Northeast,* edited by Bruce G. Trigger, pp. 394–97. Washington: Smithsonian Institution Press.

Goldstein, R. A.
1969   *French Iroquois Diplomatic and Military Relations, 1609–1701.* The Hague: Mouton.

Gramley, R. M.
1977   Deerskins and Hunting Territories: Competition for a Scarce Resource of the Northeastern Woodlands. *American Antiquity* 42:601–5.

Graymont, Barbara
1972   *The Iroquois in the American Revolution.* Syracuse, N.Y.: Syracuse University Press.

Grinde, Donald A., Jr.
1977   *The Iroquois and the Founding of the American Nation.* San Francisco: Indian Historian Press.

Guldenzopf, David
1984   Frontier Demography and Settlement Patterns of the Mohawk Iroquois. *Man in the Northeast* 27:79–94.

Haan, Richard
1980   The Problem of Iroquoian Neutrality: Suggestions for Revision. *Ethnohistory* 27:317–30.

Hagedorn, Nancy L.
1988   "A Friend to Go Between Them": The Interpreter as Cultural Broker During the Anglo-Iroquois Councils, 1740–70. *Ethnohistory* 35: 60–80.

Hale, Horatio
1963   *The Iroquois Book of Rites.* 1883. Edited by William Fenton. Toronto: University of Toronto Press.

Hamell, George R.
1987   Mohawks Abroad: The 1764 Amsterdam Etching of Synhnecta. In *Indians and Europe: An Interdisciplinary Collection of Essays,* edited by Christian Feest, pp. 175–94. Aachen: Rader Verlag.

Hamilton, J.
1986   Caughnawaga Preserves. *Canadian Geographic* 106:36–45.

Hamilton, Milton W.
1963   Sir William Johnson: Interpreter of the Iroquois. *Ethnohistory* 10:270–86.

Hauptman, Laurence M.
1986   *The Iroquois Struggle for Survival: World War II to Red Power.* Syracuse, N.Y.: Syracuse University Press.

Hayes, Charles F., ed.
1981   *The Iroquois in the American Revolution.* Research Records 14. Rochester: Rochester Museum and Science Center.

Heidenreich, Conrad E.
1971   *Huronia: A History and Geography of the Huron Indians, 1600–1650.* Toronto: McClelland and Stewart.
1972   *The Huron: A Brief Ethnography.* Toronto: York University.
1978   Huron. In *Handbook of North American Indians,* vol. 15, *Northeast,* edited by Bruce G. Trigger, pp. 368–88. Washington: Smithsonian Institution Press.

Horsman, Reginald
1958   British Indian Policy in the War of 1812. *Mississippi Valley Historical Review* 45:51–66

Hunt, George T.
1940   *The Wars of the Iroquois: A Study in Intertribal Trade Relations.* Madison: University of Wisconsin Press.

Jamieson, James B.
1983   An Examination of Prisoner-Sacrifice and Cannibalism at the St. Lawrence Iroquoian Roebuck Site. *Canadian Journal of Archaeology* 7:159–75.

Jamieson, Susan M.
1981   Economics and Ontario Iroquoian Social Organization. *Canadian Journal of Archaeology* 5:19–30.

Jennings, Francis
1984   *The Ambiguous Iroquois Empire: The Covenant Chain Confederation of Indian Tribes with English Colonies from Its Beginning to the Lancaster Treaty of 1744.* New York: Norton.
1988   *Empire of Fortune: Crowns, Colonies, and Tribes in the Seven Years War in America.* New York: W. W. Norton.

Jennings, Francis, ed.
1985   *The History and Culture of Iroquois Diplomacy: An Interdisciplinary Guide to the Treaties of the Six Nations and their League.* Syracuse, N.Y.: Syracuse University Press.

Johansen, Bruce E.
1990   Commentary on the Iroquois and the U.S. Constitution. *Ethnohistory* 37(3):279–90.

Johnston, Charles M.
1963   Joseph Brant, the Grand River Lands, and the Northwest Crisis. *Ontario History* 55:267–82.

Johnston, Charles M., ed.
1964   *The Valley of the Six Nations: A Collection of Documents on the Indian Lands of the Grand River.* Toronto: University of Toronto Press.

Jones, Dorothy V.
1982   *License for Empire: Colonialism by Treaty in Early America.* Chicago: University of Chicago Press.

Junker-Andersen, C.
1988   The Eel Fisheries of the St. Lawrence Iroquoians. *North American Archaeologist* 9(2): 97–122.

Kapches, M.
1990   The Spatial Dynamics of Ontario Longhouses. *American Antiquity* 55:49–67.

Katzer, Bruce
1988   The Caughnawaga Mohawks: The Other Side of Ironwork. *Journal of Ethnic Studies* 15(4):39–55.

Kelsay, Isabel Thompson
1984   *Joseph Brant, 1743–1807: Man of Two Worlds.* Syracuse, N.Y.: Syracuse University Press.

Konrad, V.
1981   An Iroquois Frontier: The North Shore of Lake Ontario During the Late Seventeenth Century. *Journal of Historical Geography* 7(2):129–44.

Landsman, Gail H.
1988   *Sovereignty and Symbol: Indian-White Conflict at Ganienkeh.* Albuquerque: University of New Mexico Press.

LaRocque, Robert
1980   Les maladies chez les iroquoiens préhistoriques. *Recherches amérindiennes au Québec* 10:165–80.

Lounsbury, Floyd G.
1978   Iroquoian Languages. In *Handbook of North American Indians,* vol. 15, *Northeast,* edited by Bruce G. Trigger, pp. 334–43. Washington: Smithsonian Institution Press.

Lynch, James
1985   The Iroquois Confederacy, and the Adoption and Administration of Non-Iroquoian Individuals and Groups Prior to 1756. *Man in the Northeast* 30:83–99.

Macauley, Ann Celia, et al.
1989   Breastfeeding in the Mohawk Community of Kahnawake: Revisited and Redefined. *Canadian Journal of Public Health/Revue canadienne de la santé publique* 80(3):177–81.

McIlwain, Thomas
1987   Seneca Iroquois Concepts of Time. *Canadian Journal of Native Studies/Révue canadienne des études autochtones* 7:267-77.

Mahon, John K.
1958   Anglo-American Methods of Indian Warfare, 1676–1774. *Mississippi Valley Historical Review* 45:254–75.

Mithun, Marianne
1979   Iroquoian. In *Native Languages of North America: An Historical and Comparative Assessment,* edited by Lyle Campbell and Marianne Mithun, pp. 133–212. Austin: University of Texas Press.
1984   <<Maman:>> l'évolution d'un terme de par-

enté dans les langues iroquoiennes. *Recherches amérindiennes au Québec* 14(4):17–23.

Montgomery, Malcolm
1963   The Legal Status of the Six Nations Indians in Canada. *Ontario History* 55(2):93–105.

Morgan, Lewis Henry
1851   *League of the Ho-De-No-Sau-Nee or Iroquois.* Rochester: Sage and Brothers.

Morissonneau, Christian
1978   Huron of Lorette. In *Handbook of North American Indians,* vol. 15, *Northeast,* edited by Bruce G. Trigger, pp. 389–93. Washington: Smithsonian Institution Press.

Naroll, Raoul
1969   The Causes of the Fourth Iroquois War. *Ethnohistory* 16:51–81.

Niemczycki, Mary Ann
1980   Seneca Tribalization: An Adaptive Strategy. *Man in the Northeast* 36:77–87.

Noble, William C.
1978   The Neutral Indians. In *Essays in Northeastern Anthropology in Memory of Marian E. White,* edited by William E. Engelbrecht and Donald K. Grayson, pp. 152–64. Rindge, N.H.: Franklin Pierce College.
1982   Potsherds, Potlids, and Politics: An Overview of Ontario Archaeology During the 1970's. *Canadian Journal of Archaeology* 6:167–94.
1984   Historic Neutral Iroquois Settlement Patterns. *Canadian Journal of Archaeology* 8(1):3–27.

Noon, J. A.
1949   *Law and Government of the Grand River Iroquois.* Viking Fund Publications in Anthropology, no. 12. New York.

Otterbein, Keith F.
1964   Why the Iroquois Won: An Analysis of Iroquois Military Tactics. *Ethnohistory* 11:56–63.
1979   Huron vs. Iroquois: A Case Study in Intertribal Warfare. *Ethnohistory* 26:141–52.

Pendergast, J. F.
1982   The History of the St. Lawrence Iroquois and Some Recent Research. *Anthropologica* 82(1): 2–4.

Richter, Daniel K.
1983   War and Culture: The Iroquois Experience. *William and Mary Quarterly* 40:528–59.
1985   Iroquois vs. Iroquois: Jesuit Missions and Christianity in Village Politics. *Ethnohistory* 32(1):1–16.
1988   Cultural Brokers and Intercultural Politics: New York-Iroquois Relations, 1664–1701. *Journal of American History* 75:40–67.

Richter, Daniel K., and James H. Merrell, eds.
1987   *Beyond the Covenant Chain: The Iroquois and Their Neighbors in Indian North America, 1600–1800.* Syracuse, N.Y.: Syracuse University Press.

Rustige, Rona, ed.
1988   *Tyendinaga Tales.* Kingston and Montreal: McGill-Queen's University Press.

Schlesier, Karl H.
1976   Epidemics and Indian Middlemen: Rethinking the Wars of the Iroquois, 1609–1653. *Ethnohistory* 23:129–46.

Shimony, Annemarie A.
1961   *Conservatism Among the Iroquois at the Six Nations Reserve.* Yale University Publications in Anthropology, no. 65.
1970   Iroquois Witchcraft at Six Nations. *Anthropological Monographs of the University of Idaho* 1:239–65.

Simonis, Yvan
1973   Elements d'analyse structural d'un récit cannibale seneca. *Recherches amérindiennes au Québec* 3(1–2):87–96.

Smith, Wallis M.
1970   A Re-appraisal of the Huron Kinship System. *Anthropologica* 12:191–206.

Snow, Dean R., and William A. Starna
1989   Sixteenth-century Depopulation: A View from the Mohawk Valley. *American Anthropologist* 91:142–49.

Stanley, George F. G.
1950   The Indians in the War of 1812. *Canadian Historical Review* 31:145–65.

Starna, William A.
1963   The Significance of the Six Nations Participation in the War of 1812. *Ontario History* 55:215–31.
1980   Mohawk Iroquois Populations: A Revision. *Ethnohistory* 27:371–82.

Starna, William A., George R. Hamell, and W. L. Butts
1984   Northern Iroquoian Horticulture and Insect

Infestation: A Cause for Village Removal. *Ethnohistory* 31:197–207.

Starna, William A., and Ralph Watkins
1991   Northern Iroquoian Slavery. *Ethnohistory* 38: 34–57.

Stone, Thomas
1975   Legal Mobilization and Legal Penetration: The Department of Indian Affairs and the Canadian Party at St. Regis, 1876–1918. *Ethnohistory* 23:375–408.

Sturtevant, William C.
1983   Seneca Masks. In *The Power of Symbols: Masks and Masquerade in the Americas,* edited by N. Ross Crumrine and Marjorie Halpin, pp. 39–47. Vancouver: University of British Columbia Press.

Tooker, Elisabeth
1963   The Iroquois Defeat of the Huron: A Review of Causes. *Pennsylvania Archaeologist* 33:115–23.
1964   *An Ethnography of the Huron Indians, 1615–1649.* Bureau of American Ethnology Bulletin 190. Washington.
1965   On the New Religion of Handsome Lake. *Anthropological Quarterly* 41:187–200.
1970   *The Iroquois Ceremonial of Midwinter.* Syracuse, N.Y.: Syracuse University Press.
1978a   Iroquois Since 1820. In *Handbook of North American Indians,* vol. 15, *Northeast,* edited by Bruce G. Trigger, pp. 449–65. Washington: Smithsonian Institution Press.
1978b   The League of the Iroquois: Its History, Politics, and Ritual. In *Handbook of North American Indians,* vol. 15, *Northeast,* edited by Bruce G. Trigger, pp. 418–41. Washington: Smithsonian Institution Press.
1978c   Wyandot. In *Handbook of North American Indians,* vol. 15, *Northeast,* edited by Bruce G. Trigger, pp. 398–406. Washington: Smithsonian Institution Press.
1980   Isaac N. Hurd's Ethnographic Studies of the Iroquois: Their Significance and Ethnographic Value. *Ethnohistory* 27:363–69.
1981   Eighteenth Century Political Affairs and the Iroquois League. In *The Iroquois in the American Revolution.* Research Records, no. 14. Rochester, N.Y.: Rochester Museum and Science Center.

1988   The United States Constitution and the Iroquois League. *Ethnohistory* 35:305–36.
1990   Commentary on the Iroquois and the U.S. Constitution. *Ethnohistory* 37(3):291–97.

Tooker, Elisabeth, ed.
1967   *Iroquois Culture, History, and Prehistory: Proceedings of the 1965 Conference on Iroquois Research.* Albany, N.Y.: New York State Museum and Science Service.

Trelease, Alan W.
1962   The Iroquois and the Western Fur Trade: A Problem in Interpretation. *Mississippi Valley Historical Review* 49:32–51.

Trigger, Bruce G.
1960   The Destruction of Huronia. *Transactions of the Royal Canadian Institute* 33(1):14–45.
1962   Trade and Tribal Warfare on the St. Lawrence in the 16th Century. *Ethnohistory* 9:240–56.
1963   Settlement as an Aspect of Iroquoian Adaptation at the Time of Contact. *American Anthropologist* 65:86–101.
1968   The French Presence in Huronia: The Structure of Franco-Huron Relations in the First Half of the Seventeenth Century. *Canadian Historical Review* 49:107–41.
1969   *The Huron: Farmers of the North.* New York: Holt, Rinehart and Winston.
1970   The Strategy of Iroquoian Prehistory. *Ontario Archaeology* 14:3–48.
1971   The Mohawk-Mahican War (1624–28): The Establishment of a Pattern. *Canadian Historical Review* 52:276–86.
1972   Hochelaga: History and Ethnohistory. In *Cartier's Hochelaga and the Dawson Site,* edited by J. F. Pendergast and Bruce G. Trigger, pp. 1–107. Montreal: McGill-Queen's University Press.
1976   *The Children of Aataentsic: A History of the Huron People to 1660.* 2 vols. Montreal: McGill-Queen's University Press.
1977   *The Indian and the Heroic Age of New France.* CHA Booklet #30. Ottawa: Canadian Historical Association.
1978a   Early Iroquoian Contacts with Europeans. In *Handbook of North American Indians,* vol. 15, *Northeast,* edited by Bruce G. Trigger, pp. 344–56. Washington: Smithsonian Institution Press.

1978b   Iroquoian Matriliny. *Pennsylvania Archaeologist* 48(1–2):55–65.

1978c   The Strategy of Iroquoian Prehistory. In *Archaeological Essays in Honor of Irving B. Rouse,* edited by R. C. Dunnell and E. S. Hall, pp. 275–310. The Hague: Mouton.

1979   Sixteenth Century Ontario: History, Ethnohistory, and Archaeology. *Ontario History:* 71: 205–23.

1981a   Ontario Native People and the Epidemics of 1634–1640. In *Indians, Animals, and the Fur Trade,* edited by Shepard Krech III, pp. 19–38. Athens: University of Georgia Press.

1981b   Prehistoric Social and Political Organization: An Iroquoian Case Study. In *Foundations of Northeast Archaeology,* edited by Dean Snow, pp. 1–50. New York: Academic Press.

1984   The Road to Affluence: A Reassessment of Early Huron Responses to European Contact. In *Affluence and Cultural Survival,* edited by R. F. Salisbury and E. Tooker, pp. 12–25. Washington: American Ethnological Society.

1990   *The Huron: Farmers of the North.* 2d ed. New York: Holt, Rinehart and Winston.

Trigger, Bruce G., and James F. Pendergast
1978   St. Lawrence Iroquoians. In *Handbook of North American Indians,* vol. 15, *Northeast,* edited by Bruce G. Trigger, pp. 357–61. Washington: Smithsonian Institution Press.

Tuck, James A.
1978   Northern Iroquoian Prehistory. In *Handbook of North American Indians,* vol. 15, *Northeast,* edited by Bruce G. Trigger, pp. 322–33. Washington: Smithsonian Institution Press.

Turgeon, Laurier
1982   Pêcheurs basques et indiens des côtes du Saint-Laurent au XVIe siècle. *Canadian Studies* 13:9–14.

Vecsey, Christopher
1986   The Story and Structure of the Iroquois Confederacy. *Journal of the American Academy of Religion* 54(1):79–106.

Venables, Robert W.
1980   Iroquois Environments and "We the People of the United States." In *American Indian Environments: Ecological Issues in Native American History,* edited by C. Vecsey and R. W. Venables, pp. 81–127. Syracuse, N.Y.: Syracuse University Press.

Wallace, Anthony F. C.
1957   Origins of Iroquois Neutrality: The Grand Settlement of 1701. *Pennsylvania History* 24(3): 223–35.

1969   *Death and Rebirth of the Seneca.* New York: A. A. Knopf.

1978   Origins of the Longhouse Religion. In *Handbook of North American Indians,* vol. 15, *Northeast,* edited by Bruce G. Trigger, pp. 442–48. Washington: Smithsonian Institution Press.

Waugh, Frederick W.
1916   *Iroquois Foods and Food Preparation.* Anthropological Series, no. 12. Memoirs of the Canadian Geological Survey, no. 86. Ottawa.

Weaver, Sally M.
1971   Smallpox or Chickenpox: An Iroquoian Community's Reaction to Crisis, 1901–1902. *Ethnohistory* 18:361–78.

1972   *Medicine and Politics Among the Grand River Iroquois: A Study of NonConservatives.* Publications in Ethnology, no. 4. Ottawa: National Museum of Man.

1974   *Judicial Preservation of Ethnic Group Boundaries: The Iroquois Case.* Mercury Series, Canadian Ethnology Service Paper 17. Ottawa: National Museum of Man.

1975   *The Viability of Factionalism Among the Iroquois.* Mercury Series, Canadian Ethnology Service Paper 28. Ottawa: National Museum of Man.

1978   Six Nations of the Grand River, Ontario. In *Handbook of North American Indians,* vol. 15, *Northeast,* edited by Bruce G. Trigger, pp. 525–36. Washington: Smithsonian Institution Press.

White, Marian E.
1971   Ethnic Identification and Iroquois Groups in Western New York and Ontario. *Ethnohistory* 18:19–38.

1978   Neutral and Wenro. In *Handbook of North American Indians,* vol. 15, *Northeast,* edited by Bruce G. Trigger, pp. 407–11. Washington: Smithsonian Institution Press.

White, Marian E., William E. Engelbrecht, and Elisabeth Tooker
1978   Cayuga. In *Handbook of North American In-*

dians, vol. 15, *Northeast,* edited by Bruce G. Trigger, pp. 500–504. Washington: Smithsonian Institution Press.

Wilson, Edmund
1960   *Apologies to the Iroquois.* New York: Farrar, Strauss, and Cudahy.

Wise, S. F.
1970   The American Revolution and Indian History. In *Character and Circumstance,* edited by John Moir, pp. 182–200. Toronto: Macmillan of Canada.

Wright, James V.
1966   *The Ontario Iroquois Tradition.* Anthropological Series, no. 75. Bulletin 210. Ottawa: National Museum of Canada.
1970   *Ontario Prehistory.* Ottawa: National Museum of Man.
1982   La circulation de biens archéologiques dans le bassin du Saint-Laurent au cours de la préhistoire. *Recherches amérindiennes au Québec* 12(3):193–206.

Section Seven

✤

INDIANS OF THE PRAIRIES AND PLAINS

Ahenakew, Edward
1960   An Opinion of the Frog Lake Massacre. *Alberta Historical Review,* 9–15.
1973   *Voices of the Plains Cree.* Toronto: McClelland and Stewart.

Ahenakew, Freda, ed.
1987   *wâskahikaniwiyiniw-âcimowina/Stories of the House People.* Winnipeg: University of Manitoba Press.

Allen, Robert S.
1972   Big Bear. *Saskatchewan History* 25:1–17.

Andersen, Raoul R.
1970   Alberta Stoney (Assiniboin) Origins and Adaptations: A Case for Reappraisal. *Ethnohistory* 17:49–62.

Andrews, Isabel
1975   Indian Protest Against Starvation: The Yellow Calf Incident of 1884. *Saskatchewan History* 28:41–51.

Barbeau, C. Marius
1960   *Indian Days in the Western Prairies.* Anthropological Series, no. 46. Bulletin 163. Ottawa: National Museum of Canada.

Bartlett, Richard H.
1980   Indian Reserves on the Prairies. *Canadian Native Law Reporter* 3:3–53.
1989   Hydroelectric Power and Indian Water Rights on the Prairies. *Prairie Forum* 14(2):177–94.

Bennett, John W.
1969   *Northern Plainsmen: Adaptive Strategy and Agrarian Life.* Chicago: Aldine.

Bingaman, Sandra E.
1975   The Trials of Poundmaker and Big Bear, 1885. *Saskatchewan History* 28:81–94.

Braroe, Niels Winther
1965   Reciprocal Exploitation in an Indian-White Community. *Southwestern Journal of Anthropology* 21:166–78.
1975   *Indian and White: Self-Image and Interaction in a Canadian Plains Community.* Stanford: Stanford University Press.

Brass, Eleanor
1953   The File Hills Ex-Pupil Colony. *Saskatchewan History* 6:66–69.
1987   *I Walk in Two Worlds.* Calgary: Glenbow Museum.

Brasser, Ted J. C.
1982   The Tipi as an Element in the Emergence of Historic Plains Indian Nomadism. *Plains Anthropologist* 27:309–21.

Brown, Randall J.
1982   Hobbema Sun Dance of 1923. *Alberta History Occasional Paper,* Summer, 9–18.

Bryan, Liz
1991   *The Buffalo People: Prehistoric Archaeology on the Canadian Plains.* Edmonton: University of Alaska Press.

Burley, David V., ed.
1985   *Contributions to Plains Prehistory.* Occasional Paper 26. Edmonton: Archaeological Survey of Alberta.

Burt, Larry
1987   Nowhere to Go: Montana's Crees, Metis, and Chippewas and the Creation of the Rocky Boy's Reservation. *Great Plains Quarterly* 7: 195–209.

Cameron, W. B.
1950   *Blood Red the Sun.* 1926. Reprint. Calgary: Kenway Publishing.

Carter, Sarah
1983   Agriculture and Agitation on the Oak River Dakota Reserve, 1875–1895. *Manitoba History* 6:2–9.
1985   Controlling Indian Movement: The Pass System. *NeWest Review* 10:8–9.
1988   Indian Captivity Stories Thrilled Victorian Readers—But Were They True? *Beaver* 68: 21–28.
1989a   St. Peter's and the Interpretation of the Agriculture of Manitoba's Aboriginal People. *Manitoba History* 18:46–52.
1989b   Two Acres and a Cow: "Peasant" Farming for the Indians of the Northwest, 1889–97. *Canadian Historical Review* 70:27–52.
1990   *Lost Harvests: Prairie Indian Reserve Farmers and Government Policy.* Montreal: McGill-Queen's University Press.

Cuthand, Stan
1988   Poundmaker's Surrender. *Saskatchewan Indian,* September, 12–15.

Darnell, Regna
1991   Thirty-nine Postulates of Plains Cree Conversation, "Power," and Interaction: A Culture-

Specific Model. In *Papers of the Twenty-second Algonquian Conference,* edited by William Cowan, pp. 89–102. Ottawa: Carleton University.

Davis, Leslie
1983   From Microcosm to Macrocosm: Advances in Tipi Ring Investigation and Interpretation. *Plains Anthropologist,* 28–109. Pt. 2. Memoir 19.

Dempsey, Hugh A.
n.d.   *A Blackfoot Winter Count.* Occasional Paper 1. Calgary: Glenbow Foundation.
1967   The Indians of Alberta. *Alberta Historical Review,* 1–115.
1968   *The Blackfoot Ghost Dance.* Occasional Paper 3. Calgary: Glenbow Foundation.
1972   *Crowfoot: Chief of the Blackfeet.* Norman: University of Oklahoma Press. Reprint. Edmonton: Hurtig, 1976.
1977   The Centennial of Treaty Seven. *Canadian Geographical Journal,* 10–19.
1978a   *Charcoal's World.* Lincoln: University of Nebraska Press.
1978b   *Indian Tribes of Alberta.* Calgary: Glenbow-Alberta Institute.
1980   *Red Crow, Warrior Chief.* Lincoln: University of Nebraska Press.
1981   The Snake Man. *Alberta History* 29(3):1–5.
1984   *Big Bear: The End of Freedom.* Vancouver: Douglas and McIntyre; Lincoln: University of Nebraska Press.
1986   *The Gentle Persuader: A Biography of James Gladstone, Indian Senator.* Saskatoon: Western Producer Prairie Books.
1990   Simpson's Essay on the Blackfoot, 1841. *Alberta History* 38(1):1–14.

Dempsey, James
1988   Persistence of a Warrior Ethic Among the Plains Indians. *Alberta History* 36(1):1–10.

Denig, E. T., and J. N. B. Hewitt
1930   Indian Tribes of the Upper Missouri. In *Forty-sixth Annual Report of the Bureau of American Ethnology,* 375–628. Washington.

Dickason, Olive Patricia
1980   A Historical Reconstruction for the Northwestern Plains. *Prairie Forum* 5(1):19–37.

Dion, Joe
1979   *My Tribe the Crees.* Calgary: Glenbow-Alberta Museum.

Elias, Peter Douglas
1988   *The Dakota of the Canadian North-West: Lessons for Survival.* Winnipeg: University of Manitoba Press.

Erasmus, Peter
1976   *Buffalo Days and Nights.* Edited by Irene Spry. Calgary: Glenbow-Alberta Institute.

Ewers, John C.
1955   *The Horse in Blackfoot Indian Culture.* Bureau of American Ethnology Bulletin 159. Washington.
1974   *The Blackfeet: Raiders on the Northwestern Plains.* Norman: University of Oklahoma Press.
1985   *Blackfeet: Their History.* Surrey, B.C.: Hancock House.

Fisher, Anthony D.
1965   The Algonquian Plains? *Anthropologica* 10: 219–34.
1968   Cultural Conflict on the Prairies: Indian and White. *Alberta Historical Review* 16(3):22–29.
1974   Introducing "Our Betrayed Wards," by R. N. Wilson. *Western Canadian Journal of Anthropology* 4(1):21–31.

Frantz, Donald G.
1991   *Blackfoot Grammar.* Toronto: University of Toronto Press.

Fraser, W. B.
1966   Big Bear, Indian Patriot. *Alberta Historical Review* 14:1–13.

Friesen, Gerald
1984   *The Canadian Prairies: A History.* Toronto: University of Toronto Press; Lincoln: University of Nebraska Press.

Friesen, Jean
1986   Magnificent Gifts: The Treaties of Canada with the Indians of the Northwest, 1869–76. *Transactions of the Royal Society of Canada* 5(1): 41–51.

Gibbons, Roger, and J. Rick Ponting
1977   Contemporary Prairie Perceptions of Canada's Native Peoples. *Prairie Forum* 2(1):22–23.

Goldfrank, Esther S.
1945   *Changing Configurations in the Social Organization of a Blackfoot Tribe During the Reserve Period.* American Ethnological Society Monograph 8.

Goldring, Philip
1973   The Cypress Hills Massacre—A Century's Retrospect. *Saskatchewan History* 26:81–102.

Gooderman, Kent, ed.
1969   *I Am an Indian.* Don Mills, Ont.: J. M. Dent.

Grobsmith, Elizabeth S.
1990   The Plains. In *Native North Americans: An Ethnohistorical Approach,* edited by Daniel L. Boxberger, pp. 167–213. Dubuque, Iowa: Kendall/Hunt Publishing Company.

Hanks, Lucien M., and Jane Richardson Hanks
1950   *Tribe Under Trust: A Study of the Blackfoot Reserve of Alberta.* Toronto: University of Toronto Press.

Hanson, Jeffrey R.
1988   Age-Set Theory and Plains Indian Age-Grading: A Critical Review and Revision. *American Ethnologist* 15:349–64.

Hildebrandt, Walter
1985   Battleford 1885: The Siege Mentality. *NeWest Review* 10:20–21.

Howard, James H.
1961   The Identity and Demography of the Plains-Ojibwa. *Plains Anthropologist* 6:171–78.
1965   *The Plains Ojibwa or Bungi: Hunters and Warriors of the Northern Plains with Special Reference to the Turtle Mountain Band.* Vermillion: South Dakota Museum, University of South Dakota. Reprint. Lincoln, Nebr.: J. and L. Reprint Company, 1977.
1984   *The Canadian Sioux.* Lincoln: University of Nebraska Press.

Hughes, Stuart
1976   *The Frog Lake "Massacre": Personal Perspectives on Ethnic Conflict.* Toronto: McClelland and Stewart West.

Hungry Wolf, Adolf
1977   *The Blood People: A Division of the Blackfoot Confederacy.* New York: Harper and Row.

Innes, Ross, ed.
1986   *The Sands of Time.* North Battleford, Sask.: Turner Warwick Publications.

Jenness, Diamond
1938   *The Sarcee Indians of Alberta.* Department of Mines Bulletin 90. Ottawa: National Museum of Canada.

Jobson, Valerie
1985   The Blackfoot and the Rationing System. *Alberta History* 33(4):13–17.

Kaye, Barry, and D. Wayne Moodie
1978   The "Psoralea": Food Resources of the Northern Plains. *Plains Anthropologist* 23:329–36.

Kehoe, Alice B.
1968   The Ghost Dance Religion in Saskatchewan, Canada. *Plains Anthropologist* 13:296–304.
1970   The Dakotas in Saskatchewan. In *The Modern Sioux: Social Systems and Reservation Culture,* edited by E. Nurge, pp. 148–72. Lincoln: University of Nebraska Press.
1975   Dakota Indian Ethnicity in Saskatchewan. *Journal of Ethnic Studies* 3(2):37–42.
1980   The Giveaway Ceremony of Blackfoot and Plains Cree. *Plains Anthropologist* 25–87:17–26.
1982   Plains Indians of North America: Concepts of Ultimate Reality and Meaning. *Ultimate Reality and Meaning* 5(1):5–14.
1989   *The Ghost Dance: Ethnohistory and Revitalization.* New York: Holt, Rinehart and Winston.

Kehoe, Alice B., and Thomas F. Kehoe
1979   *Solstice-aligned Boulder Configurations in Saskatchewan.* Mercury Series, Canadian Ethnology Service Paper 48. Ottawa: National Museum of Man.

Kehoe, Thomas F., and Alice B. Kehoe
1977   Stones, Solstices, and Sun Dance Structures. *Plains Anthropologist* 22(76):85–95.

Kidd, Kenneth E.
1986   *Blackfoot Ethnography.* Archaeological Survey of Alberta Manuscript Series, no. 8. Edmonton.

Landes, Ruth
1986   Dakota Warfare. *Journal of Anthropological Research* 42:239–48.

Larmour, Jean
1980   Edgar Dewdney: Indian Commissioner in the Transition Period of Indian Settlement, 1879–1884. *Saskatchewan History* 33:13–24.

Laviolette, Gontran
1944   *The Sioux Indians in Canada.* Regina: Marian Press.

Lee, David
1983   Foremost Man, and His Band. *Saskatchewan History* 36:94–101.

Lithman, Yngve Georg
1984   *The Community Apart: A Case Study of a Canadian Indian Reserve Community.* Winnipeg: University of Manitoba Press.

Looy, A. J.
1979   Saskatchewan's First Indian Agent, M. G. Dickieson. *Saskatchewan History* 32:104-15.

Lowie, Robert H.
1910   The Assiniboine. *Anthropological Papers of the American Museum of Natural History* 4:1–270.

Lupul, David
1978   The Bobtail Land Surrender. *Alberta History* 26:29–39.

Luxton, Eleanor G.
1983   Stony Indian Medicine. In *The Developing West,* edited by John Foster, pp. 101–22. Edmonton: University of Alberta Press.

McClintock, Walter
1968   *The Old North Trail; or, Life, Legends, and Religion of the Blackfeet Indians.* Lincoln: University of Nebraska Press.

Macdonald, R. H., ed.
1985   *Eyewitness to History: William Bleasdell Cameron, Frontier Journalist.* Saskatoon: Western Producer Prairie Books.

McDougall, John
1971   *Pathfinding on Plain and Prairie.* 1898. Toronto: Coles Publishing Company.
1983   *In the Days of the Red River Rebellion.* 1903. Edmonton: University of Alberta Press.

MacEwan, Grant
1969   *Tatanga Mani: Walking Buffalo of the Stonies.* Edmonton: Hurtig.
1973   *Sitting Bull: The Years in Canada.* Edmonton: Hurtig.

MacLean, John
1971   *Canadian Savage Folk.* 1896. Toronto: Coles Publishing Company.

McQuillan, D. Aidan
1980   Creation of Indian Reserves on the Canadian Prairies, 1870–1885. *Geographical Review* 70:379–96.

Mandelbaum, David G.
1940   The Plains Cree. *Anthropological Papers of*

the American Museum of Natural History 37: 155–316.

1979 *The Plains Cree: An Ethnographic, Historical, and Comparative Study.* Canadian Plains Studies, no. 9. Regina: Canadian Plains Research Center.

Meyer, David
1985 *The Red Earth Crees, 1860–1960.* Mercury Series, Canadian Ethnology Service Paper 100. Ottawa: National Museum of Man.

Milloy, John S.
1988 *The Plains Cree: Warriors, Traders, and Diplomats, 1790–1870.* Winnipeg: University of Manitoba Press.

Moodie, D. Wayne, and Arthur J. Ray
1976 Buffalo Migrations in the Canadian Plains. *Plains Anthropologist* 21:45–51.

Moore, T. A., ed.
1981 *Alberta Archaeology: Prospect and Retrospect.* Lethbridge: Archaeological Society of Alberta.

Morgan, R. Grace
1980 Bison Movement on the Canadian Plains: An Ecological Analysis. *Plains Anthropologist* 25–88:143–60.

Nicholson, B. A.
1987 Culture History of the Forest/Grassland Transition Zone of Western Manitoba and Relationships to Cultures in Adjacent Regions. *Manitoba Archaeological Quarterly* 11(2–3):1–124.
1988 Modelling Subsistence Strategies in the Forest/Grassland Transition Zone of Western Manitoba During the Late Prehistoric and Early Historic Periods. *Plains Anthropologist* 33(121): 351–68.

O'Brodovich, L.
1968 Plains Cree Acculturation in the Nineteenth Century: A Study of Injustice. *Na'Pao* 2:2–23.

Pennanen, Gary
1970 Sitting Bull: Indian Without a Country. *Canadian Historical Review* 51:123–40.

Philips, Donna, Robert Troff, and Harvey Whitecalf, eds.
1976 *Ka-ta-a-yuk Saskatchewan Indian Elders.* Saskatoon: Saskatchewan Indian Cultural College.

Price, Richard, ed.
1979 *The Spirit of the Alberta Indian Treaties.* Toronto: Butterworth.

Quigg, J. Michael
1984 A 4700-Year-Old Tool Assemblage from East-Central Alberta. *Plains Anthropologist* 29(104): 151–60.

Raby, Stewart
1973 Indian Land Surrenders in Southern Saskatchewan. *Canadian Geographer* 17:36–52.

Reeves, Brian O. K.
1983 *Culture Change in the Northern Plains: 1000 B.C.–1000 A.D.* Occasional Paper 20. Edmonton: Archaeological Survey of Alberta.

Roe, F. G.
1934 The Extermination of the Buffalo in Western Canada. *Canadian Historical Review,* 1–23.
1951 *The North American Buffalo.* Toronto: University of Toronto Press.

Samarin, W. J.
1987 Demythologizing Plains Indian Sign Language History. *International Journal of American Linguistics* 53:65–73.

Samek, Hanna
1987 *The Blackfoot Confederacy, 1880–1920: A Comparative Study of Canadian and U.S. Indian Policy.* Albuquerque: University of New Mexico Press.

Sanderson, James F.
1965 *Indian Tales of the Canadian Prairies.* Calgary: Historical Society of Alberta.

Schaeffer, Claude E.
1969 *Blackfoot Shaking Tent.* Occasional Paper 5. Calgary: Glenbow-Alberta Institute.
1982 Plains Kutenai: An Ethnological Evaluation. *Alberta History* 30(3):9–18.

Schwimmer, E. G.
1972 Symbolic Competition. *Anthropologica* 14(2): 117–55.

Sharp, Paul F.
1954 Massacre at Cypress Hills. *Saskatchewan History* 7:81–99.
1955 *Whoop-Up Country: The Canadian-American West, 1865–1885.* Norman: University of Oklahoma Press.

Sharrock, Susan R.
1974 Crees, Cree-Assiniboines, and Assiniboines: Interethnic Social Organization on the Far Northern Plains. *Ethnohistory* 21:95–122.

Sluman, Norma, and Jean Goodwill
1982   *John Tootoosis: A Biography of a Cree Leader.* Ottawa: Golden Dog Press.

Smith, Donald B.
1989   From Sylvester Long to Chief Buffalo Child Long Lance. In *Being and Becoming Indian: Biographical Studies of North American Frontiers,* edited by James Clifton, pp. 183–203. Chicago: Dorsey Press.

Snow, Chief John
1960   *These Mountains Are Our Sacred Places: The Story of the Stoney Indians.* Toronto: University of Toronto Press.

Spry, Irene M.
1968   The Transition from a Nomadic to a Settled Economy in Western Canada, 1856–96. *Transactions of the Royal Society of Canada,* 4th. ser., 6:187–201.

Tarasoff, K. J.
1980   *Persistent Ceremonialism: The Plains Cree and Saulteaux.* Mercury Series, Canadian Ethnology Service Paper 69. Ottawa: National Museum of Man.

Thurman, Melburn
1988   On the Identity of the Chariticas: Dog Eating and Pre-horse Adaptation on the High Plains. *Plains Anthropologist* 32(120):159–70.

Titley, E. Brian
1983   W. M. Graham: Indian Agent Extraordinaire. *Prairie Forum* 8(1):25–41.
1991   Fate of the Sheephead Stoneys. *Alberta History* 39(1):1–8.

Tobias, John L.
1983   Canada's Subjugation of the Plains Cree, 1879–1885. *Canadian Historical Review* 64:519–48.

Ubelaker, Douglas H., and Herman J. Viola, eds.
1982   *Plains Indian Studies: A Collection of Essays in Honor of John C. Ewers and Waldo R. Wedel.* Smithsonian Contributions to Anthropology, no. 30.

Verbicky-Todd, Eleanor
1984   *Communal Buffalo-Hunting Among the Plains Indians.* Occasional Paper 24. Edmonton: Archaeological Survey of Alberta.

Walker, Ernest G.
1983   The Woodlawn Site: A Case for Interregional Disease Transmission in the Late Prehistoric Period. *Canadian Journal of Archaeology* 7:49–59.

Wallis, Wilson D.
1947   The Canadian Dakota. *Anthropological Papers of the American Museum of Natural History* 41(1):1–225.

Watetch, Abel
1959   *Payepot and His People.* Saskatoon: Modern Press.

Whitecap, Leah
1988   The Education of Children in Pre-European Plains America. *Canadian Journal of Native Education* 15(2):33–40.

Wiebe, Rudy
1973   *The Temptations of Big Bear.* Toronto: McClelland and Stewart.
1975   On the Trail of Big Bear. In *Western Canada Past and Present,* edited by A. W. Rasporich, pp. 182–92. Calgary: McClelland and Stewart West.

Wissler, Clark
1912   The Social Life of the Blackfoot Indians. *Anthropological Papers of the American Museum of Natural History* 7:1–64.
1913   Societies and Dance Associations of the Blackfoot Indians. *Anthropological Papers of the American Museum of Natural History* 11:359–460.
1918   The Sun Dance of the Blackfoot Indians. *Anthropological Papers of the American Museum of Natural History* 16:223–70.

Wissler, Clark, and D. C. Duvall
1908   Mythology of the Blackfoot Indians. *Anthropological Papers of the American Museum of Natural History* 2:1–163.

Witmer, Robert
1982   *The Musical Life of the Blood Indians.* Mercury Series, Canadian Ethnology Service Paper 86. Ottawa: National Museum of Man.

Wolfe, Alexander
1989   *Earth Elder Stories: The Pinayzitt Path.* Saskatoon: Fifth House.

Wood, W. Raymond, and Margot Liberty, eds.
1980   *Anthropology on the Great Plains.* Lincoln: University of Nebraska Press.

Section Eight

✦

INDIANS OF THE NORTHWEST COAST AND PLATEAU (BRITISH COLUMBIA)

Abbott, Donald N., ed.
1981   *The World Is as Sharp as a Knife: An Anthology in Honour of Wilson Duff.* Victoria: British Columbia Provincial Museum.

Acheson, Steven R.
1985   "Ninstints" Village: A Case of Mistaken Identity. *BC Studies* 67:47–56.

Adams, John W.
1973   *The Gitksan Potlatch.* Toronto: Holt, Rinehart and Winston of Canada.

Ames, Kenneth M.
1981   The Evolution of Social Ranking on the Northwest Coast of North America. *American Antiquity* 46:789–805.

Amoss, Pamela
1978a   *Coast Salish Spirit Dancing.* Seattle: University of Washington Press.
1978b   Symbolic Substitution in the Indian Shaker Church. *Ethnohistory* 25:225–50.
1987   The Fish God Gave Us: The First Salmon Ceremony Revived. *Arctic Anthropology* 24(1): 56–66.
1990   The Indian Shaker Church. In *Handbook of North American Indians,* vol. 7, *Northwest Coast,* edited by Wayne Suttles, pp. 633–39. Washington: Smithsonian Institution Press.

Archer, Christon I.
1973   The Transient Presence: A Re-appraisal of Spanish Attitudes Towards the Northwest Coast in the Eighteenth Century. *BC Studies* 18:3–32.
1980   Cannibalism in the Early History of the Northwest Coast: Enduring Myths and Neglected Realities. *Canadian Historical Review* 61: 453–79.

Arima, Eugene Y.
1983   *The West Coast (Nootka) People.* Special Publication 6. Victoria: British Columbia Provincial Museum.
1988   Notes on Nootkan Sea Mammal Hunting. *Arctic Anthropology* 25(1):16–27.
1991   *Between Ports Alberni and Renfrew: Notes on West Coast Peoples.* Mercury Series, Canadian Ethnology Service Paper 121. Ottawa: Canadian Museum of Civilization.

Arima, Eugene Y., and John Dewhirst
1990   Nootkans of Vancouver Island. In *Handbook*

of North American Indians, vol. 7, *Northwest Coast,* edited by Wayne Suttles, pp. 391–411. Washington: Smithsonian Institution Press.

Assu, Harry, and Joy Inglis
1989   *Assu of Cape Mudge: Recollections of a Coastal Indian Chief.* Vancouver: University of British Columbia Press.

Barnett, Homer G.
1938   The Nature of the Potlatch. *American Anthropologist* 40:349–58.
1955   *The Coast Salish of British Columbia.* Studies in Anthropology, no. 4. Eugene: University of Oregon Press.

Barbeau, C. Marius
1973   *The Downfall of Temlahan.* 1928. Edmonton: Hurtig.

Bishop, Charles A.
1987   Coast-Interior Exchange: The Origins of Stratification in Northwestern North America. *Arctic Anthropology* 24(1):72–83.

Blackman, Margaret B.
1977   Continuity and Change in Northwest Coast Ceremonialism: Introduction. *Arctic Anthropology* 14(1):1–4.
1981   *Window on the Past: The Photographic Ethnohistory of the Northern and Kaigani Haida.* Mercury Series, Canadian Ethnology Service Paper 74. Ottawa: National Museum of Man.
1981–82   "Copying People": Northwest Coast Native Response to Early Photography. *BC Studies* 52:86–112.
1990   Haida: Traditional Culture. In *Handbook of North American Indians,* vol. 7, *Northwest Coast,* edited by Wayne Suttles, pp. 240–60. Washington: Smithsonian Institution Press.

Boas, Franz
1895   The Social Organization and the Secret Societies of the Kwakiutl Indians. In *Report of the United States National Museum for 1895,* pp. 311–738. Washington.
1909   The Kwakiutl of Vancouver Island. *Memoirs of the American Museum of Natural History* 8:307–515.
1916   Tsimshian Mythology. In *Thirty-first Annual Report of the Bureau of American Ethnology,* pp. 29–979. Washington.
1921   Ethnology of the Kwakiutl. In *Thirty-fifth An-*

nual Report of the Bureau of American Ethnology, pp. 39–794, 795–1473. Washington.
1930   *The Religion of the Kwakiutl Indians.* Columbia University Contributions to Anthropology 10. New York.
1966   *Kwakiutl Ethnography.* Edited by Helen Codere. Chicago: University of Chicago Press.

Boelscher, Marianne
1988   *The Curtain Within: Haida Social and Mythical Discourse.* Vancouver: University of British Columbia Press.

Borden, Charles E.
1979   Peopling and Early Cultures of the Pacific Northwest. *Science* 203:963–71.

Boxberger, Daniel L.
1988   The Lummi Indians and the Canadian/American Pacific Salmon Treaty. *American Indian Quarterly* 12:299–311.
1990   The Northwest Coast. In *Native North Americans: An Ethnohistorical Approach,* edited by Daniel K. Boxberger, pp. 387–410. Dubuque, Iowa: Kendall/Hunt Publishing Company.

Boyd, Robert T.
1990   Demographic History, 1774–1874. In *Handbook of North American Indians,* vol. 7, *Northwest Coast,* edited by Wayne Suttles, pp. 135–48. Washington: Smithsonian Institution Press.

Burrows, James K.
1986   "A Much-Needed Class of Labour": The Economy and Income of the Southern Interior Plateau Indian, 1897–1910. *BC Studies* 71:27–46.

Campbell, Chris K.
1989   A Study of Matrilineal Descent from the Perspective of the Tlingit NexA'di Eagles. *Arctic* 42:119–27.

Cannizzo, Jeanne
1983   George Hunt and the Invention of Kwakiutl Culture. *Canadian Review of Sociology and Anthropology* 20(1):44–58.

Carlson, Roy L.
1990a   Cultural Antecedents. In *Handbook of North American Indians,* vol. 7, *Northwest Coast,* edited by Wayne Suttles, pp. 60–69. Washington: Smithsonian Institution Press.
1990b   History of Research in Archeology. In *Handbook of North American Indians,* vol. 7, *North-*

west Coast, edited by Wayne Suttles, pp. 107–15. Washington: Smithsonian Institution Press.

Carstens, Peter
1991   *The Queen's People: A Study of Hegemony, Coercion, and Accommodation Among the Okanagan of Canada.* Toronto: University of Toronto Press.

Clutesi, G.
1969   *Potlatch.* Sidney, B.C.: Gray's Publishing.

Codere, Helen
1950   *Fighting With Property.* Monographs of the American Ethnological Society, no. 18.
1956   The Amiable Side of Kwakiutl Life. *American Anthropologist* 58:334–51.
1957   Kwakiutl Society: Rank Without Class. *American Anthropologist* 59:473–86.
1990   Kwakiutl: Traditional Culture. In *Handbook of North American Indians,* vol. 7, *Northwest Coast,* edited by Wayne Suttles, pp. 359–77. Washington: Smithsonian Institution Press.

Cole, Douglas, and Ira Chaikin
1990   *An Iron Hand upon the People: The Law Against the Potlatch on the Northwest Coast.* Seattle: University of Washington Press.

Cole, Douglas, and David Darling
1990   History of the Early Period. In *Handbook of North American Indians,* vol. 7, *Northwest Coast,* edited by Wayne Suttles, pp. 119–34. Washington: Smithsonian Institution Press.

Collins, June McC.
1974   *Valley of the Spirits.* Seattle: University of Washington Press.

Cove, John W.
1977   Back to Square One: A Reexamination of Tsimshian Cousin Marriage. *Anthropologica* 18:153–78.

Croes, Dale R., ed.
1976   *The Excavation of Water-Saturated Archaeological Sites (Wet Sites) on the Northwest Coast of North America.* Ottawa: National Museum of Man.

Cybulski, Jerome S.
1990a   History of Research in Physical Anthropology. In *Handbook of North American Indians,* vol. 7, *Northwest Coast,* edited by Wayne Sut-

tles, pp. 116–18. Washington: Smithsonian Institution Press.
1990b   Human Biology. In *Handbook of North American Indians,* vol. 7, *Northwest Coast,* edited by Wayne Suttles, pp. 52–59. Washington: Smithsonian Institution Press.

De Laguna, Frederica
1960   *The Story of a Tlingit Community.* Bureau of American Ethnology Bulletin 172. Washington.
1972   *Under Mount Saint Elias: The History and Culture of the Yakutat Tlingit.* 3 pts. Smithsonian Contributions to Anthropology, no. 7. Washington.
1983   Aboriginal Tlingit Sociopolitical Organization. In *The Development of Political Organization in Native North America,* edited by E. Tooker, pp. 71–85. Washington: American Ethnological Society.
1987   Atna and Tlingit Shamanism: Witchcraft on the Northwest Coast. *Arctic Anthropology* 24(1):84–100.
1988   Potlatch Ceremonialism on the Northwest Coast. In *Crossroads of Continents: Cultures of Siberia and Alaska,* edited by William Fitzhugh and Aron Crowell, pp. 271–80. Washington: Smithsonian Institution Press.
1990   Tlingit. In *Handbook of North American Indians,* vol. 7, *Northwest Coast,* edited by Wayne Suttles, pp. 203–28. Washington: Smithsonian Institution Press.

Donald, Leland
1983   Was Nuu-chah-nueth-aht (Nootka) Society Based on Slave Labor? In *The Development of Political Organization in Native North America,* edited by E. Tooker, pp. 108–19. Washington: American Ethnological Society.
1987   Slave Raiding on the North Pacific Coast. In *Native People, Native Lands,* edited by Bruce A. Cox, pp. 161–72. Ottawa: Carleton University.

Donald, Leland, and Donald H. Mitchell
1975   Some Correlates of Local Group Rank Among the Southern Kwakiutl. *Ethnology* 14:325–46.

Drucker, Philip
1950   Culture Element Distributions: XXVI, Northwest Coast. *Anthropological Records* 9:157–294.
1951   *The Northern and Central Nootkan Tribes.* Bureau of American Ethnology Bulletin 144. Washington.

1955   *Indians of the Northwest Coast.* New York: McGraw-Hill.

1958   *The Native Brotherhoods.* Bureau of American Ethnology Bulletin 168. Washington.

1965   *Cultures of the North Pacific Coast.* San Francisco: Chandler.

1983   Ecology and Political Organization on the Northwest Coast of America. In *The Development of Political Organization in Native North America,* edited by E. Tooker, pp. 86–96. Washington: American Ethnological Society.

Drucker, Philip, and Robert F. Heizer
1967   *To Make My Name Good: A Reexamination of the Kwakiutl Potlatch.* Berkeley: University of California Press.

Duff, Wilson
1953   *The Upper Stalo Indians of the Fraser Valley, British Columbia.* Anthropology in British Columbia Memoirs, no. 1.

1964   *The Indian History of British Columbia.* Vol. 1, *The Impact of the White Man.* British Columbia Provincial Museum, Anthropology in British Columbia, Memoir 5. Victoria.

Dundes, Alan
1979   Heads or Tails: A Psychoanalytic Study of Potlatch. *Journal of Psychological Anthropology* 2:395–424.

Dunn, John A., and Arnold Booth
1990   Tsimshian of Metlakatla, Alaska. In *Handbook of North American Indians,* vol. 7, *Northwest Coast,* edited by Wayne Suttles, pp. 294–97. Washington: Smithsonian Institution Press.

Efrat, Barbara S., and W. J. Langlois, eds.
1978   nu. tka. The History and Survival of Nootkan Culture and Contemporary Accounts of Nootkan Culture. *Sound Heritage* 7(2):1–65.

Etkin, Carol E.
1988   Sechelt Indian Band: An Analysis of a New Form of Native Self-Government. *Canadian Journal of Native Studies* 8(1):73–105.

Ferguson, Brian
1983   Warfare and Redistributive Exchange on the Northwest Coast. In *The Development of Political Organization in Native North America,* edited by E. Tooker, pp. 133–47. Washington: American Ethnological Society.

1984   A Reexamination of the Causes of Northwest Coast Warfare. In *Warfare, Culture, and Environment,* edited by R. B. Ferguson, pp. 267–328. New York: Academic Press.

Fisher, Robin
1975   An Exercise in Futility: The Joint Commission on Indian Land in British Columbia, 1875–1880. *Historical Papers/Communications historiques* (1975), 79–94.

1976   Arms and Men on the Northwest Coast. *BC Studies* 29:3–18.

1977   *Contact and Conflict: Indian-European Relations in British Columbia, 1774–1890.* Vancouver: University of British Columbia Press.

1979   Cook and the Nootka. In *Captain James Cook and His Times,* edited by Robin Fisher and Hugh Johnston, pp. 81–98. Vancouver: Douglas and McIntyre.

1980   The Impact of European Settlement on the Indigenous Peoples of Australia, New Zealand, and British Columbia: Some Comparative Dimensions. *Canadian Ethnic Studies* 12(1):1–14.

1981   Indian Warfare and Two Frontiers: A Comparison of British Columbia and Washington Territory During the Early Years of Settlement. *Pacific Historical Review* 50:31–51.

Fladmark, Knut R.
1975   *A Paleoecological Model for Northwest Coast Prehistory.* Ottawa: National Museum of Man.

1980–81a British Columbia Archaeology in the 1970s. *BC Studies* 48:11–20, 136–56.

1980–81b Paleo-Indian Artifacts from the Peace River District. *BC Studies* 48:124–56.

1982   An Introduction to the Prehistory of British Columbia. *Canadian Journal of Archaeology* 6:95–156.

Fladmark, Knut R., Kenneth M. Ames, and Patricia D. Sutherland
1990   Prehistory of the Northern Coast of British Columbia. In *Handbook of North American Indians,* vol. 7, *Northwest Coast,* edited by Wayne Suttles, pp. 229–39. Washington: Smithsonian Institution Press.

Ford, Clellan S.
1941   *Smoke from Their Fires.* New Haven: Yale University Press.

Furst, Peter T.
1989   The Water of Life: Symbolism and Natural

History on the Northwest Coast. *Dialectical Anthropology* 14:95–116.

Garfield, Viola E.
1939   Tsimshian Clan and Society. *Washington University Publications in Anthropology* 7:167–349.

Garfield, Viola E., et al.
1951   *The Tsimshian: Their Arts and Music.* American Ethnological Society Publications, no. 18.

Gerber, Peter R., and Maximillien Bruggman
1989   *Indians of the Northwest Coast.* New York: Facts on File.

Gibson, James R.
1976   Russian Sources for the Ethnohistory of the Pacific Coast of North America in the 18th and 19th Centuries. *Western Canadian Journal of Anthropology* 6:91–115.

Gladstone, Percy
1953   Native Indians and the Fishing Industry of British Columbia. *Canadian Journal of Economics and Political Science* 19:20–34.

Goldman, Irving
1975   *The Mouth of Heaven: An Introduction to Kwakiutl Religious Thought.* New York: Wiley.

Gormly, Mary
1977   Early Culture Contact on the Northwest Coast, 1774–1795: Analysis of Spanish Source Material. *Northwest Anthropological Research Notes* 11:1–80.

Gough, Barry M.
1978a   Nootka Sound in James Cook's Pacific World. *Sound Heritage* 7(1):1–31.
1978b   Official Uses of Violence Against Northwest Coast Indians in Colonial British Columbia. In *Pacific Northwest Themes: Historical Essays in Honor of Keith A. Murray,* edited by James W. Scott, pp. 43–69. Bellingham, Wash.: Center for Pacific Northwest Studies.
1980   *Distant Dominion: Britain and the Northwest Coast of North America, 1579–1809.* Vancouver: University of British Columbia Press.
1982a   The Indian Policies of Great Britain and the United States in the Pacific Northwest in the Mid-nineteenth Century. *Canadian Journal of Native Studies* 2(2):321–37.
1982b   New Light on Haida Chiefship: The Case of

Edenshaw, 1850–1853. *Ethnohistory* 29:131–39.
1984   *Gunboat Frontier: British Maritime Authority and Northwest Coast Indians, 1846–1890.* Vancouver: University of British Columbia Press.

Grumet, Robert Stephen
1975   Changes in Coast Tsimshian Redistributive Activities in the Fort Simpson Region of British Columbia, 1788–1862. *Ethnohistory* 23:295–318.

Guédon, Marie-Françoise
1982   Problèmes de definition du chamanisme chez les Amerindiens de la Côte nord-ouest, l'exemple des Tsimshian. *Culture* 2(3):129–44.
1984   La formation des sociétés secrètes amérindiennes de la Côte nord-ouest. *Recherches amérindiennes au Québec* 14(2):35–46.

Gunther, Erna
1972   *Indian Life on the Northwest Coast of North America as Seen by the Early Explorers and Fur Traders During the Last Decades of the Eighteenth Century.* Chicago: University of Chicago Press.

Haberland, Wolfgang
1987   Nine Bella Coolas in Germany. In *Indians and Europe: An Interdisciplinary Collection of Essays,* edited by Christian Feest, pp. 337–74. Aachen: Rader Verlag.

Haig-Brown, Alan
1983   British Columbia Indian Languages: A Crisis of Silence. *BC Studies* 57:57–67.

Halpin, Marjorie M., and Margaret Seguin
1990   Tsimshian Peoples: Southern Tsimshian, Coast Tsimshian, Nishga, and Gitskan. In *Handbook of North American Indians,* vol. 7, *Northwest Coast,* edited by Wayne Suttles, pp. 267–84. Washington: Smithsonian Institution Press.

Hamori-Torok, Charles
1990   Haisla. In *Handbook of North American Indians,* vol. 7, *Northwest Coast,* edited by Wayne Suttles, pp. 306–11. Washington: Smithsonian Institution Press.

Harkin, Michael
1988   History, Narrativity, and Temporality: Examples from the Northwest Coast. *Ethnohistory* 35:99–130.
1990   Mortuary Practices and the Category of the

Person Among the Heiltsuk. *Arctic Anthropology* 27:87–108.

Hawthorn, H. B., C. B. Belshaw, and S. M. Jamieson
1958   *The Indians of British Columbia: A Study of Contemporary Social Adjustment.* Toronto: University of Toronto Press.

Hayden, Brian, and June M. Ryder
1991   Prehistoric cultural collapse in the Lillooet area. *American Antiquity* 56:50–65.

Hester, James J., and Sarah M. Nelson, eds.
1978   *Studies in Bella Bella Prehistory.* Burnaby, B.C.: Simon Fraser University.

Hewlett, Edward Sleigh
1973   The Chilcotin Uprising of 1864. *BC Studies* 19:50–72.

Hilton, Susanne F.
1990   Haihais, Bella Bella, and Oowekeeno. In *Handbook of North American Indians,* vol. 7, *Northwest Coast,* edited by Wayne Suttles, pp. 312–22. Washington: Smithsonian Institution Press.

Hobler, Philip M.
1990   Prehistory of the Central Coast of British Columbia. In *Handbook of North American Indians,* vol. 7, *Northwest Coast,* edited by Wayne Suttles, pp. 298–305. Washington: Smithsonian Institution Press.

Holm, Bill
1990   Kwakiutl: Winter Ceremonies. In *Handbook of North American Indians,* vol. 7, *Northwest Coast,* edited by Wayne Suttles, pp. 378–86. Washington: Smithsonian Institution Press.

Howay, F. W.
1925   Indian Attacks upon Maritime Traders of the North-West Coast, 1785–1805. *Canadian Historical Review* 6:287–309.

Huelsback, David R.
1988   Whaling in the Precontact Economy of the Central Northwest Coast. *Arctic Anthropology* 25(1):1–15.

Hymes, Dell
1990   Mythology. In *Handbook of North American Indians,* vol. 7, *Northwest Coast,* edited by Wayne Suttles, pp. 593–601. Washington: Smithsonian Institution Press.

Ignace, Marianne Boelsher
1991   Haida public discourse and its social context.

Canadian Journal of Native Studies 11(1):113–35.

Inglis, Gordon B., Douglas R. Hudson, Barbara K. Rigsby, and Bruce Rigsby
1990   Tsimshian of British Columbia Since 1900. In *Handbook of North American Indians,* vol. 7, *Northwest Coast,* edited by Wayne Suttles, pp. 285–93. Washington: Smithsonian Institution Press.

Inglis, Richard I., and George MacDonald, eds.
1979   *Skeena River Prehistory.* Ottawa: National Museum of Man.

Jacknis, Ira
1990   Authenticity and the Mungo Martin House, Victoria, B.C.: Visual and Verbal Sources. *Arctic Anthropology* 27(2)1–12.

Kan, Sergei
1983   Words that Heal the Soul: Analysis of the Tlingit Potlatch Oratory. *Arctic Anthropology* 20(2):47–59.
1986   The 19th-century Tlingit Potlatch: A New Perspective. *American Ethnologist* 13:191–212.
1989a   Cohorts, Generations, and Their Culture: The Tlingit Potlatch in the 1980s. *Anthropos* 84:405–22.
1989b   Memory Eternal: Orthodox Christianity and the Tlingit Mortuary Complex. *Arctic Anthropology* 24(1):19–31.
1989c   *Symbolic Immortality: The Tlingit Potlatch of the Nineteenth Century.* Washington: Smithsonian Institution Press.
1989d   Why the Aristocrats were "Heavy," or How Ethnopsychology Legitimized Inequality Among the Tlingit. *Dialectical Anthropology* 14:81–94.
1990   The sacred and the secular: Tlingit potlatch songs outside the potlatch. *American Indian Quarterly* 14:355–66.
1991   Shamanism and Christianity: Modern-Day Tlingit Elders Look at the Past. *Ethnohistory* 38(4):363–87.

Kennedy, Dorothy I. D., and Randall T. Bouchard
1990a   Bella Coola. In *Handbook of North American Indians,* vol. 7, *Northwest Coast,* edited by Wayne Suttles, pp. 323–39. Washington: Smithsonian Institution Press.
1990b   Northern Coast Salish. In *Handbook of North American Indians,* vol. 7, *Northwest Coast,*

edited by Wayne Suttles, pp. 441–52. Washington: Smithsonian Institution Press.

Kenyon, Sally
1980   *The Kyoquot Way: A Study of a West Coast (Nootkan) Community.* Mercury Series, Canadian Ethnology Service Paper 61. Ottawa: National Museum of Man.

Kew, J. E. Michael
1990a   Central and Southern Coast Salish Ceremonies Since 1900. In *Handbook of North American Indians,* vol. 7, *Northwest Coast,* edited by Wayne Suttles, pp. 476–80. Washington: Smithsonian Institution Press.
1990b   History of British Columbia Since 1849. In *Handbook of North American Indians,* vol. 7, *Northwest Coast,* edited by Wayne Suttles, pp. 159–68. Washington: Smithsonian Institution Press.

Kinkade, M. Dale
1990   History of Research in Linguistics. In *Handbook of North American Indians,* vol. 7, *Northwest Coast,* edited by Wayne Suttles, pp. 98–106. Washington: Smithsonian Institution Press.

Knight, Rolf
1978   *Indians at Work: An Informal History of Native Indian Labour in British Columbia, 1858–1930.* Vancouver: New Star Books.

Kobrinsky, Vernon H.
1975   Dynamics of the Fort Rupert Class Struggle. In *Papers in Honor of Harry Hawthorn,* edited by V. Serl and H. Taylor, pp. 32–59. Bellingham: Western Washington State College Press.

Kolstee, Anton F.
1982   *Bella Coola Indian Music.* Mercury Series, Canadian Ethnology Service Paper 83. Ottawa: National Museum of Man.
1988   Historical and Musical Significance of Northwest Coast Indian Hámáca Songs. *Canadian Journal of Native Studies* 8(2):173–82.

Korovkin, M., and G. Lanoue
1988   On the Substantiality of Form: Interpreting Symbolic Expression in the Paradigm of Social Organization. *Comparative Studies in Society and History* 30:613–48.

Krause, Aurel
1956   *The Tlingit Indians.* Translated by Erna Gunther. Seattle: University of Washington Press.

Langdon, Steve
1979   Comparative Tlingit and Haida Adaptation to the West Coast of the Prince of Wales Archipelago. *Ethnology* 18:101–20.

La Violette, Forrest E.
1973   *The Struggle for Survival: Indian Cultures and the Protestant Ethic in B.C.* Toronto: University of Toronto Press.

Legros, Dominique
1984   Commerce entre tlingits et athapaskans tutchones au XIXe siècle. *Recherches amérindiennes au Québec* 14(2):11–24.

Lévi-Strauss, Claude
1967   The Story of Asdiwal. In *The Structural Study of Myth and Totemism,* edited by E. Leach, pp. 1–47. London: Tavistock.

Lewis, Claudia Louise
1970   *Indian Families of the Northwest Coast: The Impact of Change.* Chicago: University of Chicago Press.

Lohse, E. S., and Frances Sundt
1990   History of Research: Museum Collections. In *Handbook of North American Indians,* vol. 7, *Northwest Coast,* edited by Wayne Suttles, pp. 88–97. Washington: Smithsonian Institution Press.

MacDonald, George F.
1989   *Chiefs of the Sea and Sky: Haida Heritage Sites of the Queen Charlotte Islands.* Vancouver: University of British Columbia Press.

McDonald, James A.
1983   An Historic Event in the Political Economy of the Tsimshian: Information on the Ownership of the Zimacord District. *BC Studies* 57:24–37.
1987   The Marginalization of the Tsimshian Cultural Ecology: The Seasonal Cycle. In *Native People, Native Lands,* edited by Bruce A. Cox, pp. 199–218. Ottawa: Carleton University.
1990   Bleeding Day and Night: The construction of the Grand Trunk Pacific Railway across Tsimshian reserve lands. *Canadian Journal of Native Studies* 10(1):33–69.

McFeat, Tom, ed.
1966   *Indians of the North Pacific Coast.* Toronto: McClelland and Stewart.

McIlwraith, Thomas F.
1948   *The Bella Coola Indians.* 2 vols. Toronto: University of Toronto Press.

M'Gonigle, Michael
1988   Native Rights and Environmental Sustainability: Lessons from the British Columbian Wilderness. *Canadian Journal of Native Studies* 8(1):107–30.

Maranda, Lynn
1984   *Coast Salish Gambling Games.* Canadian Ethnology Service Paper 93. Ottawa: National Museum of Man.

Marr, Carolyn J.
1990   Photographers and Their Subjects on the Southern Northwest Coast: Motivations and Responses. *Arctic Anthropology* 27(2):13–26.

Miller, Jay
1981   Moieties and Cultural Amnesia: Manipulation of Knowledge in a Pacific Northwest Coast Indian Community. *Arctic Anthropology* 18: 23–32.

Miller, Jay, and Carol M. Eastman, eds.
1984   *The Tsimshian and Their Neighbors of the North Pacific Coast.* Seattle: University of Washington Press.

Mitchell, Donald H.
1981   Sebassa's Men. In *The World Is as Sharp as a Knife,* edited by D. N. Abbott, pp. 79–86. Victoria, B.C.: Provincial Museum.
1983a   Seasonal Settlements, Village Aggregations, and Political Autonomy on the Central Northwest Coast. In *The Development of Political Organization in Native North America,* edited by E. Tooker, pp. 97–107. Washington: American Ethnological Society.
1983b   Tribes and Chiefdoms of the Northwest Coast: The Tsimshian Case. In *Evolution of Maritime Cultures on the Northeast and the Northwest Coast of America,* edited by R. J. Nash, pp. 57–65. Burnaby, B.C.: Simon Fraser University.
1984   Predatory Warfare, Social Status, and the North Pacific Slave Trade. *Ethnology* 23:39–48.
1990   Prehistory of the Coasts of Southern British Columbia and Northern Washington. In *Handbook of North American Indians,* vol. 7, *Northwest Coast,* edited by Wayne Suttles, pp. 340–58. Washington: Smithsonian Institution Press.

Mooney, Kathleen
1976a   Social Distance and Exchange: The Coast Salish Case. *Ethnology* 15:323–46.
1976b   Urban and Reserve Coast Salish Employment. *Journal of Anthropological Research* 32:390–410.
1978   The Effects of Rank and Wealth on Exchange Among the Coast Salish. *Ethnology* 17:391–406.

Morinis, E. A.
1982   Skid Row Indians and the Politics of Self. *Culture* 2(3):93–106.

Murdock, George Peter
1936   *Rank and Potlatch Among the Haida.* Yale University Publications in Anthropology, no. 13.

Murray, Rebecca Anne
1982   *Analysis of Artifacts from Four Duke Point Area Sites, near Nanaimo, B.C.* Archaeological Survey of Canada Paper 113. Ottawa: National Museum of Man.

Nelson, Charles M.
1990   Prehistory of the Puget Sound Region. In *Handbook of North American Indians,* vol. 7, *Northwest Coast,* edited by Wayne Suttles, pp. 481–84. Washington: Smithsonian Institution Press.

Newton, N.
1975   On Survivals of Ancient Astronomical Ideas Among the Peoples of the Northwest Coast. *BC Studies* 26:16–38.

Oberg, Kalervo
1973   *The Social Economy of the Tlingit Indians.* Seattle: University of Washington Press.

Orans, Martin
1975   Domesticating the Functional Dragon: An Analysis of Piddocke's Potlatch. *American Anthropologist* 77:312–28.

Patterson, E. Palmer, II
1984   A Decade of Change: Origins of the Nishga and Tsimshian Land Protests in the 1880s. *Revue d'études canadiènnes/Journal of Canadian Studies* 18(3):40–54.
1985   Early Nishga-European Contact to 1860: A People for "Those who Talk of the Efficiency of Moral Lectures to Subdue the Obduracy of the Heart." *Anthropologica* 20.

1988   Early Nishga-European Contact to 1860. *Anthropologica* 25:193–220.

1989   George Kinzadah-Simoogit in His Times. *BC Studies* 82:16–38.

Pearsall, Marion

1949   Contributions of Early Explorers and Traders to the Ethnography of the Northwest. *Pacific Northwest Quarterly* 40:316–26.

1980   *The Nootka Connection: Europe and the Northwest Coast 1790–1795.* Vancouver: Douglas and MacIntyre.

Piddocke, Stuart

1965   The Potlatch System of the Southern Kwakiutl. *Southwestern Journal of Anthropology* 21: 244–64.

Pokotylo, D. L., and P. D. Froese

1983   Archaeological Evidence for Prehistoric Root Gathering in the Southern Interior Plateau of British Columbia: A Case Study for Upper Hat Creek Valley. *Canadian Journal of Archaeology* 7:127–57.

Ray, Verne F.

1939   Cultural Relations in the Plateau of Northwestern America. *Southwest Museum Publications* 3:1–154.

Reid, Martine J.

1984   Le mythe de Baxbakwalanuxsiwae: Une affaire de famille. *Recherches amérindiennes au Québec* 14(2): 25–34.

Reid, Susan

1979   The Kwakiutl Maneater. *Anthropologica* 21: 247–75.

Renker, Ann M., and Erna Gunther

1990   Makah. In *Handbook of North American Indians,* vol. 7, *Northwest Coast,* edited by Wayne Suttles, pp. 422–30. Washington: Smithsonian Institution Press.

Rettig, Andrew

1980   A Nativistic Movement at Metlakatla Mission. *BC Studies* 46:28–39.

Riches, David

1979   Ecological Variation on the Northwest Coast. In *Social and Ecological Systems,* edited by R. Ellen and P. Burnham, pp. 145–66. London: Academic Press.

1984   Hunting, Herding, and Potlatching: Towards a Sociological Account of Prestige. *Man* 19: 234–51.

Ringel, Gail

1979   The Kwakiutl Potlatch: History, Economics, and Symbols. *Ethnohistory* 26:347–62.

Robinson, Michael

1978   *Sea Otter Chiefs.* Vancouver: Friendly Cove Press.

Rohner, Ronald P.

1967   *The People of Gilford: A Contemporary Kwakiutl Village.* Bulletin 225. Ottawa: National Museum of Canada.

Rohner, Ronald P., and E. C. Rohner

1970   *The Kwakiutl: Indians of British Columbia.* New York: Holt, Rinehart and Winston.

Rosman, Abraham, and Paula G. Rubel

1971   *Feasting with Mine Enemy: Rank and Exchange Among Northwest Coast Societies.* New York: Columbia University Press.

1972   The Potlatch: A Structural Analysis. *American Anthropologist* 74:658–71.

1986   The Evolution of Central Northwest Coast Societies. *Journal of Anthropological Research* 42:557–72.

Ruyle, Eugene

1973   Slavery, Surplus, and Stratification on the Northwest Coast: The Ethnoenergetics of an Incipient Stratification System. *Current Anthropology* 14:603–31.

Sapir, Edward, and M. Swadesh

1955   *Native Accounts of Nootka Ethnography.* Research Publication 1. Bloomington: Research Center in Anthropology, Folklore, and Linguistics, Indiana University.

Seguin, Margaret

1985   *Interpretive Contexts for Traditional and Current Coast Tsimshian Feasts.* Mercury Series, Canadian Ethnology Service Paper 98. Ottawa: National Museum of Man.

Seguin, Margaret, ed.

1984   *The Tsimshian: Images of the Past; Views for the Present.* Vancouver: University of British Columbia Press.

Sheppard, Janice R.

1989   Image and Form in a Tsimshian Narrative. *Arctic Anthropology* 26(2):1–12.

Smyly, C.
1981   Anthony Island Totems. *Canadian Geographic* 101(5):26–34.

Snyder, Sally
1975   Quest for the Sacred in Northern Puget Sound. *Ethnology* 14:149–61.

Spradley, James P., ed.
1969   *Guests Never Leave Hungry: The Autobiography of James Sewid, a Kwakiutl Indian.* New Haven: Yale University Press. Reprint. McGill-Queen's University Press, 1972.

Stanbury, William T.
1975   Indians in British Columbia: Level of Income, Welfare and Dependency and the Poverty Rate. *BC Studies:* 39–64.

Stanbury, William T., and J. Siegel
1975   *Success and Failure: Indians in Urban Society.* Vancouver: University of British Columbia Press.

Stearns, Mary Lee
1981   *Haida Culture in Custody: The Masset Band.* Seattle: University of Washington Press.
1990   Haida Since 1960. In *Handbook of North American Indians,* vol. 7, *Northwest Coast,* edited by Wayne Suttles, pp. 261–66. Washington: Smithsonian Institution Press.

Steltzer, U.
1984   *A Haida Potlatch.* Seattle: University of Washington Press.

Stewart, Hilary
1987   *The Adventures and Sufferings of John R. Jewitt: Captive of Maquinna.* Vancouver: Douglas and McIntyre.

Suttles, Wayne
1960   Affinal Ties, Subsistence, and Prestige Among the Coast Salish. *American Anthropologist* 62: 296–305.
1962   Variation in Habitat and Culture in the Northwest Coast. In *Proceedings of the 34th Congress of Americanists,* pp. 522–37.
1968   Coping with Abundance. In *Man the Hunter,* edited by Richard Lee and Irven De Vore, pp. 59–69. Chicago: Aldine.
1987   *Coast Salish Essays.* Vancouver: Talon Books.
1990a   Central Coast Salish. In *Handbook of North American Indians,* vol. 7, *Northwest Coast,* edited by Wayne Suttles, pp. 453–75. Washington: Smithsonian Institution Press.
1990b   Environment. In *Handbook of North American Indians,* vol. 7, *Northwest Coast,* edited by Wayne Suttles, pp. 16–29. Washington: Smithsonian Institution Press.
1990c   History of Research: Early Sources. In *Handbook of North American Indians,* vol. 7, *Northwest Coast,* edited by Wayne Suttles, pp. 70–72. Washington: Smithsonian Institution Press.
1990d   Introduction. In *Handbook of North American Indians,* vol. 7, *Northwest Coast,* edited by Wayne Suttles, pp. 1–15. Washington: Smithsonian Institution Press.

Suttles, Wayne, ed.
1990   *Northwest Coast.* Vol. 7, *Handbook of North American Indians.* Washington: Smithsonian Institution Press.

Suttles, Wayne, and Aldona C. Jonaitis
1990   History of Research in Ethnology. In *Handbook of North American Indians,* vol. 7, *Northwest Coast,* edited by Wayne Suttles, pp. 72–87. Washington: Smithsonian Institution Press.

Swanton, John R.
1909   *Contributions to the Ethnology of the Haida.* Memoirs of the American Museum of Natural History, no. 8. New York.

Teit, James A.
1898   Traditions of the Thompson River Indians. *Memoirs of the American Folklore Society* 6:1–137.
1900   The Thompson Indians. *Memoirs of the American Museum of Natural History* 2:163–392.
1906   The Lillooet Indians. *Memoirs of the American Museum of Natural History* 4:193–300.
1909   The Shuswap. *Memoirs of the American Museum of Natural History* 4:447–758.

Tepper, Leslie, ed.
1991   *The Bella Coola Valley: Harlan I. Smith's Fieldwork Photography, 1920–1924.* Mercury Series, Canadian Ethnology Service Paper 123. Ottawa: Canadian Museum of Civilization.

Thomas, A.
1981–82   Photography of the Indian: Concept and Practice on the Northwest Coast. *BC Studies* 52:61–85.

Thompson, Laurence C., and M. Dale Kinkade
1990   Languages. In *Handbook of North American*

Indians, vol. 7, *Northwest Coast,* edited by Wayne Suttles, pp. 30–51. Washington: Smithsonian Institution Press.

Turner, N. J.
1988   "The Importance of a Rose": Evaluating the Cultural Significance of Plants in Thompson and Lillooet Interior Salish. *American Anthropologist* 90:272–90.

Turney-High, H. H.
1941   *Ethnography of the Kutenai.* Memoirs of the American Anthropological Association 56. Washington.

Van den Brink, J. H.
1974   *The Haida Indians: Cultural Change Mainly Between 1876–1970.* Leiden: E. J. Brill.

Vayda, Andrew Peter
1961   A Reexamination of Northwest Coast Economic Systems. *Transactions of the New York Academy of Sciences* 23:618–24.

Walens, Stanley
1981   *Feasting with Cannibals: Metaphor and Morality in 19th Century Kwakiutl Culture.* Princeton: Princeton University Press.
1985   Analogic Causality and the Power of Masks. In *The Power of Symbols: Masks and Masquerade in the Americas,* edited by N. Ross Crumrine and Marjorie Halpin, pp. 70–78.

Vancouver: University of British Columbia Press.

Weber, Ronald L.
1985   Photographs as Ethnographic Documents. *Arctic Anthropology* 22(1):67–78.

Webster, Gloria Cranmer
1990a   Kwakiutl Since 1980. In *Handbook of North American Indians,* vol. 7, *Northwest Coast,* edited by Wayne Suttles, pp. 387–90. Washington: Smithsonian Institution Press.
1990b   The U'mista Cultural Centre. *Massachusetts Review* 31:132–43.

Weinberg, Daniela
1965   Models of Southern Kwakiutl Social Organization. *General Systems* 10:169–81.

Wells, Oliver N.
1987   *The Chilliwacks and Their Neighbors.* Vancouver: Talon Books.

Woodcock, George
1977   *Peoples of the Coast: The Indians of the Pacific Northwest.* Bloomington: Indiana University Press.

Yarmie, Andrew H.
1968   Smallpox and the British Columbia Indians: Epidemic of 1862. *British Columbia Library Association Quarterly* 31:13–21.

Section Nine

♦

NORTHERN ATHAPASKANS
OF THE WESTERN
SUBARCTIC

Acheson, Ann W.
1981   Old Crow, Yukon Territory. In *Handbook of North American Indians,* vol. 6, *Subarctic,* edited by June Helm, pp. 694–703. Washington: Smithsonian Institution Press.

Asch, Michael I.
1975   Social Context and the Musical Analysis of Slavey Drum Dances. *Ethnomusicology* 19: 245–57.
1977   The Dene Economy. In *Dene Nation—The Colony Within,* edited by Mel Watkins, pp. 47–61. Toronto: University of Toronto Press.
1980   Steps Towards the Analysis of Aboriginal Athapaskan Social Organization. *Arctic Anthropology* 17(2):46–51.
1981   Slavey. In *Handbook of North American Indians,* vol. 6, *Subarctic,* edited by June Helm, pp. 338–49. Washington: Smithsonian Institution Press.
1988   *Kinship and the Drum Dance in a Northern Dene Community.* Edmonton: Boreal Institute for Northern Studies.
1989   Wildlife: Defining the Animals the Dene Hunt and the Settlement of Aboriginal Rights Claims. *Canadian Public Policy/Analyses de politiques* 15(2): 205–19.

Balikci, Asen
1963   *Vunta Kutchin Social Change.* Northern Coordination and Research Centre Publication 63(3). Ottawa: Department of Northern Affairs and National Resources, Canada.
1988   Old Crow: Ethnographie et histoire. *Recherches amérindiennes au Québec* 16(1):5–28.

Basso, Ellen B.
1978   The Enemy of Every Tribe: "Bushman" Images in Northern Athapaskan Narratives. *American Ethnologist* 5:690–709.

Basso, Keith H.
1972   Ice and Travel Among the Fort Norman Slave: Folk Taxonomies and Cultural Rules. *Language in Society* 1(1):31–49.

Birket-Smith, Kaj
1930   Contributions to Chipewyan Ethnology. *Report of the Fifth Thule Expedition* 6(3):1–114.

Bishop, Charles A.
1980   Kwah: A Carrier Chief. In *Old Trails and New Directions,* edited by C. M. Judd and A. J.

Ray, pp. 191–206. Toronto: University of Toronto Press.

1983   Limiting Access to Limited Goods. The Origins of Stratification in Interior British Columbia. In *The Development of Political Organization in Native North America,* edited by E. Tooker, pp. 148–61. Washington: American Ethnological Society.

1987   Coast-Interior Exchange: The Origins of Stratification in Northwestern North America. *Arctic Anthropology* 24(1):72–83.

Bone, Robert M., and Robert J. Mahnic
1984   Norman Wells: The Oil Center of the Northwest Territories. *Arctic* 37:53–60.

Bone, Robert M., Earl N. Shannon, and Steward Raby
1973   *The Chipewyan of the Stony Rapids Region: A Study of Their Changing World with Special Attention Focused upon Caribou.* Mawdsley Memoir 1. Saskatoon: Institute for Northern Studies, University of Saskatchewan.

Broch, Harald Beyer
1983   The Bluefish River Incident. In *The Politics of Indianness,* edited by Adrian Tanner, pp. 137–96. St. Johns: Memorial University of Newfoundland, Institute for Social and Economic Research.

1986   *Woodland Trappers: Hare Indians of Northwest Canada.* Bergen Studies in Social Anthropology, no. 35. Bergen, Norway: Department of Anthropology, University of Bergen.

Brody, Hugh
1981   *Maps and Dreams: A Journey into the Lives and Lands of the Beaver Indians of Northwest Canada.* New York: Pelican Books.

Brumbach, Hetty Jo, Robert Jarvenpa, and Clifford Buell
1982   An Ethnoarchaeological Approach to Chipewyan Adaptations in the Late Fur Trade Period. *Arctic Anthropology* 19(1):1–50.

Cinq-Mars, J.
1979   Bluefish Cave I: A Late Pleistocene Eastern Beringian Cave Deposit in the Northern Yukon. *Canadian Journal of Anthropology* 3:1–32.

Christian, Jane, and Peter M. Gardner
1977   *The Individual in Northern Dene Thought and Communication: A Study in Sharing and Diversity.* Mercury Series, Canadian Ethnology Service Paper 35. Ottawa: National Museum of Man.

Clark, Annette McFadyen, ed.
1975   *Proceedings: Northern Athapaskan Conference, 1971.* 2 vols. Mercury Series, Canadian Ethnology Service Paper 27. Ottawa: National Museum of Man.

Clark, Donald W.
1982   The Vanishing Edge of Today in the Northern District of Mackenzie: A View from Field Archaeology. *Canadian Journal of Anthropology* 2:107–28.

1983a   Is There a Northern Cordillera Tradition? *Canadian Journal of Archaeology* 7:23–48.

1983b   Mackenzie—River to Nowhere? *Musk-Ox* 33: 1–9.

Clark, Donald W., and Annette McFadyen Clark
1983   Paleo-Indians and Fluted Points: Subarctic Alternatives. *Plains Anthropologist* 28–102: 283–92.

Clark, Donald W., and Richard E. Morlan
1982   Western Subarctic Prehistory: Twenty Years Later. *Canadian Journal of Archaeology* 6:79–93.

Cohen, Ronald, and James W. Van Stone
1964   Dependency and Self-sufficiency in Chipewyan Stories. Anthropological Series 62. *National Museum of Canada Bulletin* 194:29–55.

Crow, John R., and Philip R. Obley
1981   Han. In *Handbook of North American Indians,* vol. 6, *Subarctic,* edited by June Helm, pp. 506–13. Washington: Smithsonian Institution Press.

Cruikshank, Julie
1981   Legend and Landscape: Convergence of Oral and Scientific Traditions in the Yukon Territory. *Arctic Anthropology* 18(2):67–93.

1984   Tagish and Tlingit Place Names in the Southern Lakes Region, Yukon Territory. *Canoma* 10(1):30–35.

1988a   Myth and Tradition as Narrative Framework: Oral Histories from Northern Canada. *International Journal of Oral History* 9:198–214.

1988b   Telling About Culture: Changing Traditions in Subarctic Anthropology. *Northern Review* 1:27–40.

1990   Getting the Words Right: Perspectives on Naming and Places in Athapaskan Oral History. *Arctic Anthropology* 27(1):52–65.

1991   *Life Lived Like a Story: Life Histories of Three Yukon Elders.* Vancouver: University of British Columbia Press.

Daniels, Doug
1987   Dreams and Realities of Dene Government. *Canadian Journal of Native Studies* 7:95–110.

De Laguna, Frederica
1975   Matrilineal Kin Groups in Northwestern North America. *Proceedings: Northern Athapaskan Conference, 1971,* edited by Annette McFadyen Clark, 1:17–145. Mercury Series, Canadian Ethnology Service Paper 27. Ottawa: National Museum of Man.

Denniston, Glenda
1981   Sekani. In *Handbook of North American Indians,* vol. 6, *Subarctic,* edited by June Helm, pp. 433–41. Washington: Smithsonian Institution Press.

Derry, David E., and Douglas R. Hudson, eds.
1975   Special Issue: Athapaskan Archeology. *Western Canadian Journal of Anthropology* 5(3–4).

Dixon, E. James
1985   Cultural Chronology of Central Interior Alaska. *Arctic Anthropology* 22(1):47–66.

Duff, Wilson
1981   Tsetsaut. In *Handbook of North American Indians,* vol. 6, *Subarctic,* edited by June Helm, pp. 454–57. Washington: Smithsonian Institution Press.

Emmons, George T.
1911   *The Tahltan Indians.* Anthropological Publications 4. Philadelphia: University of Pennsylvania Museum.

Fried, Jacob
1971   Reservation Phenomena in Canada's Northwest Territories, 1945–1962. *Northwest Anthropological Research Notes* 5(1):123

Gardner, Peter M.
1976   Birds, Words, and Requiem for the Omniscient Informant. *American Ethnologist* 3:446–68.

Gillespie, Beryl C.
1970   Yellowknives: Quo Iverunt? In *Migration and Anthropology* (proceedings of the 1970 Spring Annual Meeting of the American Ethnological Society), edited by R. F. Spencer, pp. 61–70. Seattle: University of Washington Press.

1975a   An Ethnohistory of the Yellowknives: A Northern Athapaskan Tribe. In *Contributions to Canadian Ethnology, 1975,* edited by David B. Carlisle, pp. 191–245. Mercury Series, Canadian Ethnology Service Paper 31. Ottawa: National Museum of Man.

1975b   Territorial Expansion of the Chipewyan in the 18th Century. In *Proceedings: Northern Athapaskan Conference, 1971,* edited by Annette McFadyen Clark, 2:350–88. Mercury Series, Canadian Ethnology Service Paper 27. Ottawa: National Museum of Man.

1976   Changes in Territory and Technology of the Chipewyan. *Arctic Anthropology* 13(1):6–11.

1978a   Bearlake Indians. In *Handbook of North American Indians,* vol. 6, *Subarctic,* edited by June Helm, pp. 310–13. Washington: Smithsonian Institution Press.

1978b   Mountain Indians. In *Handbook of North American Indians,* vol. 6, *Subarctic,* edited by June Helm, pp. 326–37. Washington: Smithsonian Institution Press.

1978c   Nahani. In *Handbook of North American Indians,* vol. 6, *Subarctic,* edited by June Helm, pp. 451–53. Washington: Smithsonian Institution Press.

1978d   Territorial Groups Before 1821: Athapaskans of the Shield and the Mackenzie Drainage. In *Handbook of North American Indians,* vol. 6, *Subarctic,* edited by June Helm, pp. 161–68. Washington: Smithsonian Institution Press.

1978e   Yellowknife. In *Handbook of North American Indians,* vol. 6, *Subarctic,* edited by June Helm, pp. 285–90. Washington: Smithsonian Institution Press.

Goddard, Pliny E.
1916   The Beaver Indians. *Anthropological Papers of the American Museum of Natural History* 10:201–93.

Gordon, Bryan H. C.
1975   *Of Men and Herds in Barrenland Prehistory.* Mercury Series, Canadian Archaeological Survey Paper 28. Ottawa: National Museum of Man.

1976   *Migod—8,000 Years of Barrenland Prehistory.* Mercury Series, Canadian Archaeological Survey Paper 56. Ottawa: National Museum of Man.

1981 Man-Environment Relationships in Barren-land Prehistory. *Musk-Ox* 28:1–19.

Gordon, Bryan H. C., and Howard Savage
1974 Whirl Lake: A Stratified Indian Site near the Mackenzie Delta. *Arctic* 27:175–88.

Goulet, Jean-Guy
1982 Religious Dualism Among Athapaskan Catholics. *Canadian Journal of Anthropology* 3(1): 1–18.
1988 Representation of Self and Reincarnation Among the Dene Tha. *Culture* 8:3–18.

Greer, Sheila C,. and Raymond J. Leblanc
1983 Yukon Culture History: An Update. *Musk-Ox* 33:26–36.

Gruhn, Ruth
1981 *Archaeological Research at Calling Lake, Northern Alberta.* Archaeological Survey of Canada Paper 99. Ottawa: National Museum of Canada.

Guédon, Marie-Françoise
1974 *People of Tetlin, Why Are You Singing?* Mercury Series, Canadian Ethnology Service Paper 9. Ottawa: National Museum of Man.
1988 Du rêve à l'ethnographie: Explorations sur le mode personnel du chamanisme Nabesna. *Recherches amérindiennes au Québec* 18:1–18.

Hanks, Christopher C., and Barbara J. Winter
1983 Dene Names as an Organizing Principle in Ethnoarchaeological Research. *Musk-Ox* 33: 49–55.

Hanks, Christopher C., and David L. Pokotylo
1989 The Mackenzie Basin: An Alternative Approach to Dene and Metis Archaeology. *Arctic* 42:139–47.

Hara, Hiroko Sue
1980 *The Hare Indians and Their World.* Mercury Series, Canadian Ethnology Service Paper 63. Ottawa: National Museum of Man.

Heffley, Sheri
1980 The Relationship Between Northern Athapaskan Settlement Patterns and Resource Distribution: An Application of Horn's Model. In *Hunter-Gatherer Foraging Strategies,* edited by Bruce Winterhalder and Eric Alden Smith, pp. 126–47. Chicago: University of Chicago Press.

Helm, June
1961 *The Lynx Point People: The Dynamics of a Northern Athapaskan Band.* Anthropological Series 53, Bulletin 176. Ottawa: National Museum of Canada.
1972 The Dogrib Indians. In *Hunters and Gatherers Today,* edited by M. G. Bicchieri, pp. 51–89. New York: Holt, Rinehart and Winston.
1978 On Responsible Scholarship on Culture Contact in the Mackenzie Basin. *Current Anthropology* 19:160–62.
1979 Long-term Research Among the Dogrib and Other Dene. In *Long-term Field Research in Social Anthropology,* edited by George M. Foster, Thayer Scudder, Elizabeth Colson, Robert V. Kemper, pp. 145–63. New York: Academic Press.
1980 Female Infanticide, European Diseases, and Population Levels Among the Mackenzie Dene. *American Ethnologist* 7: 259–85.
1981 Dogrib. In *Handbook of North American Indians,* vol. 6, *Subarctic,* edited by June Helm, pp. 291–309. Washington: Smithsonian Institution Press.
1989 Matonabbee's Map. *Arctic Anthropology* 26(2): 28–47.

Helm, June, Terry Alliband, Terry Birk, Virginia Lawson, Suzanne Reisner, Craig Sturtevant, and Stanley Witkowski
1975 The Contact History of the Subarctic Athapaskans: An Overview. In *Proceedings: Northern Athapaskan Conference, 1971,* edited by A. McFadyen Clark, 1:302–46. Mercury Series, Canadian Ethnology Service Paper 27. Ottawa: National Museum of Man.

Helm, June, George A. DeVos, and Teresa Carterette
1963 Variations in Personality and Ego Identification Within a Slave Indian Kin-Community. In *Contributions to Anthropology, 1960,* pt. 2, pp. 94–138. Anthropological Series 60, Bulletin 190. Ottawa: National Museum of Canada.

Helm, June, and Beryl Gillespie
1981 Dogrib Oral Tradition as History: War and Peace in the 1820s. *Journal of Anthropological Research* 37:8–27.

Helm, June, and Nancy O. Lurie
1961 *The Subsistence Economy of the Dogrib Indians of Lac La Martre in the Mackenzie District of the Northwest West Territories.* NCRC 61–3. Ottawa: Department of Northern

Affairs and National Resources, Northern Co-ordination and Research Centre.

1966   *The Dogrib Hand Game.* Anthropological Series 71, Bulletin 205. Ottawa: National Museum of Canada.

Helmer, James W., S. Van Dyke, and F. J. Kense, eds.
1977   *Prehistory of the North American Subarctic: The Athapaskan Question.* Calgary: Archaeological Association of the University of Calgary.

Honigmann, John J.
1946   *Ethnography and Acculturation of the Fort Nelson Slave.* Yale University Publications in Anthropology, no. 33. New Haven.

1947   Witch-fear in Post-contact Kaska Society. *American Anthropologist* 49(2):222–43.

1949   *Culture and Ethos of Kaska Society.* Yale University Publications in Anthropology, no. 40. New Haven.

1954   *The Kaska Indians: An Ethnographic Reconstruction.* Yale University Publications in Anthropology, no. 51. New Haven.

1970a   Field Work in Two Northern Canadian Communities. In *Marginal Natives: Anthropologists at Work,* edited by Morris Freilich, pp. 39–72. New York: Harper and Row.

1970b   Witchcraft Among Kaska Indians. In *Systems of North American Witchcraft and Sorcery,* edited by Deward E. Walker, Jr., pp. 221–38. Moscow: University of Idaho.

1971   Formation of Mackenzie Delta Frontier Culture. In *Pilot Not Commander: Essays in Memory of Diamond Jenness,* edited by Pat Lotz and Jim Lotz, pp. 185–92. *Anthropologica* 13(1–2).

1975   Psychological Traits in Northern Athapaskan Culture. In *Proceedings: Northern Athapaskan Conference, 1971,* edited by A. McFadyen Clark, 2:545–76. Mercury Series, Canadian Ethnology Service Paper 27. Ottawa: National Museum of Man.

1978   The Personal Approach in Culture and Personality Research. In *The Making of Psychological Anthropology,* edited by George D. Spindler, pp. 30–29. Berkeley: University of California Press.

1981   Kaska. In *Handbook of North American Indians,* vol. 6, *Subarctic,* edited by June Helm, pp. 442–50. Washington: Smithsonian Institution Press.

Hulbert, Janice
1962   *Age as a Factor in the Social Organization of the Hare Indian of Fort Good Hope, N.W.T.* NCRC 62–5. Ottawa: Department of Northern Affairs and National Resources, Northern Coordination and Research Centre.

Hultkrantz, Ake
1973   The Hare Indians: Notes on Their Traditional Culture and Religion, Past and Present. *Ethnos* 38(1–4):113–52.

Irimoto, Takashi
1981   The Chipewyan Caribou Hunting System. *Arctic Anthropology* 18(1):44–56.

Janes, Robert R.
1976   Culture Contact in the 19th Century Mackenzie Basin, Canada. *Current Anthropology* 17(2):344–45.

1983a   *Archaeological Ethnography Among Mackenzie Basin Dene.* Technical Paper 28. Calgary: Arctic Institute of North America.

1983b   Ethnoarchaeological Observations Among the Willow Lake Dene, Northwest Territories. *Musk-Ox* 33:56–67.

1988   Vernacular Architecture at a Contemporary Dene Hunting Camp. *Bulletin, Society for the Study of Architecture in Canada/Société pour l'étude de l'architecture au Canada* 13(2):4–10.

1989   An Ethnoarchaeological Model for the Identification of Prehistoric Tepee Remains in the Boreal Forest. *Arctic* 42:128–38.

Janes, Robert R., and J. H. Kelley
1977   Observations on Crisis Cult Activities in the Mackenzie Basin. In *Prehistory of the North American Subarctic: The Athapaskan Question,* edited by J. W. Helmer et al., pp. 153–64. Proceedings of the Ninth Annual Conference, Archaeological Association of the University of Calgary. Calgary: Archaeological Association of the University of Calgary.

Jarvenpa, Robert
1976   Spatial and Ecological Factors in the Annual Economic Cycle of the English River Band of Chipewyan. *Arctic Anthropology* 13(1):43–69.

1977   Subarctic Indian Trappers and Band Society: The Economics of Male Mobility. *Human Ecology* 5(3):223–59.

1980 *The Trappers of Patuanak: Toward a Spatial Ecology of Modern Hunters.* Mercury Series, Canadian Ethnology Service Paper 67. Ottawa: National Museum of Man.

1982 Intergroup Behavior and Imagery: The Case of Chipewyan and Cree. *Ethnology* 21:283–99.

Jarvenpa, Robert, and Hetty Jo Brumbach
1988 Socio-Spatial Organization and Decision-making Processes: Observations from the Chipewyan. *American Anthropologist* 90:598–618.

Jenness, Diamond
1937 *The Sekani Indians of British Columbia.* Anthropological Series 20, Department of Mines Bulletin 84. Ottawa: National Museum of Canada.

1943 The Carrier Indians of the Bulkley River: Their Social and Religious Life. In *Anthropological Papers,* no. 25, Bureau of American Ethnology. Bulletin 133. Washington.

Jopling, A. V., W. N. Irving, and B. F. Beebe
1981 Stratigraphic, Sedimentological, and Faunal Evidence for the Occurrence of Pre-Sangamonian Artifacts in Northern Yukon. *Arctic* 34:3–33.

Kobrinsky, Vernon H.
1977 The Tsimshianization of the Carrier Indians. In *Prehistory of the North American Subarctic,* edited by J. W. Helmer et al., pp. 201–10. Calgary: Archaeological Association of the University of Calgary.

Koolage, William W., Jr.
1974 Relocation and Culture Change: A Canadian Subarctic Case Study. In *Proceedings of the 40th International Congress of Americanists,* Rome and Genoa, 1972, 2:613–17.

1976 Differential Adaptations of Athapaskans and Other Native Ethnic Groups to a Canadian Northern Town. *Arctic Anthropology* 13(1):70–83.

Krauss, Michael E.
1973 Na-Dene. In *Current Trends in Linguistics,* edited by Thomas A. Sebeok, 10:903–78. The Hague: Mouton.

Krauss, Michael E., and Victor K. Golla
1981 Northern Athapaskan Languages. In *Handbook of North American Indians,* vol. 6, *Sub-*

arctic, edited by June Helm, pp. 67–85. Washington: Smithsonian Institution Press.

Krech, Shepard III
1978a On the Aboriginal Population of the Kutchin. *Arctic Anthropology* 15(1):89–104.

1978b Disease, Starvation, and Northern Athapaskan Social Organization. *American Ethnologist* 5:710–32.

1980 The Nakotcho Kutchin: A Tenth Aboriginal Kutchin Band? *Journal of Anthropological Research* 35:109–21.

1982 The Banditte of St. John's. *Beaver* 313(3):36–41.

1983 The Beaver Indians and the Hostilities at Fort St. Johns. *Arctic Anthropology* 20(2):35–46.

1984 "Massacre" of the Inuit. *Beaver* 315(1):52–59.

1990 The Subarctic. In *Native North Americans: An Ethnohistorical Approach,* edited by Daniel K. Boxberger, pp. 65–89. Dubuque, Iowa: Kendall/Hunt Publishing Company.

1991 The Fifth Earl of Lonsdale in the Arctic, 1888–89. *Rutland Record* 11:25–38.

Lane, Robert B.
1981 Chilcotin. In *Handbook of North American Indians,* vol. 6, *Subarctic,* edited by June Helm, pp. 402–12. Washington: Smithsonian Institution.

Lantis, Margaret, ed.
1970 *Ethnohistory in Southwestern Alaska and the Southern Yukon: Method and Content.* Lexington: University Press of Kentucky.

Legros, Dominique
1978 Dualisme de moitié et stratification sociale chez les athapaskan tutchone septentrinaux du territoire du Youkon. In *Actes du XLIIe Congrès International des Américanistes* (1976, Paris), 5:339–59.

1982 Reflexions sur l'origine des inégalités sociales à partir du cas des athapaskan tutchone. *Culture* 2(3):65–84.

1984 Commerce entre tlingits et athapaskans tutchones au XIXe siècle. *Recherches amérindiennes au Québec* 14(2):11–24.

1985 Wealth, Poverty, and Slavery Among 19th-Century Tutchone Athapaskans. *Research in Economic Anthropology* 7:37–64.

Lewis, Henry T.
1982 *A Time for Burning.* Occasional Publication 17.

Edmonton: Boreal Institute for Northern Studies, University of Alberta.

McClellan, Catharine

1954   The Interrelations of Social Structure with Northern Tlingit Ceremonialism. *Southwestern Journal of Anthropology* 10(1):75–96.

1956   Shamanistic Syncretism in Southern Yukon Territory. *Transactions of the New York Academy of Sciences,* 2d ser., 19(2):130–37.

1961   Avoidance Between Siblings of the Same Sex in North America. *Southwestern Journal of Anthropology* 17(2):103–23.

1963   Wealth Woman and Frogs Among the Tagish Indians. *Anthropos* 58(1–2):121–28.

1964   Culture Contacts in the Early Historic Period in Northwestern North America. *Arctic Anthropology* 2(2):3–15.

1970a   *The Girl Who Married the Bear: A Masterpiece of Indian Oral Tradition.* Publications in Ethnology, no. 2. Ottawa: National Museum of Man.

1970b   Indian Stories About the First Whites in Northwestern America. In *Ethnohistory in Southwestern Alaska and the Southern Yukon: Method and Content,* edited by Margaret Lantis, pp. 103–33. Lexington: University Press of Kentucky.

1970c   Introduction to Special Issue: Athapascan Studies. *Western Canadian Journal of Anthropology* 2(1):vi–xix.

1975a   Feuding and Warfare Among Northwestern Athapaskan. *Proceedings: Northern Athapaskan Conference, 1971,* edited by A. M. Clark, 1:181–258. Mercury Series, Canadian Ethnology Service Paper 27. Ottawa: National Museum of Man.

1975b   *My Old People Say: An Ethnographic Survey of Southern Yukon Territory.* 2 parts. Publications in Ethnology 6. Ottawa: National Museum of Man.

1981a   Inland Tlingit. In *Handbook of North American Indians,* vol. 6, *Subarctic,* edited by June Helm, pp. 469–80. Washington: Smithsonian Institution Press.

1981b   Intercultural Relations and Cultural Change in the Cordillera. In *Handbook of North American Indians,* vol. 6, *Subarctic,* edited by June Helm, pp. 387–401. Washington: Smithsonian Institution Press.

1981c   Tagish. In *Handbook of North American Indians,* vol. 6, *Subarctic,* edited by June Helm, pp. 481–92. Washington: Smithsonian Institution Press.

1981d   Tutchone. In *Handbook of North American Indians,* vol. 6, *Subarctic,* edited by June Helm, pp. 493–505. Washington: Smithsonian Institution Press.

1987   *Part of the Land, Part of the Water: A History of the Yukon Indians.* Vancouver: Douglas and McIntyre.

McCormack, Patricia A.

1988   *Northwind Dreaming/Kiwetin Pawâtamowin Tthisi Ni*tsi Nâts'Ete: Fort Chipewyan, 1788–1988.* Provincial Museum of Alberta Special Publication 6. Edmonton.

MacDonald, Jake

1987   The Road to Camp 10: A Chipewyan Profile. *Beaver* 67(1):42–45.

McKennan, Robert A.

1959   *The Upper Tanana Indians.* Yale University Publications in Anthropology, no. 55. New Haven.

1965   *The Chandalar Kutchin.* Technical Paper 17. Montreal: Arctic Institute of North America.

MacLachlan, Bruce B.

1981   Tahltan. In *Handbook of North American Indians,* vol. 6, *Subarctic,* edited by June Helm, pp. 458–68. Washington: Smithsonian Institution Press.

MacNeish, June Helm

1954   Contemporary Folk Beliefs of a Slave Indian Band. *Journal of American Folklore* 67(264):185–98.

1955   Folktales of the Slave Indians. *Anthropologica* 1:37–44.

1956a   Leadership Among the Northeastern Athabascans. *Anthropologica* 2:131–63.

1956b   Problems of Acculturation and Livelihood in a Northern Indian Band. *Contributions à l'étude des sciences de l'homme* 3:169–81.

1960   Kin Terms of Arctic Drainage Déné: Hare, Slavey, Chipewyan. *American Anthropologist* 62(2):279–95.

Mason, J. Alden

1946   *Notes on the Indians of the Great Slave Lake Area.* Yale University Publications in Anthropology, no. 34. New Haven.

Michéa, Jean
1963   Les Chitra-gottinéke: Essai de monographie d'un groupe Athapascan des Montagnes Rocheuses. In *Contributions to Anthropology, 1960, pt. 2.* Anthropological Series 60, Bulletin 190. Ottawa: National Museum of Canada.

Mills, Antonia C.
1986   The Meaningful Universe: Intersecting Forces in Beaver Indian Cosmology. *Culture* 6(2):81–91.
1988a   A Comparison of Wet'suwet'en Cases of the Reincarnation Type with Gitksan and Beaver. *Journal of Anthropological Research* 44:385–415.
1988b   A Preliminary Investigation of Cases of Reincarnation Among the Beaver and Gitksan Indians. *Anthropologica* 30:23–59.

Moore, Pat, and Angela Wheelock
1989   *Wolverine Myths and Visions: Dene Traditions from Northern Alberta.* Edmonton: University of Alberta Press.

Morice, Adrian G.
1893   Notes Archaeological, Industrial, and Sociological on the Western Denes. *Transactions of the Canadian Institute* 4:1–222.
1906–10 The Great Dene Race. *Anthropos* 1:229–77, 483–508, 695–730; 2:1–34, 181–96; 4:582–606; 5:113–42, 419–43, 643–53, 969–90.

Morlan, Richard E.
1970   Symposium on Northern Athabaskan Prehistory: Introductory Remarks. *Bulletin of the Canadian Archaeological Association* 2:1–2.
1972a   *The Cadzow Lake Site (MjVi-1): A Multicomponent Historic Kutchin Camp.* Mercury Series, Canadian Archaeological Survey Paper 3. Ottawa: National Museum of Man.
1972b   *NbVk-1: An Historic Fishing Camp in Old Crow Flats, Northern Yukon.* Mercury Series, Canadian Archaeological Survey Paper 5. Ottawa: National Museum of Man.
1973   *The Later Prehistory of the Middle Porcupine Drainage, Northern Yukon Territory.* Mercury Series, Canadian Archaeological Survey Paper 11. Ottawa: National Museum of Man.

Morris, Margaret W.
1972   Great Bear Lake Indians: A Historical Demography and Human Ecology, Pt. 1: The Situa-

tion Prior to European Contact. *Musk-Ox* 11:3–27.
1973   Great Bear Lake Indians: A Historical Demography and Human Ecology, Pt. 2: The Situation After European Contact. *Musk-Ox* 12:58–80.

Morrison, David A.
1984   The Late Prehistoric Period in the Mackenzie Valley. *Arctic* 37:195–209.

Müller-Wille, Ludger
1974   Caribou Never Die! Modern Caribou Hunting Economy of the Dene (Chipewyan) of Fond du Lac, Saskatchewan and N.W.T. *Musk-Ox* 14:7–19.

Nelson, Richard K.
1973   *Hunters of the Northern Forest.* Chicago: University of Chicago Press.

Osgood, Cornelius B.
1931   *The Ethnography of the Great Bear Lake Indians.* Department of Mines Bulletin 70. Ottawa: National Museum of Canada.
1936a   *Contributions to the Ethnography of the Kutchin.* Yale University Publications in Anthropology, no. 14. New Haven.
1936b   *The Distribution of the Northern Athapaskan Indians.* Yale University Publications in Anthropology, no. 7, 3–23. New Haven.
1971   *The Han Indians: A Compilation of Ethnographic and Historical Data on the Alaska-Yukon Boundary Area.* Yale University Publications in Anthropology, no. 74. New Haven.

Perry, Richard J.
1983   Proto-Athapascan Culture: The Use of Ethnographic Reconstruction. *American Ethnologist* 10:715–33.
1989   Matrilineal Descent in a Hunting Context: The Athapaskan Case. *Ethnology* 28:33–52.

Reynolds, Brad
1990   Athapaskans Along the Yukon. *National Geographic* 177(2):44–69.

Ridington, Robin
1968   The Medicine Fight: An Instrument of Political Process Among the Beaver Indians. *American Anthropologist* 70:1152–60.
1969   Kin Categories Versus Kin Groups: A Two-section System Without Sections. *Ethnology* 8(4):460–67.

1971   Beaver Dreaming and Singing. In *Pilot Not Commander: Essays in Memory of Diamond Jenness,* edited by Pat Lotz and James R. Lotz, pp. 115–28. *Anthropologica* 13:1–2.

1976a   Eye on the Wheel. *Io* 22:69–82.

1976b   Wechuge and Windigo: A Comparison of Cannibal Belief Among Boreal Forest Athapaskans and Algonkians. *Anthropologica* 18:107–29.

1977   The Prophet Dance Among the Dunne-Za. In *Problems in the Prehistory of the North American Subarctic: The Athapaskan Question,* edited by J. W. Helmer, S. Van Dyke, and F. J. Kense, pp. 211–32. Calgary: Archaeological Association of the University of Calgary.

1978a   Metaphor and Meaning: Healing in Dunne-za Music and Dance. *Western Canadian Journal of Anthropology* 8(2–4):9–17.

1978b   *Swan People: A Study of the Dunne-za Prophet Dance.* Mercury Series, Canadian Ethnology Service Paper 38. Ottawa: National Museum of Man.

1979   Changes of Mind: Dunne-za Resistance to Empire. *BC Studies* 43:65–80.

1981   Beaver. In *Handbook of North American Indians,* vol. 6, *Subarctic,* edited by June Helm, pp. 350–60. Washington: Smithsonian Institution Press.

1982a   Technology, World View, and Adaptive Strategy in a Northern Hunting Society. *Canadian Review of Sociology and Anthropology* 18:55–66.

1982b   Telling Secrets: Stories of the Vision Quest. *Canadian Journal of Native Studies* 2:213–20.

1982c   When Poison Gas Comes down Like a Fog: A Native Community's Response to Cultural Disaster. *Human Organization* 41:36–42.

1983a   From Artifice to Artifact: Stages in the Industrialization of a Northern Hunting People. *Journal of Canadian Studies* 18:55–66.

1983b   In Doig People's Ears: Portrait of a Native Community in Sound. *Anthropologica* 25(1): 9–21.

1985   The Old Wagon Road: Talking Fieldnotes from Ethnographic Fieldwork. *Canadian Journal of Native Studies* 5(2):201–16.

1987a   Fox and Chickadee. In *The American Indian and the Problem of History,* edited by Calvin Martin, pp. 128–35. New York: Oxford University Press.

1987b   From Hunt Chief to Prophet: Beaver Indian Dreamers and Christianity. *Arctic Anthropology* 24(1):8–18.

1988   Knowledge, Power, and the Individual in Subarctic Hunting Societies. *American Anthropologist* 90:98–110.

1989   *Trail to Heaven: Knowledge and Narrative in a Northern Native Community.* Iowa City: University of Iowa Press.

1990a   Culture in Conflict: The Problem of Discourse. *Canadian Literature* 124–5: 273-89.

1990b   *Little Bit Know Something: Stories in a Language of Anthropology.* Iowa City: University of Iowa Press.

Ridington, Robin, and Tonia Ridington

1970   The Inner Eye of Shamanism and Totemism. *History of Religions* 10(1):49–61.

Roth, Eric

1981   Historic Population Structure of a Northern Athapaskan Bush Community: Old Crow Village, Yukon Territory. *Arctic Anthropology* 18(1):33–43.

Rothenberger, Mel

1978   *The Chilcotin War.* Langley, B.C.: Mr. Paperback.

Rushforth, Scott

1977   Country Food. In *Dene Nation—The Colony Within,* edited by Mel Watkins, pp. 32–46. Toronto: University of Toronto Press.

1984   *Bear Lake Athapaskan Kinship and Task Group Formation.* Mercury Series, Canadian Ethnology Service Paper 96. Ottawa: National Museum of Man.

1988   Autonomy and Community Among the Bearlake Athapaskans. In *Native North American Interaction Patterns,* edited by Regna Darnell and Michael K. Foster, pp. 112–42. Ottawa: National Museum of Man.

Rushforth, Scott, and James S. Chisholm

1991   *Cultural Persistence: Continuity in Meaning and Moral Responsibility Among the Bearlake Athapaskans.* Tucson: University of Arizona Press.

Savishinsky, Joel S.

1970   Kinship and the Expression of Values in an Athabascan Bush Community. *Western Canadian Journal of Anthropology* 2(1):31–59.

1971   Mobility as an Aspect of Stress in an Arctic Community. *American Anthropologist* 73(3): 604–18.

1972   Coping with Feuding: The Missionary, the Fur Trader, and the Ethnographer. *Human Organization* 31(3):281–90.

1974   *The Trail of the Hare.* New York: Gordon and Breach.

1975   The Dog and the Hare: Canine Culture in the Athapaskan Band. In *Proceedings: Northern Athapaskan Conference, 1971,* edited by A. McFadyen Clark, 2:462–515. Mercury Series, Canadian Ethnology Service Paper 27. Ottawa: National Museum of Man.

1978   Trapping, Survival Strategies, and Environment Involvement: A Case Study from the Canadian Sub-Arctic. *Human Ecology* 6:1-25.

Savishinsky, Joel S., and Susan B. Frimmer
1973   *The Middle Ground: Social Change in an Arctic Community, 1967–1971.* Mercury Series, Canadian Ethnology Service Paper 7. Ottawa: National Museum of Man.

Savishinsky, Joel S., and Hiroko Sue Hara
1981   Hare. In *Handbook of North American Indians,* vol. 6, *Subarctic,* edited by June Helm, pp. 314–25. Washington: Smithsonian Institution Press.

Savoie, Donat, ed.
1971   The Amerindians of the Canadian North-West in the 19th Century, as Seen by Emile Petitot. Vol. 2, *The Loucheux Indians.* MDRP 10. Ottawa: Department of Indian Affairs and Northern Development, Northern Science Research Group.

Scollon, Ronald, and Suzanne B. K. Scollon
1979   *Linguistic Convergence: An Ethnography of Speaking at Fort Chipewyan, Alberta.* New York: Academic Press.

Sharp, Henry S.
1975a   Introducing the Sororate to a Northern Saskatchewan Chipewyan Village. *Ethnology* 14(1): 71–82.

1975b   Trapping and Welfare: The Economics of Trapping in a Northern Saskatchewan Chipewyan Village. *Anthropologica* 17(1):29–44.

1976   Man:Wolf::Woman:Dog. *Arctic Anthropology* 13(1):25–34.

1977a   The Chipewyan Hunting Unit. *American Ethnologist* 4(2):377–93.

1977b   The Caribou Eater Chipewyan: Bilaterality, Strategies of Caribou Hunting, and the Fur Trade. *Arctic Anthropology* 14(2):35–40.

1978   Comparative Ethology of the Wolf and the Chipewyan. In *Wolf and Man: Evolution in Parallel,* edited by R. L. Hall and H. S. Sharp, pp. 55–79. New York: Academic Press.

1979   *Chipewyan Marriage.* Mercury Series, Canadian Ethnology Service Paper 58. Ottawa: National Museum of Man.

1986   Shared Experience and Magical Death: Chipewyan Explanations of a Prophet's Decline. *Ethnology* 25:257–70.

1987   Giant Fish, Giant Otters, and Dinosaurs: "Apparently Irrational Beliefs" in a Chipewyan Community. *American Ethnologist* 14:226–35.

1988   *The Transformation of Bigfoot: Maleness, Power, and Belief Among the Chipewyan.* Washington: Smithsonian Institution Press.

1991a   Dry Meat and Gender: The Absence of Chipewyan Ritual for the Regulation of Hunting and Animal Numbers. In *Hunters and Gatherers,* vol. 2, *Property, Power and Ideology,* edited by Tim Ingold, David Riches, and James Woodburn, pp. 183–910. Oxford: Berg.

1991b   Memory, Meaning, and Imaginary Time: The Construction of Knowledge in White and Chipewyan Cultures. *Ethnohistory* 39:149–75.

Slobodin, Richard
1960a   Eastern Kutchin Warfare. *Anthropologica* 2(1): 76–94.

1960b   Some Social Functions of Kutchin Anxiety. *American Anthropologist* 62(1):122–33.

1962   *Band Organization of the Peel River Kutchin.* Bulletin 179. Ottawa: National Museum of Canada.

1969a   Criteria for Identification of Bands. In *Contributions to Anthropology: Band Societies,* edited by David Damas, pp. 191–211. Anthropological Series 84, Bulletin 228. Ottawa: National Museum of Canada.

1969b   Leadership and Participation in a Kutchin Trapping Party. In *Contributions to Anthropology: Band Societies,* edited by David Damas, pp. 56–89. Anthropological Series 84. Bulletin 228. Ottawa: National Museum of Canada.

1970   Kutchin Concepts of Reincarnation. *Western Canadian Journal of Anthropology* 2(1):67–79.

1975   Without Fire: A Kutchin Tale of Warfare, Survival, and Vengeance. *Proceedings: Northern Athapascan Conference, 1971,* edited by A. McFadyen Clark, 1:259–301. Mercury Series, Canadian Ethnology Service Paper 27. Ottawa: National Museum of Man.

1981   Kutchin. In *Handbook of North American Indians,* vol. 6, *Subarctic,* edited by June Helm, pp. 514–32. Washington: Smithsonian Institution Press.

Smith, David M.

1973   *Inkonze: Magico-Religious Beliefs of Contact-Traditional Chipewyan Trading at Fort Resolution, NWT, Canada.* Mercury Series, Canadian Ethnology Service Paper 6. Ottawa: National Museum of Man.

1976   Cultural and Ecological Change: The Chipewyan of Fort Resolution. *Arctic Anthropology* 13(1):35–42.

1977   Differential Adaptations Among the Chipewyan of the Great Slave Lake Area in the Early Twentieth Century. In *Prehistory of the North American Subarctic: The Athapaskan Question,* edited by J. W. Helmer, S. Van Dyke, J. F. Kense, pp. 184–91. Calgary: Archaeological Association of the University of Calgary.

1981   Fort Resolution, Northwest Territories. In *Handbook of North American Indians,* vol. 6, *Subarctic,* edited by June Helm, pp. 683–92. Washington: Smithsonian Institution Press.

1982   *Moose-Deer Island House People: A History of Native People of Fort Resolution.* Canadian Ethnology Service Paper 81. Ottawa: National Museum of Man.

1985   Big Stone Foundations: Manifest Meaning in Chipewyan Myths. *Journal of American Culture* 8:73–77.

1990   The Chipewyan Medicine-Fight in Cultural and Ecological Perspectives. In *Culture and the Anthropological Tradition: Essays in Honor of Robert F. Spencer.* Lanham, Md.: University Press of America.

Smith, Derek G.

1975   *Natives and Outsiders: Pluralism in the Mackenzie River Delta Northwest Territories.* MDRP12. Ottawa: Department of Indian Affairs and Northern Development, Northern Research Division.

Smith, James G. E.

1970   The Chipewyan Hunting Group in a Village Context. *Western Canadian Journal of Anthropology* 2(1):60–66.

1975   The Ecological Basis of Chipewyan Socio-Territorial Organization. *Proceedings: Northern Athapaskan Conference, 1971,* edited by A. McFadyen Clark, 2:389–461. Mercury Series, Canadian Ethnology Service Paper 27. Ottawa: National Museum of Man.

1976   Chipewyan Adaptations. Papers from a Symposium on the Chipewyan of Subarctic Canada: Variation in Ecological Adaptation. *Arctic Anthropology* 13(1).

1976a   Local Band Organization of the Caribou Chipewyan in the Eighteenth and Early Nineteenth Centuries. *Western Canadian Journal of Anthropology* 6(1):72–90.

1976b   Local Band Organization of the Caribou Eater Chipewyan. *Arctic Anthropology* 13(1):12–24.

1978a   Economic Uncertainty in an "Original Affluent Society": Caribou and Caribou Eater Chipewyan Adaptive Strategies. *Arctic Anthropology* 15(1):68–88.

1978b   The Emergence of the Micro-Urban Village Among the Caribou-Eater Chipewyan. *Human Organization* 37(1):38–49.

1981   Chipewyan. In *Handbook of North American Indians,* vol. 6, *Subarctic,* edited by June Helm, pp. 271–84. Washington: Smithsonian Institution Press.

Smith, James G. E., ed.

1976   Chipewyan Adaptations. Papers from a Symposium on the Chipewyan of Subarctic Canada: Variation in Ecological Adaptation. *Arctic Anthropology* 13(1).

Stabler, Jack C.

1990   Fur Trappers in the Northwest Territories: An Econometric Analysis of the Factors Influencing Participation. *Arctic* 43:1–8.

Steward, Julian H.

1941   Recording Culture Changes Among the Carrier Indians of British Columbia. In *Explorations and Field Work of the Smithsonian Institution in 1940,* pp. 83–90. Washington.

1960   Carrier Acculturation: The Direct Historical

Approach. In *Culture History: Essays in Honor of Paul Radin,* edited by Stanley Diamond, pp. 732–44. New York: Columbia University Press.

Teit, James A.
1956   Field Notes on the Tahltan and Kaska Indians, 1912–1915. *Anthropologica* 3:39–171.

Tetso, John
1970   *Trapping Is My Life.* Toronto: Peter Martin Associates.

Tobey, Margaret
1981   Carrier. In *Handbook of North American Indians,* vol. 6, *Subarctic,* edited by June Helm, pp. 413–32. Washington: Smithsonian Institution Press.

Van Stone, James W.
1963a   Changing Patterns of Indian Trapping in the Canadian Subarctic. *Arctic* 16(3):159–74.
1963b   *The Snowdrift Chipewyan.* NCRC 63–64. Ottawa: Department of Northern Affairs and National Resources, Northern Coordination and Research Centre.

1965   *The Changing Culture of the Snowdrift Chipewyan.* Anthropological Series 74, Bulletin 209. Ottawa: National Museum of Canada.
1974   *Athapaskan Adaptations: Hunters and Fishermen of the Subarctic Forests.* Chicago: Aldine.

Wein, Eleanor, et al.
1991   Food consumption patterns and use of country foods by native Canadians near Wood Buffalo National Park, Canada. *Arctic* 44:196–205.

Yerbury, J. Colin
1977   On Culture Contact in the Mackenzie Basin. *Current Anthropology* 18:350–52.
1978   Further Notes on the Ethnohistory of the Mackenzie Basin. *Current Anthropology* 19: 458–59.

Yesner, David R.
1989   Moose Hunters of the Boreal Forest? A Reexamination of Subsistence Patterns in the Western Subarctic. *Arctic* 42(2):97–108.

Section Ten

🍁

INUIT OF THE ARCTIC

Alexander, B., and C. Alexander
1988   Canada's U-Turn. *Geographical Magazine* 60: 10–16.

Arima, Eugene Y.
1984   Caribou Eskimo. In *Handbook of North American Indians,* vol. 6, *Subarctic,* edited by June Helm, pp. 447–62. Washington: Smithsonian Institution Press.

Arnold, Charles D.
1981   Demographic Process and Culture Change: An Example from the Western Canadian Arctic. In *Networks of the Past: Regional Interaction in Archaeology,* edited by P. D. Francis et al., pp. 311–26. Calgary: Archaeological Association of the University of Calgary.
1983   A Summary of the Prehistory of the Western Canadian Arctic. *Musk-Ox* 33:10–20.
1988   Vanishing Villages of the Past: Rescue Archaeology in the Mackenzie Delta. *Northern Review* 1:40–58.

Arnold, Charles D., and Carole Stimmel
1983   An Analysis of Thule Pottery. *Canadian Journal of Archaeology* 7:1–21.

Auger, Réginald
1987   Probabilities for a Late Eighteenth Century Inuit Occupation of the Strait of Belle Isle. *Études/Inuit/Studies* 11(1):47–66.

Balikci, Asen
1960a   Some Acculturative Trends Among the Eastern Canadian Eskimos. *Anthropologica* 2(2): 139–53.
1960b   *Suicidal Behavior Among the Netsilik Eskimos.* NCRC 60-2. Ottawa: Department of Northern Affairs and National Resources, Northern Coordination and Research Center.
1961   *Relations inter-ethniques à la Grande Rivière de la Baleine, baie d'Hudson, 1957.* Anthropological Series 50, Bulletin 173. Ottawa: National Museum of Canada.
1963   Shamanistic Behavior Among the Netsilik Eskimos. *Southwestern Journal of Anthropology* 19(4):380–96.
1967   Female Infanticide on the Arctic Coast. *Man* 2(4):615–25.
1970   *The Netsilik Eskimo.* New York: Natural History Press.
1975   Reconstructing Cultures on Film. In *Princi-

ples of Visual Anthropology, edited by Paul Hocking, pp. 191–200. The Hague: Mouton.

1978   The Netsilik Inuit Today. *Études/Inuit/Studies* 2:111–19.

1984   Netsilik. In *Handbook of North American Indians,* vol. 6, *Subarctic,* edited by June Helm, pp. 415–30. Washington: Smithsonian Institution Press.

Barkham, Selma
1984   The Basque Whaling Establishment in Labrador 1536–1632—A Summary. *Arctic* 37: 515–19.

Ben-Dor, Shmuel
1966   *Makkovik: Eskimos and Settlers in a Labrador Community.* St. Johns: Memorial University of Newfoundland, Institute for Social Economic Research.

Bernard, Alain
1975   Le context socio-économique du chômage et de l'assistance sociale au Nouveau Quebec Inuit. *Recherches amérindiennes au Québec* 5(3):16–25.

1977   Dépendence et capitalisme marchand: Le cas des inuit de la rive sud du détroit d'Hudson, 1930–1956. *Études/Inuit/Studies* 1(2):1–29.

Berry, John W.
1976   Acculturative Stress in Northern Canada: Ecological, Cultural, and Psychological Factors. In *Circumpolar Health,* edited by R. J. Shephard and S. Itoh, pp. 490–97. Toronto: University of Toronto Press.

Bielawski, Ellen
1988   Paleoeskimo Variability: The Early Arctic Small-Tool Tradition in the Central Canadian Arctic. *American Antiquity* 53:52–74.

Billson, Janet M.
1990   Opportunity or Tragedy: The Impact of Canadian Resettlement Policy on Inuit Families. *American Review of Canadian Studies* 20: 189–218.

Birket-Smith, Kaj
1929   The Caribou Eskimos; Material and Social Life and Their Cultural Position. *Report on the Fifth Thule Expedition 1921–24,* vol. 5 (1–2). Copenhagen.

1945   Ethnographical Collections from the North-west Passage. *Report of the Fifth Thule Expedition, 1921–24,* vol. 6 (2). Copenhagen.

1959   *The Eskimos.* Rev. ed. London: Methuen.

Boas, Franz
1901–7 The Eskimo of Baffin Land and Hudson Bay. *Bulletin of the American Museum of Natural History* 15:1–570.

1964   *The Central Eskimo.* 1888. Lincoln: University of Nebraska Press.

Bockstoce, John R.
1986   *Whales, Ice, and Men: The History of Commercial Whaling in the Western Arctic, 1840–1936.* Seattle: University of Washington Press.

Brantenberg, Anne, and Terje Brantenberg
1984   Coastal Northern Labrador After 1950. In *Handbook of North American Indians,* vol. 5, *Arctic,* edited by David Damas, pp. 689–99. Washington: Smithsonian Institution Press.

Briggs, Jean L.
1970   *Never in Anger: Portrait of an Eskimo Family.* Cambridge, Mass.: Harvard University Press.

1975   The Origins of Non-Violence: Aggression in Two Canadian Eskimo Groups. In *The Psychoanalytic Study of Society,* edited by Warner Muensterberger and Aaron H. Esman, 6:134–203. New York: International Universities Press.

1978   The Origins of Non-Violence: Inuit Management of Aggression. In *Learning Non-Aggression,* edited by Ashley Montagu, pp. 54–93. New York: Oxford University Press.

1982   Living Dangerously: The Contradictory Foundations of Value in Canadian Inuit Society. In *Politics and History in Band Societies,* edited by Eleanor Leacock and Richard Lee, pp. 109–32. Cambridge: Cambridge University Press.

Brody, Hugh
1975   *The People's Land: Eskimos and Whites in the Eastern Arctic.* New York: Penguin Books.

1978   Ecology, Politics, and Change: The Case of the Eskimo. *Development and Change* 9:21–40.

Bruemmer, Fred
1980   Herschel! The Big Town. *Beaver* 311(3):26–35.

Burch, Ernest S., Jr.
1977   Muskox and Man in the Central Canadian Subarctic, 1689–1974. *Arctic* 30(3):135–54.

1978   Caribou Eskimo Origins: An Old Problem Reconsidered. *Arctic Anthropology* 15(1):1–35.

1979   The Thule-Historic Eskimo Transition on the West Coast of Hudson Bay. In *Thule Eskimo Culture: An Anthropological Retrospective,* edited by Allen P. McCartney, pp. 189–211. Mercury Series, Canadian Archaeological Survey Paper 88. Ottawa: National Museum of Man.

1988a   *The Eskimos.* Norman: University of Oklahoma Press.

1988b   Knud Rasmussen and the "Original" Inland Eskimos of Southern Keewatin. *Études/Inuit/ Studies* 12(1–2):81–100.

Cavanaugh, Beverly
1982   *Music of the Netsilik Eskimos.* Vols. 1–2. Mercury Series, Canadian Ethnology Service Paper 82. Ottawa: National Museum of Man.

Chartrand, Jean-Philippe
1987   Survival and Adaptation of the Inuit Ethnic Identity: The Importance of Inuktitut. In *Native People, Native Lands,* edited by Bruce A. Cox, pp. 241–55. Ottawa: Carleton University.

Choinière, Robert, and Norbert Robitaille
1983   Evolution démographique des inuit du Nouveau-Québec, des Territoires du Nord-Ouest, du Groenland et de l'Alaska de 1930 à nos jours. *Études/Inuit/Studies* 7(2):125-50.

1987   La mobilité des inuit du Nouveau-Québec, 1977–1981. *Études/Inuit/Studies* 11(2):209–24.

Clancy, Peter
1987   The Making of Eskimo Policy in Canada, 1952–62: The Life and Times of the Eskimo Affairs Committee. *Arctic* 40:191–97.

Clark, Brenda L.
1977   *The Development of Caribou Eskimo Culture.* Mercury Series, Canadian Archaeological Survey Paper 59. Ottawa: National Museum of Man.

Cole, Douglas
1986   Franz Boas in Baffin-Land. *Beaver* 66(4):4–15.

Collin, Dominique
1983   La discrète émancipation de Talasia: Identité féminine et vision du monde d'une jeune inuk du Québec nordique. *Recherches amérindiennes au Québec* 13(4):255–64.

Condon, Richard G.
1982   Seasonal Variation and Interpersonal Conflict in the Central Canadian Arctic. *Ethnology* 21:151–64.

1983   *Inuit Behavior and Seasonal Change in the Canadian Arctic.* Ann Arbor: UMI Research Press.

1987   *Inuit Youth: Growth and Change in the Canadian Arctic.* New Brunswick, N.J.: Rutgers University Press.

1989   The History and Development of Arctic Photography. *Arctic Anthropology* 26(1):46–87.

Cowan, Susan, ed.
1981   *We Don't Live in Snowhouses Now: Reflections of Arctic Bay.* Chicago: University of Chicago Press.

Creery, Ian
1983   *The Inuit (Eskimo) of Canada.* Report 60. London: Minority Rights Group.

Damas, David
1963   *Igluligmiut Kinship and Local Groupings: A Structural Approach.* Anthropological Series 64, Bulletin 196. Ottawa: National Museum of Canada.

1969a   Characteristics of Central Eskimo Band Structure. In *Contributions to Anthropology: Band Societies,* edited by David Damas, pp. 116–34. Anthropological Series 84, Bulletin 228. Ottawa: National Museum of Canada.

1969b   Environment, History, and Central Eskimo Society. In *Contributions to Anthropology: Ecological Essays,* edited by David Damas, pp. 40–64. Bulletin 230. Ottawa: National Museum of Canada.

1971   The Problem of the Eskimo Family. In *The Canadian Family: A Book of Readings,* edited by K. Ishwaran, pp. 54–78. Toronto: Holt, Rinehart and Winston of Canada.

1972a   Central Eskimo Systems of Food Sharing. *Ethnology* 11(3):220–40.

1972b   The Copper Eskimo. In *Hunters and Gatherers Today,* edited by M. G. Bicchieri, pp. 3–50. New York: Holt, Rinehart and Winston.

1975a   Demographic Aspects of Central Eskimo Marriage Practices. *American Ethnologist* 2(3):409–18.

1975b   Three Kinship Systems from the Central Arctic. *Arctic Anthropology* 12(1):10–30.

1984a Central Eskimo: Introduction. In *Handbook of North American Indians,* vol. 5, *Arctic,* edited by David Damas, pp. 391–96. Washington: Smithsonian Institution Press.

1984b Copper Eskimo. In *Handbook of North American Indians,* vol. 5, *Arctic,* edited by David Damas, pp. 397–414. Washington: Smithsonian Institution Press.

1988a The Contact-Traditional Horizon of the Central Arctic: Reassessment of a Concept and Reexamination of an Era. *Arctic Anthropology* 25(2):101–38.

1988b Journey at the Threshold: Knud Rasmussen's Study of the Copper Eskimos, 1923–24. *Études/Inuit/Studies* 12(1–2):129–50.

Diubaldo, R. J.
1981 The Absurd Little Mouse: When Eskimos Became Indians. *Journal of Canadian Studies* 16(2):34–40.

Dorais, Louis-Jacques
1982 S'occuper de ses propres affaires afin de s'accroître: Parlons argent avec les inuit. *Recherches amérindiennes au Québec* 12(4):273–80.

1984a Humiliation et harmonie—L'expression du droit coutumier chez les inuit du Labrador. *Recherches amérindiennes au Québec* 14(4):3–8.

1984b *Les Tuvaalummit. Histoire sociale des inuit de Quaqtaq (Québec arctique).* Collection "Signes des Amériques," no. 4. Montreal: Recherches Amérindiennes au Québec.

1985 La recherche sur les inuit du Nord québécois: Bilan et perspectives. *Études/Inuit/Studies* 8(2):99–116.

Dorais, Louis-Jacques, ed.
1981 The Language of the Inuit: Historical, Phonological, and Grammatical Issues. *Études/Inuit/Studies* 5, supplement.

Duhaime, Gérard
1983 La sédentarisation au Nouveau-Québec inuit. *Études/Inuit/Studies* 7(2):25–52.

1985 *De l'igloo au H.L.M.: Les inuit sédentaires et l'état providence.* Collection Nordicana 48. Laval: Centre d'études nordiques.

1989 La catastrophe et l'État: Histoire démographique et changements sociaux dans l'Artique. *Études/Inuit/Studies* 13(1):75–114.

1991 Revenu personnel, destin collectif: La structure du revenu des inuit de l'Arctique du Québec, 1953–1983. *Canadian Ethnic Studies* 23:21–39.

Dumond, Don
1977 *The Eskimos and Aleuts.* London: Thames and Hudson.

1987 A Reexamination of Eskimo-Aleut Prehistory. *American Anthropologist* 89:32–56.

Eber, Dorothy Harley
1985 Bringing the Captain Back to the Bay. *Natural History* 94(1):66–73.

1989a Eskimo Memories. *History Today* 39:45–50.

1989b *When the Whalers Were up North: Inuit Memories from the Eastern Arctic.* Kingston and Montreal: McGill-Queens University Press.

Eckert, Penelope, and Russell Newmark
1980 Central Eskimo Song Duels: A Contextual Analysis of Ritual Ambiguity. *Ethnology* 19:191–212.

Études/Inuit/Studies
1984 Dans les traces de Boas: 100 ans d'anthropologie des inuit. *Études/Inuit/Studies* 8(1):1–80.

Ferguson, Jack
1971 Eskimo in a Satellite Society. In *Minority Canadians,* vol. 1, *Native Peoples,* edited by Jan Leonhard Elliot, pp. 15–28. Scarborough: Prentice-Hall of Canada.

Fitzhugh, William W.
1979 Les modes d'adaptation basés sur le caribou dans les régions centrales et septentrionales du Labrador. *Recherches amérindiennes au Québec* 9(1–2):55–70.

1980 A Review of Paleo-Eskimo Culture History in Southern Quebec-Labrador and Newfoundland. *Études/Inuit/Studies* 4(1–2):21–31.

1985 Early Contacts North of Newfoundland Before A.D. 1600: A Review. In *Cultures in Contact: The European Impact on Native Cultural Institutions in Eastern North America, A.D. 1000–1800,* edited by W. W. Fitzhugh, pp. 23–43. Washington: Smithsonian Institution Press.

Fitzhugh, William W., ed.
1975 *Prehistoric Maritime Adaptations of the Circumpolar Zone.* The Hague: Mouton.

Floquet, Anne
1982   Ethnohistoire des Inuit du bas Mackenzie. *Inter-Nord* 16:159–69.

Fortescue, Michael
1988   Thule and Back: A Critical Appraisal of Knud Rasmussen's Contribution to Eskimo Language Studies. *Études/Inuit/Studies* 12(1–2): 171–92.

Francis, Daniel
1984   *Arctic Chase: A History of Whaling in Canada's North.* St. John's, Nfld.: Breakwater Books.

Freeman, Milton M. R.
1967   An Ecological Study of Mobility and Settlement Patterns Among the Belcher Island Eskimo. *Arctic* 20(3):154–75.
1969   Adaptive Innovation Among Recent Eskimo Immigrants in the Eastern Canadian Arctic. *Polar Record* 14(93):769–81.
1971a   The Significance of Demographic Changes Occurring in the Canadian East Arctic. *Anthropologica* 13(1–2):215–36.
1971b   A Social and Ecological Analysis of Systematic Female Infanticide Among the Netsilik Eskimo. *American Anthropologist* 73(5):1011–18.
1976   Environment and Development: The Case of the Canadian Arctic. In *Science for Better Environment: Proceedings of the International Congress on the Human Environment,* pp. 860–66. Tokyo: Science Council of Japan.
1981   Persistence and Change: The Cultural Dimension. In *A Century of Canada's Arctic Islands,* edited by M. Zaslow, pp. 257–66. Ottawa: Royal Society of Canada.
1982   An Ecological Perspective on Man-Environment Research in the Hudson and James Bay Region. *Le naturaliste canadien* (Rev. Ecol. Syst.) 109:955–63.
1984a   Arctic Ecosystems. In *Handbook of North American Indians,* vol. 5, *Arctic,* edited by David Damas, pp. 36–48. Washington: Smithsonian Institution Press.
1984b   The Grise Fiord Project. In *Handbook of North American Indians,* vol. 5, *Arctic,* edited by David Damas, pp. 676–82. Washington: Smithsonian Institution Press.

Freeman, Milton M. R., ed.
1969   *Intermediate Adaptation in Newfoundland and the Arctic: A Strategy of Social and Economic Development.* St. John's: Memorial University of Newfoundland, Institute for Social and Economic Research.

Freeman, Milton M. R., and L. M. Hackman
1975   Bathurst Island NWT: A Test Case of Canada's Northern Policy. *Canadian Public Policy/ Analyses de Politiques* 1(3):402–14.

Freeman, Minnie Aodla
1975   *Life Among the Qallunaat.* Edmonton: Hurtig.
1981   ikumoaluminik—Living in Two Hells. In *A Century of Canada's Arctic Islands,* edited by M. Zaslow, pp. 267–74. Ottawa: Royal Society of Canada.

Gessain, Robert
1981   *Ovibos: La grande aventure des boeufs musqués et des hommes.* Paris: Éditions Robert Laffont.

Goehring, B., and J. K. Stager
1991   The intrusion of industrial time and space into Inuit lifeworld: Changing perceptions and behavior. *Environmental Behavior* 23:666–79.

Graburn, Nelson H. H.
1964   *Taqagmiut Eskimo Kinship Terminology.* NCRC 64–1. Ottawa: Department of Northern Affairs and National Resources, Northern Coordination and Research Centre.
1969   *Eskimos Without Igloos: Social and Economic Development in Sugluk.* Boston: Little, Brown.

Graburn, Nelson H. H., and Molly Lee
1990   The Arctic. In *Native North Americans: An Ethnohistorical Approach,* edited by Daniel K. Boxberger, pp. 23–64. Dubuque, Iowa: Kendall/Hunt Publishing Company.

Guemple, Lee
1969   The Eskimo Ritual Sponsor: A Problem in the Fusion of Semantic Domains. *Ethnology* 8(4): 468–83.
1972a   Alliance in Eskimo Society. In *Proceedings of the American Ethnological Society for 1971,* supplement. Seattle: University of Washington Press.
1972b   Eskimo Band Organization and the "DP Camp" Hypothesis. *Arctic Anthropology* 9(2):80–112.

Guemple, Lee, ed.
1979   *Inuit Adoption.* Mercury Series, Canadian Ethnology Service Paper 47. Ottawa: National Museum of Man.

Hawkes, Ernest W.
1916   *The Labrador Eskimo.* Geological Survey Memoirs, no. 91. Ottawa: Department of Mines.

Helmer, James W.
1991   Paleo-Eskimo prehistory of the North Devon Lowlands. *Arctic* 44:301–17.

Hickey, Clifford
1984   An Examination of Processes of Cultural Change Among Nineteenth Century Copper Inuit. *Études/Inuit/Studies* 8(1):13–36.

Hobart, Charles W.
1982   Inuit Employment at the Nanisivik Mine on Baffin Island. *Études/Inuit/Studies* 6(10):53–74.
1983   Quand cessent les emplois: Étude d'une communauté inuit canadienne. *Études/Inuit/Studies* 7:117–41.

Honigmann, John J.
1951   An Episode in the Administration of the Great Whale River Eskimo. *Human Organization* 10(2):5–14.

Honigmann, John J., and Irma Honigmann
1965   *Eskimo Townsmen.* Ottawa: Canadian Research Centre for Anthropology.

Hughes, Charles C.
1965   Under Four Flags: Recent Culture Change Among the Eskimos. *Current Anthropology* 6:3–73.

Idiens, Dale
1987   Eskimos in Scotland, c. 1682–1924. In *Indians and Europe: An Interdisciplinary Collection of Essays,* edited by Christian Feest, pp. 161–75. Aachen: Rader Verlag.

Israel, Heinz
1987   Johann Gottfried Schadow and His Inuit Portraits. In *Indians and Europe: An Interdisciplinary Collection of Essays,* edited by Christian Feest, pp. 235–42. Aachen: Rader Verlag.

Ittinuar, Peter
1981   Inuit Participation in Politics. In *A Century of Canada's Arctic Islands,* edited by M. Zaslow, pp. 291–98. Ottawa: Royal Society of Canada.

Jacob, H. K., K. Snoeijing, and R. Vaughan, eds.
1984   *Arctic Whaling: Proceedings of the International Symposium on Arctic Whaling.* Groningen: University of Groningen.

Jacobs, John D., and Douglas Stenton
1985   Environment, Resources, and Prehistoric Settlement in Upper Frobisher Bay, Baffin Island. *Arctic Anthropology* 22(2):59–76.

Jenness, Diamond
1922   The Life of the Copper Eskimos. In *Report of the Canadian Arctic Expedition, 1913–18,* vol. 12 (A). Ottawa.
1959   *The People of the Twilight.* 1928. Chicago: University of Chicago Press.
1964   *Eskimo Administration, II.* Technical Paper 14. Montreal: Arctic Institute of North America.
1965   *Eskimo Administration: III.* Technical Paper 16. Montreal: Arctic Institute of North America.
1968   *Eskimo Administration, V: Analysis and Reflections.* Technical Paper 21. Montreal: Arctic Institute of North America.

Jordan, Richard H., and Susan A. Kaplan
1980   An Anthropological View of the Inuit/European Contact Period in Central Labrador. *Études/Inuit/Studies* 4(1–2):35–45.

Kaplan, Susan A.
1980   Neo-Eskimo Occupations of the Northern Labrador Coast. *Arctic* 33:646–58.
1984   Eskimo-European Contact Archaeology in Labrador. In *Comparative Studies in the Archaeology of Colonialism,* edited by S. Dyson. Oxford: British Archaeological Reports.
1985   European Goods and Socio-Economic Change in Early Labrador Inuit Society. In *Cultures in Contact: The European Impact on Native Cultural Institutions in Eastern North America, A.D. 1000–1800,* edited by W. W. Fitzhugh, pp. 45–69. Washington: Smithsonian Institution Press.

Keenleyside, Anne
1990   Euro-American Whaling in the Canadian Arctic: Its Effects on Eskimo Health. *Arctic Anthropology* 27(1):1–19.

Kemp, William B.
1984   Baffinland Eskimo. In *Handbook of North American Indians,* vol. 5, *Arctic,* edited by David Damas, pp. 463–75. Washington: Smithsonian Institution Press.

Kennedy, John C.
1981   Productivité différentielle de la pêche à Makkovik. *Anthropologie et sociétés* 5(1):87–96.

1982   *Holding the Line—Ethnic Boundaries in a Northern Labrador Community*. St. John's: Memorial University of Newfoundland, Institute of Social and Economic Research.

Klutschak, Heinrich
1987   *Overland to Starvation Cove: With the Inuit in Search of Franklin, 1878–1880*. Edited and translated by William Barr. Toronto: University of Toronto Press.

Koster, Ditte
1974   The Emerging Confrontation Between Inuit and Kabloona in the Northwest Territories. *Western Canadian Journal of Anthropology* 4(2):1–15.

Kupfer, George, and Charles W. Hobart
1978   Impact of Oil Exploration Work on an Inuit Community. *Arctic Anthropology* 15(1):58–67.

Larochelle, Gilles
1975   Du travail salarié dans la construction à Puvirnituuq. *Recherches amérindiennes au Québec* 5(3):26–33.

Larsen, Helge
1981   Adaptation to Frigid Zones by Arctic Peoples. *Folk* 23:113–38.

Lauritzen, Philip
1983   *Oil and Amulets. Inuit: A People United at the Top of the World*. St. John's, Nfld.: Breakwater Books.

Lee, John Alan
1989   Waging the Seal War in the Media: Toward a Content Analysis of Moral Communication. *Canadian Journal of Communication* 14(1):37–56.

Lowe, Ronald
1984   L'assimilation linguistique des esquimaux de l'arctique de l'ouest. *Recherches amérindiennes au Québec* 14(4):54–57.

Lutz, M. M.
1982   *Musical Traditions of the Labrador Coast Inuit*. Mercury Series, Canadian Ethnology Service Paper 79. Ottawa: National Museum of Man.

McCartney, Allen P., ed.
1979   *Thule Eskimo Culture: An Anthropological Retrospective*. Archaeological Survey Paper 88. Ottawa: National Museum of Canada.

1984   Daniel Weetaluktuk: Contributions to Canadian Arctic Anthropology. *Études/Inuit/Studies* 8(1):103–16.

McCartney, Allen P., and James M. Savelle
1985   Thule Eskimo Whaling in the Central Canadian Arctic. *Arctic Anthropology* 22(2):37–58.

McElroy, Ann
1975   Arctic Modernization and Change in Inuit Family Organization. In *Marriage, Family, and Society*, edited by S. Parvez-Wakil, pp. 379–99. Toronto: Butterworth.

McGhee, Robert
1974   *Beluga Hunters: An Archaeological Reconstruction of the History and Culture of the Mackenzie Delta Kittegarymiut*. St. John's: Memorial University of Newfoundland, Institute for Social and Economic Research. Reprint. Ottawa: Canadian Museum of Civilization, 1988.

1980   Technological Change in the Prehistoric Eskimo Cultural Tradition. *Canadian Journal of Archaeology* 4:39–52.

1982a   The Past Ten Years in Canadian Arctic Prehistory. *Canadian Journal of Archaeology* 6:65–77.

1982b   Possible Norse-Eskimo Contacts in the Eastern Arctic. In *Early European Settlement and Exploration in Arctic Canada*, edited by G. M. Story, pp. 31–40. St. John's: Memorial University of Newfoundland.

1983   Eastern Arctic Prehistory: The Reality of a Myth? *Musk-Ox* 33:21–25.

1984a   Contact Between Native North Americans and the Medieval Norse. *American Antiquity* 49:4–26.

1984b   Thule Prehistory of Canada. In *Handbook of North American Indians*, vol. 5, *Arctic*, edited by David Damas, pp. 369–76. Washington: Smithsonian Institution Press.

1984c   *The Thule Village at Brooman Point, High Arctic Canada*. Archaeological Survey of Canada Paper 125. Ottawa: National Museum of Canada.

1986   Relics of an Arctic Life. *Beaver* 66(1):45–53.

1988   The Vikings Got Here First, But Why Did They Leave? *Canadian Geographic* 108(4):12–21.

McGrath, Robin
1984   *Canadian Inuit Literature: The Development*

of a Tradition. Ethnology Service Paper 94. Ottawa: National Museum of Canada.

Mailhot, José, J. P. Simard, and Sylvie Vincent
1980   On est toujours l'esquimau de quelqu'un. *Études/Inuit/Studies* 4(1–2):59–76.

Markoosie
1970   *Harpoon of the Hunter.* Kingston and Montreal: McGill-Queen's University Press.

Martijn, Charles A., and Norman Clermont, eds.
1980   Les inuit du Québec-Labrador. *Études/Inuit/Studies* 4(1–2).

Mary-Rousselière, Guy
1980   Qitdlarssuaq: L'histoire l'une migration polaire. Montreal: Presses de l'Université de Montréal.
1984   Iglulik. In *Handbook of North American Indians,* vol. 5, *Arctic,* edited by David Damas, pp. 431–46. Washington: Smithsonian Institution Press.

Maxwell, Moreau S.
1980a   Archaeology of the Arctic and Subarctic Zones. *Annual Review of Anthropology* 9:161–85.
1980b   The Politics of Inuit Alliance Movements in the Canadian Arctic. In *Political Organization of Native North Americans,* edited by E. L. Schusky, pp. 243–82. Washington: University Press of America.
1984   Pre-Dorset and Dorset Prehistory of Canada. In *Handbook of North American Indians,* vol. 5, *Arctic,* edited by David Damas, pp. 359–68. Washington: Smithsonian Institution Press.
1985   *Prehistory of the Eastern Arctic.* London: Academic Press.

Mayes, Robert G.
1982   Contemporary Inuit Society. *Musk-Ox* 30:36–47.

Merkur, Daniel
1987   Eagle, the Hunting Helper: The Cultic Significances of Inuit Mythological Tales. *History of Religions* 27:171–88.
1991   *Powers Which We Do Not Know: The Gods and Spirits of the Inuit.* Moscow, Idaho: University of Idaho Press.

Metayer, Maurice
1971   *I, Nuligak.* New York: Pocket Books.

Morrison, David A.
1987   Thule and Historic Copper Use in the Copper Inuit Arctic. *American Antiquity* 52:3–12.
1989   Radiocarbon Dating Thule Culture. *Arctic Anthropology* 26(2):48–77.
1990a   *Iglulualumiut Prehistory: The Lost Inuit of Franklin Bay.* Mercury Series, Canadian Ethnology Service Paper. Ottawa: Canadian Museum of Civilization.
1990b   The Lost Inuit of Franklin Bay. *Beaver* 70(4): 48–54.

Mowat, Farley
1968   *People of the Deer.* New York: Pyramid Books.

Müller-Wille, Ludger
1985   Une méthodologie pour les enquêtes toponymiques authochtones: Le répertoire de la région de Kativik et de la zone côtière. *Études/Inuit/Studies* 9(1):51–66.

Nattiez, Jean-Jacques
1980   Le disque de musique amérindienne. II. Introduction á l'écoute des disques de musique inuit. *Recherches amérindiennes au Québec* 10(1–2):110–31.

Neatby, Leslie H.
1984   Exploration and History of the Canadian Arctic. In *Handbook of North American Indians,* vol. 5, *Arctic,* edited by David Damas, pp. 377–90. Washington: Smithsonian Institution Press.

Nungak, Zehedee, and Eugene Arima
1988   *Inuit Stories, Povunguituk.* Mercury Series, Canadian Ethnology Service Paper. Ottawa: Canadian Museum of Civilization.

Oosten, Jaarich G.
1981   The Structure of the Shamanistic Complex Among the Netsilik and Iglulik. *Études/Inuit/Studies* 5(1):83–98.
1986   Male and Female in Inuit Shamanism. *Études/Inuit/Studies* 10(1–2):115–32.

Ostermann, H., ed.
1942   The Mackenzie Eskimos, after K. Rasmussen's Posthumous Notes. *Report of the Fifth Thule Expedition,* 10(2):1–166. Copenhagen.

Paine, Robert
1977a   The Nursery Game—Colonizers and Colonized in the Canadian Arctic. *Études/Inuit/Studies* 1:5–32.
1977b   *The White Arctic: Anthropological Essays on Tutelage and Ethnicity.* St. John's: Memorial

University of Newfoundland, Institute for Social and Economic Research.

Paine, Robert, ed.
1971   *Patrons and Brokers in the East Arctic.* St. John's: Memorial University of Newfoundland, Institute for Social and Economic Research.

Park, Robert W.
1987   Dog Remains from Devon Island, N.W.T.: Archaeological and Osteological Evidence for Domestic Dog Use in the Thule Culture. *Arctic* 40:184–90.

Pelinski, Ramon
1981   *La musique des inuit du Caribou: Cinq perspectives méthodologiques.* Montreal: University of Montreal Press.

Pelly, David F.
1990   In the face of adversity. *Geographical Magazine* 62 (January):16–18.
1991   Pond Inlet: A community caught between two worlds. *Canadian Geographic* 11:46–52.

Pelly, Donald M.
1991   How Inuit Find Their Way in the Trackless Arctic. *Canadian Geographic* 111(4):58–64.

Pitseolak, Peter, and D. Eber
1975   *People from Our Side: A Life Story with Photographs by Peter Pitseolak and Oral Biography by Dorothy Eber.* Edmonton: Hurtig.

Prattis, J. Ian, and Jean-Phillipe Chartrand
1990   The Cultural Division of Labour in the Canadian North: A Statistical Study of the Inuit. *Canadian Review of Sociology and Anthropology* 27:49–73.

Raine, David F.
1980   *Pitseolak: A Canadian Tragedy.* Edmonton: Hurtig.

Rasmussen, Knud
1929   Intellectual Culture of the Iglulik Eskimos. *Report of the Fifth Thule Expedition 1921–24,* 7(1):1–304. Copenhagen.
1930a Intellectual Culture of the Hudson Bay Eskimos. *Report of the Fifth Thule Expedition, 1921–24,* 7 (1–3). Copenhagen.
1930b Observations on the Intellectual Culture of the Caribou Eskimos. *Report of the Fifth Thule Expedition, 1921–24,* 7(2):1–114. Copenhagen.
1931   The Netsilik Eskimos. *Report of the Fifth Thule Expedition, 1921–24,* 8:1–542. Copenhagen.
1932   Intellectual Culture of the Copper Eskimos. *Report of the Fifth Thule Expedition, 1921–24,* 9:1–350. Copenhagen.

Remie, Cornelius H. W.
1985   Towards a New Perspective on Netjilik Inuit Female Infanticide. *Études/Inuit/Studies* 9(1):67–76.
1988   Flying Like a Butterfly, or Knud Rasmussen Among the Netsilingmiut. *Études/Inuit/Studies* 12(1–2):101–28.

Riches, David
1974   The Netsilik Eskimo: A Special Case of Selective Female Infanticide. *Ethnology* 13(4): 351–61.

Richling, Barnett
1983   Labrador Nalujuk: The Transformation of an Aboriginal Inuit Ritual Complex in a Post-contact Setting. In *The Power of Symbols: Masks and Masquerade in the Americas,* edited by N. Ross Crumrine and Marjorie Halpin, pp. 21–29. Vancouver: University of British Columbia Press.
1985   Stuck Up on a Rock: Resettlement and Community Development in Hopedale, Labrador. *Human Organization* 44:348–52.
1989a Recent Trends in the Northern Labrador Seal Hunt. *Études/Inuit/Studies* 13(1):61–74.
1989b "Very Serious Reflections": Inuit Dreams About Salvation and Loss in Eighteenth-Century Labrador. *Ethnohistory* 36:148–69.

Robitaille, Norbert, and Robert Choinière
1988   The Inuit Population of Northern Quebec: Present Situation, Future Trends. *Anthropologica* 30:137–53.

Ross, W. Gilles
1973   Whaling in Hudson Bay. Part III: The Voyage of the "Perseverance." *Beaver* 304(2):52–59.
1975   *Whaling and Eskimos: Hudson Bay, 1860–1915.* Publications in Ethnology 10. Ottawa: National Museum of Man.
1977   Whaling and the Decline of Native Populations. *Arctic Anthropology* 14(2):1–8.
1981   Whaling, Inuit, and the Arctic Islands. In *A Century of Canada's Arctic Islands,* edited by M. Zaslow, pp. 33–50. Ottawa: Royal Society of Canada.

1985   *Arctic Whalers, Icy Seas.* Toronto: Irwin Publishing.

1990   The Use and Misuse of Historical Photographs: A Case Study from Hudson Bay, Canada. *Arctic Anthropology* 27(2):93–112.

Ross, W. Gilles, ed.

1984   *An Arctic Whaling Diary: The Journal of Captain George Comer in Hudson Bay, 1903–1905.* Toronto: University of Toronto Press.

Rouland, Norbert

1979   Les modes indigènes de solution des conflits chez les inuit. *Études/Inuit/Studies* 3.

1983   L'acculturation judiciare chez les inuit du Canada (1ère et 2e parties). *Recherches amérindiennes au Québec* 13:179–92, 307–18.

Rowley, Susan

1985   Population Movements in the Canadian Arctic. *Études/Inuit/Studies* 9(1):3–22.

Sabo, George, III, and Deborah Rowland Sabo

1985   Belief Systems and the Ecology of Sea Mammal Hunting Among the Baffinland Eskimo. *Arctic Anthropology* 22(2):77–86.

Saladin d'Anglure, Bernard

1967   *L'organisation sociale traditionelle des esquimaux de Kangiusufuaaj (Nouveau-Québec).* Centre d'Études nordiques Travaux divers, no. 17. Quebec: Université Laval.

1977   Iqallijug, ou les reminiscences d'une âme-anom inuit. *Études/Inuit/Studies* 1(1):33–63.

1978   L'Homme (angut), le fils (irniq) et la lumière (qau); ou le cercle du pouvoir masculin chez les inuit de l'Arctique central. *Anthropologica* 20(1–2):104–44.

1980a   "Petit-Ventre" l'enfant-géant du cosmos inuit: Ethnographie de l'enfant et enfance de l'ethnographie dans l'Arctique central. *L'Homme* 20(1):7–46.

1980b   Violences et enfantements inuit ou les noeuds de la vie dans le fil du temps. *Anthropologie et Sociétés* 4(2):65–100.

1983   Ijiqqat: Voyage au pays de l'invisible inuit. *Études/Inuit/Studies* 7(1):67–84.

1984a   Contemporary Inuit of Quebec. In *Handbook of North American Indians,* vol. 5, *Arctic,* edited by David Damas, pp. 683–88. Washington: Smithsonian Institution Press.

1984b   Inuit of Quebec. In *Handbook of North American Indians,* vol. 5, *Arctic,* edited by David Damas, pp. 476–507. Washington: Smithsonian Institution Press.

1986   Du foetus au chamane: La construction d'un "troisième sex." *Études/Inuit/Studies* 10(1–2): 25–114.

1988   Kunut et les angakkut iglulik. *Études/Inuit/Studies* 12(1–2):57–80.

Samson, Gilles

1978   Ethnohistoire des Mushuau Innuts (1903–1910). *Recherches amérindiennes au Québec* 7(3–4):59–72.

Savelle, James M.

1981   The Nature of Nineteenth Century Inuit Occupations of the High Arctic Islands of Canada. *Études/Inuit/Studies* 5(2):109–24.

Scheffel, David

1985   From Polygyny to Cousin Marriage? Acculturation and Marriage in 19th Century Labrador Inuit Society. *Études/Inuit/Studies* 8(2): 61–76.

Schindler, Debra L.

1985   Anthropology in the Arctic: A Critique of Racial Typology and Narrative Theory. *Current Anthropology* 26:475–500.

Schledermann, Peter

1981   Inuit Prehistory and Archaeology. In *A Century of Canada's Arctic Islands,* edited by M. Zaslow, pp. 245–65. Ottawa: Royal Society of Canada.

Schrire, Carmel, and W. L. Steiger

1974   A Matter of Life and Death: An Investigation into the Practice of Female Infanticide in the Arctic. *Man* 9:161–84.

1981   Arctic Infanticide Revisited. *Études/Inuit/Studies* 5(1):111–17.

Sillitoe, Paul

1981   The Flexible Social Organization of the Labrador Eskimos: The Response to a Harsh Environment. *Arctic Anthropology* 18(1):78–86.

Smith, Derek G.

1984   Mackenzie Delta Eskimo. In *Handbook of North American Indians,* vol. 5, *Arctic,* edited by David Damas, pp. 347–58. Washington: Smithsonian Institution Press.

Smith, Eric Alden
1981   The Application of Optimal Foraging Theory to the Analysis of Hunter-Gatherer Group Size. In *Hunter-Gatherer Foraging Strategies,* edited by Bruce Winterhalder and Eric Alden Smith, pp. 36–65. Chicago: University of Chicago Press.
1984   Approaches to Inuit Socioecology. *Études/Inuit/Studies* 8(1):65–88.
1991   *Inujjuamiut Foraging Strategies.* Hawthorne, N.Y.: Aldine de Gruyter.

Steenhoven, Geert van den
1959   *Legal Concepts Among the Netsilik of Pelly Bay.* Northern Coordination and Research Centre Report 3. Ottawa: Department of Northern Affairs and National Resources.
1962   *Leadership and Law Among the Eskimos of the Keewatin District, Northwest Territories.* The Hague: Uitgeverij Excelsior.

Stefánsson, Vilhjálmur
1913   *My Life with the Eskimo.* New York: Macmillan.
1921   *The Friendly Arctic: The Story of Five Years in Polar Regions.* New York: Macmillan.

Stenbaek, Marianne
1987   Forty Years of Cultural Change Among the Inuit of Alaska, Canada, and Greenland: Some Reflections. *Arctic* 40:300–9.

Stevenson, Alex
1973   The Robert Janes Murder Trial at Pond Inlet. *Beaver* 304(2):16–23.

Sturtevant, William C., and David B. Quinn
1987   Eskimos in Europe in 1567, 1576, and 1577. In *Indians and Europe: An Interdisciplinary Collection of Essays,* edited by Christian Feest, pp. 61–140. Aachen: Rader Verlag.

Sutherland, Patricia D.
1985   *The Franklin Era in Canadian Arctic History, 1845–1859.* Mercury Series, Canadian Archaeological Survey Paper 131. Ottawa: National Museum of Man.

Taylor, J. Garth
1969   William Turner's Journey to the Caribou Country with the Labrador Eskimos in 1780. *Ethnohistory* 16:141–64.
1972   Eskimo Answers to an Eighteenth Century Questionnaire. *Ethnohistory* 19:135–46.
1974   *Labrador Eskimo Settlements of the Early Contact Period.* Canadian Ethnology Service Paper 9. Ottawa: National Museum of Man.
1975   Demography and Adaptations of Eighteenth Century Eskimo Groups in Northern Labrador and Ungava. In *Prehistoric Maritime Adaptations of the Circumpolar Zone,* edited by W. W. Fitzhugh, pp. 269–78. The Hague: Mouton.
1978   Did the First Eskimos Speak Algonquian? In *Papers of the Ninth Algonquian Conference,* edited by William Cowan, pp. 96–103. Ottawa: Carleton University.
1979   L'exploitation du caribou par les inuit de la côte du Labrador (1694–1977). *Recherches amérindiennes au Québec* 9(1–2):71–81.
1980   The Inuit of Southern Quebec—Labrador: Reviewing the Evidence. *Études/Inuit/Studies* 4(1–2):185–94.
1983   The Two Worlds of Mikak, Parts 1–2. *Beaver* 314(3):4–13; 314(4):18–25.
1984   Historical Ethnography of the Labrador Coast. In *Handbook of North American Indians,* vol. 5, *Arctic,* edited by David Damas, pp. 508–21. Washington: Smithsonian Institution Press.
1988   Labrador Inuit Whale Use During the Early Contact Period. *Arctic Anthropology* 25(1):120–35.
1990   The Labrador Inuit Kashim (Ceremonial House) Complex. *Arctic Anthropology* 27(2):51–67.

Taylor, J. Garth, and Helga Taylor
1986   Labrador Inuit Summer Ceremonies. *Études/Inuit/Studies* 10(1–2):233–44.

Tedjuk, Joe
1986   Times of Sorrow, Times of Joy. *Beaver* 66(1):28–38.

Trott, C. G.
1982   The Inuk as Object—Some Problems in the Study of Inuit Social Organization. *Études/Inuit/Studies* 6(2):93–108.

Trudel, François
1978a   The Inuit of Southern Labrador and the Development of French Sedentary Fisheries (1700–1760). In *Papers from the Fourth Annual Congress, Canadian Ethnology Society, 1977,* edited by Richard J. Preston, pp. 99–122. Canadian Ethnology Service Paper 40. Ottawa: National Museum of Man.
1978b   Les inuit du Labrador méridional face à l'ex-

ploitation canadienne et française des pêcheries (1700–1760). *Revue d'histoire de l'Amérique française* 31:481–500.

1978c   Les inuit face à l'expansion commerciale euro-
péenne dans la region du Détroit de Belle-Isle
au XVIe et XVIIe siècles. *Recherches amérindiennes au Québec* 7(3–4):49–58.

1979   L'importance du caribou dans la subsistance
et la traite chez les inuit de la côte orientale
de la baie d'Hudson (1839–1910). *Recherches
amérindiennes au Québec* 9(1–2):141–50.

1987a   Moses: Un employé inuit de la Compagnie de
la baie d'Hudson. *Études/Inuit/Studies* 11(2):
165–86.

1987b   Trolio et Jack: Deux inuit au service de
la Compagnie de la Baie d'Hudson au 18è
siècle. *Canadian Journal of Native Studies*
7:79–93.

Tuck, James A.
1976   Paleoeskimo Cultures of Northern Labrador.
In *Eastern Arctic Prehistory: Paleoeskimo
Problems.* Edited by Moreau S. Maxwell.
Memoirs of the Society for American Arche-
ology 31.

Tuck, James A., and Robert Grenier
1981   A 16th Century Basque Whaling Station in
Labrador. *Scientific American* 245(5):180–90.

Turner, Lucien M.
1888   On the Indians and Eskimos of the Ungava
District, Labrador. *Proceedings and Transactions of the Royal Society of Canada for the
Year 1887,* vol. 5, sec. 2:99–119.

1894   Ethnology of the Ungava District, Hudson
Bay Territory. Edited by John Murdoch. In
*Eleventh Annual Report of the Bureau of Amer-
ican Ethnology for the Years 1889-1890,* pp. 159–
350. Washington.

Usher, Peter J.
1970   *The Bankslanders: Economy and Ecology of a
Frontier Trapping Community.* 3 vols. NRSG
71-1. Ottawa: Department of Indian Affairs
and National Resources.

1971   The Canadian Western Arctic: A Century of
Change. *Anthropologica,* n.s. 13(1–2):169–83.

Valentine, Victor F., and Frank G. Vallee, eds.
1965   *Eskimo of the Canadian Arctic.* Toronto:
McClelland and Stewart.

Vallee, Frank G.
1966   Eskimo Theories of Mental Illness in the Hudson
Bay Region. *Anthropologica,* n.s., 8(1):53–83.

1967a   *Kabloona and Eskimo in the Central Keewatin.* Ottawa: Canadian Research Center for
Anthropology.

1967b   *Povungnetuk and Its Cooperative: A Case Study
in Community Change.* NCRC-67-2. Ottawa:
Department of Northern Affairs and National
Resources, Northern Coordination and Research Centre.

1971   Eskimos of Canada as a Minority Group. In
Minority Canadians, vol. 1, *Native Peoples,*
edited by Jean L. Elliott, pp. 75–88. Scarborough: Prentice-Hall of Canada.

1972   Eskimos of Canada as a Minority Group:
Social and Cultural Perspectives. In *Education in the North,* edited by Frank Darnell,
pp. 20–41. Fairbanks: University of Alaska,
Arctic Institute of North America.

Vallee, Frank G., Derek G. Smith, and Joseph D. Cooper
1984   Contemporary Canadian Inuit. In *Handbook
of North American Indians,* vol. 5, *Arctic,* edited by David Damas, pp. 662–75. Washington: Smithsonian Institution Press.

VanderZwaag, David L., and Cynthia Lamson, eds.
1990   *The Challenge of Arctic Shipping: Science,
Environmental Assessment, and Human
Values.* Montreal: McGill-Queen's University
Press.

Van Stone, James W., and Wendell H. Oswalt
1959   *The Caribou Eskimos of Eskimo Point.* NCRC-
59-2. Ottawa: Department of Northern Affairs and National Resources, Northern Coordination and Research Centre.

Vernon, Philip E.
1966   Educational and Intellectual Development
Among Canadian Indians and Eskimos. *Educational Review* 18:79–91, 186–95.

Vézinet, Monique
1979   L'économie traditionnelle du caribou chez les
inuit du Québec. *Recherches amérindiennes
au Québec* 9(1–2):82–92.

1980   *Les Nunamiut. Inuit au coeur des terres.* Collection Civilisation du Québec, no. 28. Quebec:
Ministère des Affaires Culturelles.

1982   Occupation humaine de l'Ungava. Perspectives ethnohistoriques et ecologiques. *Paleo-Quebec,* no. 14.

Weissling, Lee E.
1991 Inuit Life in the Eastern Canadian Arctic, 1922–42: Change as recorded by the RMCP. *Canadian Geographer* 35(1):59–69.

Wenzel, George W.
1979 Inuit and Local Control: The Case of Somerset Island. *Études/Inuit/Studies* 3(2):19–25.
1981 *Clyde Inuit Adaptation and Ecology: The Organization of Subsistence.* Canadian Ethnology Service Paper 77. Ottawa: National Museum of Man.
1983 The Integration of "Remote" Site Labor into the Inuit Economy of Clyde River, N.W.T. *Arctic Anthropology* 20(2):79–92.
1984 L'écologie culturelle et les inuit du Canada: une approche appliqué. *Études/Inuit/Studies* 8(1):89–102.
1989 Sealing at Clyde River, N.W.T.: A Discussion of Inuit Economy. *Études/Inuit/Studies* 13(1):3–23.

Williamson, Robert G.
1974 *Eskimo Underground: Socio-Cultural Change in the Canadian Central Arctic.* Uppsala: Uppsala University.

Wonders, William C.
1987 Native Claims and Place Names in Canada's Western Arctic. *Canadian Journal of Native Studies/Révue canadienne des études autochtones* 7:111–20.

Woodbury, Anthony C.
1984 Eskimo and Aleut Languages. In *Handbook of North American Indians,* vol. 5, *Arctic,* edited by David Damas, pp. 49–63. Washington: Smithsonian Institution Press.

Wright, Robin K.
1987 The Traveling Exhibition of Captain Samuel Hadlock, Jr.: Eskimos in Europe, 1822–1826. In *Indians and Europe: An Interdisciplinary Collection of Essays,* edited by Christian Feest, pp. 215–34. Aachen: Rader Verlag.

Yorga, Brian W. D.
1980 *Washout: A Western Thule Site on Herschel Island, Yukon Territory.* Archaeological Survey of Canada Paper 98. Ottawa: National Museum of Man.

Zaslow, Morris
1981 Administering the Arctic Islands, 1880–1940: Policemen, Missionaries, Fur Traders. In *A Century of Canada's Arctic Islands,* edited by M. Zaslow, pp. 61–78. Ottawa: Royal Society of Canada.

Section Eleven

✦

MÉTIS

Alberta Federation of Metis Settlement Associations
1982   *Metisism: A Canadian Identity.* Edmonton: Alberta Federation of Metis Settlement Association.

Anctil, Pierre
1981   L'exil américain de Louis Riel, 1874–1884. *Recherches amérindiennes au Québec* 11(3): 239–50.

Anderson, D. R., and A. M. Anderson
1977   *The Metis People of Canada: A History.* Edmonton: Alberta Federation of Metis Settlement Associations.

Association of Metis and Non-Status Indians of Saskatchewan
1979   *Louis Riel: Justice Must Be Done.* Winnipeg: Manitoba Metis Federation Press.

Bakker, Peter
1990   The Genesis of Michif: A First Hypothesis. In *Papers of the Twenty-first Algonquian Conference,* edited by William Cowan, pp. 12–35. Ottawa: Carleton University.
1991   The Ojibwa Element in Michif. In *Papers of the Twenty-second Algonquian Conference,* edited by William Cowan, pp. 11–20. Ottawa: Carleton University.

Barkwell, Lawrence J., et al.
1989   Status of Metis Children Within the Child Welfare System. *Canadian Journal of Native Studies* 9(1):33–53.

Barron, F. Laurie, and James B. Waldram
1986   *1885 and After: Native Society in Transition.* Regina, Sask.: Canadian Plains Research Center.

Beal, Bob, and R. C. Macleod
1984   *Prairie Fire: The 1885 North-West Rebellion.* Edmonton: Hurtig.

Beal, Bob, and Rudy Wiebe
1985   *War in the West: Voices of the 1885 Rebellion.* Toronto: McClelland and Stewart.

Bienvenue, R. M.
1990   Symbolic and material interests in language policy disputes: A Canadian case. *Social Science Quarterly* 71:729–43.

Boisvert, David, and Keith Turnbull
1985   Who Are the Métis? *Studies in Political Economy* 18:107–47.

Bone, Robert M., and Milford B. Green
1983   Housing Assistance and Maintenance for the Metis in Northern Saskatchewan. *Canadian Public Policy* 9:476–86.

Bowsfield, Hartwell
1969   *Louis Riel: Rebel of the Western Frontier or Victim of Politics and Prejudice.* Toronto: Copp Clark.
1971   *Louis Riel: The Rebel and the Hero.* Toronto: Oxford University Press.

Brown, F. Laurie
1990   CCF and the Development of Metis Colonies in Southern Saskatchewan During the Premiership of T. C. Douglas, 1944–1961. *Canadian Journal of Native Studies* 10(2):243–71.

Brown, Jennifer S. H.
1978   Ultimate Respectability: Fur Trade Children in the "Civilized World." *Beaver* 308(4):48–55.
1980   Linguistic Solitudes and Changing Social Categories. In *Old Trails and New Directions,* edited by C. M. Judd and A. J. Ray, pp. 147–59. Toronto: University of Toronto Press.
1985   Métis. In *Canadian Encyclopedia*, pp. 1124–27. Edmonton: Hurtig.
1987   The Métis: Genesis and Rebirth. In *Native People, Native Lands,* edited by Bruce A. Cox, pp. 136–47. Ottawa: Carleton University.

Charette, Guillaume, ed.
1976   *Vanishing Spaces: Memoirs of a Prairie Métis.* Winnipeg: Éditions Bois-Brûlés.

Charlebois, Peter
1975   *The Life of Louis Riel.* Toronto: NC Press.

Chislett, K. L., et al.
1987   Housing Mismatch for Metis in Northern Saskatchewan. *Canadian Geographic* 31:341–46.

Clark, W. Leland
1981   The Place of the Metis Within the Agricultural Economy of the Red River During the 1840s and 1850s. *Canadian Journal of Native Studies* 3(1):69–84.

Coutts, Robert
1988   The Role of Agriculture in an English-speaking Halfbreed Economy: The Case of St. Andrew's, Red River. *Native Studies Review* 4(1–2):67–94.

Crawford, John C.
1983   Speaking Michif in Four Metis Communities.
Canadian Journal of Native Studies 3(1):47–55.
1985   What is Michif? Language in the Métis Tradition. In *The New Peoples,* edited by Jacqueline Peterson and Jennifer S. H. Brown, pp. 231–41. Winnipeg: University of Manitoba Press; Lincoln: University of Nebraska Press.

Dempsey, Hugh A., ed.
1985   Calgary and the Riel Rebellion. *Alberta History* 33(2):7–18.

de Trémaudan, Auguste Henri
1935   *Histoire de la nation métisse dans l'Ouest canadien.* Montreal: Lévesque.
1982   *Hold High Your Heads: History of The Metis Nation in Western Canada.* Translated Elizabeth Maguet. Winnipeg: Pemmican Publications.

Dick, Lyle
1991   Seven Oaks Incident and the Construction of a Historical Tradition. *Journal of Canadian Historical Association* 2:91–113.

Dickason, Olive Patricia
1982   From "One Nation" in the Northeast to "New Nation" in the Northwest: A Look at the Emergence of the Metis. *American Indian Culture and Research Journal* 6(2):1–21.

Dobbin, Murray
1981   *The One-and-a-Half Men: The Story of Jim Brady and Malcolm Norris, Metis Patriots of the Twentieth Century.* Vancouver: New Star Books.

Douaud, Patrick C.
1980   Metis: A Case of Triadic Linguistic Economy. *Anthropological Linguistics.*
1983   Canadian Metis Identity: A Pattern of Evolution. *Anthropos* 78:71–88.
1985   *Ethnolinguistic Profile of the Canadian Metis.* Mercury Series, Canadian Ethnology Service Paper 99. Ottawa: National Museum of Man.

Driben, Paul
1975   *We Are Metis: The Ethnography of a Halfbreed Community in Northern Alberta.* New York: AMS Press.

Ens, Gerhard
1988   Dispossession or Adaptation? Migration and Persistence of the Red River Metis, 1835–

1890. *Historical Papers/Communications Historiques* 1988:120–44.

Flanagan, Thomas E.
1974a   Catastrophe and the Millennium: A New View of Louis Riel. In *Canadian Plains Studies 3: Religion and Society in the Prairie West,* edited by R. Allen, pp. 35–51. Regina, Sask.: Canadian Plains Research Center.
1974b   Louis "David" Riel: Prophet, Priest-King, Infallible Pontiff. *Journal of Canadian Studies* 9(3):15–25.
1975   The Mission of Louis Riel. *Alberta History* 23(1):1–12.
1976a   *The Diaries of Louis Riel.* Edmonton: Hurtig.
1976b   The Riel "Lunacy Commission": The Report of Dr. Valade. *Revue de l'Université d'Ottawa* 46:108–27.
1977   Louis Riel: Insanity and Prophecy. In *The Settlement of the West,* edited by Howard Palmer. Calgary: University of Calgary.
1979   *Louis "David" Riel: "Prophet of the New World."* Toronto: University of Toronto Press.
1983a   The Case Against Métis Aboriginal Rights. *Canadian Public Policy* 9 (3):314–25.
1983b   Louis Riel and Aboriginal Rights. In *As Long as the Sun Shines and Water Flows: A Reader in Canadian Native Studies,* edited by I. A. L. Getty and A. S. Lussier, pp. 247–62. Vancouver: University of British Columbia Press.
1983c   *Riel and the Rebellion of 1885 Reconsidered.* Saskatoon: Western Producer Prairie Books.
1985a   Metis Aboriginal Rights: Some Historical and Contemporary Problems. In *The Quest for Justice: Aboriginal Peoples and Aboriginal Rights,* edited by Menno Boldt and J. Anthony Long, pp. 230–45. Toronto: University of Toronto Press.
1985b   Louis Riel and the Dispersion of the American Métis. *Minnesota History* 49:179–90.
1985c   Louis Riel: Was He Really Crazy? *Humanities Association of Canada Newsletter* 13:7–27.
1987   Metis Land Claims at St. Laurent: Old Arguments and New Evidence. *Prairie Forum* 12(2): 245–56.
1991   Market for Métis Lands in Manitoba: An Exploratory Study. *Prairie Forum* 16(1):1–20.

Flanagan, Thomas E., and John Foster, eds.
1985   The Metis: Past and Present. *Canadian Ethnic Studies* 17(2).

Flanagan, Thomas E., and C. M. Rocan
1980–81 A Guide to the Louis Riel Papers. *Archivaria* 11:135–69.

Foster, John E.
1976   The Origins of the Mixed Bloods in the Canadian West. In *Essays on Western History,* edited by L. H. Thomas, pp. 69–80. Edmonton: University of Alberta Press.
1978   The Metis: The People and the Term. *Prairie Forum* 3:79–90.
1985   Paulet Paul: Metis or "House Indian" Folk Hero? *Manitoba History* 9 (Spring): 2–8.

Foster, John E., ed.
1975   Rupert's Land and the Red River Settlement, 1820–1870. In *The Prairie West to 1905,* edited by L. G. Thomas, pp. 19–72. Toronto: Oxford University Press.

Gallagher, Brian
1988   A Re-examination of Race, Class, and Society in Red River. *Native Studies Review* 4(1–2):25–66.

Gauvreau, D., F. Bernèche, and J. A. Fernandez
1982   La population des Métis et des Indiens sans statut: Essai d'estimation et de distribution spatiale. *Recherches amérindiennes au Québec* 12(2):95–104.

Giraud, Marcel
1954   Metis Settlement in the North West Territories. *Saskatchewan History* 7:1–16.
1956   The Western Metis After the Insurrection. *Saskatchewan History* 9(1):1–15.
1986   *The Métis in the Canadian West.* 1945. 2 vols. Translated by George Woodcock. Edmonton: University of Alberta Press.

Gorham, Harriet
1987   Families of Mixed Descent in the Western Great Lakes Region. In *Native People, Native Lands,* edited by Bruce A. Cox, pp. 37–55. Ottawa: Carleton University.

Hall, D. J.
1977   The Half-Breed Claims Commission. *Alberta History* 25:1–8.

Harrison, Julia D.
1985   *Metis: People Between Two Worlds.* Vancouver: Douglas and McIntyre.

Hatt, Fred K.
1971   The Canadian Metis: Recent Interpretations. *Canadian Ethnic Studies* 3:1–16.

Hildebrandt, Walter
1985a   The Battle of Batoche. *Prairie Forum* 10:17–63.
1985b   *The Battle of Batoche: British Small Warfare and the Entrenched Métis.* Studies in Archaeology, Architecture, and History. Ottawa: National Historic Parks and Sites Branch.

Howard, Joseph Kinsey
1952   *Strange Empire: Louis Riel and the Metis People.* New York: W. Morrow.

Judd, Carol M.
1982   Mixed Bloods of Moose Factory, 1730–1981: A Socio-Economic Study. *American Indian Culture and Research Journal* 6(2):65–88.

Kienetz, Alvin
1988   Metis "Nationalism" and the Concept of a Metis Land Base in Canada's Prairies Provinces. *Canadian Review of Studies in Nationalism/Révue canadienne des études sur le nationalisme* 15(1–2):11–18.

Lafontaine, Thérèse E.
1979   Louis Riel: A Preliminary Bibliography 1963–1968. In *Louis Riel and The Metis,* edited by A. S. Lussier, pp. 129–62. Winnipeg: Pemmican Publications.

Larmour, Jean
1970   Edgar Dewdney and the Aftermath of the Rebellion. *Saskatchewan History* 23:105–17.

LaRocque, Emma
1983   The Metis in English Canadian Literature. *Canadian Journal of Native Studies* 3(1):85–94.
1986   Conversations on Metis Identity. *Prairie Fire* 7(1):19–24.

Laverdure, Patline, and Ida Rose Allard
1983   *The Michif Dictionary: Turtle Mountain Chippewa Cree.* Winnipeg: Pemmican Publications.

Lee, David
1989   Métis Militant Rebels of 1885. *Canadian Ethnic Studies* 21(3):1–19.

Light, Douglas
1987   *Footprints in the Dust.* North Battleford, Sask.: Turner-Warwick Printers.

Lussier, Antoine S., ed.
1979   *Riel and the Metis: Riel Mini-conference Papers.* Winnipeg: Manitoba Metis Federation Press.
1983   *Louis Riel and the Metis.* Winnipeg: Pemmican Publications.

Lussier, Antoine S., and D. Bruce Sealey, eds.
1978–80 *The Other Natives: The Metis, 1700–1885.* 3 vols. Winnipeg: Manitoba Metis Federation Press.

McDonald, Jeanne
1982   Nous marchons dans les traces de nos ancêtres: Et pourtant il y en a encore pour dire que nous ne sommes plus indiens. *Recherches amérindiennes au Québec* 12(2):111–14.

MacEwan, Grant
1981   *Metis Makers of History.* Saskatoon: Western Producer Prairie Books.

McLean, Don
1985   *1885: Metis Rebellion or Government Conspiracy?* Regina, Sask.: Gabriel Dumont Institute.

MacLeod, Margaret, and W. L. Morton
1963   *Cuthbert Grant of Grantown.* Toronto: McClelland and Stewart.

McNab, David T.
1983   "Hearty Co-operation and Efficient Aid": The Metis and Treaty #3. *Canadian Journal of Native Studies* 3:131–50.
1985   Metis Participation in the Treaty-making Process in Ontario: A Reconnaissance. *Native Studies Review* 1(2):57–79.

Mailhot, P. R., and D. N. Sprague
1985   Persistent Settlers: The Dispersal and Resettlement of the Red River Métis, 1870–1885. *Canadian Journal of Ethnic Studies* 17:1–30.

Martel, Gilles
1978   Les indiens dans la pensée messianique de Louis Riel. *Recherches amérindiennes au Québec* 8(2):123–37.
1984   *Le messianisme de Louis Riel.* Waterloo: Wilfred Laurier University Press.

Metis Association of Alberta
1979   *Origins of the Alberta Metis: Land Claims Research Project, 1978–79.*

1980   *The Metis and the Land in Alberta: Land Claims Research Project 1979–80.*

Miller, J. R.
1988   From Riel to the Métis. *Canadian Historical Review* 69:1–20.

Morton, Arthur S.
1939   The New Nation, the Metis. *Royal Society of Canada, Proceedings and Transactions,* 137–45.

Morton, Desmond
1972   *The Last War Drum.* Toronto: Hakkert.

Morton, Desmond, ed.
1974   *The Queen vs. Louis Riel.* Toronto: University of Toronto Press.

Morton, W. L.
1949   Agriculture in the Red River Colony. *Canadian Historical Review* 30:315–21.
1950   The Canadian Metis. *Beaver* 280:3–7.

Owram, Douglas
1982   The Myth of Louis Riel. *Canadian Historical Review* 63:315–36.

Pannekoek, Frits
1976a   The Anglican Church and the Disintegration of Red River Society, 1818–1870. In *The West and the Nation,* edited by Carl Berge and Ramsay Cook. Toronto: McClelland and Stewart.
1976b   A Probe into the Demographic Structure of Nineteenth Century Red River. In *Essays on Western History,* edited by L. H. Thomas, pp. 81–95. Edmonton: University of Alberta Press.
1978   The Rev. Griffiths Owen Corbett and the Red River Civil War of 1869–70. *Canadian Historical Review* 57:133–49.
1990   *A Snug Little Flock: The Social Origins of the Riel Resistance, 1869–70.* Winnipeg: Watson and Dwyer.
1990–91 The Flock Divided: Factions and Feuds at Red River. *Beaver* 70(6):29–37.

Payment, Diane Paulette
1979   Monsieur Batoche. *Saskatchewan History* 32(3): 81–103.
1984   *Batoche (1870–1910).* St. Boniface, Man.: Editions du Blé.
1986   Batoche After 1885, a Society in Transition. In *1885 and After: Native Society in Transition,* edited by Laurie F. Barron and James B.

Waldram, pp. 173–87. Regina, Sask.: Canadian Plains Research Center.
1990   *"The Free People—Otipemisiwak": Batoche, Saskatchewan, 1870–1930.* Studies in Archaeology, Architecture, and History Series. Environment Canada, Parks Service.

Pelletier, Emile
1974   *A Social History of the Manitoba Metis: The Development and Loss of Aboriginal Rights.* Winnipeg: Manitoba Metis Federation Press.

Perrault, Isabelle
1982   Traite et métissage: Un aspect du peuplement de la Nouvelle-France. *Recherches amérindiennes au Québec* 12(2):86–94.

Peters, Evelyn, et al.
1991   Ontario Metis: Some aspects of a Metis identity. *Canadian Ethnic Studies* 23:71–84.

Peterson, Jacqueline
1978   Prelude to Red River: A Social Portrait of the Great Lakes Metis. *Ethnohistory* 25:41–68.
1982   Ethnogenesis: The Settlement and Growth of a "New People" in the Great Lakes Region, 1702–1815. *American Indian Culture and Research Journal* 6(2):23–64.

Peterson, Jacqueline, and Jennifer S. H. Brown, eds.
1985   *The New Peoples: Being and Becoming Metis in North America.* Winnipeg: University of Manitoba Press; Lincoln: University of Nebraska Press.

Purich, Donald
1988   *The Métis.* Toronto: James Lorimer.

Ray, Arthur J.
1982   Reflections on Fur Trade Social History and Metis History of Canada. *American Indian Culture and Research Journal* 6(2):91–107.

Rea, J. E.
1982   The Hudson's Bay Company and the North-West Rebellion. *Beaver* 313(1):43–57.

Redbird, Duke
1980   *We Are Metis: A Metis View of the Development of the Canadian People.* Toronto: Ontario Metis and Non-Status Indian Association.

Rhodes, Richard A.
1986   Métchif—A Second Look. In *Actes du dix-septième congrès des algonquinistes,* edited by

William Cowan, pp. 287–96. Ottawa: Carleton University.

St. Onge, Nicole
1985   The Dissolution of a Métis Community: Pointe
        à Grouette, 1860–1885. *Studies in Political
        Economy* 18:149–72.
1989   Race, Class, and Marginality in a Manitoba
        Interlake Settlement, 1850–1950. In *Race, Class,
        Gender: Bonds and Barriers,* edited by Jesse
        Vorst. Winnipeg: Society for Socialist Studies.

Sawchuk, Joe
1978   *The Metis of Manitoba: Reformulation of an
        Ethnic Identity.* Toronto: Peter Martin Associates Limited.
1982   Some Early Influences on Metis Political Organizations. *Culture* 2(3):85–92.

Schilling, Rita
1983   *Gabriel's Children.* Saskatoon: Saskatoon Metis
        Society.

Sealey, D. Bruce
1975   *Statutory Land Rights of the Manitoba Metis.*
        Winnipeg: Manitoba Metis Federation Press.
1982   Origin of the Metis. In *Readings in Canadian
        History: Pre-Confederation,* edited by R. Douglas Francis and Donald B. Smith, pp. 160–67.
        Toronto: Holt, Rinehart and Winston of Canada.

Sealey, D. Bruce, and Antoine S. Lussier
1975   *The Metis: Canada's Forgotten People.* Winnipeg: Pemmican Publications.

Silver, Arthur I.
1976   French Quebec and the Metis Question. In
        The West and the Nation, edited by Carl Berger
        and Ramsay Cook, pp. 91–113.
1988   Ontario's Alleged Fanaticism in the Riel Affair.
        Canadian Historical Review 69:21–50.

Slobodin, Richard
1964   The Subarctic Metis as Products and Agents
        of Culture Contact. *Arctic Anthropology* 2(2):
        50–55.
1966   *Metis of the Mackenzie District.* Ottawa: Canadian Research Center for Anthropology.
1981   Subarctic Métis. In *Handbook of North American Indians,* vol. 6, *Subarctic,* edited by June
        Helm, pp. 361–71. Washington: Smithsonian
        Institution Press.

Smith, Donald B.
1980   William Henry Jackson: Riel's English Cana-
        dian Disciple. In *Pelletier-Lathlin Memorial
        Lecture Series, Brandon University, 1979–1980,*
        edited by A. S. Lussier, pp. 47–81. Brandon,
        Man.: Department of Native Studies, Brandon
        University.
1984   Ordered to Winnipeg: Varsity Men Fought
        Louis Riel, but One Served as His Secretary.
        Graduate 12(2):5–9.

Sprague, Douglas N.
1980a   Government Lawlessness in the Administration of Manitoba Land Claims, 1870–1887.
        Manitoba Law Journal 10:415–41.
1980b   The Manitoba Land Question, 1870–1882. *Journal of Canadian Studies* 15(3):74–84.
1988   *Canada and the Métis, 1869–1885.* Waterloo,
        Ont.: Wilfred Laurier University Press.
1991   Dispossession vs. accommodation in plaintiff
        vs. defendant accounts of Métis dispersal from
        Manitoba, 1870–1881. *Prairie Forum* 16(2):
        137–55.

Sprague, Douglas N., and R. P. Frye, comps.
1983   *The Genealogy of the First Metis Nation: The
        Development and Dispersal of the Red River
        Settlement, 1820–1900.* Winnipeg: Pemmican
        Publications.

Stanley, George F. G.
1947   The Metis and the Conflict of Cultures in
        Western Canada. *Canadian Historical Review*
        23:428–33.
1963   *Louis Riel.* Toronto: Ryerson.
1970   *Louis Riel, Patriot or Rebel?* Ottawa: Canadian Historical Association.
1978   *The Birth of Western Canada: A History of the
        Riel Rebellions.* Toronto: University of Toronto
        Press.
1983   New Brunswick and Nova Scotia and the
        North-West Rebellion, 1885. In *The Developing West,* edited by John Foster, pp. 71–100.
        Edmonton: University of Alberta Press.

Stanley, George F. G., general ed.
1986   *The Collected Writings of Louis Riel/Les écrits
        complets de Louis Riel.* 5 vols. Edmonton:
        University of Alberta Press.

Taylor, John L.
1983   An Historical Introduction to Metis Claims in
        Canada. *Canadian Journal of Native Studies*
        3(1):151–81.

Thomas, Lewis H.
1977   A Judicial Murder—The Trial of Louis Riel. In *The Settlement of the West,* edited by Howard Palmer. Calgary: University of Calgary.
1982   Riel, Louis. *Dictionary of Canadian Biography* 11:736–52. Toronto: University of Toronto Press.

Valentine, Victor F.
1954   Some Problems of the Metis of Northern Saskatchewan. *Canadian Journal of Economics and Political Science* 20:89–95.

Waldram, James B., and F. L. Barron, eds.
1985   *1885 and After: Native Society in Transition.* Regina, Sask.: Canadian Plains Research Center.

Welsh, Christine
1991   Voices of the grandmothers: reclaiming a Metis heritage. *Canadian Literature* 131:15–24.

Wiebe, Rudy
1977   *The Scorched-Wood People: A Novel.* Toronto: McClelland and Stewart.

Wiebe, Rudy, and Bob Beal
1985   *War in the West: Voices of the 1885 Rebellion.* Toronto: McClelland and Stewart.

Woodcock, George
1975   *Gabriel Dumont: The Metis Chief and His Lost World.* Edmonton: Hurtig.

Part Three

Special Topics

Section Twelve

✦

WRITING THE HISTORY OF NATIVE CANADIANS

Axtell, James
1978   The Ethnohistory of Early America: A Review Essay. *William and Mary Quarterly* 35: 110–44.
1979   A North American Perspective for Colonial History. *History Teacher* 12.
1981   *The European and the Indian: Essays in the Ethnohistory of Colonial North America.* New York: Oxford University Press.
1983   A Moral History of Indian-White Relations Revisited. *History Teacher* 16:169–90.
1985   The Indian in American History: The Colonial Period. In *The Impact of Indian History on the Teaching of United States History* (conference, Chicago, 1984), 2:1–30. Chicago: Newberry Library.
1988   *After Columbus: Essays in the Ethnohistory of Colonial North America.* New York: Oxford University Press.

Axtell, James, and William C. Sturtevant
1980   The Unkindest Cut, or Who Invented Scalping? *William and Mary Quarterly* 37:451–72.

Berkhofer, Robert F., Jr.
1978   *The White Man's Indian.* New York: A. A. Knopf.

Bibeau, Donald F.
1984   Fur Trade Literature from a Tribal Point of View: A Critique. In *Selected Papers of the Fourth North American Fur Trade Conference,* 1981, edited by Thomas C. Buckley, pp. 83–92. St. Paul: Minnesota Historical Society.

Bruner, Edward M.
1986   Ethnography as Narrative. In *The Anthropology of Experience,* edited by V. M. Turner and E. M Bruner, pp. 135–55. Urbana: University of Illinois Press.

Clifton, James A.
1979   The Tribal History—An Obsolete Paradigm. *American Indian Culture and History Journal* 3(4):81–100.

Clifton, James A., ed.
1990   *The Invented Indian: Cultural Fictions and Government Policies.* New Brunswick, N.J.: Transaction.

Cohn, Bernard S.
1987   *An Anthropologist Among the Historians, and Other Essays.* Delhi, India: Oxford University Press.

Fausz, J. Frederick
1984   Anglo-Indian Relations in Colonial North America. In *Scholars and the Indian Experience,* edited by W. R. Swagerty, pp. 79–105. Bloomington: Indiana University Press.

Fisher, Robin
1982   Historical Writing on Native People in Canada. *History and Social Science Teacher* 17(2): 65–72.

Fogelson, Raymond D.
1985   Night Thoughts on Native American Social History. In *The Impact of Indian History on the Teaching of United States History* (conference, Chicago, 1984), 3:67–89. Chicago: Newberry Library.
1989   The Ethnohistory of Events and Nonevents. *Ethnohistory* 36:133–47.

Francis, R. Douglas
1987   From Wasteland to Utopia: Changing Images of the Canadian West in the Nineteenth Century. *Great Plains Quarterly,* summer, 178–94.

Gadacz, René R.
1982   The Language of Ethnohistory. *Anthropologica* 17:149–67.

Hobsbawm, Eric, and Terence Ranger, eds.
1983   *The Invention of Tradition.* Cambridge: Cambridge University Press.

Hoxie, Frederick E.
1988   The problems of Indian history. *Social Sciences Journal* 25:389–99.

Iverson, Peter
1984   Indian Tribal Histories. In *Scholars and the Indian Experience,* edited by W. R. Swagerty, pp. 205–22. Bloomington: Indiana University Press.

Jaenen, Cornelius J.
1978   Conceptual Frameworks for French Views of America and Amerindians. *French Colonial Studies* 2:1–22.
1983   Pelleteries et peaux-rouges: Perceptions françaises de la Nouvelle-France et de ses indigènes aux XVIe, XVIIe, XVIIIe siècles. *Recherches amérindiennes au Québec* 13(2): 107–14.
1984   L'image de l'Amerique. In *Le Monde de Jacques Cartier,* edited by Fernand Braudel, pp. 201–16. Paris: Berger-Levrault.

Jenness, Diamond
1937   *The Indian Background of Canadian History.* Canadian Department of Mines and Resources Bulletin 86. Ottawa.

Keesing, Roger
1990   Colonial History as Contested Ground: The Bell Massacre in the Solomons. *History and Anthropology* 4:279–301.

Kidd, Kenneth E.
1981   Tradition and the Canadian Indian. *Revue d'Études Canadiennes* 16:222–25.

Krech, Shepard, III
1991   The State of Ethnohistory. *Annual Review of Anthropology* 20:345–75.

McGee, Harold F. Jr.
1981   No Longer Neglected: A Decade of Writing Concerning the Native Peoples of the Maritimes. *Acadiensis* 10:135–42.

Martin, Calvin
1979   The Metaphysics of Writing Indian-White History. *Ethnohistory* 26:153–60.

Martin, Calvin, ed.
1987   *The American Indian and the Problem of History.* New York: Oxford University Press.

Merrell, James H.
1989   Some Thoughts on Colonial Historians and American Indians. *William and Mary Quarterly* 46:94–119.

Patterson, E. Palmer, II
1971   The Colonial Parallel: A View of Indian History. *Ethnohistory* 18:1–18.

Simmons, William S.
1988   Culture Theory in Contemporary Ethnohistory. *Ethnohistory* 35:1–14.

Sioui, Georges E.
1989   *Pour une autohistoire amérindienne: Essai sur les fondements d'une morale sociale.* Laval: Presses de l'Université Laval.

Smith, Donald B.
1974   *Le Sauvage: The Native People in Quebec. Historiography of the Heroic Period of New France, 1534–1663.* Ottawa: National Museum of Man.
1978   L'idée de "Sauvage" vehiculée par les historiens. *Devoir* 9:30.

Stanley, George F. G.
1952   The Indian Background of Canadian History.

Canadian Historical Association Report, 14–21.

Trigger, Bruce G.

1971   Champlain Judged by His Indian Policy: A Different View of Early Canadian History. *Anthropologica* 13–14:85–114.

1975   Brecht and Ethnohistory. *Ethnohistory* 23:51–56.

1978   Ethnohistory and Archaeology. *Ontario Archaeology* 30:17–24.

1981   Pour une histoire plus objective des relations entre colonisateurs et autochtones en Nouvelle-France. *Recherches amérindiennes au Québec* 11:199–204.

1982a   Ethnohistory: Problems and Prospects. *Ethnohistory* 29:1–19.

1982b   Indians and Ontario's History. *Ontario History* 74:246–57.

1982c   Responses of Native People to European Contact. In *Early European Settlement and Exploitation in Atlantic Canada,* edited by G. M. Story, pp. 139–55. St. John's: Memorial University of Newfoundland.

1984   Indian and White History: Two Worlds or One? In *Extending the Rafters: Interdisciplinary Approaches to Iroquoian Studies,* edited by M. K. Foster, J. Campisi, M. Mithun, pp. 17–33. Albany: State University of New York Press.

1986   Ethnohistory: The Unfinished Edifice. *Ethnohistory* 33:253–67.

1988   A Present of Their Past? Anthropologists, Native People, and Their Heritage. *Culture* 8(1):71–80.

1991   Early native North American responses to European contact: Romantic versus rationalistic interpretations. *Journal of American History* 77:1195–1215.

Vaughan, Alden T.

1982   From White Man to Red Skin: Changing Anglo-American Perceptions of the American Indian. *American Historical Review* 87:917–53.

Vincent, Sylvie, and Bernard Arcand

1979   *L'image de l'amérindien dans les manuels*

Walker, James W. St. G.

1971   The Indian in Canadian Historical Writing. *Historical Papers/Communications Historiques* 1971: 21–51.

1983   The Indian in Canadian Historical Writing, 1972–1982. In *As Long as the Sun Shines and Water Flows,* edited by I. A. L. Getty and A. S. Lussier, pp. 340–57. Vancouver: University of British Columbia Press.

Ward, W. Peter

1978   Western Canada: Recent Historical Writing. *Queen's Quarterly* 85:271–88.

White, Richard

1983   *The Roots of Dependency: Subsistence, Environment, and Social Change Among the Choctaws, Pawnees, and Navajos.* Lincoln: University of Nebraska Press.

Wolf, Eric

1982   *Europe and the People Without History.* Berkeley: University of California Press.

Section Thirteen

✦

THE FUR TRADE

Allaire, Gratien
1980   Les engagements pour la traitie des fourrures—
         evaluation de la documentation. *Revue d'his-
         toire de l'Amérique française* 34(1):3–26.

Arthur, Elizabeth
1985   The Concept of the Good Indian: An Albany
         River 19th Century Managerial Perspective.
         *Canadian Journal of Native Studies/Révue ca-
         nadiennes des études autochtones* 5(1):61–
         74.

Asch, Michael I.
1976   Some Effects of the Late Nineteenth Century
         Modernization of the Fur Trade on the Econ-
         omy of the Slavey Indians. *Western Canadian
         Journal of Anthropology* 6(4):7–16.

Bell, Georgiana
1985   The Monopoly System of Wildlife Manage-
         ment of the Indians and the Hudson's Bay
         Company in the Early History of British Co-
         lumbia. *BC Studies* 66:37–58.

Bishop, Charles A.
1972   Demography, Ecology, and Trade Among the
         Northern Ojibwa and Swampy Cree. *Western
         Canadian Journal of Anthropology* 3:58–71.
1974   *The Northern Ojibwa and the Fur Trade: An
         Historical and Ecological Study.* Toronto: Holt,
         Rinehart and Winston of Canada.
1981   Northeastern Indian Concepts of Conserva-
         tion and the Fur Trade: A Critique of Calvin
         Martin's Thesis. In *Indians, Animals, and the
         Fur Trade,* edited by Shepard Krech III, pp. 39–
         58. Athens: University of Georgia Press.
1984   The First Century: Adaptive Changes Among
         the Western James Bay Cree Between the
         Early Seventeenth and Early Eighteenth Cen-
         turies. In *The Subarctic Fur Trade,* edited by
         Shepard Krech III, pp. 21–53. Vancouver: Uni-
         versity of British Columbia Press.

Bishop, Charles A., and Arthur J. Ray
1976   Ethnohistoric Research in the Central Subarc-
         tic: Some Conceptual and Methodological Prob-
         lems. *Western Canadian Journal of Anthropol-
         ogy* 6(1):117–44.

Bolus, Malvina, ed.
1972   *People and Pelts: Selected Papers of the Sec-
         ond North American Fur Trade Conference.*
         Winnipeg: Peguis Publishers.

Brasser, Ted J. C.
1970   Group Identification Along a Moving Frontier. *Verhandlungen des XXXVII Internationalen Amerikanistenkongresses* (1968), 2: 261–65.

Brown, Jennifer S. H.
1976   A Demographic Transition in the Fur Trade Country: Family Sizes and Fertility of Company Officers and Country Wives, ca. 1750–1850. *Western Canadian Journal of Anthropology* 6:66–71.
1977   A Colony of Very Useful Hands. *Beaver* 307 (Spring):39–45.
1980   *Strangers in Blood: Fur Trade Company Families in Indian Country.* Vancouver: University of British Columbia Press.
1982   Children of the Early Fur Trades. In *Childhood and Family in Canadian History,* edited by Joy Parr, pp. 44–68. Toronto: McClelland and Stewart.
1984   "Man in His Natural State": The Indian Worlds of George Nelson. In *Rendezvous: Selected Papers of the Fourth North American Fur Trade Conference,* edited by Thomas C. Buckley, pp. 199–206. St. Paul: Minnesota Historical Society.
1986   Newman's Company of Adventurers in Two Solitudes: A Look at Reviews and Responses. *Canadian Historical Review* 67:562–71.
1987   Rejoinder to Peter C. Newman. *Canadian Historical Review* 68(2).
1988   A Parcel of Upstart Scotchmen. *Beaver* 68(1): 4–11.

Brumbach, Hetty Jo
1985   The Recent Fur Trade in Northwestern Saskatchewan. *Historical Archaeology* 19(2):19–39.

Buckley, Thomas C., ed.
1984   *Rendezvous: Selected Papers of the Fourth North American Fur Trade Conference.* St. Paul: Minnesota Historical Society.

Burley, David V.
1981   Protohistoric Ecological Effects of the Fur Trade on Micmac Culture in Northeastern New Brunswick. *Ethnohistory* 28:203–16.

Calloway, Colin G.
1987   Foundations of Sand: The Fur Trade and British-Indian Relations, 1783–1815. In *Le Castor Fait Tout: Selected Papers of the Fifth North American Fur Trade Conference, 1985,* edited by Bruce G. Trigger, Toby Morantz, and Louise Dechêne, pp. 144–63. Montreal: Lake St. Louis Historical Society.

Campbell, Marjorie Wilkins
1973   *The North West Company.* Vancouver: Douglas and McIntyre.

Carlos, Ann M.
1982   The Birth and Death of Predatory Competition in the North American Fur Trade: 1810–1821. *Explorations in Economic History* 19: 156–83.

Carlos, Ann M., and E. Hoffman
1986   The North American Fur Trade: Bargaining to a Joint Profit Maximum Under Incomplete Information, 1804–1821. *Journal of Economic History* 46:967–86.
1988   Game Theory and the North American Fur Trade: A Reply. *Journal of Economic History* 48:681–86.

Chalmers, John W.
1969   Social Stratification of the Fur Trade. *Alberta Historical Review* 12(1):10–19.

Coates, Kenneth S.
1982   Furs Along the Yukon: Hudson's Bay Company-Native Trade in the Yukon River Basin, 1830–1893. *BC Studies* 55:50–78.
1984   Protecting the Monopoly: The Hudson's Bay Company and Contemporary Knowledge of the Far Northwest, 1830–1869. *Yukon Historical and Museum Association Proceedings* 2:3–12.

Cockburn, R. H.
1990   Revillon Man: The Northern Career of A. Wallace Laird, 1924–1931. *Beaver* 70(1): 12–26.

Cox, Bruce A.
1984   Indian Middlemen and the Early Fur Trade: Reconsidering the Position of the Hudson's Bay Company's "Trading Indians." In *Rendezvous: Selected Papers of the Fourth North American Fur Trade Conference,* edited by Thomas C. Buckley, pp. 93–100. St. Paul: Minnesota Historical Society.

Dickason, Olive Patricia
1983   The Brazilian Connection: A Look at the

Origin of French Techniques for Trading with Amerindians. In *Rendezvous: Selected Papers of the Fourth North American Fur Trade Conference,* edited by Thomas C. Buckley, pp. 27–42. St. Paul: Minnesota Historical Society.

Dickinson, John A.
1987   Old Routes and New Wares: The Advent of European Goods in the St. Lawrence Valley. In *Le Castor Fait Tout: Selected Papers of the Fifth North American Fur Trade Conference, 1985,* edited by Bruce G. Trigger, Toby Morantz, and Louise Dechêne, pp. 25–41. Montreal: Lake St. Louis Historical Society.

Duckworth, Harry W., ed.
1989   *The English River Book: A Northwest Company Journal and Account Books of 1786.* Montreal and Quebec: McGill-Queen's University Press.

Eccles, William J.
1972   A Belated Review of Harold Adams Innis: The Fur Trade in Canada. *Canadian Historical Review* 50:419–41.
1981   A Response to Hugh M. Grant on Innis. *Canadian Historical Review* 62:323–29.
1983   The Fur Trade and Eighteenth Century Imperialism. *William and Mary Quarterly* 40:341–62.
1988   The Fur Trade in the Colonial Northeast. In *Handbook of North American Indians,* vol. 4, *History of Indian-White Relations,* edited by Wilcomb E. Washburn, pp. 324–34. Washington: Smithsonian Institution Press.

Eiman, Charles R.
1986   Fur Trade Archaeology: A Study of Frontier Hierarchies. *Historical Archaeology* 20(1):15–28.

Ewers, John C.
1972   The Influence of the Fur Trade upon the Indians of the Northern Plains. In *People and Pelts: Selected Papers of the Second North American Fur Trade Conference,* edited by Malvina Bolus, pp. 1–26. Winnipeg: Peguis Publishers.

Filion, Michel
1987   La traite des fourrures au XVIIIe siècle: Essai d'analyse statistique et d'interprétation d'un processus. *Histoire sociale/Social History* 20(4):279–98.

Fisher, Robin
1977   Indian Control of the Maritime Fur Trade and the Northwest Coast. In *Approaches to Native History in Canada,* edited by D. A. Muise, pp. 65–85. Ottawa: National Museum of Canada.
1988   Trading in Mythology: A Review of [Peter C. Newman's] *Caesars of the Wilderness. Beaver* 68(1):51–55.

Fladmark, Knut R.
1985   Early Fur-trade Forts of the Peace River Area of British Columbia. *BC Studies* 65:48–65.

Francis, Daniel, and Toby Morantz
1983   *Partners in Furs: A History of the Fur Trade in Eastern James Bay, 1600–1870.* Kingston: McGill-Queen's University Press.

Freeman, Donald B., and Frances L. Dungey
1981   A Spatial Duopoly: Competition in the Western Canadian Fur Trade, 1770–1835. *Journal of Historical Geography* 7:252–70.

Frennette, Jacques
1987   Commerce de fourrures et compétition à Betsiamites de 1850 à 1880. *Canadian Journal of Native Studies* 7:41–56.

Gibson, James R.
1988   The Maritime Trade of the North Pacific Coast. In *Handbook of North American Indians,* vol. 4, *History of Indian-White Relations,* edited by Wilcomb E. Washburn, pp. 375–90. Washington: Smithsonian Institution Press.

Gilman, Carolyn
1981   *Where Two Worlds Meet: The Great Lakes Fur Trade.* St. Paul: Minnesota Historical Society.

Grant, Hugh M.
1981   One Step Forward, Two Steps Back: Innis, Eccles, and the Canadian Fur Trade. *Canadian Historical Review* 62:304–22.

Grumet, Robert Stephen
1984   Managing the Fur Trade: The Coast Tsimshian to 1862. In *Proceedings of the 1981 American Ethnological Society,* pp. 26–39. Washington.

Harper-Fender, Ann
1987   A Transaction-Cost Analysis of the Hudson's Bay Company. In *Le Castor Fait Tout: Selected Papers of the Fifth North American Fur Trade Conference, 1985,* edited by Bruce G.

Trigger, Toby Morantz, and Louise Dechêne, pp. 359–81. Montreal: Lake St. Louis Historical Society.

Harris, Donald A., and George C. Ingram
1972   New Caledonia and the Fur Trade: A Status Report. *Western Canadian Journal of Anthropology* 3(1):179–94.

Heidenreich, Conrad E., and Arthur J. Ray
1976   *The Early Fur Trades: A Study in Cultural Interaction.* Toronto: McClelland and Stewart.

Hickerson, Harold
1956   The Genesis of the Trading Post Band: The Pembina Chippewa. *Ethnohistory* 3:289–345.
1973   Fur Trade Colonialism and the North American Indians. *Journal of Ethnic Studies* 1(2):15–44.

Hobler, Philip M.
1986   Measures of the Acculturative Response to Trade on the Central Coast of British Columbia. *Historical Archaeology* 20(2):16–26.

Holmgren, Eric J.
1984   Fort Dunvegan and the Fur Trade on the Upper Peace River. In *Rendezvous: Selected Papers of the Fourth North American Fur Trade Conference,* edited by Thomas C. Buckley, pp. 175–84. St. Paul: Minnesota Historical Society.

Inglis, Richard I., and James Haggarty
1987   Cook to Jewitt: Three Decades of Change in Nootka Sound. In *Le Castor Fait Tout: Selected Papers of the Fifth North American Fur Trade Conference, 1985,* edited by Bruce G. Trigger, Toby Morantz, and Louise Dechêne, pp. 193–222. Montreal: Lake St. Louis Historical Society.

Innis, Harold A.
1970   *The Fur Trade in Canada.* Rev. ed. Toronto: University of Toronto Press.

Jaenen, Cornelius J.
1985   The Role of Presents in French-Amerindian Trade. In *Explorations in Canadian Economic History: Essays in Honour of Irene M. Spry,* edited by Duncan Cameron. Ottawa: University of Ottawa Press.

James, William C.
1985   *A Fur Trader's Photographs: A. A. Chesterfield in the District of Ungava, 1901–4.* Kings-

ton and Montreal: McGill-Queen's University Press.

Janes, Robert R.
1975   The Athapascan and the Fur Trade: Observations from Archaeology and Ethnohistory. *Western Canadian Journal of Anthropology* 5(3–4):159–86.

Janes, Robert R., and T. C. Losey
1974   Recent Discoveries in Fur Trade Archaeology of Upper and Central Mackenzie River Regions. *Canadian Archaeological Association Bulletin* 6:93–120.

Jarvenpa, Robert
1987   The Hudson's Bay Company, the Roman Catholic Church, and the Chipewyan in the Late Fur Trade Period. In *Le Castor Fait Tout: Selected Papers of the Fifth North American Fur Trade Conference, 1985,* edited by Bruce G. Trigger, Toby Morantz, and Louise Dechêne, pp. 485–517. Montreal: Lake St. Louis Historical Society.

Jarvenpa, Robert, and Hetty Jo Brumbach
1984   The Microeconomics of Southern Chipewyan Fur Trade History. In *The Subarctic Fur Trade,* edited by Shepard Krech III, pp. 147–83. Vancouver: University of British Columbia Press.

Jarvenpa, Robert, and Walter P. Zenner
1979   Scot Trader/Indian Worker Relations and Ethnic Segregation: A Subarctic Example. *Ethnos* 44(1–2):58–77.

Judd, Carol M.
1980   Native Labour and Social Stratification in the Hudson's Bay Company's Northern Department (1770–1870). *Canadian Review of Sociology and Anthropology* 17:305–314.
1982   Mixt Bands of Many Nations: 1821–70. In *Old Trails and New Directions: Papers of the Third North American Fur Trade Conference,* edited by C. M. Judd and A. J. Ray, pp. 127–46. Toronto: University of Toronto Press.
1984   Sakie, Esquawenoe, and the Foundation of a Dual-Native Tradition at Moose Factory. In *The Subarctic Fur Trade,* edited by Shepard Krech III, pp. 82–97. Vancouver: University of British Columbia Press.

Judd, Carol M., and Arthur J. Ray, eds.
1980   *Old Trails and New Directions.* Toronto: University of Toronto Press.

Karamanski, Theodore J.
1982   The Iroquois and the Fur Trade of the Far West. *Beaver* 312(4):4–13.
1983   *Fur Trade and Exploration: Opening the Far Northwest, 1821–1852.* Norman: University of Oklahoma Press.

Keighley, Sydney Augustus
1989   *Trader, Tripper, Trapper: The Life of a Bay Man.* Winnipeg: Rupert's Land Research Centre, University of Winnipeg; Watson and Dwyer.

Kemp, David D.
1987   Attitudes to Winter in the Northwest Fur Trade. *Canadian Geographer/Géographe Canadien* 31:49–56.

Klein, Laura F.
1987   Demystifying the Opposition: The Hudson's Bay Company and the Tlingit. *Arctic Anthropology* 24(1):101–14.

Krech, Shepard, III
1976   The Eastern Kutchin and the Fur Trade, 1800–1860. *Ethnohistory* 23:213–36.
1981   "Throwing Bad Medicine": Sorcery, Disease, and the Fur Trade Among the Kutchin and Other Northern Athapaskans. In *Indians, Animals, and the Fur Trade,* edited by Shepard Krech III, pp. 73–108. Athens: University of Georgia Press.
1982   The Death of Barbue, a Kutchin Trading Chief. *Arctic* 35:429–37.
1983   The Influence of Disease and the Fur Trade on Arctic Drainage Lowlands Dene, 1800–1850. *Journal of Anthropological Research* 39:123–46.
1984   The Trade of the Slavey and Dogrib at Fort Simpson in the Early Nineteenth Century. In *The Subarctic Fur Trade,* edited by Shepard Krech III, pp. 99–146. Vancouver: University of British Columbia Press.
1987   The Early Fur Trade in the Northwestern Subarctic: The Kutchin and the Trade in Beads. In *Le Castor Fait Tout: Selected Papers of the Fifth North American Fur Trade Conference, 1985,* edited by Bruce G. Trigger, Toby Morantz, and Louise Dechêne, pp. 236–77. Montreal: Lake St. Louis Historical Society.
1988   The Hudson's Bay Company and Dependency Among Subarctic Tribes Before 1900. In *Overcoming Economic Dependency,* pp. 62–70. Occasional Papers in Curriculum Series, no. 9. Chicago: Newberry Library.

Krech, Shepard III, ed.
1981   *Indians, Animals, and the Fur Trade: A Critique of "Keepers of the Game."* Athens: University of Georgia Press.
1984   *The Subarctic Fur Trade: Native Social and Economic Adaptations.* Vancouver: University of British Columbia Press.

Leechman, Douglas
1974   "Commodeties Besides Furres." *Beaver* 304(4): 46–52.

Lewis, Oscar
1966   *The Effects of White Contact upon Blackfoot Culture with Special References to the Fur Trade.* Seattle and London: University of Washington Press.

Lomasny, Patrick J.
1933   The Canadian Jesuits and the Fur Trade. *Mid-American* 15:139–50.

Lytwyn, Victor P.
1986   *The Fur Trade of the Little North: Indians, Pedlars, and Englishmen East of Lake Winnipeg, 1760–1821.* Winnipeg: Rupert's Land Research Centre, University of Winnipeg.

McCormack, Patricia A.
1984   The Transformation to a Fur Trade Mode of Production at Fort Chipewyan. In *Rendezvous: Selected Papers of the Fourth North American Fur Trade Conference,* edited by Thomas C. Buckley, pp. 155–74. St. Paul: Minnesota Historical Society.

McGillivray, Duncan
1969   The Impact of the Fur Trade. In *The Prairies,* edited by Kenneth Osborne. Toronto: McClelland and Stewart.

Makahonuk, Glen
1988   Wage-labour in the Northwest Fur Trade Economy, 1760–1849. *Saskatchewan History* 41(1):1–17.

Mancke, Elizabeth
1988   *A Company of Businessmen: The Hudson's Bay Company and Long-distance Trade, 1670–1730.* Winnipeg: Rupert's Land Research Centre, University of Winnipeg.

Martin, Calvin
1975   The Four Lives of a Micmac Copper Pot. *Ethnohistory* 23:111–34.
1978   *Keepers of the Game: Indian-Animal Relationships and the Fur Trade.* Berkeley: University of California Press.

Miller, Christopher, and George R. Hamell
1986   A New Perspective on Indian-White Contact: Cultural Symbols and Colonial Trade. *Journal of American History* 73:311–28.

Mitchell, Elaine Allan
1977   *Fort Timiskaming and the Fur Trade.* Toronto: University of Toronto Press.

Moodie, D. Wayne
1987   The Trading Post Settlement of the Canadian Northwest, 1774–1821. *Journal of Historical Geography* 13:360–74.

Morantz, Toby
1980   The Fur Trade and the Cree of James Bay. In *Old Trails and New Directions,* edited by C. M. Judd and A. J. Ray, pp. 39–58. Toronto: University of Toronto Press.
1982   Northern Algonquian Concepts of Status and Leadership Reviewed: A Case Study of the Eighteenth Century Trading Captain System. *Canadian Review of Sociology and Anthropology* 19:482–500.
1983   "Not Annual Visitors"—The Drawing into Trade of Northern Algonquian Caribou Hunters. In *Actes du quatorzième congrès des algonquinistes,* edited by William Cowan, pp. 57–74. Ottawa: Carleton University.
1984   Economic and Social Adaptations of the James Bay Inlanders to the Fur Trade. In *The Subarctic Fur Trade,* edited by Shepard Krech III, pp. 55–79. Vancouver: University of British Columbia Press.
1987   Dwindling Animals and Diminished Lands: Early Twentieth Century Developments in Eastern James Bay. In *Papers of the Eighteenth Algonquian Conference,* edited by William Cowan, pp. 209–27. Ottawa: Carleton University.
1988   "Gift-Offerings to Their Own Importance and Superiority": Fur Trade Relations, 1700–1940. In *Papers of the Nineteenth Algonquian Conference,* edited by William Cowan, pp. 133–45. Ottawa: Carleton University.

Morton, Arthur S.
1973   *A History of the Canadian West to 1870–71.* 2d ed. Edited by Lewis G. Thomas. Toronto: University of Toronto Press.

Murray, Richard
1988   Rendering unto Caesar. *Beaver* 68(3):62.

Newman, Peter C.
1985   *Company of Adventurers: The Story of the Hudson's Bay Company.* Vol. 1. New York: Viking.
1987   *Caesars of the Wilderness: The Story of the Hudson's Bay Company.* Vol. 2. New York: Viking.

Nicks, Trudy
1980   The Iroquois and the Fur Trade in Western Canada. In *Old Trails and New Directions,* edited by C. M. Judd and A. J. Ray, pp. 85–101. Toronto: University of Toronto Press.
1987   Native Responses to the Early Fur Trade at Lesser Slave Lake. In *Le Castor Fait Tout: Selected Papers of the Fifth North American Fur Trade Conference, 1985,* edited by Bruce G. Trigger, Toby Morantz, and Louise Dechêne, pp. 278–310. Montreal: Lake St. Louis Historical Society.

Norton, Thomas Eliot
1974   *The Fur Trade in Colonial New York, 1686–1776.* Madison: University of Wisconsin Press.

Nye, John Vincent
1988   Game Theory and the North American Fur Trade: A Comment. *Journal of Economic History* 48:677–81.

Pannekoek, Frits
1974   The Rev. James Evans and the Social Antagonisms of the Fur Trade Society, 1840–1846. In *Religion and Society in the Prairie West,* edited by Richard Allen. Regina, Sask.: Canadian Plains Research Centre.

Parker, James M.
1976   The Struggle for the Athabasca. In *Essays on Western History,* edited by Lewis H. Thomas, pp. 31–46. Edmonton: University of Alberta Press.
1987   *Emporium of the North: Fort Chipewyan and the Fur Trade to 1835.* Regina, Sask.: Canadian Plains Research Center.

Payne, Michael
1989   "The Most Respectable Place in the Terri-

tory": Everyday Life in Hudson's Bay Company Service at York Factory, 1788–1870. Studies in Archaeology, Architecture, and History. Ottawa: Environment Canada, Park Service.

Peterson, Jacqueline, and John Anfinson
1984   The Indian and the Fur Trade. In *Scholars and the Indian Experience,* edited by W. R. Swagerty, pp. 223–58. Bloomington: Indiana University Press.
1985   The Indian and the Fur Trade: A Review of Recent Literature. *Manitoba History* 10:10–18.

Phillips, Paul Chrisler
1961   *The Fur Trade.* 2 vols. Norman: University of Oklahoma Press.

Potvin, Joseph
1988   *Fur and First Canadians.* Ottawa: Canadian Arctic Resources Committee.

Preston, Richard J., III
1975   Eastern Cree Community in Relation to Fur Trade Post in the 1830s: The Background of the Posting Process. In *Papers of the Sixth Algonquian Conference,* edited by William Cowan, pp. 324–35. Mercury Series, Canadian Ethnology Service Paper 23. Ottawa: National Museum of Man.

Quimby, George I.
1966   *Indian Culture and European Trade Goods: The Archaeology of the Historic Period in the Western Great Lakes Region.* Madison: University of Wisconsin Press.

Ray, Arthur J.
1974   *Indians in the Fur Trade: Their Role as Hunters, Trappers, and Middlemen in the Lands Southwest of Hudson Bay, 1660–1870.* Toronto: University of Toronto Press.
1975a The Factor and the Trading Captain in the Hudson's Bay Company Fur Trade Before 1763. In *Proceedings of the Second Congress, Canadian Ethnological Society,* edited by Jim Freedman and Jerome H. Barkow, 2:586–602. Mercury Series, Canadian Ethnology Service Paper 28. Ottawa: National Museum of Man.
1975b Some Conservation Schemes of the Hudson's Bay Company, 1821–50: An Examination of the Problems of Resource Management in the Fur Trade. *Journal of Historical Geography* 1(1):49–68.

1978a Competition and Conservation in the Early Subarctic Fur Trade. *Ethnohistory* 25:347–58.
1978b Fur Trade History as an Aspect of Native History. In *One Century Later,* edited by I. A. L. Getty and D. B. Smith, pp. 7–19. Vancouver: University of British Columbia Press.
1978c History and Archaeology of the Northern Fur Trade. *American Antiquity* 43:26–34.
1978d The Hudson's Bay Company Fur Trade in the Eighteenth Century: A Comparative Study. In *European Settlement and Development in North America: Essays on Geographic Change in Honour and Memory of Andrew Hill Clark,* edited by James R. Gibson, pp. 116–35. Toronto: University of Toronto Press.
1980   Indians as Consumers in the Eighteenth Century. In *Old Trails and New Directions,* edited by C. M. Judd and A. J. Ray, pp. 255–71. Toronto: University of Toronto Press.
1982a Reflections on Fur Trade Social History and Metis History in Canada. *American Indian Culture and Research Journal* 6(2):91–107.
1982b York Factory: The Crises of Transition, 1870–1880. *Beaver* 313(2):26–31.
1984a The Northern Great Plains: Pantry of the Northwestern Fur Trade, 1774–1885. *Prairie Forum* 9(2):263–80.
1984b Periodic Shortages, Native Welfare, and the Hudson's Bay Company, 1670–1930. In *The Subarctic Fur Trade,* edited by Shepard Krech III, pp. 1–20. Vancouver: University of British Columbia Press.
1985   Buying and Selling Hudson's Bay Company Furs in the Eighteenth Century. In *Explorations in Canadian Economic History: Essays in Honour of Irene M. Spry,* edited by Duncan Cameron, pp. 95–115. Ottawa: University of Ottawa Press.
1988   The Hudson's Bay Company and Native People. In *Handbook of North American Indians,* vol. 4, *History of Indian-White Relations,* edited by Wilcomb E. Washburn, pp. 335–50. Washington: Smithsonian Institution Press.
1990a *The Canadian Fur Trade in the Industrial Age.* Toronto: University of Toronto Press.
1990b Rivals for Fur. *Beaver* 70(2):30–44.

Ray, Arthur J., and Donald Freeman
1978   *"Give Us Good Measure": An Economic Anal-*

ysis of Relations Between the Indians and the Hudson's Bay Company Before 1763. Toronto: University of Toronto Press.

Rich, E. E.
1958–59 *The History of the Hudson's Bay Company, 1670–1870.* 3 vols. London: Hudson's Bay Record Society.
1960   Trade Habits and Economic Motivation Among the Indians of North America. *Canadian Journal of Economics and Political Science* 26:35–53.
1966   *Montreal and the Fur Trade.* Montreal: McGill University Press.
1967   *The Fur Trade and the Northwest to 1857.* Toronto: McClelland and Stewart.
1970   The Indian Traders. *Beaver* 301:4–20.

Richling, Barnett
1988   Not by Seals Alone: The Moravians in the Fur Trade—Souls and Skins. *Beaver* 68(1):29–35.

Rogers, Edward S.
1983   Cultural Adaptations: The Northern Ojibwa of the Boreal Forest, 1670–1980. In *Boreal Forest Adaptations,* edited by A. Theodore Steegmann, Jr., pp. 85–142. New York: Plenum Press.

Rotstein, Abraham
1972   Trade and Politics: An Institutional Approach. *Western Canadian Journal of Anthropology* 3:10–28.

Ruggles, Richard I.
1990   *A Country So Interesting: The Hudson's Bay Company and Two Centuries of Mapping, 1670–1870.* Montreal: McGill-Queen's University Press.

Saum, Lewis O.
1965   *The Fur Trader and the Indian.* Seattle: University of Washington Press.

Schilz, Thomas F.
1984   Brandy and Beaver Pelts: Assiniboine-European Trading Patterns, 1695–1805. *Saskatchewan History* 27(3):95–102.
1988   The Gros Ventres and the Canadian Fur Trade, 1754–1831. *American Indian Quarterly* 12:41–56.

Sloan, William A.
1979   The Native Response to the Extension of the European Traders into the Athabasca and Mackenzie Basins, 1770–1814. *Canadian Historical Review* 60:281–99.

Smith, Wallis M.
1973   The Fur Trade and the Frontier: A Study of an Inter-cultural Alliance. *Anthropologica* 15:21–35.

Smyth, David
1984–85 The Yellowhead Pass and the Fur Trade. *BC Studies* 64:48–73.
1989a   Jacques Berger, Fur Trader. *Beaver* 69(3):39–50.
1989b   Rivals Among the Blackfoot: Jacques Berger, Fur Trader. *Beaver* 69(3):39–50.

Spry, Irene M.
1968   The Transition from a Nomadic to a Settled Economy in Western Canada, 1856–96. *Transactions of the Royal Society of Canada* 187–201.
1983   The "Private Adventurers" of Rupert's Land. In *The Developing West,* edited by John E. Foster, pp. 49–70. Edmonton: University of Alberta Press.

Swagerty, William R.
1988   Indian Trade in the Trans-Mississippi West to 1870. In *Handbook of North American Indians,* vol. 4, *History of Indian-White Relations,* edited by Wilcomb E. Washburn, pp. 351–74. Washington: Smithsonian Institution Press.

Tanner, Adrian
1978   Game Shortage and the Inland Fur Trade in Northern Quebec, 1915–1940. In *Papers of the Ninth Algonquian Conference,* edited by William Cowan, pp. 146–59. Ottawa: Carleton University.
1983   The End of Fur Trade History. *Queen's Quarterly* 90(1):176–91.

Thistle, Paul C.
1986   *Indian-European Trade Relations in the Lower Saskatchewan River Region to 1840.* Winnipeg: University of Manitoba Press.

Tough, Frank
1988   Northern Fur Trade: A Review Of Conceptual and Methodological Problems. *Musk-Ox* 36:66–79.
1990   Indian economic behavior, exchange and profits in northern Manitoba during the decline of monopoly, 1870–1930. *Journal of Historical Geography* 16:385–401.

145

Trelease, Alan W.
1962   The Iroquois of the Western Fur Trade: A Problem of Interpretation. *Mississippi Valley Historical Review* 99:32–51.

Trigger, Bruce G.
1965   The Jesuits and the Fur Trade. *Ethnohistory* 12:30–53.

Trigger, Bruce G., Toby Morantz, and Louise Dechêne, eds.
1987   *Le Castor Fait Tout: Selected Papers of the Fifth North American Fur Trade Conference, 1985.* Montreal: Lake St. Louis Historical Society.

Trudel, François
1989   Les inuit de l'est de la baie d'Hudson et la traite à Fort George (1837–1851). *Études/Inuit/Studies* 13(2):3–32.

Turgeon, Laurier, et Evelyne Picot-Bermond
1987   Pêcheurs basques et la traite de la fourrure dans le Saint-Laurent au XVIe siècle. In *Le Castor Fait Tout: Selected Papers of the Fifth North American Fur Trade Conference, 1985,* edited by Bruce G. Trigger, Toby Morantz, and Louise Dechêne, pp. 14–24. Montreal: Lake St. Louis Historical Society.

Van Kirk, Sylvia
1980   Fur Trade Social History: Some Recent Trends. In *Old Trails and New Directions,* edited by C. M. Judd and A. J. Ray, pp. 160–76. Toronto: University of Toronto Press.

Warburton, Rennie, and Stephen Scott
1985   The Fur Trade and Early Capitalist Development in British Columbia. *Canadian Journal of Native Studies/Révue canadienne des études autochtones* 5(1):27–46.

White, Bruce M.
1984   "Give Us a Little Milk": Social and Cultural Significance of Gift Giving in the Lake Superior Fur Trade. In *Rendezvous: Selected Papers of the Fourth North American Fur Trade Conference,* edited by Thomas C. Buckley, pp. 185–98. St. Paul: Minnesota Historical Society.
1987   A Skilled Game of Exchange: Ojibway Fur Trade Protocol. *Minnesota History* 50(6):229–40.

Williams, Glyndwr
1983   The Hudson's Bay Company and the Fur Trade: 1670–1870. *Beaver* 314(2):1–86.

Yerbury, J. Colin
1976   The Post-contact Chipewyan: Trade Rivalries and Changing Territorial Boundaries. *Ethnohistory* 23:237–64.
1981   Lake Athabasca Region Before 1765. *Alberta Historical Review* 29(1):31–35.
1985   *The Subarctic Indian and the Fur Trade, 1680–1860.* Vancouver: University of British Columbia Press.

Zenner, Walter P., and Robert Jarvenpa
1980   Scots in the Northern Fur Trade: A Middleman Minority Perspective. *Ethnic Groups* 2:189–210.

Section Fourteen

MISSIONARIES

Abel, Kerry
1986   Prophets, Priests, and Preachers: Dene Shamans and Christian Missions in the Nineteenth Century. *Historical Papers/Communications Historiques* 1986.

Archer, John H., ed.
1986   Rupert's Land Issue. *Journal of the Canadian Church Historical Society* 28(1):3–43.

Axtell, James
1982   Some Thoughts on the Ethnohistory of Missions. *Ethnohistory* 29:35–41.
1985   *The Invasion Within: The Contest of Cultures in Colonial North America.* New York: Oxford University Press.
1984   Invading America: Puritans and Jesuits. *Journal of Interdisciplinary History* 14:635–46.

Barnett-Cowan, Alyson, ed.
1991   Henry Budd and His Contemporaries: Canadian Indians. Papers from the second Rupert's Land Conference. *Journal of the Canadian Church Historical Society* 33(1):7–118.

Benoit, Barbara
1980   Mission at Île-à-la-Crosse. *Beaver* 311(3):40–50.

Berkhofer, Robert F., Jr.
1965a   Faith and Factionalism Among the Senecas: Theory and Ethnohistory. *Ethnohistory* 12:99–112.
1965b   *Salvation and the Savage: An Analysis of Protestant Missions and American Indian Response, 1787–1862.* Lexington: University of Kentucky Press.

Blanchard, David
1982   To the other side of the sky: Catholicism at Kahnawake, 1667–1700. *Anthropologica* 24:77–102.

Bolt, Clarence R.
1983   The Conversion of the Port Simpson Tsimshian: Indian Control or Missionary Manipulation? *BC Studies* 57:38–56.

Bowden, Henry Warner
1981   *American Indians and Christian Missions: Studies in Cultural Conflict.* Chicago: University of Chicago Press.

Brown, Jennifer S. H.
1982   The Track to Heaven: The Hudson Bay Cree Religious Movement of 1842–1843. In *Papers*

of the Thirteenth Algonquian Conference, edited by William Cowan, pp. 53–64. Ottawa: Carleton University.

1987   "I Wish to Be as I See You": An Ojibwa-Methodist Encounter in Fur Trade Country, Rainy Lake, 1854–1855. *Arctic Anthropology* 24(1):19–31.

Brown, Joseph Epes
1982   *The Spiritual Legacy of the American Indian.* New York: Crossroads.

Burns, Robert J.
1966   *The Jesuits and the Indian Wars of the Northwest.* New Haven: Yale University Press.

Campeau, Lucien
1967   *Monumenta Novae Franciae I: La première mission d'Acadie, 1602–1616.* Quebec: Presses de l'Université Laval.
1972   *La première mission des Jesuits en Nouvelle Franciae (1611–1613).* Montreal: Bellarmin.
1979   *Monumenta Novae Franciae II: Établissement à Quebec, 1616–1634.* Quebec: Presses de l'Université Laval.
1987   *La mission des Jésuits chez les hurons, 1634–1650.* Montreal: Éditions Bellarmin; Rome: Institutum Historicum S. J.

Carrière, Gaston
1966   L'Honorable Compagnie de la Baie-d'Hudson et les missions dans l'Ouest canadien. *Revue de l'Université d'Ottawa,* 15–39, 232–57.
1971   Fondation et développement des missions catholiques dans la terre de Rupert et les territoires du Nord-Ouest (1845–1861). *Revue de l'Université d'Ottawa,* 253–81, 397–427.
1979   The Early Efforts of the Oblate Missionaries in Western Canada. *Prairie Forum* 4:1–25.

Carrière, Gaston, trans.
1978   Letter from Bishop Alexandre Taché to His Mother, Concerning His Life with the Chipewyan Nation. *Prairie Forum* 3:131–56.

Carter, Sarah
1983   The Missionaries' Indian: The Publications of John McDougall, John Maclean, and Egerton Ryerson Young. *Prairie Forum* 9:27–43.

Champagne, Claude
1983   *Les débuts de la mission dans le Nord-Ouest Canadien.* Ottawa: Editions de l'Université Saint-Paul.

Coates, Kenneth S.
1984–85   "Betwixt and Between": The Anglican Church and the Children of the Carcross (Chooutla) Residential School, 1911–1954. *BC Studies* 64: 27–47.

Conkling, Robert
1974   Legitimacy and Conversion in Social Change: The Case of French Missionaries and the Northeastern Algonkian. *Ethnohistory* 21:1–24.

Delâge, Denys
1982   Conversion et identité: Le cas des hurons et des iroquois. *Culture* 2(1):75–82.

Dooling, D. M., and Paul Jordan-Smith, eds.
1989   *I Become Part of It: Sacred Dimensions in Native American Life.* New York: Parabola Books.

Dorais, Louis-Jacques, and Bernard Saladin d'Anglure
1988   Roman Catholic Missions in the Arctic. In *Handbook of North American Indians,* vol. 4, *History of Indian-White Relations,* edited by Wilcomb E. Washburn, pp. 501–5. Washington: Smithsonian Institution Press.

Fisher, Robin
1977   Missions to the Indians of British Columbia. In *Early Indian Village Churches: Wooden Frontier Architecture in British Columbia,* edited by John Veillette and Gary White, pp. 1–11. Vancouver: University of British Columbia Press.

Freeman, J.
1965   The Indian Convert: Theme and Variation. *Ethnohistory* 12:113–28.

Fumoleau, René
1982   Missionaries chez les denes. *Interculture* 15(1): 9–31.

Gagnon, François-Marc
1975   *La conversion par l'image: Un aspect de la mission des Jésuites auprès des indiens du Canada au XVIIe siècle.* Montreal: Éditions Bellarmin.

Gagnon, François-Marc, with Laurier Lacroix
1984   La France apportant la foix aux hurons de Nouvelle France: Un tableau conservé chez les Ursulines de Quebec. *Journal of Canadian Studies* 18(3):5–20.

George, Leonard
1991   Native Spirituality, past, present, and future. *BC Studies* 89:160–68.

Getty, Ian A. L.
1974   The Failure of the Native Church Policy of the CMS in the North-West. In *Canadian Plains Studies 3: Religion and Society in the Prairie West,* edited by R. Allen, pp. 19–33. Regina, Sask.: Canadian Plains Research Center.

Gill, Sam
1982   *Native American Religions.* Belmont, Calif.: Wadsworth.

1983   *Native American Traditions.* Belmont, Calif.: Wadsworth.

1987   *Mother Earth: An American Story.* Chicago: University of Chicago Press.

Gosselin, Ronald
1984   La christianisation de la forêt boréale. In *L'eglise Catholique et la societé du Québec,* pp. 31–61. Quebec: Musée du Quebec.

Gough, Barry M.
1982   A Priest Versus the Potlatch: The Reverend Alfred James Hall and the Fort Rupert Kwakiutl, 1878–1880. *Journal of the Canadian Church Historical Society* 24(2):75–89.

1983   Father Brabant and the Hesquiat of Vancouver Island. *Study Sessions, Canadian Catholic Historical Association* 50:553–68.

1984   Pioneer Missionaries to the Nishga: The Crosscurrents of Demon Rum and British Gunboats, 1860–1871. *Journal of the Canadian Church Historical Society* 26(2):81–95.

Goulet, Jean-Guy
1982   Religious Dualism Among Athapaskan Catholics. *Canadian Journal of Anthropology* 3(1): 1–18.

1984   Liberation theology and missions in Canada. *Eglise et Theologie* 15:293–319.

Graham, Elizabeth
1975   *Medicine Man to Missionary: Missionaries as Agents of Social Change Among the Indians of Southern Ontario, 1764–1867.* Toronto: Peter Martin Associates.

Grant, John Webster
1980   Missionaries and Messiahs in the Northwest. *Studies in Religion* 9(2):125–36.

1984   *Moon of Wintertime: Missionaries and the Indians of Canada in Encounter Since 1534.* Toronto: University of Toronto Press.

Gray, Elma E.
1956   *Wilderness Christians: The Moravian Mission to the Delaware Indians.* Toronto: Macmillan.

Gresko, Jacqueline
1982   Roman Catholic Missions to the Indians of British Columbia: A Reappraisal of the Lemert Thesis. *Journal of the Canadian Church Historical Society* 24(2):51–62.

Gualtieri, Antonio R.
1980a   Canadian Missionary Perceptions of Indian and Inuit Culture and Religious Tradition. *Studies in Religion* 9(3):299–314.

1980b   Indigenization of Christianity and Syncretism Among the Indians and Inuit of the Western Arctic. *Canadian Ethnic Studies* 12(1):47–57.

1984   *Christianity and Native Traditions: Indigenization and Syncretism Among the Inuit and Dene of the Western Arctic.* Notre Dame, Ind.: Cross Roads Books.

Harper, Kenn
1981   The Moravian Mission at Cumberland Sound. *Beaver* 312(1):43–47.

1985   The Early Development of Inuktituk Syllabic Orthography. *Études/Inuit/Studies* 9(1):141–62.

Harrod, Howard L.
1984   Missionary Life-World and Native Responses: Jesuits in New France. *Studies in Religion* 13(2):179–92.

Henderson, John R.
1974   Missionary Influence on the Haida Settlement and Subsistence Patterns, 1876–1920. *Ethnohistory* 22:303–16.

Hendry, Charles E.
1969   *Beyond Traplines: Towards an Assessment of the Work of the Anglican Church with Canada's Native People.* Toronto: Anglican Church of Canada.

Hiller, James
1971   Early Patrons of the Labrador Eskimos: The Moravian Mission in Labrador, 1764–1805. In *Patrons and Brokers in the East Arctic,* edited by Robert Paine. St. John's: Memorial University of Newfoundland, Institute for Social and Economic Research.

Hultkrantz, Ake
1979   *The Religions of the American Indians.* Berkeley: University of California Press.
1980   The Problem of Christian Influence on Northern Algonkian Eschatology. *Studies in Religion* 9(2):161–83.
1987   *Native Religions of North America: The Power of Visions and Fertility.* San Francisco: Harper and Row.

Jaenen, Cornelius J.
1969   The Frenchification and Evangelization of the Amerindians in Seventeenth Century New France. *Study Sessions of the Canadian Catholic Historical Association* 55:57–71.
1970   The Catholic Clergy and the Fur Trade, 1585–1685. *Historical Papers* 1970:60–80.
1976   *The Role of the Church in New France.* Toronto: McGraw-Hill-Ryerson.
1977   Missionary Approaches to Native People. In *Approaches to Native History in Canada,* edited by D. A. Muise, pp. 5–15. Ottawa: National Museums of Canada.
1980   Missionaries as Explorers: The Recollects of New France. *Journal of the Canadian Church Historical Society* 22(3):32–45.
1985   Amerindian Responses to French Missionary Intrusion, 1611–1760: A Categorization. In *Religion/Culture: Comparative Canadian Studies/Études canadiennes comparées,* edited by William Westfall and L. Rousseau, pp. 182–97. Ottawa: Association for Canadian Studies.

Jarvenpa, Robert
1985   Northern Pilgrimage. *Beaver* 315(4): 54–9.
1990   The development of pilgrimage in an intercultural frontier. In *Culture and the Anthropological Tradition,* edited by Robert H. Winthrop, pp. 177–203. Lanham, Md.: University Press of America.

Kan, Sergei
1985   Russian Orthodox Brotherhoods Among the Tlingit: Missionary Goals and Native Response. *Ethnohistory* 32:196–223.
1990   Russian Orthodox Missionaries and the Tlingit Indians of Alaska, 1800–1890. In *New Directions in Ethnohistory,* edited by B. M. Gough. Mercury Series. Ottawa: Canadian Museum of Civilization.

Kennedy, John C.
1988   The Impact of the Grenfell Mission on Southeastern Labrador Communities. *Polar Record* 24(150):199–206.

Krieger, Carlo J.
1989   Ethnogenesis or Cultural Interference? Catholic Missionaries and the Micmac. In *Actes du vingtième congrès des algonquinistes,* edited by William Cowan, pp. 193–200. Ottawa: Carleton University.

Lafleche, Guy
1980   Le chamanisme des amérindiens et des missionaires de la Nouvelle-France. *Studies in Religion/Sciences religieuses* 9(2):137–60.

LaViolette, Forrest E.
1951   Missionaries and the Potlatch. *Queen's Quarterly* 237–51.

Le Blanc, Peter G.
1968   Indian-Missionary Contact in Huronia, 1615–1649. *Ontario History* 60:133–46.

Leighton, Douglas
1984   The Ethnohistory of Missions in Southwestern Ontario. *Journal of the Canadian Church Historical Society* 26(2):50–57.

Lemert, Edwin M.
1954   The Life and Death of an Indian State. *Human Organization* 13(3):23–27.

Lewis, Clifford M.
1988   Roman Catholic Missions in the Southeast and Northeast. In *Handbook of North American Indians,* vol. 4, *History of Indian-White Relations,* edited by Wilcomb E. Washburn, pp. 481–93. Washington: Smithsonian Institution Press.

Long, John S.
1985   Rev. Edwin Watkins: Missionary to the Cree, 1852–1857. In *Papers of the Sixteenth Algonquian Conference,* edited by William Cowan, pp. 91–118. Ottawa: Carleton University.

Mary-Rousselière, Guy
1984   Exploration and Evangelization of the Great Canadian North: Vikings, Coureurs de Bois, and Missionaries. *Arctic* 37:590–602.

Miller, Christopher L.
1985   *Prophetic Worlds: Indians and Whites on the*

Columbia Plateau. New Brunswick, N.J.: Rutgers University Press.

Miller, Virginia P.
1980   Silas Rand, 19th Century Anthropologist Among the Micmac. *Anthropologica* 22:235–50.

Milliea, Mildred
1989   Micmac Catholicism in My Community. In *Actes du vingtième congrès des algonquinistes,* edited by William Cowan, pp. 262–66. Ottawa: Carleton University.

Moore, J. T.
1982   *Indian and Jesuit: A Seventeenth-century Encounter.* Chicago: Loyola University Press.

Morrison, Kenneth M.
1981   The mythological sources of Abenaki Catholicism: A case study of the social history of power. *Religion: Journal of Religion and Religions* 11:235–63.
1985   Discourse and the accommodation of values: Toward a revision of mission history. *Journal of the American Academy of Religion* 53:365–82.

Mulhall, David
1986   *Will to Power: The Missionary Career of Father A. G. Morice.* Vancouver: University of British Columbia Press.

Murray, Peter
1988   *The Devil and Mr. Duncan: A History of the Two Metlakatlas.* Vancouver: Sono Nis Press.

Nock, David A.
1980   The failure of the CMS native church policy in southwestern Ontario and Algoma. *Studies in Religion/Sciences religieuses* 9(3):269–85.
1988   *A Victorian Missionary and Canadian Indian Policy: Cultural Synthesis vs. Cultural Replacement.* Waterloo, Ont.: Wilfred Laurier University Press.

Norwood, Frederick A.
1984   Caught Between Two Cultures. *Drew Gateway* 54(22–3):76–84.

Pannekoek, Frits
1972   Protestant Agricultural Zions for the Western Indian. *Journal of the Canadian Church Historical Society.*

Patterson, E. Palmer, II
1981   Nishga Initiative and Missionary Response:

Robert Doolan at Quinwoch, B.C. *Missiology: An International Review* 9(3):337–44.
1982a   Kincolith, B.C.: Leadership Continuity in a Native Christian Village, 1867–1887. *Canadian Journal of Anthropology* 3:45–55.
1982b   *Mission on the Nass: The Evangelization of the Nishga (1860–1890).* Waterloo, Ont.: Eulachon Press.
1988   Nishga Perceptions of Their First Resident Missionary, the Reverend R. R. A. Doolan (1864–1867). *Anthropologica* 30:119–136.

Peacock, F. W.
1964   The cultural change among the Labrador Eskimos incident to the coming of the Moravian Mission. In *Le Nouveau-Quebec,* edited by J. Malaurie and J. Rousseau, pp. 439–56.

Peake, Frank A.
1972   Fur Traders and Missionaries: Some Reflections on the Attitudes of the Hudson's Bay Company Towards Missionary Work Among the Indians. *Western Canadian Journal of Anthropology* 3(1):72–93.
1977   The Achievements and Frustrations of James Hunter. *Journal of the Canadian Church Historical Society* 19(3–4):138–65.
1988   Church Missionary Society Personnel and Policy in Rupert's Land. *Journal of the Canadian Church Historical Society* 30(2):59–74.
1989   From the Red River to the Arctic: Essays on Anglican Missionary Expansion in the Nineteenth Century. *Journal of the Canadian Church Historical Society* 31(3):1–47.

Pomedli, Michael
1987   Beyond Unbelief: Early Jesuit Interpretations of Native Religions. *Studies in Religion/Sciences religieuses* 16:275–88.

Pratt, Edwin J.
1972   *Brebeuf and His Brethren.* Toronto: Macmillan of Canada.

Preston, Richard J., III
1987   Catholicism at Attawapiskat: A Case of Culture Change. In *Papers of the Eighteenth Algonquian Conference,* edited by William Cowan, pp. 271–86. Ottawa: Carleton University.

Remie, Cornelius H. W.
1983   Culture Change and Religious Continuity

Among the Arviligdjuarmiut of Pelly Bay, N.W.T. *Études/Inuit/Studies* 7(2):53–78.

Rettig, Andrew
1980   A Nativist Movement at Metlakatla Mission. *BC Studies* 46:28–39.

Ronda, James P.
1972   The European Indian: Jesuit Planning in New France. *Church History* 41:385–95.
1977   We Are Well as We Are: An Indian Critique of Seventeenth Century Christian Missions. *William and Mary Quarterly* 34:68–82.
1979   The Sillery Experiment: A Jesuit Indian Village in New France, 1637–1663. *American Indian Culture and Research Journal* 3(1):1–18.

Simonson, Gayle
1988   The Prayer Man: Ojibwa Henry Bird Steinhauer Brought Religion to the Cree. *Beaver* 68(5):28–33.

Smith, Donald B.
1987   *Sacred Feathers: The Reverend Peter Jones (Kahkewaquonaby) and the Missisauga Indians.* Toronto: University of Toronto Press.

Stevenson, John C.
1986   Metlakatla: William Duncan on the Northwest Coast Bringing Jesus to the Tsimshians. *Beaver* 66(4):35–41.
1990   William Duncan: Missionary to the Tsimshian. *Canadian West* 6(2):52–60.

Stocken, Cannon H. W.
1976   *Among the Blackfoot and Sarcee.* Calgary: Glenbow-Alberta Institute.

Stone, Thomas
1981   Whalers and Missionaries at Herschel Island. *Ethnohistory* 28:101–24.

Sullivan, Lawrence E., ed.
1989   *Native American Religions in North America.* Readings from the Encyclopedia of Religion Series, edited by Mircea Eliade. New York: Macmillan.

Tedlock, Dennis, and Barbara Tedlock, eds.
1975   *Teachings from the American Earth: Indian Religion and Philosophy.* New York: Liveright.

Tooker, Elisabeth, ed.
1979   *Native North American Spirituality of the Eastern Woodlands.* New York and Toronto: Parkhurst Press.

Usher, Jean
1968   Duncan of Metlakatla: The Victorian Origins of a Model Indian Community. In *The Shield of Achilles: Aspects of Canada in the Victorian Age,* edited by W. L. Morton, pp. 286–310. Toronto: McClelland and Stewart.
1971a   Apostles and Aborigines: The Social Theory of Church Missionary Society. *Social History* 7:28–52.
1971b   The Long Slumbering Offspring of Adam: The Evangelical Approach to the Tsimshian. *Anthropologica* 13(1–2):37–61.
1974   *William Duncan of Metlakatla: A Victorian Missionary in British Columbia.* Ottawa: National Museum of Man.

Vecsey, Christopher, ed.
1990   *Religion in Native North America.* Moscow, Idaho: University of Idaho Press.

Whitehead, Margaret
1981a   *The Cariboo Mission: A History of the Oblates.* Victoria, B.C.: Sononis.
1981b   Christianity, A Matter of Choice. *Pacific Northwest Quarterly,* July, 98–106.

Whitehead, Margaret, ed.
1988   *They Call Me Father: Memoirs of Father Nicholas Coccola.* Vancouver: University of British Columbia Press.

Whiteley, W. H.
1964   The establishment of the Moravian Mission in Labrador and British Policy, 1763–1783. *Canadian Historical Review* 45:29–50.

Williamson, Norman James
1980   Abishabis the Cree. *Studies in Religion* 9(2):217–45.

Zaslow, Morris
1966   The Missionary as Social Reformer: The Case of William Duncan. *Journal of the Canadian Church Historical Society* 8:52–69.

Section Fifteen

♦

EDUCATION

Allison, Derek J.
1983   Fourth World Education in Canada and the Faltering Promise of Native Teacher Education Programs. *Journal of Canadian Studies* 18:102–18.

Barman, Jean, Yvonne Hébert, and Don McCaskill, eds.
1986a   *Indian Education in Canada.* Vol. 1, *The Legacy.* Vancouver: University of British Columbia Press.
1986b   *Indian Education in Canada.* Vol. 2, *The Challenge.* Vancouver: University of British Columbia Press.

Basran, G. S.
1990   History and rationale of the affirmative action program, College of Arts and Sciences, University of Saskatchewan. *Canadian Journal of Native Studies* 10(2):273–88.

Beaudoin, Jean
1977a   Les droits des autochtones en matière d'education. *Recherches amérindiennes au Québec* 6(3–4):24–28.
1977b   Pourquoi La Macaza? *Recherches amérindiennes au Québec* 6(3–4):30–32.
1977c   La société amérindienne et ses besoins d'ordre educatif. *Recherches amérindiennes au Québec* 6(3–4):17–22.

Bennett, Jo Anne, and John W. Berry
1986   The Future of Cree Syllabic Literacy in Northern Canada. In *The Future of Literacy in a Changing World,* edited by David Wagner. Oxford: Pergamon Press.
1989a   Cree Literacy in the Syllabic Script. In *Orality and Literacy,* edited by David Olson. Cambridge: Cambridge University Press.
1989b   The Meaning and Value of the Syllabic Script for Native People. In *Actes du vingtième congrès des algonquinistes,* edited by William Cowan, pp. 31–42. Ottawa: Carleton University.

Berry, John W., and Jo Anne Bennett
1989   Syllabic Literacy and Cognitive Performance Among the Cree. In *Scripts and Literacy: East and West,* edited by Insup Taylor and David Olson. Toronto: Hogrete.

Bezeau, Laurence M.
1984   The Constitutional and Legal Basis for the Education of Canadian Indians. *Canadian Journal of Native Education* 12(1):38–46.

Born, D. O.
1970   Eskimo Education and the Trauma of Social Change. NSRG Notes 1. Ottawa: Northern Science Research Group, Department of Indian Affairs and Northern Development.

Bowd, Alan D.
1974   Practical Abilities of Indians and Eskimos. *Canadian Psychologist* 15:281–90.
1977   Ten Years After the Hawthorn Report: Changing Psychological Implications for the Education of Canadian Native Peoples. *Canadian Psychological Review* 18:332–45.

Brant, C., and Charles W. Hobart
1966   The Educational System in the Western Arctic. *Canadian Review of Sociology and Anthropology* 2:47–66.

Brantenberg, Anne
1977   The Marginal School and the Children of Nain. In *The White Arctic,* edited by R. Paine, pp. 344–58. St. John's: Memorial University of Newfoundland, Institute for Social and Economic Research.

Briggs, Jean L.
1983   Le modèle traditionnel d'education chez les inuit: Différentes formes d'expérimentation face à l'inconnu. *Recherches amérindiennes au Québec* 13(1):13–26.

Bringhurst, Robert
1990   That is also you: Some classics of native Canadian literature. *Canadian Literature* 124–25:32–47.

Brooks, Ian R.
1977   L'école et l'enfant indien, source de conflit culturel. *Recherches amérindiennes au Québec* 6(3–4):46–50.

Bundock, Germaine
1973   L'école-residence de Rae-Edzo. *North* 20(1):1–8.

Burnaby, Barbara
1976   Algonquian Language in Indian Education. In *Papers of the Seventh Algonquian Conference,* edited by William Cowan, pp. 436–49. Ottawa: Carleton University.
1980   Writing in Recently Alphabetized Languages. In *Papers of the Eleventh Algonquian Conference,* edited by W. Cowan, pp. 159–65. Ottawa: Carleton University.

1981   Education: Language Shift in Northern Ontario. In *Papers of the Twelfth Algonquian Conference,* edited by William Cowan, pp. 114–20. Ottawa: Carleton University.
1982   On the Success of School Programmes Involving a Native Language. In *Papers of the Thirteenth Algonquian Conference,* edited by William Cowan, pp. 251–60. Ottawa: Carleton University.
1983   Towards a National Policy for Language in Native Education. In *Actes du quatorzième congrès des algonquinistes,* edited by William Cowan, pp. 3–12. Ottawa: Carleton University.
1984   Orthography Characteristics for Real Readers. In *Papers of the Fifteenth Algonquian Conference,* edited by William Cowan, pp. 1–14. Ottawa: Carleton University.
1985   *Promoting Writing Systems for Canadian Native Languages.* Toronto: Ontario Institute for Studies in Education Press.
1987   English Language Curriculum Development for Algonquian-speaking Children. In *Papers of the Eighteenth Algonquian Conference,* edited by William Cowan, pp. 39–48. Ottawa: Carleton University.

Burnaby, Barbara, ed.
1985   *Promoting Native Writing Systems in Canada.* Toronto: Ontario Institute for Studies in Education Press.

Canadian Association in Support of Native Peoples
1975   Education: Special Issue. *Canadian Association in Support of the Native Peoples Bulletin* 16(2):2–31.

Carney, Robert
1981   The Native-Wilderness Equation: Catholic and Other School Orientations in the Western Arctic. *Canadian Historical Association Study Sessions* 48:61–78.
1982   The Road to Heart Lake—Native People: Adult Learners and the Future. *Canadian Journal of Native Education* 9(3):1–13.
1983   The Canadian Inuit and Vocational Education. *Études/Inuit/Studies* 7:85–116.

Chalmers, John W.
1976   Federal, Provincial, and Territorial Strategies for Canadian Native Education, 1960–1970. *Journal of Canadian Studies* 11(3):37–49.
1983   Missions and Schools in the Athabasca. *Alberta History* 31(1):24–29.

Chance, Norman A.
1973   Minority Education and the Transformation of Consciousness. In *Learning and Culture,* edited by Solon T. Kimball and Jacquetta H. Burnett, pp. 175–84. Seattle: University of Washington Press.

Clarke, Sandra, and Marguerite Mackenzie
1980   Education in the Mother Tongue: Tokenism Versus Cultural Autonomy in Canadian Indian Schools. *Canadian Journal of Anthropology* 1:205–18.

Clifton, R. A.
1972   The Social Adjustment of Native Students in a Northern Canadian Hostel. *Canadian Review of Sociology and Anthropology* 9:163–66.
1975   Self-concept and Attitudes: A Comparison of Canadian Indian and Non-Indian Students. *Canadian Review of Sociology and Anthropology* 12:577–84.
1976   Factors Which Affect the Education of Canadian Indian Students. In *Education, Change, and Society,* edited by R. A. Carleton et al., pp. 183–205. Toronto: Gage.

Coldevin, Gary, and Thomas Wilson
1982   Education, télévision par satellite et impuissance apprise chez les adolescents inuit du Canada. *Études/Inuit/Studies* 6(1):29–38.

Common, R. W.
1990   Toward a More Equitable Post-secondary Educational System for Natives in Canada. In *Papers of the Twenty-first Algonquian Conference,* edited by William Cowan, pp. 84–99. Ottawa: Carleton University.

Dawson, Janis
1988   "If My Children Are Proud": Native Education and the Problem of Self-esteem. *Canadian Journal of Native Education* 15(1):43–50.

Deprez, Paul
1973   *Education and Economic Development: The Case of Indian Reserves in Canada.* Occasional Paper 5. Winnipeg: University of Manitoba, Center for Settlement Studies.

Dieleman, Marinus
1983   Some Trends in Native Adult Education: Should We Be Optimistic? In *Actes du quatorzième congrès des algonquinistes,* edited by William Cowan, pp. 13–26. Ottawa: Carleton University.

Elofston, Betty-Lou, and W. Elofston
1988   Improving Native Education in the Province of Alberta. *Canadian Journal of Native Education* 15(1):31–38.

Fisher, Anthony D.
1981   A Colonial Education System: Historical Changes and Schooling in Fort Chipewyan. *Canadian Journal of Anthropology* 2(1):37–44.

Foley, Denis P.
1977   L'education des minorités. *Recherches amérindiennes au Québec* 6(3–4):34–38.

Friesen, John W.
1987   Multicultural Policy and Practice: What About the Indians? *Canadian Journal of Native Education* 14(1):30–40.

Friesen, John W., and Louise C. Lyon
1970   Progress of Southern Alberta Native Peoples. *Journal of American Indian Education* 9(3):15–23.

Gill, Aurelien
1975   Indian Concern in Indian Education Management. *Northian* 11(2):20–25.

Gladstone, James
1967   Indian School Days. *Alberta Historical Review* 15:18–24.

Godard, Barbara
1990   The politics of representation. *Canadian Literature* 124–25:183–225.

Graburn, Nelson H. H.
1982   Television and the Canadian Inuit. *Études/Inuit/Studies* 6(1):7–17.

Grantham, E. N.
1951   Education Goes North. *Canadian Geographical Journal* 42:45–49.

Granzberg, Gary
1982   Television as Storyteller. *Journal of Communication* 32(1):43–52.
1983   Key Factors of Native Culture Affecting the Impact of Television. *Laurentian University Review* 15(2):31–50.
1985   Television and Self-Concept Formation in Developing Areas: The Central Canadian Algonkian Experience. *Journal of Cross-cultural Psychology* 16(3).

Granzberg, Gary, and Jack H. Steinbring, eds.
1980   *TV and the Canadian Indian: Impact and*

Meaning Among Algonkians of Central Canada. Winnipeg: University of Winnipeg.

Green, Charlie
1990   Coming of Age: Native Education in the 21st Century. *Education Canada* 30(1):35–39.

Gresko, Jacqueline
1975   White "Rites" and Indian "Rites": Indian Education and Native Responses in the West, 1870–1910. In *Western Canada Past and Present,* edited by A. W. Rasporich, pp. 163–81. Calgary: McClelland and Stewart West.

Guemple, Lee
1988   Teaching Social Relations to Inuit Children. In *Hunters and Gatherers: Property, Power, and Ideology,* edited by Tim Ingold, David Riches, James Woodburn, pp. 131–49. Oxford: Berg Publications.

Haig-Brown, Celia
1988   *Resistance and Renewal: Surviving the Indian Residential School.* Vancouver: Tillacum Library/Arsenal Pulp Press.

Hanks, Christopher C.
1981   Perception and Utilization of Television: A Comparison Between a Saulteaux Reserve and a Rural White Community. *Musk-Ox* 28:20–25.

Hanks, Christopher C., et al.
1983   Social Changes and the Mass Media: The Oxford House Cree, 1909–83. *Polar Record* 21(134):459–65.

Hobart, Charles W.
1970   Some Consequences of Residential Schooling of Eskimos in the Canadian Arctic. *Arctic Anthropology* 6(2):123–35.

Hodgkinson, Jean
1970   Is Northern Education Meaningful? *Western Canadian Journal of Anthropology* 2(1):156–63.

Jaenen, Cornelius J.
1983   Education for Francisation: The Case of New France in the Seventeenth Century. *Canadian Journal of Native Education* 11(1):1–19.

Jaine, Linda
1991   Industrial and residential school administration: The attempt to undermine indigenous self-de-

termination. *Journal of Indigenous Studies* 2(2):37–48.

Jenness, Diamond
1929   The Ancient Education of a Carrier Indian. Annual Report for 1928. *National Museum of Canada Bulletin* 62:22–27.

Johns, Robert E.
1973   A History of St. Peter's Mission and of Education in Hay River, N.W.T., Prior to 1950. *Musk-Ox* 13:22–32.
1976   History of Administration of Schools, N.W.T. *Musk-Ox* 18:42–57.

Johnston, Basil
1988   *Indian School Days.* Toronto: Key Porter Books. Reprint. Norman: University of Oklahoma Press, 1989.
1991   Is that all there is? Tribal literature. *Canadian Literature* 128:54–62.

Katz, Richard, and Verna St. Denis
1991   Teacher as healer. *Journal of Indigenous Studies* 2(2):23–36.

King, A. J. C.
1968   Ethnicity and School Adjustment. *Canadian Review of Sociology and Anthropology* 5:84–91.

King, A. Richard
1967   *The School at Mopass: A Problem of Identity.* New York: Holt, Rinehart and Winston.

Kirkness, Verna J.
1981   The Education of Canadian Indian Children. *Child Welfare* 60:447–55.

Klokeid, Terry J., and Solomon Ratt
1989   Using Computer Adventures to Teach Cree. In *Actes du vingtième congrès des algonquinistes,* edited by William Cowan, pp. 161–78. Ottawa: Carleton University.

Krech, Shepard, III
1978   Nutritional Evolution of a Mission Residential School Diet: The Accuracy of Informant Recall. *Human Organization* 37:186–90.

Leavitt, Robert M.
1983   Storytelling as Language Curriculum. In *Actes du quatorzième congrès des algonquinistes,* edited by William Cowan, pp. 27–36. Ottawa: Carleton University.
1987   Fluency Is not Enough: Reassessing the Goals of Native Language Instruction. In *Papers of*

the Eighteenth Algonquian Conference, edited by William Cowan, pp. 165–72. Ottawa: Carleton University.

1989 Passwords: Writing Native Studies Curriculum. In *Actes du vingtième congrès des algonquinistes,* edited by William Cowan, pp. 201–7. Ottawa: Carleton University.

1991 Language and cultural contact in native education. *Canadian Modern Language Review* 47(2):266–79.

Long, John S.
1986 The Politics of Education in Moose Factory, Ontario. In *Actes du dix-septième congrès des algonquinistes,* edited by William Cowan, pp. 183–208. Ottawa: Carleton University.

1990 Schooling at Kashechewan: Then and Now. In *Papers of the Twenty-first Algonquian Conference,* edited by William Cowan, pp. 197–215. Ottawa: Carleton University.

Lotz, James R.
1972 Socio-Economic Development in the Canadian North: Some Perspectives and Problems. In *Education in the North,* edited by Frank Darnell, pp. 228–39. Fairbanks: University of Alaska, Arctic Institute of North America.

McElroy, Ann
1979 The Assessment of Role Identity: Use of the Instrumental Activities Inventory in Studying Inuit Children. In *Childhood and Adolescence in Canada,* edited by K. Ishwaran, pp. 54–71. Toronto: McGraw Hill Ryerson.

McGrath, Robin
1991–92 History of Inuit literacy in Labrador. *Newfoundland Quarterly* 87(1):35–40.

McPhie, Judith L., and June Benyon
1989 Attitude Change Through Cultural Immersion: A Grade Four Southwest Curriculum. *Canadian Ethnic Studies* 21(1):65–76.

Maloney, T.
1987 Native Network Spreading News in Northern Ontario. *Canadian Geographic* 107: 60–64.

Maranda, E. K.
1975 B.C. Indian Myth and Education: A Review Article. *BC Studies* 26:125–34.

Marshall, Lionel George
1955 The Development of Education in Northern Saskatchewan. *Musk-Ox* 1:19–25.

Matthiasson, John
1979 But Teacher, Why Can't I Be a Hunter?: Inuit Adolescence as a Double-bind Situation. In *Childhood and Adolescence in Canada,* edited by K. Ishwaran, pp. 72–82. Toronto: McGraw Hill Ryerson.

Mellow, J. Dean
1991 Integrating Language and Culture in Native Language Teaching. In *Papers of the Twenty-second Algonquian Conference,* edited by William Cowan, pp. 203–12. Ottawa: Carleton University.

Miller, J. R.
1987 The Irony of Residential Schooling. *Canadian Journal of Native Education* 14:3–14

1991 Owen Glendower, Hotspur, and Canadian Indian Policy. *Ethnohistory* 37(4):386–415.

Mitchell, Mary L.
1986 Algonquian Language Education. In *Actes du dix-septième congrès des algonquinistes,* edited by William Cowan, pp. 209–14. Ottawa: Carleton University.

1987 Ojibwa Vocabulary Acquisition. In *Papers of the Eighteenth Algonquian Conference,* edited by William Cowan, pp. 201–8. Ottawa: Carleton University.

Molohon, Kathryn T.
1984a Attitudes Toward Formal Education Among Swampy Cree. In *Actes du quatorzième congrès des algonquinistes,* edited by William Cowan, pp. 49–68. Ottawa: Carleton University.

1984b Responses to the Introduction of Television in Two Swampy Cree Communities on the West Coast of James Bay. *Kroeber Anthropological Society Papers* 63–64:95–103.

Murdoch, John
1982 Cree Literacy in Formal Education: A Problem in Educational Motivation. In *Papers of the Thirteenth Algonquian Conference,* edited by William Cowan, pp. 23–28. Ottawa: Carleton University.

National Indian Brotherhood
1974 Indian Control of Indian Education. *Northian* 10(2):11–25.

O'Connell, S.
1975 Television and the Eskimo People of Frobisher Bay. *Arctic* 28:155–58.

Paquette, Jerald
1989   Policy, Power, and Purpose: Lessons from Two Indian Education Scenarios. *Journal of Canadian Studies/Révue d' études canadiennes* 24(2):78–94.

Paul, Léonard
1983   La résistance culturelle des montagnais et le cas de Betsiamites. *Recherches amérindiennes au Québec* 13(1):5–12.

Pauls, Syd
1984   The Case for Band Controlled Schools. *Canadian Journal of Native Education* 12(1):31–37.

Petrone, Penny
1983   *First People, First Voices.* Toronto: University of Toronto Press.
1985   *Northern Voices: Inuit Writing in English.* Toronto: University of Toronto Press.

Poonwassie, D. H.
1991   Training of substitute teachers in Northern Manitoba, Canada. *Journal of Indigenous Studies* 2(1):43–45.

Preston, Richard J., III
1974   The Means to Academic Success for Eastern Cree Students. In *Proceedings of the First Congress, Canadian Ethnology Society,* edited by Jerome H. Barkow, pp. 87–96. Mercury Series, Canadian Ethnology Service Paper 17. Ottawa: National Museum of Man.
1979   The Cree Way Project: An Experiment in Grassroots Curriculum Development. In *Papers of the Tenth Algonquian Conference,* edited by William Cowan, pp. 92–101. Ottawa: Carleton University.
1982   Toward a General Statement on the Eastern Cree Structure of Knowledge. In *Papers of the Thirteenth Algonquian Conference,* edited by William Cowan, pp. 299–306. Ottawa: Carleton University.

Proulx, Paul
1986   Anxiety Management in Native Language Instruction. In *Actes du dix-septième congrès des algonquinistes,* edited by William Cowan, pp. 279–86. Ottawa: Carleton University.

Ralston, Helen
1981   Religion, Public Policy, and the Education of Micmac Indians of Nova Scotia, 1605–1872. *Canadian Review of Sociology and Anthropology* 18:470–98.

Robinson, P.
1985   Language Retention Among Canadian Indians: A Simultaneous Equations Model with Dichotomous Endogenous Variables. *American Sociological Review* 50:515–29.

Rohner, Ronald P.
1965   Factors Influencing the Academic Performance of Kwakiutl Children in Canada. *Comparative Education Review* 9:331–40.

Scott-Brown, Joan
1989   The Short Life of St. Dunstan's Calgary Indian Industrial School, 1896–1907. *Canadian Journal of Native Education* 14(1):41–49.

Sindell, Peter S.
1974   Some Discontinuities in the Enculturation of Mistassini Cree Children. In *Conflict in Culture: Problems in Developmental Change Among the Cree,* edited by Norman Chance, pp. 83–92. Ottawa: Canadian Research Center for Anthropology.

Sindell, Peter S., and Ronald M. Wintrob
1972   Cross-cultural Education in the North and Its Implications for Personal Identity: The Canadian Case. In *Education in the North,* edited by Frank Darnell, pp. 42–53. Fairbanks: University of Alaska, Arctic Institute of North America.

Smith, Ann F. V., and J. M. Pace
1988   Micmac Bachelor of Social Work Program: Policy Direction and Development. *Canadian Journal of Native Studies* 8(1):147–54.

Smith, B. M.
1988   Anti-Catholicism, Indian Education, and Thomas Jefferson Morgan, Commissioner of Indian Affairs. *Canadian Journal of History* 23:213–33.

Smith, Derek G.
1974   *Occupational Preferences of Northern Students.* SSN-5. Ottawa: Department of Indian Affairs and Northern Development, Northern Science Research Group.
1975   *Natives and Outsiders: Pluralism in the Mackenzie Delta, Northwest Territories.* MDRP 12. Ottawa: Department of Indian Affairs and Northern Development, Northern Science Research Group.

Stairs, Arlene
1991   Learning process and teaching roles in native

education: Cultural base and cultural broker-age. *Canadian Modern Language Review* 47(2): 280–94.

Stanbury, William T.
1973   *The Education Gap: Urban Indians in British Columbia.* Vancouver: University of British Columbia Press.

Stenbaek, Marianne
1988   The Politics of Cultural Survival: Towards a Model of Indigenous Television. *American Review of Canadian Studies* 18:331–40.

Stevenson, Winona
1988   The Red River Indian Mission School and John West's "Little Charges," 1820–1833. *Native Studies Review* 4(1–2):129–66.

Toohey, Kelleen
1983   English as a Second Language in a Northern Ontario Native Community. *Laurentian University Review* 15:115–21.
1985   Northern Native Canadian Language Education. *Canadian Review of Sociology and Anthropology* 22:93–101.

Tremblay, Marc-Adélard, et al.
1968   Education of the Indian Child. In *A Survey of the Contemporary Indians of Canada,* edited by H. B. Hawthorn, 2:105–61. Ottawa: Indian Affairs Branch.

Tschanz, Linda
1980   *Native Languages and Government Policy: An Historical Examination.* Center for Research and Teaching of Canadian Native Languages, Native Language Research Series, no. 2. London, Ont.: University of Western Ontario.

Valaskakis, G.
1982   Communication and Control in the Canadian North—The Potential of Interactive Satellites. *Études/Inuit/Studies* 6(1):19–28.

Vernon, Philip E.
1966   Educational and Intellectual Development Among Canadian Indians and Eskimos, Parts I–II. *Educational Review* 18:79–91, 186–95.

Watson, L.
1980   Television and Its Early Social Effects Among Rankin Inlet Inuit. *Musk-Ox* 27:60–66.

Waller, L. G. P., ed.
1965   *The Education of Indian Children in Canada.* Toronto: Ryerson Press.

Willis, Jane
1973   *Geneish: An Indian Girlhood.* Toronto: New Press.

Wilson, J. D.
1974a   "No Blanket to Be Worn in School": The Education of Indians in Early Nineteenth-Century Ontario. *Histoire Sociale/Social History* 4:293–305.
1974b   Notes on the Shingawauk Industrial Home for Indians. *Journal of the Canadian Church Historical Society* 16(4):66–71.

Wolcott, Harry
1967   *A Kwakiutl Village and School.* New York: Holt, Rinehart and Winston.

Woloshyn, S., and L. V. Sloan
1984   Kitaskinaw School: A Case Study in the Development of Tolerance and Understanding. *Canadian Journal of Native Education* 12(1): 47–57.

Wyatt, J. D.
1978   Self-determination Through Education: A Canadian Indian Example. In *Bilingual Education,* edited by H. Lafontaine, B. Persky, L. H. Golubchick, pp. 279–84. Wayne, N.J.: Avery Publishing Group.
1978–79 Native Involvement in Curriculum Development: The Native Teacher as Cultural Broker. *Interchange* 9(1):17–28.

Wyatt-Beynon, June
1991   Career paths of Simon Fraser University Native teacher education graduates. *Journal of Indigenous Studies* 2(2):49–70.

Zentner, Henry
1963   Value Congruence Among Indian and Non-Indian High School Students in Southern Alberta. *Alberta Journal of Education Research* 9:168–78.

Section Sixteen

✦

HEALTH AND DISEASE

Badgley, Robin F.
1973   Social Policy and Indian Health Services in Canada. *Anthropological Quarterly* 46:50–59.

Bagley, C.
1991   Poverty and suicide among native Canadians: A replication. *Psychological Reports* 69:149–50.

Balikci, Asen
1968   Bad Friends. *Human Organization* 27:191–99.

Brady, Paul
1983   The Underdevelopment of the Health Status of Treaty Indians. In *Racial Minorities in Multicultural Canada,* edited by Peter S. Li and B. S. Bolaria, pp. 39–55. Toronto: Garamond Press.

Brody, Hugh
1971   *Indians on Skid Row: The Role of Alcohol and Community in the Adaptive Process of Indian Urban Migrants.* NSRG 70-2. Ottawa: Department of Indian Affairs and Northern Development, Northern Science Research Group.
1977   Alcohol, Change, and the Industrial Frontier. *Études/Inuit/Studies* 1:31–46.

Carey, Maria
1988   An Overview of the Mental Health Services Being Provided to Treaty Indians in Alberta. *Saskatchewan Indian Federated College Journal* 4(1):13–18.

Christie, L., and J. M. Halpern
1990   Temporal Constructs and Inuit Mental Health. *Social Science and Medicine* 30(6):739–49.

Clairmont, D. H.
1962   *Notes on the Drinking Behavior of the Eskimos and Indians in the Aklavik Area.* NCRC 62-4. Ottawa: Department of Northern Affairs and National Resources, Northern Coordination and Research Centre.

Condon, Richard G.
1983   Seasonal Photoperiodism, Activity Rhythms, and Disease Susceptibility in the Central Canadian Arctic. *Arctic Anthropology* 20(1):33–48.

Culhane, Dara
1989   Error in Judgement: The Politics of Medical Care in an Indian/White Community. *BC Studies* 80:73.

Cuthand-Goodwill, Jean
1988   Indian and Inuit Nurses of Canada. *Saskatchewan Indian Federated College Journal* 4(1): 93–104.

Dailey, R. C.
1968   The Role of Alcohol Among North American Indian Tribes as Reported in the Jesuit Relations. *Anthropologica* 10:45–57.

Decker, Jody F.
1988   Tracing Historical Diffusion Patterns: The Case of the 1780–82 Smallpox Epidemic Among the Indians of Western Canada. *Native Studies Review* 4(1–2):1–24.

1991   Depopulation of the northern Plains natives. *Social Science and Medicine* 33:381–93.

Dufour, Rose
1984   Les menstruations et la grossesse chez les iglulingmiut (T.N.-O.). *Recherches amérindiennes au Québec* 14(3):17–25.

1985   L'otite chez les enfants inuit: Une question de mode alimentaire. *Études/Inuit/Studies* 8(2): 77–90.

Dufrene, Phoebe
1990   Utilizing the arts for healing from a Native American perspective: Implications for creative arts therapies. *Canadian Journal of Native Studies* 10(1):121–31.

Duval, Bernard, and François Thérien
1982   Natalité, mortalité et morbidité chez les inuit du Québec arctique. *Recherches amérindiennes au Québec* 12(1):41–50.

Edouard, Lindsay, et al.
1991   Pregnancy outcome among native Indians in Saskatchewan. *Canadian Medicine Association Journal* 144(12):1623–25.

Edwards, Grant Thomas
1980   Bella Coola: Indian and European Medicines. *Beaver* 311(3):4–11.

Fenton, William N.
1941   Iroquois Suicide: A Study in the Stability of a Culture Pattern. *Bureau of American Ethnology Bulletin* 128(14):80–137.

1986   A Further Note on Iroquois Suicide. *Ethnohistory* 33:448–57.

Foggin, P. M., and N. Aurillon
1989   Respiratory Health Indicators and Accultura-tion Among the Inuit and Cree of Northern Quebec: A Regional Approach Using Geographic Seriation Analysis. *Social Science and Medicine* 29:617–26.

Forsius, Harriet
1980   Behavior. In *The Human Biology of Circumpolar Populations,* edited by F. A. Milan, pp. 339–58. Cambridge: Cambridge University Press.

Fortuine, Robert, ed.
1985   *Circumpolar Health '84.* Seattle: University of Washington Press.

Fritz, Wayne, and Carl D'Arcy
1983   Comparisons: Indian and Non-Indian Use of Psychiatric Services. In *Racial Minorities in Multicultural Canada,* edited by Peter S. Li and B. S. Bolaria, pp. 68–85. Toronto: Garamond Press.

Gagné, Gérard
1982   La paléopathologie humaine en Amérique du Nord: un aperçu. *Recherches amérindiennes au Québec* 12(1):3–12.

Garro, L. C.
1988   Explaining High Blood Pressure: Variation in Knowledge About Illness. *American Ethnologist* 15:98–119.

Gfellner, Barbara M.
1991   Profile of aboriginal youth in a community drug program. *Canadian Journal of Native Studies* 11(1):25–48.

Gibson, James R.
1982–83 Smallpox on the Northwest Coast, 1835–1838. *BC Studies* 56:61–81.

Graham-Cumming, G.
1967   Health of the Original Canadians, 1867–1967. *Medical Services Journal, Canada,* 3:115–66.

Grondin, Jacques
1989   Social Support and Decision-making: The Inuit in the Biomedical System. *Native Studies Review* 5(1):17–40.

Hagey, R.
1984   The Phenomenon, the Explanations, and the Responses: Metaphors Surrounding Diabetes in Urban Canadian Indians. *Social Science and Medicine* 18(3):265–72.

Hamer, John, and Jack H. Steinbring, eds.
1980   *Alcohol and Native Peoples of the North.* Lanham, Md.: University Press of America.

Harvald, Brent, and J. P. Hart Hansen, eds.
1982   *Circumpolar Health '81: Proceedings of the 45th International Symposium on Circumpolar Health, Copenhagen, 9–13 August 1981.* Report Series 33. Copenhagen: Nordic Council for Arctic Medical Research.

Haworth, James C., et al.
1991   Increased prevalence of hereditary metabolic diseases among native Indians in Manitoba and northwestern Ontario. *Canadian Medical Association Journal* 143(2):123–29.

Hobart, Charles W.
1978   Economic Development, Liquor Consumption, and Offence Rates in the Northwest Territories. *Canadian Journal of Criminology* 20:259–78.

Hodgson, Corinne
1982   The Social and Political Implications of Tuberculosis Among Native Canadians. *Canadian Review of Sociology and Anthropology* 19:502–12.
1983   Cancer Surveillance in a Remote Indian Population. *American Journal of Public Health* 73:515–20.

Honigmann, John J., and Irma Honigmann
1945   Drinking in an Indian-White Community. *Quarterly Journal of Studies on Alcohol* 5:575–619.

Hurlich, Marshall G.
1983   Historical and Recent Demography of the Algonkians of Northern Ontario. In *Boreal Forest Adaptations,* edited by A. Theodore Steegmann, Jr., pp. 143–200. New York: Plenum Press.

Jarvis, George K., and Menno Boldt
1982   Death Styles Among Canada's Indians. *Social Science and Medicine* 16:1345–52.

Jilek, Wolfgang
1974   *Coast Salish Mental Health and Culture Change.* Toronto: Holt, Rinehart, and Winston.
1980   *Salish Indian Mental Health and Culture Change.* 2d ed. Vancouver: University of British Columbia Press.
1982   *Indian Healing: Shamanic Ceremonialism in*

the Pacific Northwest Today. Surrey, B.C.: Hancock House.

Johnston, Susan
1987   Epidemics: The Forgotten Factor in Seventeenth Century Native Warfare in the St. Lawrence Region. In *Native People, Native Lands,* edited by Bruce A. Cox, pp. 14–31. Ottawa: Carleton University.

Kaufert, J. M., and W. W. Koolage
1984   Role Conflict Among Culture Brokers: The Experience of Native Canadian Medical Interpreters. *Social Science and Medicine* 18:283–86.

Kennedy, Dorothy I. D.
1984   The Quest for a Cure: A Case Study in the Use of Health Care Alternatives. *Culture* 4(2): 21–32.

Kistabish, Richard
1982   La santé chez les algonquins. *Recherches amérindiennes au Québec* 12(1):29–32.

Labbé, J.
1981   La santé au Nouveau-Québec inuit: Réflexions sur les problèmes de santé et le système mis en place pour les régler. *Études/Inuit/Studies* 5(2):63–82.

Lacasse, Fernande
1982   La conception de la santé chez les indiens montagnais. *Recherches amérindiennes au Québec* 12(1):25–28.

Lacey, Laurie
1978   Npisun: Changes over Time in the Micmac Indian Approach to Health and the Maintenance of Well-being. In *Papers from the Fourth Annual Congress of the Canadian Ethnology Society, 1977,* pp. 179–88. Mercury Series, Canadian Ethnology Service Paper 40. Ottawa: National Museum of Man.

Lantis, Margaret
1981   Zoonotic Diseases in the Canadian and Alaskan North. *Études/Inuit/Studies* 5:83–107.

Larocque, Robert
1982   L'introduction de maladies européenes chez les autochtones des XVIIe et XVIIIe siècles. *Recherches amérindiennes au Québec* 12(1): 13–24.

Lavallée, Claudette, et al.
1991   Evaluation of a community health representa-

tive program among the Cree of Northern Quebec. *Canadian Journal of Public Health/ Revue canadiènne de santé publique* 82(3): 181–84.

Lemert, Edwin M.
1954   *Alcohol and the Northwest Coast Indians.* Berkeley: University of California Press.

Lithman, Yngve Georg
1979   Feeling Good and Getting Smashed: On the Symbolism of Alcohol and Drunkenness Among Canadian Indians. *Ethnos* 44(1–2):119–33.

Lurie, Nancy O.
1969   The World's Oldest On-going Protest Demonstration: North American Drinking Patterns. *Pacific Historical Review* 40:311–32.

MacAndrew, Craig, and Robert J. Edgerton
1969   *Drunken Comportment: A Social Explanation.* Chicago: Aldine.

McLeod, D. M.
1963   Liquor Control in the North-West Territories: The Permit System, 1870–1891. *Saskatchewan History* 16(3):81–89.

Malloch, Lesley
1989   Indian Medicine, Indian Health: Study Between Red and White Medicine. *Canadian Woman Studies* 10(2–3):105–12.

Melbye, Jerry
1982   Advances in the Contribution of Physical Anthropology to Archaeology in Canada: The Past Decade. *Canadian Journal of Archaeology* 6:55–64.

Milan, F. A.
1980   The Demography of Selected Circumpolar Populations. In *The Human Biology of Circumpolar Populations,* edited by F. A. Milan, pp. 13–35. Cambridge: Cambridge University Press.

Milan, F. A., ed.
1980   *The Human Biology of Circumpolar Populations.* Cambridge: Cambridge University Press.

Minorr, J. B., et al.
1991   Looking in, looking out: Coping with adolescent suicide in the Cree and Ojibway communities of northern Ontario. *Canadian Journal of Native Studies* 11(1):1–24.

Morgan, William
1987   Subsistence Strategy and Demographic Im-

pact of Virgin Soil Epidemics. In *Papers of the Eighteenth Algonquian Conference,* edited by William Cowan, pp. 229–37. Ottawa: Carleton University.

Morse, J. M., et al.
1991   Cree Indian healing practices and western health care: A comparative analysis. *Social Science and Medicine* 32(12):1361–66.

O'Neil, J. D.
1981   Beyond Healers and Patients: The Emergence of Local Responsibility in Inuit Health Care. *Études/Inuit/Studies* 5(1):17–26.
1986   The Politics of Health in the Fourth World: A Northern Canadian Example. *Human Organization* 45:119–28.

Piche, Victor, and M. V. George
1973   Estimates of Vital Rates for the Canadian Indians, 1960–1970. *Demography* 10:367–82.

Popeski, Dianne, et al.
1991   Blood pressure during pregnancy in Canadian Inuit: Community differences related to diet. *Canadian Medical Association Journal* 145: 445–54.

Ray, Arthur J.
1976   Diffusion of Diseases in the Western Interior of Canada, 1830–1850. *Geographic Review* 66:139–57.

Robbins, Richard H.
1973   Alcohol and the Identity Struggle: Some Effects of Economic Change on Interpersonal Relations. *American Anthropologist* 75:99–122.

Ross, Philip, Stas Olpinski, and Mark Curtis
1989   Relationships between dietary practice and parasite zoonoses in Northern Quebec Inuit Communities. *Études/Inuit/Studies* 13(2):33–48.

Ruderman, A. P., and G. R. Weller
1981   Health Services for the Keewatin Inuit in a Period of Transition: The View from 1980. *Études/Inuit/Studies* 5(2):49–62.

Savishinsky, Joel S.
1977   A Thematic Analysis of Drinking Behavior in a Hare Indian Community. *Papers in Anthropology* (Department of Anthropology, University of Oklahoma), 18(2):43–59.

Schaefer, Otto
1976   Socio-Cultural Change and Health in Cana-

dian Inuit. In *Les facettes de l'identité amérindienne,* edited by Marc-Adélard Tremblay, pp. 280–300. Quebec: Presses de l'Université Laval.

Schmitt, N., and W. S. Barclay
1962   Accidental Deaths Among West Coast Indians. *Canada Journal of Public Health* 53: 409–12.

Schumann, Jill R.
1982   The Diffusion of Alcohol: Through Membrane into Culture. In *Papers of the Thirteenth Algonquian Conference,* edited by William Cowan, pp. 37–46. Ottawa: Carleton University.

Shepherd, R. J., and S. Itoh, eds.
1976   *Circumpolar Health.* Toronto: University of Toronto Press.

Snow, Dean R., and Kim Lanphear
1988   European Contact and Indian Depopulation in the Northeast: The Timing of the First Epidemics. *Ethnohistory* 35:15–33.

So, J. K.
1980   Human Biological Adaptation to Arctic and Subarctic Zones. *Annual Review of Anthropology* 9:63–82.

Spady, D. W., et al.
1982   *Between two worlds: The reports of the Northwest Territories perinatal and infant mortality and morbidity study.* Occasional Publication 16. Edmonton: Boreal Institute for Northern Studies, University of Alberta.

Steinbring, Jack H.
1980   Alcoholics Anonymous: Cultural Reform Among the Saulteaux. In *Alcohol and Native Peoples of the North,* edited by John Hamer and Jack H. Steinbring, pp. 89–107. Washington: University Press of America.

Stymeist, David H.
1976   Indian Health in the North. In *Les facettes de l'identité amérindienne,* edited by Marc-Adélard Tremblay, pp. 237–78. Quebec: Presses de l'Université Laval.

Szathmary, Emöke J. E.
1984   Human Biology of the Arctic. In *Handbook of North American Indians,* vol. 5, *Arctic,* edited by David Damas, pp. 64–71. Washington: Smithsonian Institution Press.

Szathmary, Emöke J. E., and Nancy S. Ossenberg
1978   Are the Biological Differences Between North American Indians and Eskimos Truly Profound? *Current Anthropology* 19(4):673–701.

Szathmary, Emöke J. E., et al.
1987   Dietary Change and Plasma Glucose Levels in an Amerindian Population Undergoing Cultural Transition. *Social Science and Medicine* 24:791–804.

Thouez, J.-P., A. Rannou, and P. M. Foggin
1989   The Other Face of Development: Native Population, Health Status, and Indicators of Malnutrition—the Case of the Cree and Inuit of Northern Quebec. *Social Science and Medicine* 29(8):965–74.

Thouez, J.-P., P. M. Foggin, and A. Rannou
1989   Hypertension et "modernité" chez les cris et les inuit du Nord du Québec. *Canadian Geographer/Géographe Canadien* 33:19–31.
1990   Correlates of Health-Care Use: Inuit and Cree of Northern Quebec. *Social Science and Medicine* 30(1):25–34.

Tremblay, Normand
1981   *Natalité et mortalité chez les inuit de la baie d'Ungava (Nouveau-Québec).* Collection Nordicana 44. Laval: Centre d'études nordiques.
1985   La fècondité dans un village inuit. *Études/Inuit/Studies* 9(1):93–115.

Trimble, Michael K.
1989   Infectious Disease and the Northern Plains Horticulturalists: A Human Behavioral Model. *Plains Anthropologist* 34–124. Memoir 23, Part 2:41–60.

Trovato, F.
1987   A macrosociological analysis of native Indian fertility in Canada: 1961, 1971, and 1981. *Social Forces* 66:463–85.
1991   Analysis of Native mortality. *Journal of Indigenous Studies* 2(1):1–15.

Vachon, André
1960   L'eau de vie dans la société indienne. *Canadian Historical Association Report* 1960:22–32.

Vallee, Frank G.
1968   Stresses of Change and Mental Health Among the Canadian Eskimos. *Archives of Environmental Health* 17(October):565–70.

Waddell, Jack O.
1985   Malhiot's Journal: An Ethnohistoric Assessment of Chippewa Alcohol Behavior in the Early Nineteenth Century. *Ethnohistory* 32: 246–68.

Waldram, James B.
1990   Physician Utilization and Urban Native People in Saskatoon, Canada. *Social Science and Medicine* 30(5):579–89.

Weller, G. R.
1981   The Delivery of Health Services in the Canadian North. *Journal of Canadian Studies* 16(2): 69–80.

Wenzel, George W.
1981   Inuit Health and the Health Care System: Change and Status Quo. *Études/Inuit/Studies* 5(1):7–17.

Wheatley, M., and B. Wheatley
1981   The Effect of Eating Habits on Mercury Levels Among Inuit Residents of Sugluk, P.Q. *Études/ Inuit/Studies* 5(1):27–43.

Young, David E., ed.
1990   *Health Care Issues in the Canadian North.* Occasional Publication 26. Edmonton, Alta.: Boreal Institute for Northern Studies, University of Alberta.

Young, T. Kue
1979   Changing Patterns of Health and Sickness Among the Cree-Ojibwa of Northwestern Ontario. *Medical Anthropology* 3:191–223.
1983   Mortality Patterns of Isolated Indians in Northwestern Ontario. *Public Health Report* 98: 467–75.

1984   Indian Health Services in Canada: A Sociohistorical Perspective. *Social Science and Medicine* 18(3):257–64.
1988a   Are Subarctic Indians Undergoing the Epidemiological Transition? *Social Science and Medicine* 26:659–71.
1988b   *Health Care and Cultural Change: The Indian Experience in the Central Subarctic.* Toronto: University of Toronto Press.

Young, T. Kue, and R. I. Casson
1988   The Decline and Persistence of Tuberculosis in a Canadian Indian Population: Implications for Control. *Canadian Journal of Public Health/ Révue Canadienne de santé publique* 79:302– 8.

Young, T. Kue, et al.
1990   Determinants of Plasma Glucose Level and Diabetic Status in a Northern Canadian Indian Population. *Canadian Medical Association Journal* 142(8):821–30.

Young, T. Kue, Joseph M. Kaufert, and John K. McKenzie
1989   Excessive burden of end-state renal disease among Canadian Indians: A national survey. *American Journal of Public Health* 79:756– 58.

Young, T. Kue, Emöke J. E. Szathmary, and Susan Enos
1990   Geographical distribution of diabetes among the native population of Canada: A national survey. *Social Science and Medicine* 31(2): 129–39.

Zubrow, E.
1990   The depopulation of native America. *Antiquity* 64:754–65.

Section Seventeen

🍁

ART AND MATERIAL CULTURE

Ames, Michael M.

1981 Museum anthropologists and the arts of acculturation on the Northwest Coast. *BC Studies* 49:3–14.

1984–85 Bill Holm, Willie Seaweed, and the Problem of Northwest Coast Indian "Art": A Review Article. *BC Studies* 64:74–81.

1985a De-schooling the museum: A proposal to increase public access to museums and their resources. *Museum* 145:25–31.

1985b *Museums, the Public, and Anthropology: A Study in the Anthropology of Anthropology.* Vancouver: University of British Columbia Press; Delhi: Concept Publishing Co.

1987 Free Indians from Their Ethnological Fate: The Emergence of the Indian Point of View in Exhibitions of Indians. *Muse* 5(2):14–19.

1988a Daring to be Different: An Alternative. *Muse* 6(1):38–42.

1988b The Liberation of Anthropology: A Rejoinder to Professor Trigger's "A Present of their Past." *Culture* 8(1).

1988c Museum and Politics: The Spirit Sings and the Lubicon Boycott. Boycott the Politics of Suppression! *Muse* 6(3):15–16.

Ames, Michael M., and Claudia Haagen

1988 A New Native Peoples' History for Museums. *Native Studies Review* 4(1–2):119–28.

Ames, Michael M., Julia D. Harrison, and Trudy Nicks

1988 Proposed Museum Policies for Ethnological Collections and the Peoples They Represent. *Muse* 6(3):47–52.

Anderson, Marcia, and Kathy Hussy-Arntson

1986 Ojibwe Bandolier Bags in the Collection of the Minnesota Historical Society. *American Indian Art Magazine* 11(4):46–57.

Arima, Eugene Y.

1963 *Report on an Eskimo Umiak Built at Ivujivik, P.Q., in the Summer of 1960.* Anthropological Series 59, *Bulletin* 189. Ottawa: National Museum of Canada.

1964 Notes on the Kayak and Its Equipment at Ivujivik, P.Q. Anthropological Series 62, *Bulletin* 196:221–61. Ottawa: National Museum of Canada.

1967 Itivimiut Sled Construction. Anthropological Series 70, *Bulletin* 204:100–123. Ottawa: National Museum of Canada.

1975   *A Contextual Study of the Caribou Eskimo Kayak.* Mercury Series, Canadian Ethnology Service Paper 25. Ottawa: National Museum of Man.

Arima, Eugene Y., ed.
1991   *Contributions to Kayak Studies.* Mercury Series, Canadian Ethnology Service Paper 122. Ottawa: Canadian Museum of Civilization.

Arts Canada
1973–74   *Stones, Bones, and Skin: Ritual Shamanistic Art.* Thirteenth Anniversary Issue of *Artscanada.*
1974   *The Athapaskans: Strangers of the North.* Ottawa: National Museum of Canada.

Atleo, Richard E.
1991   Policy development for museums: A First Nations perspective. *BC Studies* 89:48–61.

Barbeau, C. Marius
1951   *Totem Poles.* 2 vols. Anthropological Series 30, *Bulletin* 119. Ottawa: National Museum of Canada.

Bardwell, Kathryn
1986   The Case for an Aboriginal Origin of Northeast Indian Woodsplint Basketry. *Man in the Northeast* 31:49–67.

Bebbington, Julia M.
1982   *Quillwork of the Plains.* Calgary: Glenbow-Alberta Institute.

Berlo, Janet Catherine
1990   The Power of the Pencil: Inuit Women in the Graphic Arts. *Inuit Art Quarterly* 5(1):16–26.

Birket-Smith, Kaj
1945   Ethnographic Collections from the Northwest Passage. *Report of the Fifth Thule Expedition, 1921–24,* 6(2). Copenhagen.

Black, Martha
1989   Looking for Bella Bella: the R. W. Lange collection and Heiltsuk art history. *Canadian Journal of Native Studies* 9(2):273–91.

Blackman, Margaret B.
1973   Totems to Tombstones: Culture Change as Viewed Through the Haida Mortuary Complex, 1877–1971. *Ethnology* 12:47–56.
1975   Mortuary Art from the Northwest Coast. *Beaver* (Winter):54–57.
1976a   Blankets, Bracelets, and Boas: The Potlatch in Photographs. *Anthropological Papers of the University of Alaska* 18:43–67.
1976b   Creativity in Acculturation: Art, Architecture, and Ceremony from the Northwest Coast. *Ethnohistory* 23:387–414.
1985   Contemporary Northwest Coast Art for Ceremonial Use. *American Indian Art Magazine* 10(3):24–37.
1990   Facing the Future, Envisioning the Past: Visual Literature and Contemporary Northwest Coast Masks. *Arctic Anthropology* 27(2):27–39.

Blackman, Margaret B., and Edwin S. Hall, Jr.
1981   Contemporary Northwest Coast Art: Tradition and Innovation in Serigraphy. *American Indian Art Magazine* 6(3):54–61.
1982   The Afterimage and Image After: Visual Documents and the Renaissance in Northwest Coast Art. *American Indian Art Magazine* 7(2):30–39.
1986   Snakes and Clowns: Art Thompson and the Westcoast Heritage. *American Indian Art Magazine* 11(2):30–45.

Blodgett, Jean
1979a   *The Coming and Going of the Shaman: Eskimo Shamanism and Art.* Winnipeg: Winnipeg Art Gallery.
1979b   The Historic Period in Canadian Eskimo Art. *Beaver* 310(1):17–27.
1982   Whale Bone. *Beaver* 313(2):4–11.
1983   *Grasp Tight the Old Ways: Selections from the Klauer Family Collection of Inuit Art.* Toronto: Art Gallery of Toronto.
1984   Christianity and Inuit Art. *Beaver* 315(2):16–25.
1985   *Kenojuak: Canada's renowned Eskimo artist.* Toronto: University of Toronto Press.

Boas, Franz
1927   *Primitive Art.* Cambridge: Harvard University Press.

Boreal Institute for Northern Studies
1986   *Keeveeok awake: Mamngugsualuk and the rebirth of legend at Baker Lake.* Occasional Publication 19. Edmonton: Boreal Institute for Northern Studies and University of Alberta Collections.

Bradley, Ian, and Patricia Bradley
1977   *A Bibliography of Canadian Native Arts: In-*

dian and Eskimo Arts, Crafts, Dance, and Music. Victoria: GLC Publications.

Brandson, Lorraine E.
1981 *From Tundra to Forest: A Chipewyan Resource Manual.* Winnipeg: Manitoba Museum of Man and Nature.

Brasser, Ted J. C.
1976 *Bo'jou, Neejee! Profiles of Canadian Indian Art.* Ottawa: National Museums of Canada.
1984 Backrest Banners Among the Plains Cree and Plains Ojibwa. *American Indian Art Magazine* 10(1):56–77.

Bringhurst, Robert
1991 *The Black Canoe: Bill Reid and the Spirit of Haide Gwaii.* Seattle: University of Hawaii Press.

British Columbia Indian Arts Society
1982 *Mungo Martin, Man of Two Cultures.* Sidney, B.C.: Gray's Publishing.

Brown, Ian
1985 Soft Gold: A Northwest Coast Exhibition at the Peabody Museum, Harvard University. *American Indian Art Magazine* 19(4):24–29.

Brundege, Barbara, and Eugene Fisher
1990 Old Masters: Turning Stone into Spirit, Cape Dorset's Hunters Carve a Stunning Record of Their Lives on the Land. *Equinox* 9(1):36–51.

Burnham, Dorothy K.
1981 *The Comfortable Arts: Traditional Spinning and Weaving in Canada.* Ottawa: National Gallery of Canada.

Canada, National Museum of
1974 *The Athapaskans: Strangers of the North.* Ottawa.
1977 *The Inuit Print.* Ottawa.

Canada House Cultural Centre Gallery
1985 *Mohawk, Micmac, Maliseet, and Other Indian Souvenir Art from Victorian Canada.* London: Canada House Cultural Centre Gallery.

Carlson, Roy L., ed.
1983 *Indian Art Traditions of the Northwest Coast.* Burnaby, B.C.: Simon Fraser University Press.

Carpenter, Edmund C.
1973 *Eskimo Realities.* New York: Holt, Rinehart and Winston.

Ceci, Lynn
1982 The Value of Wampum Among the New York

Iroquois: A Case Study in Artifact Analysis. *Journal of Anthropological Research* 38:97–107.

Clark, Ian Christie
1982 The Cultural Property Export and Import Act of Canada: A Progress Report. *International Journal of Museum Management and Curatorship* 1:5–15.
1986 Illicit traffic in cultural property: Canada seeks a bilateral agreement with the United States. *Museum* 151:182–87.

Coe, Ralph T.
1986 *Lost and Found Traditions: Native American Art, 1965–1985.* Seattle: University of Washington Press and American Federation of Arts.

Cole, Douglas
1982 Tricks of the Trade: Northwest Coast Artifact Collecting, 1875–1925. *Canadian Historical Review* 63:439–60.
1985 *Captured Heritage: The Scramble for Northwest Coast Artifacts.* Vancouver and London: Douglas and McIntyre.

Collins, Henry B., Frederica De Laguna, Edmund Carpenter, and Peter Stone
1973 *The Far North: 2,000 Years of American Eskimo and Indian Art.* Washington: National Gallery of Art. Reprint. Indiana University Press, Bloomington, 1977.

Cooke, Lanny
1983 Don Cardinal—Bush Painter of the North. *Beaver* 313(4):54–57.

Cooper, John M.
1938 *Snares, Deadfalls, and Other Traps of the Northern Algonquian and Northern Athapaskans.* Anthropological Series 5. Washington: Catholic University of America.

Crumrine, N. Ross, and Marjorie Halpin, eds.
1983 *The Power of Symbols: Masks and Masquerade in the Americas.* Vancouver: University of British Columbia Press.

Danford, Joanne
1989 Will the "real" false face please stand up? *Canadian Journal of Native Studies* 9(2):253–72.

Danzker, Jo-Anne B.
1990 Cultural Apartheid/Apartheid culturel. *Muse* 8(3):20–34.

Darragh, Ian
1987   The killing cliffs: Early buffalo-hunting technique preserved at world heritage sites. *Canadian Geographic* 107 (October/November):55–61.

Davis, Robert
1949   *Native Arts of the Pacific Northwest from the Rasmussen Collection of the Portland Art Museum.* Stanford: Stanford University Press.

Dewdney, Selwyn
1970   *Dating Rock Art in the Canadian Shield Region.* Art and Archaeology Division Occasional Paper 24. Toronto: Royal Ontario Museum.
1975   *The Sacred Scrolls of the Southern Ojibway.* Toronto: University of Toronto Press.
1978   Birth of a Cree-Ojibwa Style of Contemporary Art. In *One Century Later,* edited by I. A. L. Getty and D. B. Smith, pp. 117–25. Vancouver: University of British Columbia Press.

Dickason, Olive Patricia
1972   *Indian Arts in Canada.* Ottawa: Department of Indian Affairs and Northern Development.

Doxtator, Deborah
1988   The Home of the Indian and Other Stories in the Museum. *Muse* 6(3):26–28.

Driscoll, Bernadette
1984   Sapangat: Inuit Beadwork in the Canadian Arctic. *Expedition* 26(2):40–47.

Duff, Wilson
1967   *Arts of the Raven.* Vancouver: Vancouver Art Gallery.
1975   *Images Stone B.C.: Thirty Centuries of Northwest Coast Indian Sculpture.* Saanichton, B.C.: Hancock House.
1981a   Stone Clubs from the Skeena River Area. In *The World Is as Sharp as a Knife,* edited by Donald W. Abbott, pp. 95–104. Victoria: British Columbia Provincial Museum.
1981b   Thoughts on the Nootka Canoe. In *The World Is as Sharp as a Knife,* edited by Donald W. Abbott, pp. 201–6. Victoria: British Columbia Provincial Museum.
1981c   The World Is as Sharp as a Knife: Meaning in Northern Northwest Coast Art. In *The World Is as Sharp as a Knife,* edited by Donald W. Abbott, pp. 209–24. Victoria: British Columbia Provincial Museum.

Duffek, Karen
1983   "Authenticity" and the Contemporary Northwest Coast Indian Art Market. *BC Studies* 57:99–111.
1986   *Bill Reid: Beyond the Essential Form.* Vancouver: University of British Columbia Press.
1988   Exhibitions of Contemporary Native Art/Expositions d'art autochtone contemporain. *Muse* 2(3):26–28, 37–39.

Duncan, Kate C.
1981   The Metis and the Production of Embroidery in the Subarctic. *Museum of the Fur Trade Quarterly* 17(3):1–8.
1984   *Some Warmer Tone: Bead Embroidery of the Alaska Athabaskans.* Fairbanks: University of Alaska Museum.
1989   *Northern Athapaskan Art: A Beadwork Tradition.* Seattle: University of Washington Press.

Duncan, Kate C., with Eunice Carney
1988   *A Special Gift: The Kutchin Beadwork Tradition.* Seattle: University of Washington Press.

Eber, Dorothy Harley
1971   *Pitseolak: Pictures Out of My Life.* Seattle: University of Washington Press.
1983   Visits with Pia. *Beaver* 314(3):20–27.
1984   Wall Hangings at Whale Cove. *Beaver* 315(1):26–29.
1990   Images of Justice. *Natural History,* January, 32–41.

Ewers, John C.
1981   Water Monsters in Plains Indian Art. *American Indian Art Magazine* 6(4):38–45.
1982   The Awesome Bear in Plains Indian Art. *American Indian Art Magazine* 7(3):36–45.
1983a   A Century and a Half of Blackfeet Picture Writing. *American Indian Art Magazine* 8(3):52–61.
1983b   Plains Indian Artists and Anthropologists: A Fruitful Collaboration. *American Indian Art Magazine* 9(1):36–49.
1986   *Plains Indian Sculpture: A Traditional Art from America's Homeland.* Washington: Smithsonian Institution Press.

Feder, Norman
1985   Museum Exhibition: The Jasper Grant Collection. *American Indian Art Magazine* 10(3):46–51.

1987   Bird Quillwork. *American Indian Art Magazine* 12(3):46–57.

Feest, Christian
1989   The Spirit Sings: Last Song? *European Review of Native American Studies* 1(1):51–53.

Fenton, William N.
1971   The New York State Wampum Collection: The Case for the Integrity of Cultural Treasures. *Proceedings of the American Philosophical Society* 115(6):437–61.
1987   *The False Faces of the Iroquois.* Norman: University of Oklahoma Press.
1989   Return of Eleven Wampum Belts to the Six Nations Iroquois Confederacy on Grand River, Canada. *Ethnohistory* 36(4):392–410.

Fieber, Frank
1978   Birch-bark Biting. *Beaver* 308(4):56–57.

Fitzhugh, William W.
1985   The Nulliak Pendants and Their Relation to Spiritual Traditions in Northeast Prehistory. *Arctic Anthropology* 22(2):87–110.
1988   Comparative Art of the North Pacific Rim. In *Crossroads of Continents: Cultures of Siberia and Alaska,* edited by William W. Fitzhugh and Aron Crowell, pp. 294–312. Washington: Smithsonian Institution Press.

Fulford, George
1989   A Structural Analysis of Mide Song Scrolls. In *Actes du vingtième congrès des algonquinistes,* edited by William Cowan, pp. 132–53. Ottawa: Carleton University.

Garfield, Viola E., and Paul S. Wingert
1966   *The Tsimshian Indians and Their Arts.* Seattle: University of Washington Press.

Garte, Edna J.
1985   Living Tradition in Ojibwa Beadwork and Quillwork. In *Papers of the Sixteenth Algonquian Conference,* edited by William Cowan, pp. 9–24. Ottawa: Carleton University.

Gidmark, David
1985   Algonquin Birchbark Canoe Construction. In *Papers of the Sixteenth Algonquian Conference,* edited by William Cowan, pp. 25–46. Ottawa: Carleton University.
1988a   *The Algonquin Birchbark Canoe.* Aylesbury, Bucks., U.K.: Shire Ethnography.

1988b   The Birchbark Canoe Makers of Lac Barrière. In *Papers of the Nineteenth Algonquian Conference,* edited by William Cowan, pp. 75–79. Ottawa: Carleton University.

Gilman, Carolyn, and Mary Jane Schneider
1987   *The Way to Independence: Memories of a Hidatsa Indian Family, 1840–1920.* St Paul: Minnesota Historical Society Press.

Graburn, Nelson H. H.
1967   The Eskimo and Airport Art. *Trans-Action* 4(10):28–33.
1976a   Eskimo Art: The Eastern Canadian Arctic. In *Ethnic and Tourist Arts,* edited by Nelson H. H. Graburn, pp. 39–55. Berkeley: University of California Press.
1976b   "I like things to look more different than that stuff did": An experiment in cross-cultural art appreciation. In *Art in Society,* edited by M. Greenhalgh and V. Megaw, pp. 51–70. London: Duckworth.
1978a   Commercial Inuit Art. *Inter-Nord* 15:131–39.
1978b   Inuit pivalliajut: The Cultural and Identity Consequences of the Commercialization of Canadian Inuit Art. In *Consequences of Economic Change in Circumpolar Regions,* edited by L. Müller-Wille, P. J. Pelto, and R. Darnell, pp. 185–200. Occasional Paper 4. Edmonton: University of Alberta, Boreal Institute for Northern Studies.
1986   White Evaluation of the Quality of Inuit Sculpture. *Études/Inuit/Studies* 10(1–2):271–84.

Graburn, Nelson H. H., and Molly Lee
1988   The Living Arctic, Doing What The Spirit Sings Didn't. *Inuit Art Quarterly* 3(4):10–13.

Gunther, Erna
1966   *Art in the Life of the Northwest Coast Indians, with a Catalogue of the Rasmussen Collection of Northwest Indian Art at the Portland Art Museum.* Portland: Portland Art Museum.

Gustafson, Paul
1982   Ancient Salish Weaving: An Art Revived. *Beaver* 313(1):10–13.

Hail, Barbara A., and Kate C. Duncan
1989   *Out of the North: The Subarctic Collections of the Haffenreffer Museum of Anthropology.* Bristol, R.I.: Haffenreffer Museum of Anthropology, Brown University.

Hall, Edwin S., Margaret B. Blackman, and Vincent Richard
1981   *Northwest Coast Indian Graphics: An Introduction to Silk Screen Prints.* Seattle: University of Washington Press.

Hallett, Susan
1981   The Comfortable Arts: Traditional Spinning and Weaving in Canada. *Beaver* 312(3):36–41.

Halpin, Marjorie M.
1978   Some Implications of Connoisseurship for Northwest Coast Art. *BC Studies* 37:48–59.
1981a   "Seeing" in Stone: Tsimshian Masking and the Twin Stone Masks. In *The World Is as Sharp as a Knife,* edited by Donald N. Abbott, pp. 269–88. Victoria: British Columbia Provincial Museum.
1981b   *Totem Poles: An Illustrated Guide.* Vancouver: UBC Museum of Anthropology.
1984   "Seeing" in Stone. Tsimshian Masking and the Twin Stone Masks. In *The Tsimshian: Images of the Past; Views for the Present,* edited by Margaret Seguin, pp. 281–308. Vancouver: University of British Columbia Press.

Hamell, George R.
1983   Trading in Metaphors: The Magic of Beads. In *Proceedings of the 1982 Glass Trade Bead Conference,* edited by C. F. Hayes, pp. 5–28. Research Records 16. Rochester, N.Y.: Rochester Museum and Science Center.

Harp, Elmer, Jr.
1969–70 Late Dorset Eskimo Art from Newfoundland. *Folk* 11–12:109–24.

Harrison, Julia D.
1986   Métis: A Glenbow Museum Exhibition. *American Indian Art Magazine* 11(2):54–59.
1987   De-colonizing Museum Classification Systems: A case in point—the Metis. *Muse* 4(4):46–50.
1988a   Museums and Politics: The Spirit Sings and the Lubicon Boycott. Co-ordinating Curator's Statement. *Muse* 6(3):12–13.
1988b   The Spirit Sings: Artistic Traditions of Canada's First Peoples. *American Indian Art Magazine* 13(3):32–39.
1988c   The Spirit Sings: The Last Song? *International Journal Of Museum Management and Curatorship* 7:353–63.

Harrison, Julia D., et al.
1987   *The Spirit Sings: Artistic Traditions of Canada's First Peoples.* Toronto: McClelland and Stewart with the Glenbow Museum.

Hawley, Carolyn T.
1990   A New School of Iroquois Sculpture. *American Indian Art Magazine* 15(2):48–57.

Hawthorne, Audrey
1967   *Art of the Kwakiutl Indians and Other Northwest Coast Tribes.* Seattle: University of Washington Press.
1979   *Kwakiutl Art.* Seattle: University of Washington Press.

Helmer, James W.
1986   A Face from the Past: an Early Pre-Dorset Ivory Maskette from Devon Island, N.W.T. *Études/Inuit/Studies* 10(1–2):179–202.

Henry, Victoria
1989   Breaking the Bonds of Art History: Robert Houle Puts His Art Beyond the Reach of Anthropologists. *Canadian Forum* 68(783):22–23.

Hessel, Ingo
1990   Arviat Stone Sculpture: Born of the Struggle with an Uncompromising Medium. *Inuit Art Quarterly* 5(1):4–15.

Hildebrandt, Walter
1985   Official Images of 1885. *Prairie Fire* 6:31–38.

Hill, Beth
1981   Bedrock and Boulder Bowls. In *The World Is as Sharp as a Knife,* edited by Donald W. Abbott, pp. 127–42. Victoria: British Columbia Provincial Museum.

Hill, Rick
1988   Sacred Trust: Cultural Obligations of Museums to Native People. *Muse* 6(3):32–33.
1989   À notre propre image: Les image stéréotypées des indiens mènent à une nouvelle forme d'art autochtone. *Muse* 6(4): 38–43.

Holm, Bill
1970   *Northwest Coast Indian Art: An Analysis of Form.* Seattle: University of Washington Press.
1972   *Crooked Beak of Heaven: Masks and Other Ceremonial Art of the Northwest Coast.* Seattle: University of Washington Press.
1974   The Art of Willie Seaweed, A Kwakiutl Mas-

ter. In *The Human Mirror,* edited by M. Richardson. New Orleans: Louisiana State University Press.

1981 Will the Real Charles Edenshaw Please Stand Up?: The Problem of Attribution in Northwest Coast Indian Art. In *The World Is as Sharp as a Knife,* edited by Donald N. Abbott, pp. 175–200. Victoria: British Columbia Provincial Museum.

1982 A Wooling Mantle Neatly Wrought: The Early Historic Record of Northwest Coast Pattern-Twined Textiles—1774–1850. *American Indian Art Magazine* 8(1):34–47.

1983a *The Box of Daylight: Northwest Coast Indian Art.* Seattle: University of Washington Press.

1983b *Smoky-Top: The Art and Times of Willie Seaweed.* Seattle: University of Washington Press.

1987 *Spirit and Ancestor: A Century of Northwest Coast Indian Art.* Vancouver: Douglas and McIntyre.

1990 Art. In *Handbook of North American Indians,* vol. 7, *Northwest Coast,* edited by Wayne Suttles, pp. 602–32. Washington: Smithsonian Institution Press.

Hoover, Alan L.
1981 Notes on the Iconography of the Haida Moon. In *The World Is as Sharp as a Knife,* edited by Donald N. Abbott, pp. 143–52. Victoria: British Columbia Provincial Museum.

1983 Charles Edenshaw and the Creation of Human Beings. *American Indian Art Magazine* 8(3): 62–67.

Houle, Robert
1991 Sovereignty and subjectivity. *C Magazine* 30: 28–35.

Houle, Robert, and Clara Hargittay
1988 The Struggle Against Cultural Apartheid. *Muse* 6(3):58–60.

Houston, Alma, ed.
1988 *Anthology of Inuit Art.* Winnipeg: Watson and Dwyer.

Houston, James A.
1952 In Search of Contemporary Eskimo Art. *Canadian Art* 9(3):99–104.

1955 *Eskimo Prints.* Barre Mass.: Barre Publishers.

1980 Eskimo Sculptors. *Beaver* 311(2):24–29.

Howard, James H.
1980 Birch Bark and Paper Cutouts from the Northern Woodlands and Prairie Border. *American Indian Art Magazine* 5(4):54–61.

Hughes, Kenneth James
1979 *The Life and Art of Jackson Beardy.* Toronto: James Lorimer.

Idiens, Dale
1987 Northwest Coast Artifacts in the Perth Museum and Art Gallery: The Colin Robinson Collection. *American Indian Art Magazine* 13(1):46–53.

Inverarity, R. B.
1950 *Art of the Northwest Coast Indians.* Berkeley: University of California Press.

Ipellie, Alootook
1980 Old Man Carver: A Short Story. *Beaver* 311(1): 49–52.

Irving, Sue, and Lynette Harper
1988 Not Another Fur Trade Exhibit? An Inside Look at Trapline Lifeline. *Muse* 6(3):38–40.

Issenman, Betty
1991 Inuit power and museums. *Information North* 17(3):1–7.

Jackson, Marion E., and David F. Pelly
1986 *The Vital Vision: Drawings by Ruth Annaqtuusi Tuluuialik.* Windsor: Art Gallery of Windsor.

Janes, Robert R.
1987 Museum Ideology and Practice in Canada's Third World. *Muse* 4(4):33–39.

Jasper, Cynthia R.
1988 Changes in Ojibwa (Chippewa) Dress, 1820–1980. *American Indian Culture and Research Journal* 12(3):17–38.

Jenness, Diamond
1946 Material Culture of the Copper Eskimos. In *Report of the Canadian Arctic Expedition, 1913–18,* vol. 16. Ottawa.

Jensen, Doreen, and Polly Sargent
1987 *Robes of Power: Totem Poles on Cloth.* Vancouver: University of British Columbia Press.

Jonaitis, Aldona
1978 Land Otters and Shamans: Some Interpretations of Tlingit Charms. *American Indian Art Magazine* 4(1):62–71.

1980   The Devilfish in Tlingit Sacred Art. *American Indian Art Magazine* 5(3):42–47.

1981a   Creations of Mystics and Philosophers: The White Man's Perceptions of Northwest Coast Indian Art from the 1930s to the Present. *American Indian Culture and Research Journal* 5(1):1–45.

1981b   Tlingit Halibut Hooks: An Analysis of the Visual Symbols of a Rite of Passage. *Anthropological Papers of the American Museum of Natural History* 57, pt. 1.

1983   Liminality and Incorporation in the Art of the Tlingit Shaman. *American Indian Quarterly* 7(3):41–68.

1985   *Art of the Northern Tlingit.* Seattle: University of Washington Press.

1988   *From the Land of the Totem Poles: The Northwest Coast Indian Art Collection at the American Museum of Natural History.* New York and Seattle: American Museum of Natural History and University of Washington Press.

1989   Totem poles and the Indian new deal. *Canadian Journal of Native Studies* 9(2):237–52.

Jopling, Carol F.
1989   The Coppers of the Northwest Coast Indians: Their Origin, Development, and Possible Antecedents. *Transactions of the American Philosophical Society* 79, pt. 1. Philadelphia.

Jordan, Richard H.
1979–80 Dorset Art from Labrador. *Folk* 21–22:397–418.

Kaufmann, Carole N.
1976   Functional Aspects of Haida Argillite Carvings. In *Ethnic and Tourist Arts,* edited by Nelson H. H. Graburn, pp. 56–69. Berkeley: University of California Press.

Kausche, Rolf
1986   The Origin of the Mask Concept in the Eastern Woodlands of North America. Annemarie Shimony and William C. Sturtevant, trans. *Man in the Northeast* 31:1–47.

Kenyon, Ian T., and Thomas Kenyon
1983   Comments on Seventeenth Century Glass Trade Beads From Ontario. In *Proceedings of the 1982 Glass Trade Bead Conference,* edited by C. F. Hayes, pp. 59–74. Research Records 16. Rochester, N.Y.: Rochester Museum and Science Center.

King, Jonathan C. H.
1979   *Portrait Masks from the Northwest Coast of North America.* London: Blacker Calmann Cooper Ltd.

1981   *Artificial Curiosities from the Northwest Coast of America.* London: British Museum.

1982   *Thunderbird and Lightning: Indian Life in Northeastern North America, 1600–1900.* London: British Museum.

King, Jonathan C. H., ed.
1989   *Living Arctic: Hunters of the Canadian North.* London and Ottawa: British Museum and Indigenous Survival International.

Krech, Shepard, III
1989a   Living Arctic: Hunters of the Canadian North. *European Review of Native American Studies* 3(1): 49–51.

1989b   *A Victorian Earl in the Arctic: The Travels and Collections of the Fifth Earl of Lonsdale, 1888–9.* Seattle: University of Washington Press.

1990   The Yellow Earl at the Museum of Mankind. *American Indian Art Magazine* 15(4):64–75.

Krech, Shepard, III, and Barbara A. Hail, eds.
1991   Art and Material Culture of the Subarctic and Adjacent Regions. *Arctic Anthropology* 28(1). Special issue.

Laforet, Andrea
1984   Tsimshian Basketry. In *The Tsimshian: Images of the Past; Views for the Present,* edited by Margaret Seguin, pp. 215–80. Vancouver: University of British Columbia Press.

Laforet, Andrea, and Annie York
1981   Notes on the Thompson River Dwelling. In *The World Is as Sharp as a Knife,* edited by Donald N. Abbott, pp. 115–22. Victoria: British Columbia Provincial Museum.

Lanford, Benson L.
1986   Great Lakes Woven Beadwork: An Introduction. *American Indian Art Magazine* 11(3):62–67, 75.

Lebrecht, Sue
1989   Angelique Merasty: Birch Bark Artist. *Canadian Woman Studies* 10(2–3):65–68.

Lee, Molly, and Nelson H. H. Graburn
1988   The Living Arctic: Hunters of the Canadian

North. *American Indian Art Magazine* 14(1): 54–59.

Lessard, F. Dennis
1986   Great Lakes Indian "Loom" Beadwork. *American Indian Art Magazine* 11(3):54–61.

Levesque, Carole
1976   *La culture matérielle des Indiens du Québec: Une étude de raquettes, moccasins et toboggans.* Canadian Ethnology Service Paper 33. Ottawa: National Museum of Man.

Lévi-Strauss, Claude
1979   *The Way of the Masks.* Seattle: University of Washington Press.

Lindgren, Charlotte, and Edward Lindgren
1981   The Pangnirtung Tapestries. *Beaver* 312(2): 34–39.

Lips, Julius E.
1936   Trap Systems Among the Montagnais-Naskapi Indians of Labrador Peninsula. *Statens Ethnografiska Museum, Smarre Meddelanden* 13. Stockholm.

Lipton, Barbara, ed.
1984   *Art of the Canadian Inuit.* Ottawa: Canadian Arctic Producers.

Livingstone, Donna
1988   The Spirit Sings: Artistic Traditions of Canada's First Peoples. *Journal of the West* 27:84–88.

Low, Jean
1982   Dr. Charles Frederick Newcombe. *Beaver* 312(4):32–39.

Luegar, Richard
1981   Tamarack Geese. *Beaver* 312(1):4–7.

MacDonald, George F.
1981a   Cosmic Equations in Northwest Coast Indian Art. In *The World Is as Sharp as a Knife,* edited by Donald N. Abbott, pp. 225–38. Victoria: British Columbia Provincial Museum.
1981b   Painted Houses and Woven Blankets: Symbols of Wealth in Tsimshian Art. In *The Tsimshian and Their Neighbors of the North Pacific Coast,* edited by Jay Miller and Carol M. Eastman, pp. 109–37. Seattle: University of Washington Press.
1983a   *Haida Monumental Art.* Vancouver: University of British Columbia Press.

1983b   *Ninstints: Haida World Heritage Site.* Vancouver: University of British Columbia Museum Press.
1984   *The Totem Poles and Monuments of Gitwangak Village.* Ottawa: Parks Canada.
1987   The future of museums in the Global Village. *Museum* 155:209–16.
1988   Epcot Center in Museological Perspective. *Muse* 6(1):27–31.

Macdonald, Max
1990   Chronicles of the Cree: Allen Sapp Paints the Story of His People. *Canadian Geographic* 110(4):36–41.

McFeat, Tom
1987   Space and Work in Maliseet Basket-Making. In *A Key into the Language of Woodsplint Baskets,* edited by Ann McMullen and Russell G. Handsman, pp. 60–73. Washington, Conn.: American Indian Archaeological Institute.

McGhee, Robert
1981   The Prehistory and Prehistoric Art of the Canadian Inuit. *Beaver* 312:23–30.

McLaren, Carol S.
1978   Moment of Death: Gift of Life. A Reinterpretation of the Northwest Coast Image "Hawk." *Anthropologica* 20:65–90.

McLuhan, Elizabeth, and Tom Hill
1984   *Norval Morrisseau and the Emergence of the Image Makers.* Toronto: Methuen.

McMaster, Gerald R.
1989   Tenuous lines of descent: Indian arts and crafts of the reservation period. *Canadian Journal of Native Studies* 9(2):205–36.
1990   Problems of representation: Our home, but the Natives' land/Problèmes de représentation: La terre des vos a ïeuls, ou de l'Autochtone. *Muse* 8(3):35–42.

Macnair, Peter, and Alan Hoover
1984   *The Magic Leaves: A History of Haida Argillite Carving.* Victoria: British Columbia Provincial Museum.

Macnair, Peter, Alan Hoover, and Kevin Neary
1984   *The Legacy: Tradition and Innovation in Northwest Coast Indian Art.* Vancouver: Douglas and McIntyre.

Malloy, Mary
1986   Souvenirs of the Fur Trade, 1799–1832: The Northwest Coast Indian Collections of the Salem East Indian Marine Society. *American Indian Art Magazine* 11(4):30–35, 74.

Marr, Carolyn J.
1984   Salish Baskets from the Wilkes Expedition. *American Indian Art Magazine* 9(3):44–51.
1988   Wrapped Twined Baskets of the Southern Northwest Coast: A New Form with an Ancient Past. *American Indian Art Magazine* 13(3):54–63.

Marshall, Ingeborg C. L.
1985   *Beothuk Bark Canoes: An Analysis and Comparative Study.* Mercury Series, Canadian Ethnology Service Paper 102. Ottawa: National Museum of Man.

Martijn, Charles A.
1964   Canadian Eskimo Carving in Historical Perspective. *Anthropos* 59:546–96.

Mary-Rousselière, Guy
1985   Une remarquable industrie dorsétienne de l'os de caribou dans le nord de Baffin. *Études/Inuit/Studies* 8(2):41–59.

Mathews, Zena Pearlstone
1979   Pipes with Human Figures from Ontario and Western New York. *American Indian Art Magazine* 4(3):41–59.
1980   Of Man and Beast: The Chronology of Effigy Pipes Among Ontario Iroquoians. *Ethnohistory* 27:295–307.
1981a   Art Historical Photodocumentation of Iroquoian Effigy Pipes. In *The Research Potential of Anthropological Museum Collections,* edited by A. M. E. Cantwell, J. B. Griffin, N. A. Rothschild, pp. 161–76. Annals of the New York Academy of Sciences 376. New York.
1981b   The Identification of Animals on Ontario Iroquois Pipes. *Canadian Journal of Archaeology* 5:31–48.
1982   On Dreams and Journeys: Iroquoian Boat Pipes. *American Indian Art Magazine* 7(3):46–51.

Mathiassen, T.
1928   Material Culture of the Iglulik Eskimos. *Report of the Fifth Thule Expedition 1921–24,* 6(1):1–242. Copenhagen.

Maxwell, Moreau S.
1983   A Contemporary Ethnography from the Thule Period. *Arctic Anthropology* 20(1):79–88.

Mills, Jeannette C.
1989   The Meares Island Controversy and Joe David: Art In Support of a Cause. *American Indian Art Magazine* 14(4):60–69.

Morier, Jan
1979   Metis Decorative Art and Its Inspiration. *Dawson and Hind* 8(1):28–32.

Morrison, David A.
1991   Copper Inuit Soapstone Trade. *Arctic* 44:239–46.

Munro, Margaret
1988   Faded Indian Art Comes to Light with Use of Infra-red Photography. *Canadian Geographic* 108(4):66–75.

Myers, Marybelle
1982   Josie Papialook. *Beaver* 313(1):22–29.

Nabokov, Peter, and Robert Easton
1989   *Native American Architecture.* New York: Oxford University Press.

Nelson, Richard K.
1983   Inscribed Birch Bark Scrolls and Other Objects of the Midewiwin. In *Actes du quatorzième congrès des algonquinistes,* edited by William Cowan, pp. 219–38. Ottawa: Carleton University.
1984   Midewiwin Medicine Bags of the Ojibwa. In *Papers of the Fifteenth Algonquian Conference,* edited by William Cowan, pp. 397–408. Ottawa: Carleton University.

Nicks, Trudy
1982   *The Creative Tradition: Indian Handicrafts and Tourist Art.* Edmonton: Alberta Cultural Provincial Museum of Alberta.

Oakes, Jillian E.
1991a   Caribou needles and sealskin thimbles. *Musk-Ox* 38:49–55.
1991b   *Copper and Caribou: Inuit Skin Clothing Production.* Mercury Series, Canadian Ethnology Service Paper 118. Ottawa: Canadian Museum of Civilization.
1991c   Inuit clothing in transition. *Musk-Ox* 38:45–49.

Oberholtzer, Cath
1989   If Bears Could Talk. In *Actes du vingtième con-*

grès des algonquinistes, edited by William Cowan, pp. 267–78. Ottawa: Carleton University.

1990   Pipe Dreams: Pipe Cleaners and Dream Motifs. In *Papers of the Twenty-first Algonquian Conference,* edited by William Cowan, pp. 279–94. Ottawa: Carleton University.

1991   Beaded Hoods of the James Bay Cree: Origins and Developments. In *Papers of the Twenty-second Algonquian Conference,* edited by William Cowan, pp. 264–78. Ottawa: Carleton University.

Osborne, Carolyn, et al.
1977   A Technical Analysis of Three Forms of Sub-Arctic Snowshoes. *Arctic Anthropology* 14(2): 41–78.

Patterson, Nancy-Lou
1973   *Canadian Native Art.* Don Mills, Ont.: Collier Macmillan.

Pearce, Susan M.
1987   Ivory, Antler, Feather, and Wood: Material Culture and the Cosmology of the Cumberland Sound Inuit, Baffin Island, Canada. *Canadian Journal of Native Studies* 7:307–21.

Pelletier, Gaby
1979   From Animal Skins to Polyester: Four Hundred Years of Micmac and Maliseet Clothing Styles and Ornamentation. In *Papers of the Tenth Algonquian Conference,* edited by William Cowan, pp. 203–17. Ottawa: Carleton University.

1982   *Abenaki Basketry.* Canadian Ethnology Service Paper 85. Ottawa: National Museum of Man.

Penney, D. W.
1986–87   The Origins of an Indigenous Ontario Arts Tradition: Ontario Art from the Late Archaic Through the Woodland Periods, 1500 B.C.–A.D. 600. *Journal of Canadian Studies* 21:37–55.

Phillips, Ruth B.
1984a   *Patterns of Power: The Jasper Grant Collection and Great Lakes Indian Art of the Early Nineteenth Century.* Kleinburg, Ont.: McMichael Canadian Collection.

1984b   Zigzag and Spiral: Geometric Motifs in Great Lakes Indian Costume. In *Papers of the Fifteenth Algonquian Conference,* edited by Wil-

liam Cowan, pp. 409–24. Ottawa: Carleton University.

1986–87   Jasper Grant and Edward Walsh: The gentleman-soldier as early collector of Great Lakes Indian art. *Journal of Canadian Studies* 21 (Winter):56–71.

1988   Indian Art: Where do you put it? *Muse* 6(3): 64–67.

1989a   Souvenirs from North America: The Miniature as Image of Woodlands Indian Life. *American Indian Art Magazine* 14(2):52–63, 78–79.

1989b   What is "Huron art"?: Native American art and the new art history. *Canadian Journal of Native Studies* 9(2):161–86.

Podedworny, Carol
1991   First Nations art and the Canadian Mainstream. *C Magazine* 31:23–32.

Pohrt, Richard A.
1986   Nineteenth Century Michigan Chippewa Costume: Photographs of David Shoppenagons. *American Indian Art Magazine* 11(3):44–53.

1989   Tribal Identification of Northern Plains Beadwork. *American Indian Art Magazine* 15(1): 72–79.

Raczka, Paul M.
1980   Blackfoot Artists: Rights and Power. *American Indian Art Magazine* 5(2):30–35.

Regular, Keith
1986   On Public Display. *Alberta History* 34(1):1–10.

Reid, Bill
1988   *Raven Steals the Light.* Vancouver: Douglas and McIntyre.

Reid, Dennis, and Joan Vastokas
1984   *From the Four Quarters: Native and European Art in Ontario, 5000 BC to AD 1867.* Toronto: Art Gallery of Ontario.

Rivard, René, and Paule Renard
1989   Musées et les cultures autochtones. *Vie des arts* 34(137):42–43.

Robertson, Clive
1989   Art and Issues of Native Identity. *FUSE Magazine* 12(6):3–4.

Rogers, Edward S.
1967   *The Material Culture of the Mistassini.* Anthropological Series 80, Bulletin 218. Ottawa: National Museum of Canada.

Rosman, Abraham, and Paula G. Rubel
1990   Structural patterning in Kwakiutl art and ritual. *Man* 25:620–39.

Saladin d'Anglure, Bernard
1978   *La parole changée en pierre: Vie et oeuvre de Davidialuk Alasuaq, artiste inuit de Québec arctique.* Cahier du Patrimoine 11. Quebec: Ministère des Affaires Culturelles.
1983   Ijiqqat: Voyage au pays de l'invisible inuit. *Études/Inuit/Studies* 7(1):67–84.

Samuel, Cheryl
1987   *The Raven's Tail.* Vancouver: University of British Columbia Press.

Shackleton, Philip, and Kenneth Roberts
1983   The Skin Boats: Kayaks and Umiaks. *Beaver* 314(1):52–57.

Sheehan, Carol
1981   *Pipes That Don't Smoke; Coal That Won't Burn: Haida Sculpture in Argillite.* Alberta: Glenbow-Alberta Foundation.

Sherman, Glen
1972   Tobacco Pipes of the Western Eskimos. *Beaver* 303(1):49–51.

Siebert, Erna V.
1980   Northern Athapaskan Collections of the First Half of the Nineteenth Century. *Arctic Anthropology* 17(1):49–76.

Simard, Jean-Jacques
1982   La production coopératif d'art et d'artisinat inuit au Nouveau-Québec inuit. *Études/Inuit/Studies* 6(2):61–92.

Simeone, William E., and James W. Van Stone
1986   *"And He Was Beautiful": Contemporary Athapaskan Material Culture in the Collection of the Field Museum of Natural History.* Fieldiana: Anthropology, no. 10. Chicago: Field Museum of Natural History.

Sinclair, Lester, and Jack Pollock
1979   *The Art of Norval Morrisseau.* Toronto: Methuen.

Sioui, Anne-Marie
1979   Les amérindiens et les musées du Quebec: Bilan de la situation actuelle et perspectives d'avenir. *Recherches amérindiennes au Québec* 8(4):249–65.

Smith, James G. E., ed.
1980   *Arctic Art: Eskimo Ivory.* New York: Museum of the American Indian.

Smith, Nicholas N.
1989   The Economics of the Wabanaki Basket Industry. In *Actes du vingtième congrès des algonquinistes,* edited by William Cowan, pp. 306–16. Ottawa: Carleton University.

Southcott, Mary E.
1984   *The Sound of the Drum: The Sacred Art of the Anishnabec.* Erin, Ont.: Boston Mills Press.

Speck, Frank G.
1914   *The Double-curve Motive in Northeastern Algonkian Art.* Anthropological Series, no. 1. Memoirs of the Canadian Geological Survey, no. 42. Ottawa.
1925   Central Eskimo and Indian Dot Ornamentation. *Museum of the American Indian, Heye Foundation, Indian Notes* 2(3):151–72.
1937   Montagnais Art in Birch-bark: A Circumpolar Trait. *Museum of the American Indian, Heye Foundation, Indian Notes and Monographs* 11(2):45–125.

Speck, Frank G., and George G. Heye
1921   Hunting Charms of the Montagnais and the Mistassini. *Museum of the American Indian, Heye Foundation, Indian Notes and Monographs,* misc. ser., 13(1).

Steinbring, Jack H.
1978   Ethnological Identification in Rock Pictography of the Canadian Shield. In *Manitoba Rock Art, II: Rock Paintings,* pp. 3–35. Papers in Manitoba Archaeology, Miscellaneous Paper 8. Winnipeg.

Stewart, Hilary
1973   *Indian Artifacts of the Northwest Coast.* Seattle: University of Washington Press.
1977   *Indian Fishing: Early Methods on the Northwest Coast.* Seattle: University of Washington Press.
1979a   *Looking at Indian Art of the Northwest Coast.* Seattle: University of Washington Press.
1979b   *Robert Davidson: Haida Printmaker.* Vancouver: Douglas and McIntyre.
1984   *Cedar: Tree of Life to the Northwest Coast Indians.* Toronto: Douglas and McIntyre.
1990   *Totem Poles.* Seattle: University of Washington Press.

Stott, Margaret
1975   *Bella Coola Art and Ceremony.* Ottawa: National Museum of Man.

Stuart, Donald
1972   Weaving in the Arctic. *Beaver* 303(1):60–62.

Sturtevant, William C.
1974   *Boxes and Bowls: Decorated Containers by Nineteenth Century Haida, Tlingit, Bella Bella, and Tsimshian Artists.* Washington: Smithsonian Institution Press.

Swinton, George
1972   *Sculpture of the Eskimo.* Toronto: McClelland and Stewart.
1978   Touch and the real: Contemporary Inuit aesthetics—theory, usage, and relevance. In *Art in Society,* edited by Michael Greenhalgh and Vincent Megaw, pp. 71–88. New York: St. Martin's Press.

Tacon, P. S. C.
1983   An analysis of Dorset Art in relation to prehistoric culture stress. *Études/Inuit/Studies* 7(1):41–66.

Tanner, Adrian
1984   Notes on the Ceremonial Hide. In *Papers of the Fifteenth Algonquian Conference,* edited by William Cowan, pp. 91–106. Ottawa: Carleton University.

Taylor, J. Garth
1974   *Netsilik Eskimo Material Culture: The Roald Amundson Collection from King William Island.* Oslo: Universitetsforlaget.
1980   *Canoe Construction in a Cree Cultural Tradition.* Canadian Ethnology Service Paper 64. Ottawa: National Museum of Man.

Thompson, Judy
1972   *Preliminary Study of Traditional Kutchin Clothing in Museums.* Canadian Ethnology Service Paper 1. Ottawa: National Museum of Man.
1983   Turn-of-the-century Metis Decorative Art from the Frederick Bell Collection. *American Indian Art Magazine* 8(4):36–45.
1990   *Pride of the Indian Wardrobe: Northern Athapaskan Footwear.* Toronto: University of Toronto Press.

Thomson, Jane Sproull
1990   The Traces Experience: A Museum Ethnology Project. In *Papers of the Twenty-first Algonquian Conference,* edited by William Cowan, pp. 345–55. Ottawa: Carleton University.

Townsend-Gault, Charlotte
1991   Having voices and using them: First Nations artists and "native art." *Arts Magazine* 65(February):65–70.

Trevelyan, Amelie M.
1989   Continuity of form and function in the art of the Eastern Woodlands. *Canadian Journal of Native Studies* 9(2):187–203.

Trigger, Bruce G.
1988   Museums and Politics: The Spirit Sings and the Lubicon Boycott. Who Owns the Past? *Muse* 6(3):13–15.

Tulurialik, R. A., and David F. Pelly
1986   *Qikaaluktut: Images of Inuit Life.* Toronto: Oxford University Press.

Turner, Geoffrey
1976   *Hair Embroidery in Siberia and North America.* Oxford: Pitt-Rivers Museum.

Van Stone, James W.
1981   *Athapaskan Clothing and Related Objects in the Collections of Field Museum of Natural History.* Fieldiana: Anthropology, n.s., no. 4. Chicago: Field Museum of Natural History.
1982a   Southern Tutchone Clothing and Tlingit Trade. *Arctic Anthropology* 19(1):51–62.
1982b   *The Speck Collection of Montagnais Material Culture from the Lower St. Lawrence Drainage, Quebec.* Fieldiana: Anthropology, no. 5. Chicago: Field Museum of Natural History.
1983   *The Simms Collection of Plains Cree Material Culture from Southeast Saskatchewan.* Fieldiana: Anthropology, no. 6. Chicago: Field Museum of Natural History.
1985   *Material Culture of the Davis Inlet and Barren Ground Naskapi: The William Duncan Strong Collection.* Fieldiana: Anthropology, n.s., no. 7. Chicago: Field Museum of Natural History.
1988   *The Simms Collection of Southwest Chippewa Material Culture.* Fieldiana: Anthropology, no. 11. Chicago: Field Museum of Natural History.

Vastokas, Joan M.
1971   Continuities in Eskimo Graphic Style. *Artscanada* 162–63:69–83.
1984   Interpreting Birch Bark Scrolls. In *Papers of the Fifteenth Algonquian Conference,* edited by William Cowan, pp. 425–44. Ottawa: Carleton University.

1986–87 Native Art as Art History: Meaning and Time from Unwritten Sources. *Journal of Canadian Studies* 21:7–36.

Vastokas, Joan M., and Romas K. Vastokas
1973 *Sacred Art of the Algonkians.* Peterborough, N.H.: Mansard Press.

Vaughn, Thomas, and Bill Holm
1982 *Soft Gold: The Fur Trade and Cultural Exchange on the Northwest Coast of America.* Oregon Historical Society.

Veisse, Jeannine
1981 The Eskimo Museum at Churchill, Canada. *Museum* 33(1):22–29.

Wade, Edwin L., ed.
1986 *The Arts of the North American Indian: Native Traditions in Evolution.* New York: Hudson Hills Press and Philbrook Art Center.

Wade, Edwin L., and Lorraine Laurel Wade
1976 Voices of the Supernaturals: Rattles of the Northwest Coast. *American Indian Art Magazine* 2(1):32–39.

Waite, Deborah
1966 Kwakiutl Transformation Masks. In *The Many Faces of Primitive Art,* edited by D. Fraser, pp. 266–300. Englewood Cliffs, N.J.: Prentice-Hall.

Walker, Willard
1984 Wabanaki Wampum Protocol. In *Papers of the Fifteenth Algonquian Conference,* edited by William Cowan, pp. 107–24. Ottawa: Carleton University.

Walters, Anna Lee
1989 *The Spirit of Native America: Beauty and Mysticism in American Indian Art.* San Francisco: Chronicle Books.

Walton, Ann T., John C. Ewers, and Royal B. Hassrick
1985 *After the Buffalo Were Gone: The Louis Warren Hill, Sr., Collections of Indian Art.* Washington and St. Paul: Indian Arts and Crafts Board, U.S. Department of the Interior, and Northwest Area Foundation.

Wardwell, Glen, and L. Lebov
1970 *Annotated Bibliography of Northwest Coast Indian Art.* New York: Library of the Museum of Primitive Art.

Warner, John Anson
1978 Contemporary Algonkian Legend Painting. *American Indian Art Magazine* 3(3):58–69.
1985 New Visions in Canadian Plains Painting. *American Indian Art Magazine* 10(2):46–53.
1990a Continuity and Change in Modern Plains Cree Moccasins. *American Indian Art Magazine* 15(3):36–47
1990b Nature and Spirit in Contemporary Northern Manitoba Painting. *American Indian Art Magazine* 15(2):38–47.

Webster, Gloria Cranmer
1988 The "R" Word. *Muse* 6(3):43–44.

Whiteford, Andrew Hunter
1986 The Origins of Great Lakes Beaded Bandolier Bags. *American Indian Art Magazine* 11(3):32–43.

Whitehead, Ruth Holmes
1978 Micmac Porcupine Quillwork, 1750–1950. In *Papers from the Fourth Annual Congress Canadian Ethnology Society,* 1977, pp. 156–66. Ottawa: National Museums of Canada.
1980 *Elitekey: Micmac Material Culture from 1600 to the Present.* Halifax: Nova Scotia Museum.
1982 *Micmac Quillwork, Micmac Indian Techniques of Porcupine Quill Decoration: 1600–1950.* Halifax: Nova Scotia Museum.

Wight, Darlene
1989 *Out of Tradition: Abraham Anghik/David Ruben Piqtoukun.* Winnipeg: Winnipeg Art Gallery.

Wissler, Clark
1910 Material Culture of the Blackfoot Indians. *Anthropological Papers of the American Museum of Natural History* 5:1–175.
1917 Ceremonial Bundles of the Blackfoot Indians. *Anthropological Papers of the American Museum of Natural History* 7:65–289.

Wright, Robin K.
1979 Haida Argillite Ship Pipes. *American Indian Art Magazine* 5(1):40–47.
1980 Haida Argillite Pipes: The Influence of Clay Pipes. *American Indian Art Magazine* 5(4):42–47.
1983 Haida Argillite: Carved for Sale. *American Indian Art Magazine* 8(1):48–55.
1986 The Depiction of Women in Nineteenth Century Haida Argillite Carving. *American Indian Art Magazine* 11(4):36–45.

1988   The Burke Museum: Northwest Coast Collection. *American Indian Art Magazine* 13(2):32–37.

Wyatt, Victoria
1984   *Shapes of Their Thoughts: Reflections of Culture Contact in Northwest Coast Indian Art.* Norman: University of Oklahoma Press.
1989   *Images from the Inside Passage: An Alaskan Portrait by Winter and Pond.* Seattle and Juneau: University of Washington Press and Alaska State Library.

Wyman, Max
1986   New Dawn at Skidegate: Bill Reid and the Haida. *Beaver* 66(3):48–56.

Zapp, Norman, and Michael Parke-Taylor
1984   *Horses Fly Too: Bob Boyer/Edward Poitras.* Regina, Sask.: Norman Mackenzie Art Gallery, University of Regina.

Section Eighteen

🍁

GENDER

Albers, Patricia, and Beatrice Medicine, eds.
1983 *The Hidden Half: Studies of Plains Indian Women.* Washington: University Press of America.

Anderson, Karen
1985 Commodity Exchange and Subordination: Montagnais-Naskapi and Huron Women, 1600–1650. *Signs* 2(1):48–62.
1988 As Gentle as Little Lambs: Images of Huron and Montagnais-Naskapi Women in the Writings of 17th Century Jesuits. *Canadian Review of Sociology and Anthropology* 25:560–76.
1991 *Chain Her by One Foot: The Subjugation of Women in Seventeenth-century New France.* London: Routledge.

Beaudet, Christiane
1984 Mes moccasins, ton canot, nos raquettes: La division sexuelle du travail et la transmission des connaissances chez les Montagnais de la Romaine. *Recherches amérindiennes au Québec* 14(3):37–44.

Berlo, Janet Catherine
1989 Inuit women and graphic arts: Female creativity and its cultural context. *Canadian Journal of Native Studies* 9(2):293–315.

Bernick, K.
1975 The Socio-Economic Role of the Carrier Woman. *Kamtucks Review.*

Blackman, Margaret B.
1981 The Changing Status of Haida Women: An Ethnohistorical and Life History Approach. In *The World Is as Sharp as a Knife,* edited by Donald N. Abbott, pp. 65–77. Victoria: British Columbia Provincial Museum.
1982 *During My Time: Florence Edenshaw Davidson, a Haida Woman.* Seattle: University of Washington Press.

Bonvillain, Nancy
1989 Gender Relations in Native North America. *American Indian Culture and Research Journal* 13:1–28.

Bourgeault, Ron
1989 Race, Class, and Gender: Colonial Domination of Indian Women. In *Race, Class, Gender: Bonds and Barriers,* edited by Jesse Vorst. Winnipeg: Society for Socialist Studies.

Brant, Beth (Degonwadonti), ed.
1988   *A Gathering of Spirit.* Toronto: University of Toronto Press.

Brizinski, Peggy Martin
1981   Les femmes dans le Nord: Problématique et devenir. *Recherches amérindiennes au Québec* 10(4):261–68.

Brodniff, Somen
1984   The Traditional Roles of Native Women in Canada and the Impact of Colonization. *Canadian Journal of Native Studies* 4(1):85–103.

Brown, Jennifer S. H.
1983   Woman as Centre and Symbol in the Emergence of Metis Communities. *Canadian Journal of Native Studies* 3(1):39–46.
1987   A Cree Nurse in a Cradle of Methodism: Little Mary and the Egerton R. Young Family at Norway House and Berens River. In *First Days, Fighting Day: Women in Manitoba History,* edited by Mary Kinnear, pp. 18–40. Regina, Sask.: Canadian Plains Research Centre.

Brown, Judith K.
1970   Economic Organization and the Position of Women Among the Iroquois. *Ethnohistory* 17:151–68.
1975   Iroquois Women: An Ethnohistoric Note. In *Toward An Anthropology of Women,* edited by R. Reiter, pp. 237–51. New York: Monthly Review Press.

Buffalohead, Priscilla
1983   Farmers, Warriors, and Traders: A Fresh Look at Ojibwa Women. *Minnesota History* 48(6):236–44.

Campbell, Maria
1973   *Halfbreed.* Toronto: McClelland and Stewart. Reprint. Lincoln: University of Nebraska Press, 1982.

Canada, Department of Indian Affairs and Northern Development
1982   *The Elimination of Sex Discrimination from Indian Art.* Ottawa.

Canadian Association in Support of Native Peoples
1978   On Native Women: Special Issue. CASNP *Bulletin* 18(4).

Castellano, M. B.
1989   Women in Huron and Ojibwa Societies. *Canadian Woman Studies* 10(2–3):95–100.

Cheda, Sherrill
1973   Indian Women: An historical example and a contemporary view. In *Women in Canada,* edited by Marylee Stephenson. Toronto: New Press.

Clermont, Norman
1983   La place de femme dans les sociétés iroquoiennes de la période du contact. *Recherches amérindiennes au Québec* 13(4):286–90.

Collin, Dominique
1983   La discrète émancipation de Talasia. Identité féminine et vision du monde d'une jeune inuk du Québec nordique. *Recherches amérindiennes au Québec* 13(4):255–64.

Corrigan, Sam
1974   A Note on Canadian Indian Marriage Law. *Western Canadian Journal of Anthropology* 4(2):17–28.

Crnkovich, Mary, ed.
1990   *"Gossip": A Spoken History of Women in the North.* Ottawa: Canadian Arctic Resources Committee.

Cruikshank, Julie
1975   Becoming a Woman in Athapaskan Society: Changing Traditions on the Upper Yukon River. *Western Canadian Journal of Anthropology* 5(2):1–14.
1976   Matrifocal Families in the Canadian North. In *The Canadian Family,* rev. ed., edited by K. Ishwaran, pp. 105–19. Toronto: Holt, Rinehart and Winston of Canada.
1979   *Athapaskan Women: Lives and Legends.* Mercury Series, Canadian Ethnology Service Paper 57. Ottawa: National Museum of Man.
1983   *The Stolen Women: Female Journeys in Tagish and Tutchone.* Mercury Series, Canadian Ethnology Series Paper 87. Ottawa: National Museum of Man.

Devens, Carol
1986   Separate Confrontations: Gender as a Factor in Indian Adaptation to European Colonization in New France. *American Quarterly* 38(3):61–80.

Drapeau, Lynn
1984   L'émancipation des femmes dans le vocabulaire montagnais. *Recherches amérindiennes au Québec* 14(3):45–54.

Gender

Ezzo, David A.
1988   Female Status in the Northeast. In *Papers of the Nineteenth Algonquian Conference,* edited by William Cowan, pp. 49–62. Ottawa: Carleton University.

Fiske, Jo-Anne
1987   Fishing Is Women's Business: Changing Economic Roles of Carrier Women and Men. In *Native People, Native Lands,* edited by Bruce A. Cox, pp. 186–98. Ottawa: Carleton University.
1991   Colonization and the decline of women's status: The Tsimshian case. *Feminist Studies* 17:509–35.

Gerber, Linda M.
1990   Multiple Jeopardy: A socio-economic comparison of men and women among the Indian, Métis, and Inuit peoples of Canada. *Canadian Ethnic Studies* 22(3):69–84.

Godard, Barbara
1990   Politics of Representation: Some Native Canadian Women Writers. *Canadian Literature* 124–5:183–225.

Gonzales, Ellice B.
1981   *Changing Economic Roles for Micmac Men and Women: An Ethnohistorical Analysis.* Mercury Series, Canadian Ethnology Service Paper 72. Ottawa: National Museum of Man.
1982   An Ethnohistorical Analysis of Micmac Male and Female Roles. *Ethnohistory* 29:117–29.

Goodwill, Jean
1975   *Speaking Together: Canada's Native Women.* Ottawa: Secretary of State.

Grant, Agnes
1990   Contemporary Native Women's Voices in Literature. *Canadian Literature* 124–5:124–32.

Green, Gretchen
1989   Molly Brant, Catherine Brant, and Their Daughters: A Study in Colonial Acculturation. *Ontario History* 81:235–50.

Green, Joyce
1985   Sexual Equality and Indian Government: An Analysis of Bill C-31 Amendments to the Indian Act. *Native Studies Review* 1(2):81–96.

Guemple, Lee
1986   Men and Women, Husbands and Wives: The Role of Gender in Traditional Inuit Society. *Études/Inuit/Studies* 10(1–2):9–24.

Guérin, Yvonne
1982   La femme inuit dominée: Création mythique allochtone? *Anthropologie et Sociétés* 6(3):129–54.

Hungry Wolf, Beverly
1982   *The Ways of My Grandmothers.* New York: Quill.

Jamieson, Kathleen
1978   *Indian Women and the Law in Canada: Citizens Minus.* Ottawa: Advisory Council on the Status of Women.
1984   Plus ça change, plus c'est pareil? Les femmes autochtones et la question du gouvernement indien autonome et du droit coutumier. *Recherches amérindiennes au Québec* 14(3):65–74.
n.d.   Multiple Jeopardy: The Evolution of a Native Women's Movement. *Atlantis* 4(2), pt. 2:157–78.

Jeffries, Theresa M.
1991   Seechelt Women and Self-Government. *BC Studies* 89:81–86.

Kapesh, An Antane
1976   *Je suis une maudite sauvagesse.* Paris: Éditions des femmes.

Kirkness, Verna J.
1987–88 Emerging Native Women. *Canadian Journal of Women and the Law* 2(2):408–15.

Labrecque, Marie France
1984a   Des femmes de Weymontachie. *Recherches amérindiennes au Québec* 14(3):3–16.
1984b   Développement du capitalisme dans la région de Weymontachie (Haute-Mauricie). Incidences sur la condition des femmes attikaméques. *Recherches amérindiennes au Québec* 14(3):75–87.

Lachapelle, Caroline
n.d.   Beyond Barriers: Native Women and the Women's Movement. In *Still Ain't Satisfied: Canadian Feminism Today.*

Laframboise, T. D., et al.
1990   Changing and Diverse Roles of Women in American Indian Cultures. *Sex Roles* 22:455–76.

183

Landes, Ruth
1938   *The Ojibwa Woman.* Columbia University Contributions to Anthropology 31. New York.

La Prairie, Carol P.
1987   Native Women and Crime: A Theoretical Model. *Canadian Journal of Native Studies* 7:121–37.

Leacock, Eleanor B.
1978   Woman's Status in Egalitarian Society: Implications for Social Evolution. *Current Anthropology* 19:247–75.
1980   Montagnais Women and the Jesuit Program for Colonization. In *Women and Colonization: Anthropological Perspectives,* edited by Mona Ettienne and Eleanor Leacock, pp. 25–41. New York: Praeger Publishing.
1981   Women in an Egalitarian Society: The Montagnais-Naskapi of Canada. In *Myths of Male Dominance: Collected Articles on Woman Cross-culturally,* edited by E. B. Leacock, pp. 31–81. New York: Monthly Review Press.
1986   Montagnais Women and the Jesuit Program for Colonization. In *Rethinking Canada: The Promise of Women's History,* edited by Veronica Strong-Boag and Anita C. Fellman, pp. 7–22. Toronto: Copp Clark Pitman.

Littlefield, Loraine
1987   Women Traders in the Maritime Fur Trade. In *Native People, Native Lands,* edited by Bruce A. Cox, pp. 173–85. Ottawa: Carleton University.

McDonald, Linda
1989   First Nations Women and Education. *Women's Education des femmes* 7(3):25–28.

McElroy, Ann
1975   Canadian Arctic Modernization and Change in Female Inuit Role Identification. *American Ethnologist* 2:662–86.
1989   Oopeeleeka and Mina: Contrasting Responses to Modernization of Two Baffin Island Inuit Women. In *Being and Becoming Indian: Biographical Studies of North American Frontiers,* edited by James Clifton, pp. 290–318. Chicago: Dorsey Press.

McElroy, Ann, and Carolyn J. Mattiasson, eds.
1979   *Sex Roles in Changing Cultures.* Occasional Papers, no. 1. Buffalo: State University of New York.

Mitchell, Marjorie, and Anna Franklin
1984   When You Don't Know the Language, Listen to the Silence: An Historical Overview of Native Women in B.C. In *Not Just Pin Money,* edited by Barbara Latham. Victoria.

Perry, Richard J.
1979   The Fur Trade and the Status of Women in the Western Subarctic. *Ethnohistory* 26:363–76.

Preston, Sarah C.
1980   Why Did Alice Go Fishing?: Narrative from the Life of a Cree Woman. In *Papers of the Eleventh Algonquian Conference,* edited by William Cowan, pp. 71–81. Ottawa: Carleton University.
1982   Competent Social Behavior Within the Context of Childbirth: A Cree Example. In *Papers of the Thirteenth Algonquian Conference,* edited by William Cowan, pp. 211–18. Ottawa: Carleton University.

Ridington, Robin
1983   Stories of the Vision Quest Among Dunne-za Women. *Atlantis* 9(1):68–78.

Rothenberg, Diane
1976   Erosion of Power. *Western Canadian Journal of Anthropology* 6:106–22.
1980   The Mothers of the Nation. In *Women and Colonization,* edited by Mona Etienne and Eleanor Leacock, pp. 67–87. New York: Praeger Publishers.

Routhier, Marie-Josée
1984   Que sont devenues les sages-femmes d'antan? L'accouchement chez les femmes attikamèques de Manouane. *Recherches amérindiennes au Québec* 14(3):26–36.

Sanders, Douglas E.
1975   Indian Women: A Brief History of Their Roles and Rights. *McGill Law Journal* 21(4):656–72.

Séguin, Claire
1981   Essai sur la condition de la femme indienne au Canada. *Recherches amérindiennes au Québec* 10(4):251–60.

Silman, Janet, ed.
1987   *Enough Is Enough: Aboriginal Women Speak Out.* Toronto: Women's Press.

Sugar, Fran, and Lana Fox
1989–90 Nistum Peyako Séht'wawin Iskwewak [First

Nations Women]: Breaking Chains. *Canadian Journal of Women and the Law* 3(2):465–82.

Swampy, Grace Marie
1982   The Role of Native Women in a Native Society. *Canadian Journal of Native Education* 9(2):2–20.

Tooker, Elisabeth
1984   Women in Iroquois Society. In *Extending the Rafters,* edited by M. K. Foster, J. Campisi, M. Mithun, pp. 109–23. Albany: State University of New York Press.

Vanderburgh, Rosamond M.
1977   *I Am Nokomis, Too: The Biography of Verna Patronella Johnston.* Don Mills, Ont.: General Publishing.
1978   The Southern Ojibwe of Ontario. *Canadian Newsletter of Research on Women* 7(3):14–17.
1982   Tradition and Transition in the Lives of Ojibwa Women. *Resources for Feminist Research* 11(2): 218–20.

Van Kirk, Sylvia
1972   Women and the Fur Trade. *Beaver* 303(3):4–21.
1976   "The Custom of the Country": An Examination of Fur Trade Marriage Practices. In *Essays on Western History,* edited by L. H. Thomas, pp. 49–70. Edmonton: University of Alberta Press.
1977   "Women in Between": Indian Women in Fur Trade Society in Western Canada. *Historical Papers* 1977:31–46.
1980   *"Many Tender Ties": Women in Fur Trade Society, 1670–1870.* Winnipeg: Watson and Dwyer; Norman, Okla.: University of Oklahoma Press, 1983.
1983   "What if Mama Is an Indian?": The Cultural Ambivalence of the Alexander Ross Family. In *The Developing West,* edited by John Foster, pp. 123–36. Edmonton: University of Alberta Press.
1986a   "The Reputation of a Lady": Sarah Ballenden and the Foss-Pelly Scandal. *Manitoba History* 11:4–11.
1986b   The Role of Native Women in the Fur Trade Society of Western Canada, 1670–1830. In *Rethinking Canada: The Promise of Women's History,* edited by Veronica Strong-Boag and Anita C. Fellman, pp. 59–66. Toronto.
1987   Toward a Feminist Perspective in Native History. In *Papers of the Eighteenth Algonquian Conference,* edited by William Cowan, pp. 377–89. Ottawa: Carleton University.

Vincent, Sylvie
1983   Mistamaninuesh au temps de la mouvance. Notes inspirées par l'autobiographie d'une femme montagnaise. *Recherches amérindiennes au Québec* 13(4):243–54.

Wallace, Anthony F. C.
1947   Women, Land, and Society. *Pennsylvania Archaeologist* 17:1 35.

Weaver, Sally M.
1983   The Status of Indian Women. In *Two Nations, Many Cultures,* edited by Jean Elliott, pp. 56–79. Scarborough: Prentice-Hall.

Whyte, John D.
1974   The Lavell Case and Equality in Canada. *Queen's Quarterly* 81:28–42.

Willis, Jane
1972   *Geneish: An Indian Girlhood.* Toronto: New Press.

Section Nineteen

✦

POLITICAL, LEGAL, AND CONSTITUTIONAL ISSUES

Abeele, Frances
1987   Canadian Contradictions: Forty Years of North-
        ern Political Development. *Arctic* 40:310–20.

Aki-Kwe (Mary Ellen Turpel)
1989   Aboriginal Peoples and the Canadian Charter
        of Rights and Freedoms: Contradictions and
        Challenges. *Canadian Woman Studies* 10(2–
        3):149–57.

Alison, R. M.
1977   Native Rights and Wildlife: An Historical Per-
        spective. *Chitty's Law Journal* 25(7):235–39.

Ames, Randy, et al., eds.
1988   *On the Land: A Study of the Feasibility of a
        Comprehensive Wildlife Harvest Support Pro-
        gramme in the Northwest Territories.* Ottawa:
        Canadian Arctic Resources Committee.

Anderson, Ellen
1982   The Saskatchewan Indians and Canada's New
        Constitution. *Journal of International Affairs*
        36:125–48.

Asch, Michael I.
1979   The Economics of Dene Self-Determination.
        In *Challenging Anthropology,* edited by David
        H. Turner and Gavin Smith, pp. 339–52. To-
        ronto: McGraw Hill Ryerson.
1982a   Capital and Economic Development: A Criti-
        cal Appraisal of the Recommendations of the
        Mackenzie Valley Pipeline Commission. *Cul-
        ture* 2(3):1–3.
1982b   Dene Self-determination and the Study of
        Hunter-Gatherers in the Modern World. In
        Politics and History in Band Societies, edited
        by Eleanor Leacock and Richard Lee, pp. 347–
        72. Cambridge: Cambridge University Press.
1983   Regard anthropologique sur la definition judi-
        caire des droits autochtones. *Recherches amér-
        indiennes au Québec* 13(3):169–78.
1984   *Home and Native Land: Aboriginal Rights and
        the Canadian Constitution.* Toronto: Methuen.
1985   Dene Political Rights. *Cultural Survival Quart-
        erly* 8(4):33–37.

Badcock, William T.
1976   *Who Owns Canada? Aboriginal Title and Ca-
        nadian Courts.* Ottawa: Canadian Association
        in Support of the Native Peoples.

Barber, Lloyd I.
1976   Indian Land Rights and Claims. In *Les fa-*

cettes de l'identité amérindienne, edited by Marc-Adélard Tremblay, pp. 65–80. Quebec: Presses de l'Université Laval.

Bariteau, Claude
1991 Construction de barrages: La voix perdante du Québec de demain. *Action nationale* 81(8): 1065–75.

Barsh, Russel L., and James Y. Henderson
1982 Aboriginal Rights, Treaty Rights, and Human Rights: Indian Tribes and "Constitutional Renewal." *Journal of Canadian Studies* 17(2):55–81.

Bartlett, Richard H.
1978 The Indian Act of Canada. *Buffalo Law Review* 27:581–615.
1989 Hydroelectric Power and Indian Water Rights on the Prairies. *Prairie Forum* 14(2):177–93.

Berger, Thomas R.
1977 *Northern Frontier Northern Homeland: The Report of the Mackenzie Valley Pipeline Inquiry.* Vols. 1–2. Ottawa: Queens Printer.
1979 Native Rights in the New World: A Glance at History. *Northern Perspectives* 7(4):1–6.
1981 *Fragile Freedoms.* Toronto: Clarke, Irwin.
1983 Native History, Native Claims, and Self-Determination. *BC Studies* 57:10–23.

Berkes, Fikret
1988 Subsistence Fishing in Canada: A Note on Terminology. *Arctic* 41:319–20.

Bickenbach, Jerome E.
1980 The Baker Lake Cree: A Partial Recognition of Inuit Aboriginal Title. *University of Toronto Faculty of Law Review* 38:232–49.

Bissett, Don
1973 *Regional Impact of a Northern Gas Pipeline.* Vol. 5, *Impact of Pipelines on Traditional Activities of Hunter-Trappers in the Territories.* Northern Economic Development Branch, Department of Indian Affairs and Northern Development, Environmental-Social Committee, Northern Pipelines, Task Force on Northern Oil Development Report 73-32. Ottawa: Information Canada.
1974 *Regional Impact of a Northern Gas Pipeline.* Vol. 4, *Impact of Pipelines on Selected Territorial Communities.* Northern Economic Development Branch, Department of Indian Affairs and Northern Development, Environmental-

Social Committee, Northern Pipelines, Task Force on Northern Oil Development Report 73-31. Ottawa: Information Canada.

Bissonnette, Alain
1981 Les droits des autochtones et les Territoires du Nord-Ouest. I et II. *Recherches amérindiennes au Québec* 11:133–47, 181–92.

Bissonnette, Alain, and Serge Bouchard
1983 Les luttes autochtones et l'exigence de la lucidité. *Recherches amérindiennes au Québec* 13(3):163–68.

Bliss, L. C.
1978 The Report of the Mackenzie Valley Pipeline Inquiry, vol. 1: An Environmental Critique. *Musk-Ox* 21:28–33.

Boldt, Menno, and J. Anthony Long
1984–86 Tribal Traditions and European-Western Political Ideologies: The Dilemma of Canada's Native Indians. *Canadian Journal of Political Science* 17:537–53, 18:367–74, 19:151–53.
1985a Tribal Philosophies and the Canadian Charter of Rights and Freedoms. In *The Quest for Justice: Aboriginal Peoples and Aboriginal Rights,* edited by Menno Boldt and J. Anthony Long, pp. 165–79. Toronto: University of Toronto Press.
1985b *The Quest for Justice: Aboriginal Peoples and Aboriginal Rights.* Toronto: University of Toronto Press.

Boucher, Philip
1979 Righting the Balance: A New Historical Approach to European-Amerindian Relations. *Canadian Ethnic Studies* 11(1):151–56.

Brice-Bennett, Carol, ed.
1977 *Our Footprints Are Everywhere: Inuit Land Use and Occupancy in Labrador.* Nain: Labrador Inuit Association.

Brock, Cathy L.
1991 Politics of Aboriginal Self-Government: A Canadian paradox. *Canadian Public Administration* 34:272–85.

Brown, Dougald
1981 Indian Hunting Rights and Provincial Law: Some Recent Developments. *University of Toronto Faculty of Law Review* 39:121–32.

Calloway, Colin G.
1987 *Crown and Calumet: British-Indian Relations,*

1783–1815. Norman: University of Oklahoma Press.

Canada
1971   *Indian Treaties and Surrenders.* 1891. 3 vols. Toronto: Coles Publishing Company.
1982   *Outstanding Business: A Native Claims Policy.* Ottawa: Minister of Supply and Services.

Canada, Department of Indian and Northern Affairs
1978   *The Historical Development of the Indian Act.* Ottawa: Treaties and Historical Research Centre, P.R.E. Group.
1979   *Indian Treaties in Historical Perspective.* Prepared by George Brown and Ron Maguire for the Research Branch. Ottawa.
1980a   *A History of Native Claims Processes in Canada, 1867–1979.* Prepared by Richard C. Daniel for the Research Branch. Ottawa: Department of Indian and Northern Affairs.
1980b   *Indian Government Under Indian Act Legislation.* Prepared by Wayne Daugherty and Dennis Madill for the Research Branch. Ottawa.
1981   *Indian Acts and Amendments, 1868–1950.* Ottawa: Department of Indian and Northern Affairs.

Canadian Arctic Resources Committee
1984   *National and Regional Interests in the North.* Third National Workshop on People, Resources, and the Environment North. Ottawa.
1988a   *Aboriginal Self-Government and Constitutional Reform: Setbacks, Opportunities, and Arctic Experiences.* Ottawa.
1988b   *Changing Times, Challenging Agendas: Economic and Political Issues in Canada's North.* Ottawa.

Canadian Forum
1976   *Native Land Claim and the Mackenzie Pipeline.* Special Issue, November, 3–41.

Cassidy, Frank, and Norman Dale
1988   *After Native Claims? The Implications of Comprehensive Claims for National Resources in British Columbia.* Lantzville, B.C.: Oolichan Books.

Chalmers, John W.
1977   Treaty No. Six. *Alberta History,* 23–27.

Chamberlin, J. E.
1982   Homeland and Frontier. *Queen's Quarterly* 89:325–37.

Chance, Norman A.
1974   The Future of James Bay: Who Will it Serve? In *James Bay Forum* (Montreal), edited by F. Berkes, pp. 84–86.

Chance, Norman A., and R. Pothier
1967   Une étude du développement chez les Indiens cris. In *Proceedings, James Bay Conference,* edited by F. Berkes. Quebec: Presses de l'Université Laval.

Charest, Paul
1980   Les barrages hydro-électriques en territoire montagnais et leurs effets sur les communautés amérindiennes. *Recherches amérindiennes au Québec* 9(4):323–38.
1981   Contraints ecologiques et pêcheries sédentaires sur la Basse Côte-Nord du Saint Laurent. *Anthropologie et Sociétés* 5(1):29–56.
1982a   Hydroelectric Dam Construction and the Foraging Activities of Eastern Quebec Montagnais. In *Politics and History in Band Societies,* edited by Eleanor Leacock and Richard Lee, pp. 413–26. Cambridge: Cambridge University Press.
1982b   Recherches anthropologiques et contexte politique en milieu attikamek et montagnaise. *Culture* 2(3):11–24.

Clark, Bruce
1987   *Indian Title in Canada: Native Land Claims.* Toronto: University of Toronto Press.
1990   *Native Liberty, Crown Sovereignty: The Existing Aboriginal Right of Self-government in Canada.* Montreal: McGill-Queen's University Press.

Cloutier, Joe
1988   Is History Repeating Itself at Lubicon Lake? *Canadian Journal of Native Education* 15(1): 1–17.

Coates, Kenneth S.
1987   Controlling the Periphery: The Territorial Administration of the Yukon and Alaska, 1867–1959. *Pacific Historical Quarterly* 78:145–51.
1991   *Aboriginal Land Rights and Claims in Canada.* Toronto: Copp Clark and Pitman.

Coates, Kenneth S., and Judith Powell
1989   *The Modern North: People, Politics, and the Struggle Against Colonialism.* Toronto: James Lorimer.

Cohen, Fay G.
1986   *Treaties on Trial: The Continuing Controversy over Northwest Indian Fishing Rights.* Seattle: University of Washington Press.

Coon-Come, Matthew
1988   Indian Rights in Canada: An International Issue. *Saskatchewan Indian Federated College Journal* 4(2):91–98.
1991   Shafted by Hydro: The Cree, the environment, and Quebec. *Canadian Speeches* 5(6):3–10.

Cox, Bruce A.
1971   Land Rights of the Slavey Indians at Hay River, Northwest Territories. *Western Canadian Journal of Anthropology* 2(1):150–55.

Crowe, Keith J.
1979   A Summary of Northern Native Claims in Canada: The Process and Progress of Negotiations. *Études/Inuit/Studies* 3(1):31–39.
1990   Claims on the land. *Arctic Circle* 1(3):14–23.

Cumming, Peter A.
1977   *Canada: Native Land Rights and Northern Development.* Document 26. Copenhagen: International Work Group for Indigenous Affairs.

Cumming, Peter A., and Kevin Aalton
1973–74 Inuit Hunting Rights in the Northwest Territories. *Saskatchewan Law Review* 38:251–323.

Cumming, Peter A., and Neil H. Mickenberg, eds.
1972   *Native Rights in Canada.* 2d ed. Toronto: Indian-Eskimo Association of Canada.

Dacks, Gurston
1977   Lost in the Shuffle? Land Claims and the Alcan Pipeline. *Canadian Forum* (August):13–14.
1979   Northern Native Claims: Will Ottawa Default? *Canadian Forum* (March):6–10.
1981   *A Choice of Futures: Politics in the Canadian North.* Toronto: Methuen.
1986   Politics on the Last Frontier: Consociationalism in the Northwest Territories. *Canadian Journal of Political Science* 19:345–61.

Daniels, Harry W.
1981   *Native People and the Constitution of Canada: The Report of the Metis and Non-Status Indian Constitutional Review Commission.* Ottawa: Mutual Press.

Davis, Rex, ed.
1977   Dene nation: The struggle of Canada's internal colony for self-determination. *Risk* 13(2):1–43.

Diamond, Billy
1991   Renewed Struggle of the Cree for control of their northern land. *Canadian Speeches* 5(4): 27–34.

Dickason, Olive Patricia
1977   Renaissance Europe's View of Amerindian Sovereignty and Territoriality. *Plural Societies* 8(3–4):97–107.

Donohue, Maureen Ann
1991   Aboriginal land rights in Canada: A historical perspective on the fiduciary relationship. *American Indian Law Review* 15:369–89.

Duff, Wilson
1969   The Fort Victoria Treaties. *BC Studies* 14:3–57.

Duffy, R. Quinn
1988   *The Road to Nunavut: The Progress of the Eastern Arctic Inuit Since the Second World War.* Kingston and Montreal: McGill-Queen's University Press.

Dunning, R. W.
1962   Some Aspects of Governmental Indian Policy and Administration. *Anthropologica* 4:209–31.
1976   Some Speculations on the Canadian Indian Socio-Political Reality. In *Les facettes de l'identité amérindienne,* edited by Marc-Adélard Tremblay, pp. 107–30. Quebec: Presses de l'Université Laval.

Dyck, Noel
1980   Indian, Metis, Native: Some Implications of Special Status. *Canadian Ethnic Studies* 12(1): 34–46.
1981   The Politics of Special Status: Indian Associations and the Administration of Indian Affairs. In *Ethnicity, Power, and Politics in Canada,* edited by J. Dahlie and T. Fernando, pp. 279–91. Toronto: Methuen.
1983a   The Negotiation of Indian Treaties and Land Rights in Saskatchewan. In *Aborigines, Land, and Land Rights,* edited by N. Peterson and M. Langton, pp. 405–15. Canberra: Australian Institute of Aboriginal Studies.

1983b Representation and Leadership of a Provincial Indian Association. In *The Politics of Indianness,* edited by Adrian Tanner, pp. 197–306. St. John's: Memorial University of Newfoundland, Institute of Social and Economic Research.

Dyck, Noel, ed.
1985 *Indigenous Peoples and the Nation-State: Fourth-World Politics in Canada, Australia, and Norway.* St. John's: Memorial University of Newfoundland, Institute for Social and Economic Research.

Eccles, William J.
1984 Sovereignty—Association, 1500–1783. *Canadian Historical Review* 64:475–510.

Elias, Peter Douglas
1976 Indian Politics in the Canadian Political System. In *Les facettes de l'identité amérindienne,* edited by Marc Adélard Tremblay, pp. 35–61. Quebec: Presses de l'Université Laval.
1989 Aboriginal Rights and Litigation: History and Future of Court Decisions in Canada. *Polar Record* 25(152):1–9.

Ervin, Alexander M.
1983 Contrasts Between the Resolution of Native Land Claims in the United States and Canada Based on Observations of the Alaska Native Land Claims Movement. *Canadian Journal of Native Studies* 3:123–39.

Feit, Harvey A.
1979 Political Articulations of Hunters to the State: Means of Resisting Threats to Subsistence Production in the James Bay and Northern Quebec Agreement. *Études/Inuit/Studies* 3(2):37–52.
1980 Negotiating Recognition of Aboriginal Rights: History, Strategies, and Reactions to the James Bay and Northern Quebec Agreement. *Canadian Journal of Anthropology* 1(2):159–72.
1982 The Future of Hunters Within Nation-States: Anthropology and the James Bay Cree. In *Politics and History in Band Societies,* edited by Eleanor Leacock and Richard Lee, pp. 373–412. Cambridge: Cambridge University Press.

Fisher, Robin
1971–72 Joseph Trutch and Indian Land Policy. *BC Studies* 12:3–33.

Flanagan, Thomas E.
1985 The Sovereignty and Nationhood of Canadian Indians: A Comment on Boldt and Long. *Canadian Journal of Political Science* 18:367–74.
1988 Francisco de Vitoria and the Meaning of Aboriginal Rights. *Queen's Quarterly* 95:421–30.

Freeman, Milton M. R.
1976 *Report: Inuit Land Use and Occupancy Project.* 3 vols. Ottawa: Department of Indian Affairs and Northern Development.

Frideres, James S.
1981 Native Settlements and Native Rights: A Comparison of the Alaska Native Settlement, the James Bay Indian/Inuit Settlement, and the Western Canadian Inuit Settlement. *Canadian Journal of Native Studies* 1(1):59–88.
1990 Native rights and the 21st century: The making of red power. *Canadian Ethnic Studies* 22(3):1–7.

Frideres, James S., and W. J. Reeves
1987 Northwest Territories Political Development and the Plebiscite. *Études/Inuit/Studies* 11(1):107–34.

Fumoleau, René
1975 *As Long as This Land Shall Last: A History of Treaty #8 and Treaty #11.* Toronto: McClelland and Stewart.
1988 The challenge of justice in the Canadian North. *Grail: An Ecumenical Journal* 4:7–20.

Gottesmann, Dan
1983 Native Hunting and Migratory Bird Convention Act: Historical, Political, and Ideological Perspectives. *Journal of Canadian Studies* 18(3):67–89.

Gould, G. P., and A. J. Semple
1980 *Our Land: The Maritimes: The Basis of the Indian Claim in the Maritime Province of Canada.* Fredericton, N.B.: Saint Annes Point Press.

Grant, Shelagh D.
1984 Indian Affairs Under Duncan Campbell Scott: The Plains Cree of Saskatchewan, 1913–1931. *Journal of Canadian Studies* 18(3):21–39.
1988 *Sovereignty or Security? Government Policy in the Canadian North.* Vancouver: University of British Columbia Press.

Green, L. C.
1970 Canada's Indians: Federal Policy, International

and Constitutional Law. *Ottawa Law Review* 4:101–31.

1972   Legal Significance of Treaties Affecting Canada's Indians. *Anglo-American Law Review* 1:119–35.

1983   Aboriginal Peoples, International Law, and the Canadian Charter of Rights and Freedoms. *Canadian Bar Review* 61:339–53.

Green, L. C., and Olive P. Dickason
1989   *The Law of Nations and the New World.* Edmonton: University of Alberta Press.

Hall, D. J.
1977   Clifford Sifton and Canadian Indian Administration, 1896–1905. *Prairie Forum* 2:127–51.

Hall, Tony
1986   Self-Government or Self-Delusion: Brian Mulrony and Aboriginal Rights. *Canadian Journal of Native Studies/Révue canadienne des études autochtones* 6(1):77–90.

Hamelin, Louis-Edmond
1976   Manifestations amérindiennes de caractère politique dans les Territoires-du-Nord-Ouest. In *Les facettes de l'identité amérindienne,* edited by Marc-Adélard Tremblay, pp. 81–106. Quebec: Presses de l'Université Laval.

1982   Originalité culturelle et régionalisation politique: Le project Nunavut des T.N.O. *Recherches amérindiennes au Québec* 12(4):251–82.

1991   Politique autochtoniste: Suggestions aux non-autochtones. *Environments* 21(2):8–15.

Harper, Alan G.
1945   Canada's Indian Administration: Basic Concepts and Objectives. *America Indigena* 5:119–32.

1946   Canada's Indian Administration: The Indian Act. *America Indigena* 6:297–314.

1947   Canada's Indian Administration: The Treaty System. *America Indigena* 7:129–48.

Harris, Michael
1987   *Justice Denied: The Law versus Donald Marshall.* Toronto: Totem.

Hawkes, David C.
1989   *Aboriginal Peoples and Government Responsibility in Exploring Federal and Provincial Roles.* Ottawa: Carleton University.

Haysom, Veryan, and Jeff Richstone
1987   Customizing Law in the Territories: Proposal for a Task Force on Customary Law in Nunavut. *Études/Inuit/Studies* 11(1):91–106.

Helm, June
1980   Indian Dependency and Indian Self-determination: Problems and Paradoxes in Canada's Northwest Territories. In *Political Organization in Native North America,* edited by E. L. Schusky, pp. 215–42. Lanham, Md.: University Press of America.

Holzkamm, Tim E.
1988   Ojibwa Knowledge of Minerals and Treaty #3. In *Papers of the Nineteenth Algonquian Conference,* edited by William Cowan, pp. 89–97. Ottawa: Carleton University.

Imai, Shin, and Katherine Laird
1982   The Indian Status Question: A Problem of Definition. *Canadian Legal Aid Bulletin* 5(1):113–23.

Jarvenpa, Robert
1985   The Political Economy and Political Ethnicity of American Indian Adaptations and Identities. *Ethnic and Racial Studies* 8:29–48.

Johnston, Hugh
1988   The Surveillance of Indian Nationalists in North America. *BC Studies* 78:3–27.

Jull, Peter
1981   Aboriginal Peoples and Political Change in the North Atlantic Area. *Journal of Canadian Studies* 16(2):41–52.

1986   *Politics, Development, and Conservation in the International North.* Ottawa: Canadian Arctic Resources Committee.

1988   Building Nunavut: A Story of Inuit Self-government. *Northern Review* 1:59–72.

1989   L'arctique et l'internationalism inuit. *Études internationales* 20(1):115–30.

1991   Redefining Aboriginal-White Relations: Canada's Inuit. *International Journal of Canadian Studies/Revue internationale d'études canadienne* 3:11–25.

Keeping, Sarah
1989   *The Inuvialuit Final Agreement.* Calgary: Canada Institute of Resources.

Keller, Robert H.
1990   Haida Indian Land Claims and South Moresby State Park. *American Review of Canadian Studies* 20(1):7–30.

Kennedy, John C.
1987   Aboriginal Organizations and Their Claims: The Case of Newfoundland and Labrador. *Canadian Ethnic Studies/Études ethnique au Canada* 19(2):13–25.

Knoll, David
1979   Treaty and Aboriginal Hunting and Fishing Rights. *Canadian Native Law Reporter* 1:1–29.
1987   Unfinished Business: Treaty Land Entitlement and Surrender Claims in Saskatchewan. *Saskatchewan Indian Federated College Journal* 3(2):21–52.

Krech, Shepard, III
1984   Land Rights and Political Development—The Case of the Dene. *Cultural Survival Quarterly* 8(3):41–43.

Leigh, L. H.
1970   The Indian Act, the Supremacy of Parliament, and the Equal Protection of the Laws. *McGill Law Journal* 16(2):389–98.

Lepage, Pierre
1983   Rôle et défi de la Commission des droits de la personne du Québec face aux droits des peuples autochtones. *Recherches amérindiennes au Québec* 13(3): 201–8.

Little Bear, Leroy, Menno Boldt, and J. Anthony Long
1984   *Pathways to Self-Determination: Canadian Indians and the Canadian State.* Toronto: University of Toronto Press.

Long, J. Anthony
1990   Political revitalization in Canadian Native Indian Studies. *Canadian Journal of Political Science/Revue canadienne de science politique* 23:751–73.

Long, J. Anthony, and Menno Boldt
1988   Self-determination and Extra-legal Action: The Foundations of Native Indian Protest. *Canadian Review of Studies in Nationalism/Révue canadienne des études sur le nationalisme* 15(1–2):111–20.

Long, J. Anthony, and Menno Boldt, eds.
1988   *Governments in Conflict? Provinces and Indian Nations in Canada.* Toronto: University of Toronto Press.

Long, J. Anthony, Leroy Little Bear and Menno Boldt
1982   Federal Indian Policy and Indian Self-govern-

ment in Canada: An Analysis of a Current Proposal. *Canadian Public Policy* 8:189–99.

Lotz, James R.
1970   *Northern Realities: The Future of Northern Development in Canada.* Toronto: New Press.

Lysyk, Kenneth
1966   Indian Hunting Rights: Constitutional Considerations and the Role of Indian Treaties in British Columbia. *University of British Columbia Law Review* 2:401–21.
1967   The Unique Constitutional Position of the Canadian Indian. *Canadian Bar Review* 45:513–53.
1968   Canadian Bill of Rights—Irreconcilable Conflict with Another Federal Enactment—"Equality before the Law" and the Liquor Provisions of the Indian Act. *Canadian Bar Review* 46:141–49.
1973a   Approaches to Settlement of Indian Title Claims: The Alaska Model. *U.B.C. Law Review* 8(2):51–58.
1973b   The Indian Title Question in Canada: An Appraisal in the Light of Calder. *Canadian Bar Review* 51:450–80.
1982   The Rights and Freedoms of the Aboriginal Peoples of Canada. In *The Canadian Charter of Rights and Freedoms,* edited by W. S. Tarnopolsky and G. A. Beaudoin, pp. 467–88. Toronto: Carswell.

McCardle, Bennett Ellen
1982   *Indian History and Claims: A Research Handbook.* 2 volumes. Ottawa: Department of Indian and Northern Affairs.

McConnell, W. H.
1978   The Report of the Mackenzie Valley Pipeline Inquiry, vol. 1: Summary and Critique of the Final Two Chapters and Epilogue. *Musk-Ox* 21:18–25.

McCullum, Hugh, and Karmel McCullum
1975   *This Land Is Not for Sale: Canada's Original People and Their Land.* Toronto: Anglican Book Center.

MacDonald, John A.
1967–78 The Canadian Bill of Rights: Canadian Indians and the Courts. *Criminal Law Quarterly* 10: 305–19.

McDonnell, R. F.
1991   Justice for the Cree: Research in progress in

James Bay. *Canadian Journal of Criminology* 33:171–74.

MacGregor, Roy
1989   *Chief: The Fearless Vision of Billy Diamond.* New York: Viking.

McInnes, R. W.
1969   Indian Treaties and Related Disputes. *University of Toronto Faculty Law Review* 17:52–71.

McInnis, S.
1981   The Inuit and the Constitutional Process, 1978–81. *Journal of Canadian Studies* 16(2):53–68.

McNab, David T.
1981   Herman Merivale and Colonial Office Indian Policy in the Mid-nineteenth Century. *Canadian Journal of Native Studies* 1(2):277–302.

Madill, D.
1981   *B.C. Indian Treaties in Historical Perspective.* Ottawa: Research Branch, Department of Indian and Northern Affairs.

Manyfingers, Wallace
1981   Commentary: Aboriginal Peoples and the Constitution. *Alberta Law Review* 19:428–32.

Mathias, Joe, and Gary R. Yabsley
1991   Conspiracy of legislation: The suppression of Indian rights in Canada. *BC Studies* 89:34–45.

Melling, J.
1966   Recent Developments in Official Policy Towards Canadian Indians and Eskimos. *Race* 7:379–99.

Merritt, John, et al.
1989   *Nunavut: Political Choices and Manifest Destiny.* Ottawa: Canadian Arctic Resources Committee.

Moisan, Gaston
1982   Les droits des autochtones et les activités de chasse et de pêche. *Recherches amérindiennes au Québec* 12(4):269–72.

Montgomery, Malcolm
1963   The Legal Status of the Six Nations Indians in Canada. *Ontario History* 55(2):93–105.

Morisset, Jean
1979   The Demand for Ethnic Autonomy in the Canadian Northwest. *Journal of Social and Political Studies* 4:345–57.
1981   The Aboriginal Nationhood, the Northern Chal-

lenge, and the Construction of Canadian Unity. *Queen's Quarterly* 88:237–50.

Morris, Alexander
1971   *The Treaties of Canada with the Indians of Manitoba and the North-West Territories.* 1880. Toronto: Coles Publishing Company.

Morrison, James
1979–80 Archives and Native Claims. *Archivaria* 9:15–32.

Morrison, William R.
1986   Canadian Sovereignty and the Inuit of the Central and Eastern Arctic. *Études/Inuit/Studies* 10(1–2):245–60.

Morse, Bradford N., ed.
1985   *Aboriginal Peoples and the Law: Indian, Metis, and Inuit Rights in Canada.* Ottawa: Carleton University.

Moss, John E.
1980–81 Native Proposals for Constitutional Reform. *Journal of Canadian Studies* 15(4):85–92.

Müller-Wille, Ludger, and Pertti Pelto, eds.
1979   Political Expressions in the Northern Fourth World: Inuit, Cree, Sami. *Études/Inuit/Studies* 3(2):5–72.

Musk-Ox
1976   Nunavut—A Comprehensive Claim. Special Feature. 18:3–41.

Neel, David
1991   Life in the 18th hole. *BC Studies* 89:132–39.

Nichols, Roger L.
1989   The United States, Canada, and the Indians: 1865–1876. *Social Sciences Journal* 26:249–63.

Niedermeyer, Lynn
1980–81 Aboriginal Rights: Definition or Denial? *Queens Law Journal* 6:568–86.

O'Malley, Martin
1976   *The Past and Future Land: An Account of the Berger Inquiry into the Mackenzie Valley Pipeline.* Toronto: Peter Martin Associates.

Opekoken, D., ed.
1980   *The First Nations: Indian Government and the Canadian Constitution.* Saskatoon: Federation of Saskatchewan Indians.

Page, Robert
1986   *Northern Development: The Canadian Dilemma.* Toronto: McClelland and Stewart.

Patterson, E. Palmer, II
1983   A Decade of Change: Origins of the Nishga and Tsimshian Land Protests in the 1880s. *Journal of Canadian Studies* 18(3):40–54.

Payne, R. J., and R. Graham
1985   Non-hierarchical Alternatives in Northern Resource Management. *Études/Inuit/Studies* 8(2): 117–30.

Pearce, Hannah
1991   The flooding of a nation. *Geographical Magazine* 63(November):18–21.

Pibus, Christopher J.
1983   The Fisheries Act and Native Fishing Rights in Canada: 1970–1980. *University of Toronto Faculty Law Review* 39(1):43–54.

Pillipow, William
1988a   "Fact Is on Your Side": An Historical Analysis of Canadian Indian Treaties. *Saskatchewan Indian Federated College Journal* 4(2):79–90.
1988b   Indian Government: An Historical and Legal Perspective. *Saskatchewan Indian,* July/August:10–16.

Pinkerton, Evelyn
1983   Taking the Minister to Court: Changes in Public Opinion About Forest Management and Their Expression in Haida Land Claims. *BC Studies* 57:58–85.
1984   Les réactions du gouvernement de Colombie-Britannique face aux poursuites judiciaries des Haidas sur la mise en valeur des ressources. *Recherches amérindiennes au Québec* 14(2):47–56.

Point, Stephen
1991   Understanding Native activism. *BC Studies* 89:124–29.

Ponting, J. Rick
1986   *Arduous Journey: Canadian Indians and Decolonization.* Toronto: McClelland and Stewart.
1990   Internationalization: Perspectives on an emerging direction in aboriginal affairs. *Canadian Ethnic Studies* 22(3):85–109.

Ponting, J. Rick, and R. Gibbens
1980   *Out of Irrelevance: A Socio-Political Introduction to Indian Affairs in Canada.* Toronto: Butterworths.

Preston, Richard J., III
1983   Algonquian People and Energy Development in the Subarctic. In *Actes du quatorzième congrès des algonquinistes,* edited by William Cowan, pp. 169–80. Ottawa: Carleton University.

Pretes, Michael
1988   Underdevelopment in two Norths: The Brazilian Amazon and the Canadian Arctic. *Arctic* 41:109–16.

Price, Richard, ed.
1987   *The Spirit of the Alberta Indian Treaties.* 2d. ed. Alberta: Institute for Research on Public Policy.

Puddicombe, Stephen
1991   Realpolitik in arctic Quebec: Why Makivik Corporation won't fight this time. *Arctic Circle* 2(2):14–21.

Purich, Donald
1986   *Our Land: Native Rights in Canada.* Toronto: James Lorimer.

Pylypchuk, Mary Ann
1991   Value of aboriginal records as legal evidence in Canada: An examination of sources. *Archivaria* 32:51–77.

Quinn, Frank
1991   As long as the rivers run: The impact of corporate water development on Native communities in Canada. *Canadian Journal of Native Studies* 11(1):137–54.

Raby, Stewart
1972   Indian Treaty No. 5 and the Pas Agency, Saskatchewan, N.W.T. *Saskatchewan History* 25: 92–114.
1973   Indian Land Surrender in Southern Saskatchewan. *Canadian Geographer* 17:36–52.

Raunet, Daniel
1984   *Without Surrender, Without Consent: A History of Nishga Land Claims.* Vancouver: Douglas and McIntyre.

Rea, K. J.
1968   *The Political Economy of the Canadian North.* Toronto: University of Toronto Press.

Richardson, Boyce
1975   *Strangers Devour the Land: A Chronicle of the Assault upon the Last Coherent Hunting Culture in North America, the Cree Indians of Northern Quebec, and Their Vast Primeval*

Homelands. New York: Knopf, distributed by Random House.

Robinson, Eric, and Henry Bird Quinney
1985   *The Infested Blanket: Canada's Constitution—Genocide of Indian Nations.* Winnipeg: Queenston House.

Rostaing, Jean-Pierre
1985   Native Regional Autonomy: The Initial Experience of the Kativik Regional Government. *Études/Inuit/Studies* 8(2):3–39.

Rouland, Norbert
1978   *Les inuit du Nouveau-Québec et la Convention de la baie James et du Nord Quebécois.* Quebec: Association Iniksiutiit Katimajiit and Centre d'Études Nordiques, Université Laval.

Salisbury, Richard F.
1979   Application and Theory in Canadian Anthropology: The James Bay Agreement. *Transactions of the Royal Society of Canada,* 4th ser., 17:229–41.
1986   *A Homeland for the Cree: Regional Development in James Bay 1971–1981.* Kingston and Montreal: McGill-Queen's University Press.

Sanders, Douglas E.
1972   The Bill of Rights and Indian Status. *University of British Columbia Law Review* 7(1):81–105.
1973a   *Native People in Areas of Internal Expansion: Indians and Inuit in Canada.* Document 14. Copenhagen: International Work Group for Indigenous Affairs.
1973b   The Nishga Case. *BC Studies* 19:3–20.
1973–74 Indian Hunting and Fishing Rights. *Saskatchewan Law Review* 38:45–62.
1978   The Unique Constitutional Position of the Indian. *Native Perspective* 2(9):26–34.
1981   Aboriginal Peoples and the Constitution. *Alberta Law Review* 19:410–27.
1983a   The Indian Lobby. In *And No One Cheered: Federalism, Democracy, and the Constitution Act,* edited by K. Banting and R. Simeon, pp. 301–32. Toronto: Methuen.
1983b   Prior Claims: Aboriginal People in the Constitution of Canada. In *Canada and the New Constitution: The Unfinished Agenda,* edited by S. M. Beck and I. Bernier, 1:225–79. Montreal: Institute for Research on Public Policy.

1983c   The Rights of the Aboriginal Peoples of Canada. *Canadian Bar Review* 61(1):314–38.
1990   Supreme Court of Canada and the "legal and political struggle" over indigenous rights. *Canadian Ethnic Studies* 22(3):122–32.

Schmeiser, Douglas A.
1965   Indians, Eskimos, and the Law. *Musk-Ox* 3:1–23.

Schwartz, Bryan
1986   *First Principles, Second Thoughts: Aboriginal Peoples, Constitutional Reform, and Canadian Statecraft.* Montreal: Institute for Research on Public Policy.

Shapcott, Catherine
1989   Environmental Impact Assessment and Resource Management, a Haida Case: Implications for Native People of the North. *Canadian Journal of Native Studies* 9(1):55–83.

Slattery, Brian
1985   The Hidden Constitution: Aboriginal Rights in Canada. In *The Quest for Justice: Aboriginal Peoples and Aboriginal Rights,* edited by Menno Boldt and J. Anthony Long, pp. 114–38. Toronto: University of Toronto Press.
1987   Understanding Aboriginal Rights. *Canadian Bar Review* 66(4):727–83.

Smith, Derek G., ed.
1975   *Canadian Indians and the Law: Selected Documents, 1663–1972.* Toronto: McClelland and Stewart.

Smith, Donald B.
1987   Aboriginal Rights a Century Ago: The St. Catharine's Milling Case of 1885 Hardened Attitudes Toward Native Land Claims. *Beaver* 67(1):4–15.

Sprague, Douglas N.
1980   The Manitoba Land Question, 1870–1882. *Journal of Canadian Studies* 15(3):74–84.

Stabler, Jack C.
1977   The Report of the Mackenzie Valley Pipeline Inquiry, vol. 1: A Socio-Economic Critique. *Musk-Ox* 20:57–65.

Stanley, George F. G.
1973   The First Indian "Reserves" in Canada. *Révue d'histoire de l'Amérique française* 4(3):178–210.

Surtees, Robert J.
1968   The Development of an Indian Reserve Policy in Canada. *Ontario History* 60:87–98.

Tanner, Adrian
1980   La politique du Quatrième Monde et les autochtones du Canada: Remarques. *Anthropologie et sociétés* 4(3):45–58.

Tanner, Adrian, ed.
1983   *The Politics of Indianness: Case Studies of Native Ethnopolitics in Canada.* St. John's: Memorial University of Newfoundland, Institute for Social and Economic Research.

Tennant, Paul
1982   Native Indian Political Organization in British Columbia, 1900–1969: A Response to Internal Colonialism. *BC Studies* 55:3–49.
1983   Native Indian Political Activity in British Columbia. *BC Studies* 57:112–36.
1990   *Aboriginal Peoples and Politics: The Indian Land Question in British Columbia, 1849–1989.* Vancouver: University of British Columbia Press.

Thompson, Ruth, ed.
1987   *The Rights of Indigenous Peoples in International Law: Selected Essays on Self-determination.* Saskatoon: University of Saskatchewan Native Law Centre.

Titley, E. Brian
1983   W. M. Graham: Indian Agent Extraordinaire. *Prairie Forum* 8(1):25–41.
1986   *A Narrow Vision: Duncan Campbell Scott and the Administration of Indian Affairs in Canada.* Vancouver: University of British Columbia Press.

Tobias, John L.
1976   Protection, Civilization, Assimilation: An Outline History of Canada's Indian Policy. *Western Canadian Journal of Anthropology* 6(2): 13–30.

Tough, Frank
1988   Economic Aspects of Aboriginal Title in Northern Manitoba: Treaty 5 Adhesions and Metis Scrip. *Manitoba History* 15:3–16.

Trudel, Pierre
1977   Comparaison entre le Traité de la baie James et la Convention de la Baie James. *Recherches amérindiennes au Québec* 9(3):237–53.

Turpel, Mary Ellen
1991   Further travails of Canada's Human Rights Record: The Marshall case. *International Journal of Canadian Studies/Revue internationale d'études canadienne* 3:27–48.

Upton, L. F. S.
1973   The Origins of Canadian Indian Policy. *Journal of Canadian Studies* 8:51–61.

Usher, Peter J.
1973   Evaluating Country Food in the Northern Native Economy. *Arctic* 29:105–20.
1982a   Les autochtones et les chasseurs sportifs peuvent-ils coexister? *Recherches amérindiennes au Québec* 12(4):263–67.
1982b   Unfinished Business on the Frontier. *Canadian Geographer* 26:187–90.

Ware, R.
1974   *The Lands We Lost: A History of Cut-off Lands and Land Losses From Indian Reserves in BC.* Vancouver: Union of B.C. Indian Chiefs, Land Claims Research Center.

Watkins, Mel
1977   Aboriginal People and Staple Production: A Comment on the Berger Report. *Western Canadian Journal of Anthropology* 7(3):83–94.

Watkins, Mel, ed.
1977   *Dene Nation: The Colony Within.* Toronto: University of Toronto Press.

Watson, Graham
1981   The Reification of Ethnicity and Its Political Consequences in the North. *Canadian Review of Sociology and Anthropology* 18:453–69.

Weaver, Sally M.
1981   *Making Canadian Indian Policy: The Hidden Agenda, 1968–70.* Toronto: University of Toronto Press.
1982   The Joint Cabinet/National Indian Brotherhood Committee: A Unique Experiment in Pressure Group Relations. *Canadian Public Administration* 25:211–39.
1983   Les attitudes du gouvernement fédéral face aux revendications autochtones. *Recherches amérindiennes au Québec* 13(3): 193–200.
1984   Struggles of the Nation-State to Define Indigenous Ethnicity: Canada and Australia. In *Ethnicity and the Mother Country,* edited by G. Gold. St. John's: Memorial University of

Newfoundland, Institute for Social and Economics Research.

1985   Federal Policy Making for Métis and Non-Status Indians in the Context of Native Policy. *Canadian Ethnic Studies* 27:80–102.

1986   Indian Policy in the New Conservative Government. *Native Studies Review* 2(1):1–43.

1990   New paradigm in Canadian Indian policy for the 1990s. *Canadian Ethnic Studies* 22(3):8–18.

Weller, R.

1988   Self-government for Canada's Inuit: The Nunavut Proposal. *American Review of Canadian Studies* 18:341–58.

Wenzel, George W.

1985   Marooned in a Blizzard of Contradictions: Inuit and the Anti-Sealing Movement. *Études/Inuit/Studies* 9(1):77–93.

1991   *Animal Rights, Human Rights: Ecology, Economy, and Ideology in the Canadian Arctic.* Toronto: University of Toronto Press.

Whitehead, G. R. B.

1966   Indian Treaties and the Indian Act—the Sa-

credness of Treaties? *Chitty's Law Journal* 14:121–25.

Wildsmith, Bruce Harris

1988   *Aboriginal Peoples and Section 25 of the Canadian Charter of Rights and Freedoms.* Saskatoon: University of Saskatchewan Native Law Center.

Wonders, William C.

1987   The Changing Role and Significance of Native People in Canada's Northwest Territories. *Polar Record* 23(147):661–72.

1988   Overlapping Native Land Claims in the Northwest Territories. *American Review of Canadian Studies* 18:359–68.

Woodward, Michael, and Bruce George

1984   The Canadian Indian Lobby of Westminster, 1979–1982. *Journal of Canadian Studies* 18(3):119–43.

Young, Oran

1989   The Politics of Animal Rights: Preservationists vs. Consumptive Users in the North. *Études/Inuit/Studies* 13(1):43–60.

INDEX OF AUTHORS